MW00562754

Queer Public History

Queer Public History

Essays on Scholarly Activism

Marc Stein

UNIVERSITY OF CALIFORNIA PRESS

University of California Press
Oakland, California

© 2022 by Marc Stein

Library of Congress Cataloging-in-Publication Data

Names: Stein, Marc, author.
Title: Queer public history : essays on scholarly activism /
    Marc Stein.
Description: Oakland, California : University of California Press,
    [2022] | Includes bibliographical references and index.
Identifiers: LCCN 2021046159 (print) | LCCN 2021046160
    (ebook) | ISBN 9780520304307 (cloth) | ISBN 9780520304314
    (paperback) | ISBN 9780520973039 (epub)
Subjects: LCSH: Gays—United States—History—20th century. |
    Gays—United States—History—21st century. | Public
    history—United States.
Classification: LCC HQ76.3.U6 S74 2022 (print) | LCC HQ76.3.U6
    (ebook) | DDC 306.76/609730904—dc23/eng/20211021
LC record available at https://lccn.loc.gov/2021046159
LC ebook record available at https://lccn.loc.gov/2021046160

31 30 29 28 27 26 25 24 23 22
10 9 8 7 6 5 4 3 2 1

Contents

Illustrations

Introduction

Historians have long participated in public debates and discussions, interacting with audiences that extend well beyond the students who take their classes and the specialists who read their work. This is perhaps most evident in politics and law, but it is also common in other domains. Historians regularly share their work in newspapers, magazines, radio, television, and film. They contribute to archives, libraries, and museums and influence historical houses, landmarks, monuments, and parks. Genealogists and demographers make use of scholarship on the past, as do those who work in architectural preservation, urban planning, economic development, and historical tourism. Creative artists are informed and inspired by historical research, as are those who work in science, health, technology, and business. Community-based historians typically orient themselves to the public, but so do many academic historians.[1]

Members of the public are more than just passive recipients of historical scholarship; they actively produce knowledge about the past. Public audiences influence the work of historians in the questions they ask, the interpretations they develop, the affirmations they provide, and the criticisms they offer. Their choices have consequences in the books and films that are bought and sold, the texts that are praised and panned, and the narratives that are considered and consumed. Ordinary and extraordinary people save and discard historical artifacts, engage and disengage with oral history projects, and support and oppose history education. With respect to archives, landmarks, monuments, and museums, members of the public wield power in the volunteer work they do, the physical sites they visit, the financial support they provide, and the actions they take to influence memory and commemoration. When historical professionals fail to do justice to people whose lives are not deemed worthy of recognition and remembrance, public audiences develop alternative and oppositional narratives that can transform our understanding of the past.

Queer historians—defined here as those who study nonnormative genders and sexualities in the past—have been distinctly active in the public sphere. Their work has influenced popular understandings of affection, intimacy, and eroticism; collective conversations about freedom, equality, and democracy; and global conceptions of political change, social justice, and cultural transformation. Prominent recent examples include the historians' briefs cited by the US Supreme Court when it invalidated state sodomy laws, bans on same-sex marriage, and restrictions on the use of antidiscrimination statutes.[2] LGBT historical research also has influenced mass media and popular culture, most notably in film, literature, television, and theater. Excluded and marginalized by academia in the past and present, LGBT historians—based at first in queer communities and only later in colleges and universities—have succeeded in reaching large public audiences.[3]

Just as queer historians have been distinctly active in the public sphere, queer publics have been distinctly powerful in shaping the production of historical knowledge. They have engaged in extensive discussions about the past, making meaning in the movements they remember, the moments they commemorate, the sites they recognize, and the legacies they claim. Paradoxically, this may be due in part to the fact that most LGBT people do not learn about queer history in their families and schools. LGBT marginalization, in and beyond formal systems of education, incites desires for queer history. In turn, social hierarchies within LGBT cultures incite desires for queer histories of people of color, poor people, religious minorities, people with disabilities, bisexuals, lesbians, and trans people. Queer publics have influenced scholarship on the past by supporting projects that others might ignore or reject, including an extensive network of LGBT archives, libraries, and museums. LGBT communities also have inspired historically informed creative works that have moved, motivated, and mobilized. Most importantly, queer people have made LGBT history in the stories they have shared, the interviews they have recorded, the artifacts they have saved, and the memories they have passed down. It is difficult to imagine what queer history as a field of inquiry would look like without the formative contributions of diverse LGBT communities.[4]

QUEERING PUBLIC HISTORY

Notwithstanding the developments and dynamics just described, queer historians have rarely been recognized as significant in the world of public history. The field's key journal, *The Public Historian*, began publication in 1978, but did not publish a major article about LGBT history until 2010.[5] The National Register of Historic Places, which includes tens of thousands of sites, was established by the US Congress in 1966, but did not list a location because of its importance for LGBT history until 1999.[6] The 1986 anthology *Presenting the Past: Essays on History and the Public* included Lisa Duggan's essay "History's Gay Ghetto: The Contradictions of Growth in Lesbian and Gay History," but ironically ghettoized LGBT history by ignoring the field in seventeen other chapters. The book also passed up an obvious opportunity for queer self-reflection when contributor Terence O'Donnell began his chapter by writing (with sarcasm), "The news could not be better. Clio has come out of the closet and now, with the other muses, consorts in the marketplace. History has gone public." Nor did O'Donnell's chapter take queer sensibilities into consideration when concluding that "it is wonderful to have Clio out of the closet and into the marketplace, but we must not turn her into a tart working the depths of heinous compromise." Several decades later, queer public history has come a long way, but it continues to be excluded, marginalized, and ghettoized in the larger domain of public history.[7]

Public history, defined in this study to include research, writing, and communication aimed at audiences beyond academia, has been growing as a subfield. Many college and university history departments now offer public history courses or include public history assignments in other classes. Countless instructors encourage students to use community-based archives, visit historical landmarks, participate in historical walking-tours, conduct oral histories, and pursue history-oriented internships. Multiple institutions advertise faculty positions in public history, mention public history as a preferred specialization in faculty recruitment, and reference public history in tenure and promotion policies. Many describe public history as an applied field that can open up promising career paths for students.

In part, the growth of public history within academic history builds on the discipline's long-standing interest in reaching broad audiences, arguably to a greater extent than is the case in many other fields. In contrast to scholars in disciplines that tend to use highly technical and specialized language, most academic historians write in relatively accessible prose and their works are commonly assigned to undergraduates. This is not necessarily the case in, say, economics, literature, mathematics, philosophy, or physics, where academic scholarship typically is aimed at more advanced specialists. History as an institutionalized discipline also does less to police its boundaries than do many other fields of study and certainly less than many professional fields. Anyone who studies the past can call themselves a historian, whereas not everyone who studies law, medicine, nursing, or psychology can call themselves a lawyer, doctor, nurse, or psychologist; if they do so without certification, there can be negative legal consequences. These claims should not be overstated: historical scholarship is less accessible than many academic historians imagine it to be; history majors continue to be disproportionately white and male; and the discipline has not adopted the academic equivalents of open-borders policies. Nevertheless, compared to academics in many other fields, historians orient much of their work to broad public audiences. Though there are costs to this in the power and prestige that history and historians are granted, the benefits make it unlikely that the discipline will abandon its self-conception as a democratic field of inquiry open to participation by all.

While the rise of public history as an academic specialty reflects the field's long-standing commitment to broad public audiences, it also responds to great and growing anxieties about declines in the numbers of students taking history courses and majoring in history.[8] These declines are often said to reflect changing patterns of student interest and job opportunities, but there is limited evidence to support these theories. From long-term perspectives, the reductions more likely reflect factors such as the shift from history to social studies in primary and secondary education, the reorientation of teacher training away from subject-based courses, changes in general education requirements, the rise of interdisciplinary programs, and the decline in public funding for education in general and humanities education in particular. Regardless of the reasons, academic historians could turn to LGBT specialists for ideas about how to engage large public audiences, but scholars of the queer past are rarely consulted in broader conversations about the past, present, and future of public history.

LGBT academic historians generally have had greater appreciation for public history, but they, too, have contributed to its marginalization. College- and university-based queer historians, for example, tend to date the origins of LGBT history as a field of inquiry to the 1970s and 1980s. Like most origin stories, this one is a revealing myth. In the late nineteenth and early twentieth centuries, there were biographers, bibliophiles, sexologists, and others who explored the queer past. In the 1950s and 1960s, North American LGBT publications featured many articles about history; LGBT movement lectures and conferences routinely included discussions about the past. This was a period when college and university history departments had little interest in, or were deeply hostile to, the study of gender and sexuality, but instead of acknowledging this history and recognizing the contributions of community-based scholars, academic historians tend to congratulate themselves for launching the study of the LGBT past.[9]

It is true that LGBT history as a field of inquiry began to grow and change in the 1970s and 1980s. Many factors were at play in this process. The powerful social movements of the 1950s and 1960s—especially those that challenged capitalism, colonialism, white supremacy, and male supremacy—inspired new historical scholarship on oppression and resistance. The civil rights, feminist, and anti-war movements were particularly influential. By the 1970s, more and more sexual revolutionaries, gay liberationists, lesbian feminists, and trans people were interested in learning about gender and sexual histories. Many LGBT people in the 1970s and 1980s looked to the past to help them understand the growth of queer cultures, the mobilization of LGBT movements, the politics of conservative backlash, and the conflicts surrounding HIV/AIDS. Meanwhile, the discipline of history changed in the 1960s and 1970s, creating new possibilities for studying gender and sexuality. Proponents of the New Social History emphasized ordinary people, everyday experience, private life, and the importance of class, race, and gender. The field of women's history provided useful models. More generally, democratization in higher education promoted the growth of LGBT history.[10]

PARTNERSHIPS AND COLLABORATIONS

LGBT historical knowledge developed in the 1970s and 1980s in the context of extraordinary collaborations between community-based historians and their academic counterparts.[11] In part because the professional discipline of history generally ignored and opposed research on the LGBT past, queer history was sustained by community-based contributors and audiences. Historical discussions, presentations, slideshows, and workshops took place in LGBT bookstores, centers, libraries, and other community spaces. LGBT newspapers and magazines published hundreds of articles about the queer past.[12] An early example was Maurice Kenney's groundbreaking 1975 essay on Native American history in *Gay Sunshine*. Jim Kepner's wide-ranging three-part series, "200 Years of Oppression," was published in 1978 in *Philadelphia Gay News*. Several influential feminist and queer anthologies of the 1980s, published by nonacademic presses and showcasing the work of community-based writers, featured historical research by and about LGBT people of color; these included *This Bridge Called My Back*, *Home Girls*, *In the Life*, *Compañeras*, and *Living the Spirit*. Essays by Gloria Hull in *Home Girls* and Charles Michael Smith in *In the Life*, for example, explored queer lives and loves in the Harlem Renaissance.[13] These works were joined by the scholarship of Allan Bérubé on World War Two, Michael Bronski on popular culture, Madeline Davis and Joan Nestle on butch-fem communities, Eric Garber on the Harlem Renaissance, and Judith Schwarz on Greenwich Village radicals. Bérubé's work was later recognized by a MacArthur Foundation "genius" grant. One of the most influential community-based LGBT historians was Jonathan Ned Katz, author of *Gay American History* in 1976 and *Gay/Lesbian Almanac* in 1983. Most of these researchers did not have advanced degrees in history or work as professors, but together they made LGBT history.[14]

The challenges of doing this work without academic affiliations, professional privileges, disciplinary advantages, and financial compensation were substantial in the 1970s and 1980s. Even access to academic research libraries could be difficult. Women and people of color faced distinct challenges because of sexism, racism, and economic inequality in higher education, scholarly publishing, and society more generally. Much of this work would not have been completed without the complementary work of LGBT community-based archives, libraries, and history projects and the enthusiastic engagement of queer public audiences. Many community-based historians persevered despite ever-present risks of rejection by academic elites and ever-present threats of anti-LGBT bias, discrimination, and prejudice. In the world of queer public history, however, they were recognized for their valuable contributions.

Community-based queer historians were joined by academic researchers, most of whom had strong ties to LGBT communities in the 1970s and

1980s. Of those who turned to LGBT history after writing dissertations on other topics, many were influenced by the rise of women's studies and feminist activism. Carroll Smith-Rosenberg was among the first, publishing on urban evangelicals before researching nineteenth-century women's relationships. Lillian Faderman, who began her career by writing about Victorian literature, also became fascinated by the history of lesbianism. Blanche Wiesen Cook finished a dissertation on Woodrow Wilson and antimilitarism and then published on female political networks in the same era. Nancy Sahli studied Dr. Elizabeth Blackwell before exploring "smashing" among college women. Estelle Freedman initially worked on women's prison reform and later turned to feminist separatism and sexual psychopathy. Leila J. Rupp wrote about women and war mobilization before studying lesbianism among women's rights activists. Paula Gunn Allen authored a dissertation on Native American history and culture before completing work on Native American lesbian history. Elizabeth Lapovsky Kennedy earned a PhD in anthropology with research on indigenous Central Americans, after which she initiated a collaborative project on bar-based lesbian communities. Esther Newton was a somewhat different case; her dissertation was an anthropological study of contemporary female impersonators, but a few years later she began producing historical work on early twentieth-century mannish lesbians.[15]

A smaller group of academic men similarly turned to LGBT history in the 1970s and 1980s after beginning their careers with research on other topics. Vern Bullough wrote about medieval European medical education before publishing wide-ranging scholarship on LGBT history, much of which focused on sexology. John Burnham's dissertation addressed the history of psychoanalysis; he later researched early medical writings about gay communities. Robert Oaks worked on the American Revolution before publishing on sodomy in colonial New England. One of the most influential academics in the field's early development was Martin Duberman, who wrote about antislavery activism, African American history, and political radicalism before publishing essays on antebellum male homoeroticism and Hopi Indian sexualities, a collection of LGBT historical documents and essays, and a transnational anthology on the "gay past." Ronald Bayer's work on drug policy was followed by research on homosexuality and psychiatry. Henry Abelove studied early Methodism before publishing on the history of psychoanalysis and homosexuality. Walter Williams completed a dissertation on African American attitudes toward Africa; his fourth book was a historical study of American Indian sexual diversity.[16]

These scholars were joined by the first generation of researchers to earn PhDs based on LGBT history projects. Salvatore Licata's 1978 dissertation was titled "Gay Power: A History of the American Gay Movement, 1908–1974." One year later, Robert Marotta completed "The Politics of Homosexuality: Homophile and Early Gay Liberation Organizations in New York City." Three years later, John D'Emilio authored "Out of the Shadows: The Homosexual Emancipation Movement in the United States." Interestingly, all three of these projects focused on movement politics. After a bit of a lull that perhaps can be attributed to the country's conservative turn and the impact of AIDS, George Chauncey completed "Gay New York: Urban Culture and the Making of the Gay Male World, 1890–1940" in 1989. In the next few years, these men were joined by the first women to write dissertations addressing US LGBT history: Susan Cahn for "Coming on Strong: Gender and Sexuality in Women's Sport" (1990); Sharon Ullman for "Broken Silences: Sex and Culture in Turn of the Century America" (1990); and Lisa Duggan for "The Trials of Alice Mitchell: Sex, Science, and Sensationalism in Turn of the Century America" (1992).[17]

LGBT academic historians may have been relatively privileged compared to their community-based counterparts, but they confronted enormous challenges in the 1970s and 1980s. Several have written about the hostility they encountered in academic institutions and professional pursuits. Freedman and Newton, for example, experienced anti-feminist, anti-lesbian, and anti-queer employment discrimination. Both are now esteemed senior scholars with multiple award-winning publications, but they nearly had their academic careers derailed by initial denials of tenure (the academic equivalent of firing). They are not the only ones, but referencing those who have not spoken or written publicly about their experiences might cause further harm. Duberman's memoirs offer harrowing accounts of micro- and macro-aggressions against LGBT faculty and LGBT studies. These included attacks in print after he came out as gay and began writing about LGBT history, research obstacles when archives tried to block his use of erotic materials, and professional rejection when disciplinary organizations and academic departments marginalized LGBT historians and histories. John D'Emilio and Lisa Duggan have described multiple types of anti-LGBT animus in the discipline of history in the 1970s and 1980s; this included opposition to the very idea of hiring specialists in LGBT history for faculty positions.[18] Intersectional hostility created distinct challenges for people of color who might otherwise have pursued LGBT historical research; this helps explain the small number of people of color who entered the field in the 1970s and 1980s.[19]

A series of episodes involving the American Historical Association illustrates the anti-LGBT biases of the discipline just a few decades ago. At the annual business meeting of the AHA in 1974, historian Dennis Rubini of Temple University (seconded by Duberman of Lehman College and Charles Shively of Boston State College) proposed a resolution that would put the organization on record as affirming "the right of gay historians and others to engage in the research and teaching of the history of single and gay people as well as members of all sexual minorities." The proposed statement also declared that "attempts by colleagues, administrators, and others designed to subvert such research and teaching are to be considered violations of academic freedom." While the resolution garnered support at the business meeting, the AHA Council later voted "not to concur," claiming that it "singles out for separate support one particular group of historians" rather than upholding "the academic freedom of all historians." Using a term already outdated in the 1970s, the Council noted that "homosexual historians" were protected by the AHA Statement on Professional Standards, which rejected discrimination based on sexual orientation. Rubini and Duberman's response in the *AHA Newsletter* referenced ongoing problems of homophobia in the discipline, rejections of course proposals at various institutions, and "the paucity of gay history offerings throughout the country." When the AHA then conducted an extraordinary membership vote, 641 people supported the Council's non-concurrence, 164 supported the business meeting's action, and 3 abstained.[20]

In the same newsletter that announced these results, the AHA published an essay by PhD students Michael Lodwick and Thomas Fiehrer, who began by noting that they found themselves "moved to new heights of alarm and despair at the general drift of the discipline." After mentioning various reasons for this, they turned to signs that the discipline was now "placing a premium upon the odd, the unusual, even the suspect, research angle." One of their primary illustrations was the "manifesto" by Rubini and Duberman, which demonstrated that "sexual minorities" were "on the prowl." After quoting Rubini and Duberman, Lodwick and Fiehrer wrote, "Dare we suggest that the paucity of courses in gay history owes to the obvious fact that the history of this and other 'sexual minorities' is unimportant." They then complained that historians in America were in danger of "shrinking our focus to the absurdly narrow interests of the faddists." Among the absurd topics that scholars might similarly soon pursue, they warned, were the history of consorts, neurotics, ugly people, and unemployed historians.[21]

In the aftermath of what may have been the AHA's first queer controversy, changes in the discipline made it possible to imagine a nightmare scenario for Lodwick and Fiehrer: scholarship on the history of unemployed gay historians, some of whom may have been consorts, neurotics, or ugly. In 2001, my analysis of the academic careers of forty-four employed and unemployed LGBT historians documented pervasive patterns of bias, prejudice, and discrimination in the history job market (see chapter 3). A few years later, I published an autobiographical essay about my own close encounters with academic unemployment (see chapter 4). While the situation has improved in the last two decades, these problems have not disappeared: in 2015, the AHA's LGBTQ Task Force documented multiple challenges faced by LGBTQ historians in publishing, research, teaching, employment, and the AHA itself.[22]

In short, LGBT academic historians may have enjoyed privileges that queer public historians did not, but they confronted major obstacles in the 1970s and 1980s. In addition, there are many reasons to avoid drawing sharp lines between academic and public historians. Joan Nestle and Michael Bronski began their work as community-based writers, but both later taught college and university courses. Will Roscoe compiled *Living the Spirit* on behalf of Gay American Indians, but then completed a PhD. Cheryl Clark, whose research was published in *This Bridge Called My Back* and *Home Girls*, worked as a university administrator and later earned a PhD. Important LGBT studies anthologies of the 1970s and 1980s, including *This Bridge*, *Home Girls*, and *In the Life*, were edited by public intellectuals but included the work of academics. Many LGBT public historians appeared on the conference programs of the AHA and the Organization of American Historians; many were invited to present their work at colleges and universities. The Committee on LGBT History, a historical society affiliated with the AHA, was cofounded in 1979 by academic historian Walter Williams and public historian Gregory Sprague. Three of its prizes are named for public historians—Bérubé, Nestle, and Sprague—and the Bérubé Prize recognizes work in public history. Notwithstanding its name, the Gay Academic Union, founded in New York in 1973, welcomed the participation of community-based scholars. Multiple LGBT history organizations founded in the 1970s and 1980s, including the GLBT Historical Society in San Francisco, the History Project in Boston, the Gerber/Hart Library and Archives in Chicago, and the Lesbian Herstory Archives in

New York, were collaborative projects that brought together academic and public historians.

Distinctions between community-based historians and their academic counterparts also should not be overstated because many of the latter saw themselves as community-based scholars, were influenced by community-based developments, and imagined their audiences as extending beyond colleges and universities. Much of the early scholarship on US lesbian history, for example, was inspired by the politics of lesbian feminism and the participation of lesbian academics in community-based feminist movements. In autobiographical reflections, Newton, D'Emilio, and Duberman have emphasized that they often wrote for nonacademic audiences. Duberman and Duggan published regularly in nonacademic periodicals such as the *Nation* and *Village Voice*; Duberman also wrote for *Harper's*, *New Republic*, *New York Times*, *Christopher Street*, and *New York Native*. Duberman reached large public audiences through his work as a playwright; his service on the boards of the National Gay Task Force, Lambda Legal Defense, and the New York Civil Liberties Union; and his vision for the Center for Lesbian and Gay Studies, established at the City University of New York in 1991. Several LGBT academic historians played founding and leading roles in community history projects; Kennedy did so for the Buffalo Women's Oral History Project, and Ullman did so for the GLBT Historical Society in San Francisco. Major LGBT history anthologies were edited by academic scholars but featured the work of nonacademic historians; *Hidden from History* (1989), for example, was edited by three academics but included multiple essays by nonacademic historians.

D'Emilio offers an instructive example. D'Emilio's 1983 book *Sexual Politics, Sexual Communities*, which was based on his PhD dissertation, is commonly recognized as the first major scholarly work on the homophile movement of the 1950s and 1960s. As noted above, there were two earlier dissertations on pre-Stonewall activism. More to the point for the argument here is the fact that these were preceded by community-based works, many published in the LGBT press, that anticipated academic scholarship.[23] Moreover, D'Emilio's work on the homophile movement was first published in *The Body Politic*, a community-based gay periodical in Toronto. This is not to say that D'Emilio's scholarship was perfectly aligned with popular LGBT sensibilities; much of his work challenged mainstream LGBT politics and perspectives. The point is rather that even as D'Emilio embarked on a successful university career, he maintained his commitments to community-based scholarship. In the 1990s he left academia for several years to become the founding director of the National Gay and Lesbian Task Force's Policy Institute. In 2000 he coedited (with NGLTF executive director Urvashi Vaid and historian William Turner) a book on LGBT politics and policy. In 2001 he coedited a posthumous collection of essays by Allan Bérubé; and he later chaired the board of directors of the Gerber/Hart Library and Archives. As is the case with many LGBT historians, D'Emilio defies simple categorization as either a university-based scholar or a community-based one.[24]

Whether employed by academic institutions or not, LGBT historians of the 1970s and 1980s joined together in creating a powerful movement of activist scholars. Mainstream academics sometimes claim that scholars should not be activists, asserting that political commitments can compromise scholarly objectivity. This is untenable for queer historians. LGBT historians have analyzed activism; their activism has influenced their scholarship; and their scholarship has materialized in activism. Indeed, queer activism was required to make a place for LGBT histories and historians in the academy. In the 1970s and 1980s, queer scholars fought for the inclusion of LGBT history in the courses offered by colleges and universities, the essays published by academic journals, the books published by university and trade presses, and the conference programs of academic organizations. They fought to establish academic programs in gay and lesbian, LGBT, queer, feminist, women's, sexuality, and gender studies. They fought for grants, fellowships, and library resources. They fought for jobs, tenure, and promotion; health care and partner benefits; and inclusion in nondiscrimination, anti-harassment, and anti-bullying policies. In many contexts, LGBT historians used their skills and experiences as scholars to challenge academic departments, institutions, and organizations, further illustrating the impossibility of policing boundaries between activism and academia.

Thirty years later, queer public history is thriving, notwithstanding new and ongoing struggles. In the United States alone, thousands participate in LGBT public history projects; millions engage with the results. This book's conclusion reflects on queer public history today, but the chapters that follow this introduction explore the field's growth and development from the late 1980s through the 2010s, using my experiences as a lens. Before turning to those experiences, the remainder of the introduction revisits the 1960s, 1970s, and 1980s to explore how I came to identify as a queer public historian and LGBT scholarly activist.

[handwritten marginalia: similar to gen / first few pgs / of schol]

AUTOBIOGRAPHICAL REFLECTIONS

In the last few decades, I have been an engaged participant-observer in queer public history and LGBT scholarly activism. While not unique in this respect, my experiences have positioned me to reflect critically on the politics and poetics of these fields. The following autobiographical narrative sets the stage for the chapters that follow by linking my personal history to broader developments.

Born in 1963 and raised by middle-class Jewish parents in the northern suburbs of New York City, I learned many lessons about the history of sex, marriage, and reproduction in relation to my extended family, which had migrated from Eastern Europe in the early twentieth century. Norms were fairly clear, but there was a mystery that surrounded my work on a family tree for a school assignment. When I questioned my maternal grandfather, he indicated that his father's first name was the same as his, which I knew was unusual in Jewish families of our time and place. Children were typically named for family members who recently had died (my names, Marc and Robert, honored my great-grandmothers Marcia and Rose), so naming a son after a living relative was seen as a death-wish. When I queried him about this, my grandfather noted that his father had died before he was born, which I initially had trouble understanding. Only later, after I became a historian of sexuality, did it occur to me that my grandfather might have been trying to avoid talking openly about his origins in a non-marital pregnancy.

There were other intriguing family mysteries. I occasionally heard gossip about a paternal great-grandfather's many girlfriends and the appearances of impropriety when his stepdaughter moved in with him after he was widowed. There were hints of risqué stories about my favorite great aunt, who married late in life and did not have children. Another great aunt had traveled to Mexico to meet the man her yenta had found, a Jewish immigrant to Cuba. There was awkward laughter about the time my maternal grandparents, both born in Poland, mistakenly believed that their niece was dating an African American man because his name, common among Hungarian Jews, was unfamiliar to them. There was tense talk when family members divorced, especially when my great uncle's third wife abandoned him after he began losing his memory. There were intimations of transgression when we navigated the boundaries between Ashkenazi and Sephardic culinary traditions; my family was mostly Ashkenazi (from Eastern Europe), but one of my mother's first cousins had married a Sephardic Jew whose family had emigrated from Turkey. There was nothing ambiguous about the family's feelings about marriages to non-Jewish "goys" and "shiksas," though there was rejoicing when this was preceded by conversion to Judaism. As some of this suggests, I also learned familial lessons about race, class, and religion and the ways these could interact with sex, gender, and sexuality. Some of this was bigoted, but my working-class maternal grandparents, active in left and labor politics since arriving in the United States as teenagers in 1929, introduced me to more progressive perspectives.

Decades later, it is difficult to reconstruct what I learned about other types of gender and sexual transgressions when I was growing up in Shrub Oak, but I am confident that in my family and community, same-sex desires and cross-gender identifications were commonly regarded as embarrassing and shameful. I had no sense that they were worthy of historical exploration. I certainly did not know that in those very years, LGBT activists were transforming the politics of gender and sexuality, mobilizing movements and moments that would greatly influence my life. Nor did I know that historians were transforming the study of the LGBT past. In 1976, the year of my bar mitzvah, I knew that the United States was celebrating its two-hundredth birthday, but I did not know that Jonathan Ned Katz's *Gay American History* was giving birth to a new field of scholarly inquiry that I would later claim as my own.

By 1977, I was old enough to understand that I had lost family members, including great-aunts and great-uncles, in the Holocaust, and that one of my mother's first cousins, whom we saw regularly for Passover, Chanukah, and other family events, was an orphaned survivor who had been raised by my great-grandparents in New York. I sensed that there were reasons for concern about the rising tide of racism and sexism in and beyond the United States. I had several direct experiences with anti-Jewish harassment and hatred, including questions from a neighbor's father about why the Jews had killed Jesus, pennies tossed in front of me to see if I would pick them up, and beatings on my way to Hebrew school. I remember feeling worried about the growth of the Christian Right and the politics of right-wing backlash, but I did not know that social conservatives such as Florida's Anita Bryant were winning victories in their efforts to repeal recently enacted gay rights laws. Nor did I know that Harvey Milk was campaigning successfully to win election as the first openly gay member of the San Francisco Board of Supervisors or that someday I would live in the district he had represented. I was focused instead on my first year at Lakeland Senior High

School, which was disrupted by the longest teachers' strike in New York state history (forty-one days). This was when I first shared my political views in the public sphere, writing a letter about the strike that was published in the *Peekskill Evening Star* (after my first encounters with an exacting editor: my mother). While my intervention in local labor politics cannot be described as a work of queer public history or an example of scholarly activism, it anticipated my later interest in writing about political matters for public audiences (and I am proud to say that I sided with the teachers!).[25]

As far as I can recall, I first encountered the work of gay and lesbian historians during my first year at Wesleyan University, a liberal arts college in Connecticut that I attended from 1981 to 1985. I did not consistently think of myself as gay at this point (I had two long and happy relationships with women in my high school and college years and another while in graduate school), but I was fascinated by the history, politics, psychology, and sociology of oppression and resistance. I took no general US history surveys while in college, but enrolled in courses on African American history and US women's history. Neither of these topics had received much attention in my high school history classes, which concluded with World War Two. I likely had a self-congratulatory attitude about studying these topics as a white man. My women's history professor assigned Carroll Smith-Rosenberg's 1975 essay "The Female World of Love and Ritual: Relations between Women in Nineteenth-Century America," which had been published in the first issue of *Signs*, an interdisciplinary women's studies journal. I also read Lillian Faderman's *Surpassing the Love of Men*, Gayle Rubin's early essays on gender and sexuality, and Adrienne Rich's work on "compulsory heterosexuality." As a young man with sexual secrets, I was intrigued by the ways that scholars such as Smith-Rosenberg were making the private public, though I could not have known that she would later serve as my PhD supervisor.

Notwithstanding my interests in history, politics, and sociology, I was a psychology major for most of my time at Wesleyan. In the 1980s, this was still commonly seen as the most appropriate discipline for studying sexuality. In fact, I wrote my first gay-themed paper for an introductory psychology course (taught by a professor whose young son would become the queer historian Timothy Stewart-Winter). The essay explored psychological theories about the origins of homosexuality, but at the last minute, after panicking about the fact that other students might see my cover page, I changed the title (but not the contents) to

"The Origins of Heterosexuality." I laugh about this now, but my fears speak volumes about the challenges of writing about LGBT topics in the 1980s. In any event, I soon began to understand, as Smith-Rosenberg had pointed out, that it might be beneficial to approach sexuality from historical rather than psychological perspectives. I first read Michel Foucault's 1976 book *The History of Sexuality*, translated into English in 1978, in a psychology course. My mentor Henry Abelove, a history professor who was beginning to publish on queer topics, also encouraged me to read Katz's *Gay American History* (1976) and *Gay/Lesbian Almanac* (1983), along with Ronald Bayer's *Homosexuality and American Psychiatry* (1981), Toby Marotta's *The Politics of Homosexuality* (1981), and John D'Emilio's *Sexual Politics* (1983). By 1984–85, I was a history major and willing to go public as a historian of the gay past, but not as a gay-identified historian. For the senior project required of all history majors, I wrote about early twentieth-century psychoanalytic ideas about homosexuality in the United States.

In truth, I spent my undergraduate years focused more on student politics than academic work, but here, too, I began to take my first steps in the direction of queer public history and LGBT scholarly activism. I participated in protests and teach-ins that challenged US military interventions in Central America, criticized US support for South African apartheid, advocated for nuclear disarmament, opposed military draft registration, and supported ratification of the Equal Rights Amendment. One of my friends, the son of a National Abortion Rights Action League leader, persuaded a group of us to form "Students for Choice."[26] I was particularly active in the Wesleyan chapter of a national organization called the Coalition of Private University Students (COPUS), helping to mobilize participation in two marches on Washington that challenged the Reagan administration's plans for massive reductions in student financial aid.[27] I was not personally affected by these cutbacks (as corporate-based merit scholarships, which I later would criticize for reproducing economic inequality, covered approximately half of my college expenses), but my class politics were aligned with redistributive economics and my high school experiences had taught me about the ramifications of declining government support for education. All of this inspired me to undertake my first efforts as a scholarly activist: in my junior year, I coauthored a fifty-page study (single-spaced!), based on oral interviews and student surveys, of the economic challenges and financial aid experiences of Wesleyan students. I worked on this not as a paper for a course, but as a report for the COPUS chapter, and it proved effective in lobbying administrators for improvements in financial aid.[28] For me, this was an eye-opening experience that offered valuable lessons about using scholarly research to promote social justice.

My second significant project as an activist scholar focused on gay and lesbian issues. During my college years, I was very interested in gender and sexual politics and a strong supporter of feminism, but I did not generally think of myself as gay or describe myself as such to family or friends, notwithstanding my first sexual relationship with a man (between my first and second years of college) and some early conversations about that with friends. In my sophomore year, I wrote a tortured letter to the editor of the *Wesleyan Argus*, the university's main student newspaper, about the challenges of being gay on campus. At the time I was the paper's editorial page editor, but I was so afraid of being identified as the letter's author that I submitted it anonymously, in the middle of the night, to the newspaper office. The letter was then passed on to me, as the editorial page editor, giving me plausible deniability about being its author.[29] By my senior year, I was willing to be identified publicly as a gay ally, but not as gay. While serving as one of the two coordinators of the Wesleyan Student Assembly, I coauthored a thirty-page (single-spaced!) student government report on campus gay and lesbian issues. As was the case with my financial aid project, this was based on extensive interviews, and some of the reforms we supported (including adoption of official nondiscrimination statements, improvements in student and health services, and curricular reforms) influenced subsequent developments.[30] While neither of these initiatives were works of queer public history, both were examples of scholarly activism, and in this respect they anticipated my later efforts to use queer studies research for activist purposes.[31]

After graduating in 1985 and spending ten months working and traveling in Europe and Israel with my girlfriend, I moved to Boston, where I found work at the Institute for Defense and Disarmament Studies. IDDS was the brainchild of Randall Forsberg, a founder and leader of the nuclear freeze movement; Forsberg had used a MacArthur Foundation "genius" grant to establish the small think-tank. IDDS positioned itself at the intersection of peace movement activism, arms control policymaking, and research on military affairs; it provided me with additional lessons about scholarly activism.[32] I also was coming out more fully, joining the gay movement, and participating in AIDS activism. After working for more than a year as a volunteer writer, proofreader, and board member at *Gay Community News*, a national weekly based

FIGURE 1. *Gay Community News* coordinating editor Marc Stein at Boston Lesbian and Gay Pride, Boston Common, June 1989. Photographer unknown.

in Boston, I resigned my IDDS job to become the newspaper's coordinating editor. I was twenty-four years old and only recently out as gay, but the egalitarian staff salary ($10,000/year, equivalent to approximately $22,000/year in 2021 dollars) failed to attract more experienced applicants. GCN, which was founded in 1973 and launched the careers of many national LGBT leaders, provided me with an extraordinary opportunity to learn about gender and sexual politics.[33]

GCN focused primarily on contemporary politics during the Reagan and Bush eras, but we regularly published articles on historical topics, which fueled my interest in the queer past. During my time as GCN's editor, for example, we published an interview with historian Estelle Freedman and a large number of history book reviews, including one of D'Emilio and Freedman's *Intimate Matters*.[34] In 1988, GCN published an edited transcript of my interview with British historical sociologist Jeffrey Weeks, a leading gay and lesbian studies scholar in the 1970s and 1980s; this was my first venture in queer public history. One year later, GCN published my critical review of Larry Kramer's book about AIDS, *Reports from the Holocaust*. The author of *Faggots* and *The Normal Heart*, Kramer was a cofounder of New York's Gay Men's Health Crisis and a catalyst in the formation of ACT UP, the AIDS Coalition to

Unleash Power. My review objected to Kramer's anachronistic conceptions of homosexuality in the past, his uses of the holocaust analogy,
and his Johnny-come-lately attitudes about gay activism.[35] After leaving *GCN* to begin my PhD studies in 1989, I continued to write for
the paper, seeing it as an outstanding venue for queer public history.
In 1990 and 1991, *GCN* published my reviews of Bérubé's *Coming
Out under Fire*, David Halperin's *One Hundred Years of Homosexuality*, Eve Kosofsky Sedgwick's *Epistemology of the Closet*, and Abelove's *The Evangelist of Desire*. In 1994 I contributed to a special issue
commemorating the twenty-fifth anniversary of the Stonewall Riots (see
chapter 8).[36]

My 1989 decision to leave my position at *GCN*, which I thought of
as a movement job, and begin a PhD program at the University of Pennsylvania, which I hoped would prepare me for an academic career, was
not easy. I first had applied to PhD history programs in 1987, around the
same time that I pursued the position at *GCN*. My application emphasized my interests in social movements, with gay and lesbian activism
referenced as an example. I was definitely interested in gay and lesbian
history, but thought it best to take a cautious approach, since there
might be faculty opposition. This was the case even though, following
Abelove's advice, I applied to six departments with tenured US women's
historians who had worked on sexual topics. Abelove had explained to
me that with possibly one exception, there were no PhD programs with
tenured specialists in US gay, as distinct from lesbian, history. In the end,
however, I deferred my three offers of admission.

Some of my reasons related to pragmatic concerns about whether
specializing in LGBT history would make it impossible to secure a long-
term faculty position. This was in spite of the fact that in the second half
of the 1980s there were predictions of impending faculty shortages in
US colleges and universities.[37] I remember reading some of these reports
and thinking that this might be a good time to begin graduate studies in
history. At the same time, I knew enough about the discipline's biases to
suspect that specializing in LGBT history might be held against me. At
this point I was aware of only one person—D'Emilio—who had completed a PhD with a dissertation on LGBT history and then been hired
in a tenure-track faculty position. I recall telling myself that I should
not go to graduate school unless I could convince myself that four years
of PhD studies would be time well spent, whether or not it led to a faculty job. Having gone to a liberal arts college, I was woefully ignorant
about the fact that it would take more than four years! While mulling

advantage of experimental history outside of academia [handwritten margin note]

this over, I was offered the *GCN* position. Editing a gay and lesbian newspaper was appealing in its own right but also promised to broaden and deepen my knowledge of LGBT politics and culture, which I knew would benefit my future work as a historian. In this context, I decided to accept *GCN*'s offer and defer my graduate school plans.

interesting how we was in academia already [handwritten margin note]

By 1989, my feelings about this had changed. After more than a year of editing *GCN*, I was burned out. Leading *GCN*, which was constantly teetering on the edge of bankruptcy, internally divided, and struggling with weekly deadlines, was incredibly stressful. As if this were not enough, the AIDS epidemic was raging; the *GCN* community was suffering tremendous losses; and it felt like the entire progressive nonprofit sector was under grave threat. I still wanted to devote my life to social change, but it was becoming increasingly evident that if I was going to commit my life to political activism and social justice, I had to find a way to make that work sustainable. Some of these dynamics were captured in the affectionate farewell published by *GCN*, which began by noting that I had shown that "working at GCN is a twenty-four-hour-a-day-job." The announcement continued, "'Just because you have to sleep at night,' he seems to have said, 'doesn't mean you can't fundraise while you're doing so.'" After indicating that the staff would miss my laughter and the "reams of memos composed just for us," the farewell concluded by noting, "Mr. Stein is off to gradual school, where he will be working on some sort of high-falutin' advanced history degree. No one will forget the history he made here when he established *GCN*'s first-ever Promotions Fund, to get this old dog of a rag into more hands."[38]

My subsequent colleagues may laugh about the references to my frequent and lengthy memos. Few readers, however, are likely to get the inside joke about fundraising while sleeping, which was meant to tease me about the short relationship I had with *GCN*'s most generous donor. While this may have exaggerated the number of hours I devoted to *GCN* (and for the record, my coworkers also worked long days and nights, which I say with no sexual innuendo intended!), it captures the reality, then and now, that many people with movement jobs struggle to limit their work hours and achieve healthy work-life balances. Decades later, I would say the same about professors, many of whom work six or seven days a week, twelve months a year, notwithstanding the regular comments we receive about long weekends and summer vacations.

GCN's farewell also captured a sentiment expressed by others: that I was "selling out" by choosing an "elite" graduate program over "democratic" movement work. It is true that my annual income actually rose when I left *GCN*; my pay as a teaching assistant, combined with my PhD stipend, was greater than my salary in the "real" world. But I did not exactly feel as though I was selling out by pursuing graduate studies on a topic that likely would never land me an academic job. I also knew from my experiences at Wesleyan that educational institutions could and should be targets of political activism. Indeed, I fully expected that my mere presence as a graduate student focusing on LGBT history would be seen as political. In addition, it was sadly the case that most people who could afford to live on *GCN*'s salaries were white and middle class, whereas my graduate teachers and classmates were more diverse. And it was not as though *GCN*ers were not highly educated: for example, Mike Riegle, the leader of the paper's Prisoners Project and one of its greatest advocates of egalitarian class politics, had completed a PhD, and the paper's news and features editors were Stanford graduates. For me, the more meaningful questions were how and whether I could retain the political commitments I had developed over the previous decade and apply them to new situations. Queer public history and LGBT scholarly activism provided some of the best answers. In any case, back to school I went in 1989, and in many respects I have never left.

OVERVIEW AND ORGANIZATION

The chapters that follow draw from my work as a queer public historian and LGBT scholarly activist over the last three decades. In that time, I have taught at five colleges and universities, authored four scholarly books, and edited a three-volume encyclopedia, but I also have worked on public history projects. I have served as a volunteer and advisory board member of the John J. Wilcox Jr. LGBT Archives in Philadelphia (1991–96, 2015–present); contributing editor and advisory board member of the OutHistory website in New York (2008–present); and board member of the GLBT Historical Society in San Francisco (2016–19). I have regularly shared my work with public audiences, most frequently in LGBT newspapers and public history venues such as OutHistory and History News Network. My scholarship has been used in the designation of historical landmarks; featured on radio programs, television shows, and documentary films; and referenced in museum exhibits, internet blogs, and media stories. This type of work is not consistently recognized in academic institutions, but engagement in queer public history has energized, enriched, and enlivened my scholarly work.

The chapters that follow also capture some of my work as a queer scholarly activist. Since 1989, I have fought for change at the colleges and universities where I have taught, helped found and lead the Sexuality Studies Program at York University in Toronto (2005–09), and served as chair and steward of the York University Faculty Association's Queer Caucus (2011–14). I also served a three-year term as chair of the Committee on Lesbian and Gay History (now called the Committee on LGBT History), which has several hundred members and is recognized as an affiliated society of the American Historical Association (2000–03). For six years I was a member of the AHA's five-person LGBTQ Task Force (2009–15). For three years I was the chair and then a member of the Organization of American Historian's Committee on the Status of LGBTQ Historians and Histories (2013–16). Like many other LGBT scholars, I have participated in multifaceted campaigns to queer the discipline of history and transform higher education more generally.

Queer Public History reprints and reconsiders a collection of my previously published works. Introductions to the book's eight parts explore what I was attempting to accomplish and achieve, what the inspirations and influences were, what research and writing strategies I adopted, who my intended audiences and readers were, how I chose the venues and vehicles, what changed in the submission and editing process, and what I see as the successes and failures. They also situate my work within the broader field of queer public history, address some of the distinct ways that queer historians participate in the public sphere, and highlight problems and possibilities that emerge when queer academic work is shared with broader audiences. The book's narrative arc begins with the conditions of possibility for queer public history and LGBT scholarly activism in the 1980s and 1990s, when many of my contributions were aimed at LGBT readers, and concludes in the first two decades of the twenty-first century, when new technologies and changing circumstances encouraged me to imagine broader audiences. Each of the eight sections is organized around a particular theme; within each section, the essays are presented in order of original publication to show how my work developed over time. Because the book reprints previously published works not originally envisioned as parts of a whole and because the general organization is thematic, there is a little repetition and some movement back and forth in time, but I have tried to minimize that. While the autobiographical sections focus on a white gay man who has benefitted from many social privileges, the essays also address immigrants, lesbians, people of color, people with disabilities, trans people, and working-class people. I encourage my readers to question reading practices that make problematic assumptions about class, race, and gender if these are not explicitly addressed; many of the people discussed in my essays were not middle class, white, or men.

Some parts of this book explore and expose the inner workings of academic institutions, at least as I have experienced them, and I hope this will not be off-putting to nonacademic readers. Some may find it awkward and uncomfortable to read about book sales, blog views, editorial negotiations, job interviews, and professional gossip. There may be something distinctively queer about my interest in sharing information commonly treated as secrets, but my impulses in this regard also relate to the democratizing sensibilities of public history. Many of my first-generation students and colleagues experience academic cultures as foreign, intimidating, and strange; it might be helpful to highlight the bizarre characteristics and cultures of what sociologist Pierre Bourdieu, without explicit references to queer issues, calls *homo academicus*.[39] At the risk of mixing my metaphors, there are moments in this book when I attempt to pull back the curtains and open the closet doors to expose the mysteries of academia. As for references to my achievements and successes, some might see these as narcissistic (a common antigay trope), but I have attempted to be equally honest about my many failures, which I hope sends a message about the importance of perseverance and resiliency.

Part 1, "Queer Memories of the 1980s," features two essays that link my personal history to broader developments in the decade when I became a queer public historian and LGBT scholarly activist. Part 2, "Discipline, Punish, and Protest," brings together four works that address the problematic politics of academic history and the challenges that LGBT historians have experienced in struggles for fair treatment in higher education. Part 3, "Histories of Queer Activism," includes five articles on Philadelphia LGBT history. Part 4, "Queer Historical Interventions," reprints five essays that used historical arguments to intervene in political struggles during the Clinton, Bush, and Obama administrations. Part 5, "Queer Immigration," features four works on LGBT immigration law. Part 6, "Sex, Law, and the Supreme Court," includes five articles on other aspects of legal history. Part 7, "Exhibiting Queer History," brings together three essays linked to digital humanities projects. Part 8, "Stonewall, Popularity, and Publicity," features five works that historicize the Stonewall Riots era. The conclusion reflects on recent developments in queer public history, commenting on signs

[handwritten margin note: chapter summaries]

of positive change and reasons for concern. While the book has much to say about the evolution of queer public history and the history of my contributions to the field, I hope it will be read as a manifesto for the future, advocating for renewed partnerships between academic and community-based historians, strengthened links between queer public history and LGBT scholarly activism, and increased public support for historical projects on gender and sexuality.

PART ONE

Queer Memories of the 1980s

Historians often find it strange when they become the objects of historical inquiry. I remember sharing a draft of the final chapter of my 1994 PhD dissertation with my supervisor, Carroll Smith-Rosenberg, and reading her comments on my discussion of a feminist event that had taken place at the University of Pennsylvania in the 1970s. "I was there," she wrote in the margins. I regularly share this story when talking with students about the informal disciplinary rule that says that historians should avoid projects that concentrate on the last twenty years. Let scholars in other disciplines or interdisciplinary fields write about the very recent past, some historians say; we will get our turn when more time has gone by, when the dust has settled and we can offer longer-term perspectives.[1] Many historians address the present when writing about the past or offering historical perspectives on recent developments, but that is not the same thing as concentrating primarily on events so new that they feel more like the present than the past.

I recall thinking in 1994 that if my supervisor could add the authority of personal memory to all of the other power she had over my work, I was glad this was my last chapter. This was not because she misused her authority in any way, but how could I critically evaluate my sources when the source was my teacher, especially when I was a younger gay man, she was an older lesbian, and the chapter was about lesbian feminism in the 1970s? It was challenging enough to include her partner as one of my oral history narrators! I may have been a little defensive about this because around the same time a medieval European history specialist in my graduate program jokingly referred to all work on the twentieth century as "current events." If in many other fields there is a special cachet associated with work on the present, in history there is distinct admiration for studies of the distant past, partly because research on earlier periods generally is more difficult.

Years later, I was simultaneously pleased and troubled when my students began to research things I remember from the 1980s and 1990s. This was especially true when they found traces of my personal past. One student found my 1989 review of Larry Kramer's book *Reports from the Holocaust* in *Gay Community News*. Another found letters from the 1990s that I had written to Joan Nestle at the Lesbian Herstory Archives in New York. It is not unusual for students to find published academic works by their professors, but it felt different when they began to find archival evidence of my life. Maybe it just made me feel old.

I am now close to the age that Smith-Rosenberg was when she wrote "I was there" on my chapter draft. More of my students are interested in historical developments I remember, some of which occurred before they were born. In the last decade, I have begun to write about the late 1970s and 1980s, but for a long time I avoided this. My first book, published in 2000, concluded in 1972, when I was nine years old. My second, published in 2010, concluded in 1973. At the rate I was going, I was barely going to reach 1976, the year of the US Bicentennial and my bar mitzvah, before retirement. But then I leaped into the great (un)known and agreed to write a third book that would focus on the years from 1950 to 1990 (*Rethinking the Gay and Lesbian Movement*). Sure enough, I raced through the process of drafting the first few chapters, but stalled when I reached the years I remember well. I found it uncomfortable to complete those chapters, partly because my memories kept interfering with the strategies I had used for writing about earlier periods. This was a synthetic work that relied heavily on the scholarship of others, but historians had not yet written about MASS ACT OUT in Boston and ACT UP and Queer Action in Philadelphia. I found this profoundly disconcerting. Writing journalistically about those years, which I had done, was one thing; writing about them as an academic historian was more difficult.

"Queer Memories of the 1980s" reprints two essays originally published in the 2010s. Together they capture historical moments when "I was there" and historiographic moments when I was reconsidering a transformational decade. Today the 1980s is commonly remembered for the Reagan Revolution; the AIDS pandemic; and cultural wars about abortion, drugs, homosexuality, and pornography. Many gay men of my generation recall this as a strange and confusing time—we came out into a world shaped by the sexual revolution and gay liberation, but newly challenged by AIDS and the New Right. I experienced this period as a student at Wesleyan (1981–85), a traveler in Europe and the Middle East (1985–86), and an activist in Greater Boston (1986–89). In the 2010s, the publications reprinted here created opportunities for me to reflect on the 1980s as both participant and historian. Today, they allow me to revisit the era when I first became a queer public historian. In focusing on the 1980s, these essays also establish a foundation for the remainder of the book, which highlights my intensified engagement with queer public history in the 1990s and 2000s.

context

The first chapter, "Jonathan Ned Katz Murdered Me: History and Suicide," was published in 2016 on the Organization of American Historians' *Process* blog. The OAH, founded in 1907, has seven thousand members and is "the largest professional society dedicated to the teaching and study of American history." The blog was created in 2015 to explore "the process of doing history and the multifaceted ways of engaging with the U.S. past."[2] With a variety of short essays on diverse topics, it engages larger and broader audiences than those who typically read the OAH's *Journal of American History*, which publishes lengthy scholarly essays. I presented an early version of this essay in 2008 at the OAH's annual conference; academic historian Jim Downs had organized a panel to mark the seventieth birthday of public historian Jonathan Ned Katz. For the panel, attended by between fifty and a hundred people, I decided to speak publicly about my 1982 suicide attempt. I had tried several times before to write about this episode, but the conference provided me with an opportunity to talk publicly about how much Katz's work had helped me during a difficult time in my life. While I was anxious about sharing this story with an academic audience and concerned about distracting attention away from Katz, I wanted to honor his work, published by a historian without a PhD or academic appointment, by displaying the type of courage it must have taken for him to write *Gay American History*. Survivors of suicide attempts rarely write about their experiences; coming out about that can be more difficult than coming out as gay. I also wanted to speak out about an ongoing social problem: LGBT youth continue to attempt and commit suicide at staggering rates. My voice broke once during the presentation, but I was pleased by the audience responses and touched by Katz's reactions.

As brave as I may have been in 2008, it took eight more years before I shared the essay, slightly revised, with a larger audience. When I did so, I did not choose a queer history venue, which might have been easier, but offered it to *Process*, which reaches mainstream historians. In doing so I worried about whether there would be professional costs, whether I would contribute to negative stereotypes about homosexuality, and whether my language would problematically disavow relationships between homosexuality and "madness." In this context, I did not share the link with my department chair, my faculty colleagues, or my college's communications staff, as I ordinarily might have done. Nonetheless I am proud of this essay, primarily for honoring Katz's work, challenging the silences that surround suicide, and capturing a moment in the history of the 1980s, when the work of LGBT historians saved lives.

The second essay, "Memories of the 1987 March on Washington," was published in 2013 on the queer history website OutHistory, which was founded by Katz and led at the time by Katz, John D'Emilio, and Claire Potter. I introduced Katz and D'Emilio previously. Potter, a professor of history in the Schools of Public Engagement and director of the Digital Humanities Initiative at the New School in New York, is best known for her work from 2007 to 2015 as the "tenured radical," through which she "harnessed the power of blogging to address big changes in academic life, political writing and scholarship."[3] As for OutHistory, founded in 2008 by Katz, the website explains: "When the Internet became part of the everyday life of millions—even billions—of people in the 21st century, Katz understood that the work of archiving, establishing LGBTQ chronologies, and highlighting new discoveries begun in *Gay American History* should continue on a digital platform. Katz's longtime history as an activist and community scholar also caused him to imagine the site as a place of active community participation in the process of discovering and writing LGBTQ histories. . . . Katz's vision embraced the work of amateur and professional historians; researchers based in colleges and universities and those working on their own; historians focused on a particular topic and those with wide interests."[4]

I wrote my account of participating in the 1987 March on Washington in response to D'Emilio's public call for people who remembered the march to share their personal narratives for an OutHistory exhibit. In writing this essay in 2013, I was struck by the fact that I could not reconstruct the precise chronology of my involvement with *GCN*, the 1987 March, and MASS ACT OUT. Rereading it today, I am struck by the fact that I was wrong about one thing: I thought I had lost the yellow rubber gloves that I had worn during the week when hundreds of us committed civil disobedience at the US Supreme Court in 1987, but I recently found them. This makes me think about the fallibility of memory and the need to take that into consideration when interpreting oral histories and other types of autobiographical narratives. I say this not because of the need to correct mistakes, though sometimes that might be useful, and more to encourage questions about why people remember and misremember in the ways they do.

In reconsidering the essay now, I see that it was published in 2013, one year before I moved back to the United States after sixteen years of teaching in Canada. For more than a decade, I had shared with Canadian students the story of my 1987 arrest at the Supreme Court. Activists had selected the Court as a target because of its infamous 1986 decision in *Bowers v. Hardwick*, which upheld state sodomy laws. In 2004, when I first wrote for a public audience about my participation in the protest (see chapter 4), I avoided affirming explicitly that I had been arrested. At the time I was a legal resident but not a citizen of Canada and feared that my arrest record might endanger my status. By 2010, I was apparently less concerned about this, writing more explicitly about it in my book *Sexual Injustice*. Three years later, I shared additional details in the essay reprinted here. By this time I was willing to let caution go to the wind, trusting (naively perhaps) that Canada (unlike the United States) would not deport a gay man who had been arrested while protesting an antigay decision by the US Supreme Court. I probably would not have felt the same if I had not been the beneficiary of white middle-class privilege. In any case, this essay, like the previous one, highlights formative experiences in the 1980s that very much influenced my later work as a queer public historian.

Jonathan Ned Katz Murdered Me

History and Suicide

In 1982, after my first year of college, I was murdered. The weapon was seven inches long and two inches thick. It was mostly beige, but also featured the reddish color of blood. It may look old today, but when I first encountered its massive volume, it was in perfect condition. It was almost too large, long, and powerful to handle, but eventually I absorbed all of it. And then, after an unexpected twist, it was among the weapons that killed me. Or perhaps I should say it killed a certain version of me, a version that could not quite figure out how to be happy, how to be gay, or how to live in this world.

The weapon that helped kill me was Jonathan Ned Katz's groundbreaking 1976 book *Gay American History*. I do not offer here a comprehensive review, a critical analysis, or a celebratory account. Instead I provide a set of personal reflections on what this book meant to me when I encountered it more than thirty years ago, when I was eighteen years old. I first read *Gay American History* during my first year in college, 1981–82. This was the year I attempted suicide, or, as I sometimes prefer to say, the year I committed suicide. When I was younger I used to talk with friends and acquaintances more regularly about what happened to me during the summer of 1982, when I was living at home with my family in the New York suburbs after an emotionally

This essay, drafted in 2008, was published originally on *Process: A Blog for American History*, 8 Mar. 2016, http://www.processhistory.org/stein-katz/.

devastating year. Over time, the stories multiplied. In one, I committed suicide because of homophobic self-hatred. In another, the causes were antigay prejudice, discrimination, and oppression. There were stories of family violence turned inward, a traumatic breakup with a girlfriend, unrequited feelings for a male friend, and chemical imbalances. There was even a story of corporate workplace alienation, which focused on the soul-destroying effects of working for my father's company that summer. On my suicide's tenth anniversary, which occurred just after I passed my Ph.D. comprehensive examinations, I rented a cabin in Maine, where I invited my closest friends to join me as I marked a decade of life that I almost did not have.

Since that time I have been less inclined to share the stories of my suicide and in the last decade or two I have been repeatedly surprised to realize that some of my closest friends do not know that I almost did not live to my nineteenth birthday. Certainly most of my professional friends and colleagues have not heard these stories. So why did I offer to speak about this episode on a 2008 conference panel celebrating Jonathan Ned Katz and why am I now sharing this revised version more widely? One reason is captured in my title: this book helped kill my suicidal self. The historian in me is impressed by any work of scholarship that can have such a powerful effect on a reader. But I also want to honor this remarkable book by echoing, in a small and personal way, the courage that it must have taken for Katz to produce this extraordinary work. This is difficult for me to do, but I am inspired to speak about the unspoken by Katz's book.

My copy of *Gay American History* is now so old and tattered that each time I turn one of its 1,063 pages I find myself holding a page no longer attached to the rest. It is one of just a few of my books that are now held together with a rubber band. I no longer recall the circumstances that led me to buy *Gay American History* during my first year of college. I think it's the first gay-themed book I ever owned. If I had to guess I would say that I purchased it at Atticus Books in Middletown, Connecticut, but it might have been at a feminist bookstore in Hartford or New Haven; or one of the bookstores that I used to frequent in Harvard Square; or Glad Day Books in Boston. Either way, I am sure that when I took the book off the shelf, carried it to the checkout line, interacted with the sales clerk, and paid the bill, my heart was racing and I was overwhelmed by a combination of terror and excitement. I know this because the same thing happened to me for years whenever I purchased a gay or lesbian book. Sometimes it still does.

In the early 1980s, when I purchased *Gay American History*, Ronald Reagan was the U.S. president, I became eligible to vote, and I was legally required to register for the military draft. I was straight and had a girlfriend, though that year I also fell for a fellow male student, who also happened to be named Jonathan. I may have bought the book because I was working on a paper on "the origins of homosexuality" for an introductory psychology class. I remember that paper well because at the last minute, when I realized that someone would actually be reading what I had written (and that other students might see the title page), I changed the title to "the origins of heterosexuality" without changing the paper's contents. Who knows what the teaching assistant thought as he or she read a paper with a mismatched title, though I sometimes joke that years before Katz helped establish another field of historical inquiry with the publication of his 1995 book *The Invention of Heterosexuality*, I precociously gestured in the same direction. Today it does not surprise me that I wrote my first gay studies paper in a psychology course; in the early 1980s psychology was still the dominant discipline in studies of homosexuality. John D'Emilio's *Sexual Politics, Sexual Communities* (1983), which also changed my life, was not yet published. *Gay American History* was unique.

That year, as I descended into the depths of a depression that culminated in my suicide, Katz's book became my lifeline. Each night, as I lay in bed in my dormitory room, I would read one of the hundreds of primary documents collected in *Gay American History* and my head, heart, and body would respond to the results of Jonathan's archival research and introductory commentary. I have a vague memory of deciding to ignore Katz's thematic organization and instead read the documents in chronological order, which may be why even today I remember not only the first document, which tells the story of the murder of a sixteenth-century French interpreter, but also the first item in the book's Native American section, a sixteenth-century account of "devilish" practices in Florida. In the last few years, as I have returned to *Gay American History*, I have tried to recall, without success, how I reacted when I first read several items that later were critical to my work on Philadelphia gay and lesbian history. In the end, I do not think it was any particular document that affected me; it was more the combined and cumulative effects of the whole, which helped bring me back to life after I died.

What is it that so moved and inspired me when I first read *Gay American History*? One answer is that Katz's book helped me move beyond the psychological frameworks that were the primary means available for interpreting my desires. As the book's introduction explained, "The prevailing notion of homosexuality as a purely psychological phenomenon has limited discussion, focusing research almost exclusively on . . . the causation, character, and treatment of homosexuality as a psychosexual orientation disturbance" (11). I took no history classes during my first year of college. For a long time my major was psychology, and by the time I reached my fourth undergraduate year, I was one course shy of finishing that major. But something happened along the way, and instead of taking that final psychology class, I selected six history courses and completed a history degree. To fulfill my new major's requirements, I embarked on a research project on the history of psychological perspectives on homosexuality. As *Gay American History* taught me before Michel Foucault did, "The dominance of the psychological model has meant that this model itself was not seen as a historical invention. A temporal perspective emphasizes that homosexuality was once thought of by theologians as essentially a moral issue, a sin; by legislators as a legal problem, a crime; only later, by a rising class of medical entrepreneurs, as a psychological phenomenon, a psychic disturbance. If the traditional psychological model is to be transcended, homosexuality must be reconceived as a historical, social, political, and economic phenomenon, as well as a psychological one" (11–12).

What is it that history offered to me that psychology did not? Among the things I found in *Gay American History* were stories that encouraged me to imagine possible ways of living a gay life, stories of passion and power, love and lust, camaraderie and companionship. They also offered visions of social change and political transformation. Even the stories that did not turn out so well, and there were many, helped me understand that there were others with desires like mine, that we were not diseased and pathological, that it was possible to live lives beyond the ones determined by the expectations of hostile and hateful others. As Katz wrote in his introduction, "Knowledge of Gay history . . . extends the range of human possibilities, suggests new ways of living, new ways of loving" (14). For me, document after document in *Gay American History* opened up worlds of possibilities about how to live and love.

There were also the lives and loves I imagined for the storyteller, his comrades, and his audience. Katz wrote in the first pages of *Gay American History*, "Those of us affected by [the gay and lesbian] movement have experienced a basic change in our sense of self. As we acted upon our society we acted upon ourselves. . . . From a sense of our homosexuality as a personal and devastating fate, a private, secret shame, we moved with often dizzying speed to the consciousness of ourselves as members of an oppressed social group. . . . We moved . . . from a sense that there was something deeply wrong with us to the realization that there was something radically wrong with . . . society. . . . Starting with a sense of ourselves as . . . the passive victims of a family tragedy, we experienced ourselves as . . . assertive actors in a movement for social change" (1–2).

As I read these words today, I think about what it must have meant to my suicidal self, who felt so isolated and alone even when surrounded by friends, to come across these collective pronouns, which placed the individual within larger narratives of history and politics. Critics may object to the ways that Katz presumed to speak for an entire generation of gay men and lesbians, but what a difference it made to readers like me to imagine the possibility of joining the worlds of the author and his audience!

Was *Gay American History* essentialist in the ways it imagined homosexuality in the past? Sure, though today that has to be among the most trite and boring things one could say about this book. Any serious consideration of this issue would have to acknowledge Katz's emphasis on "the existence of many Gay voices, many Gay lives, many homosexualities" (9–10), his assertion that "there is no such thing as homosexuality in general, only particular historical forms of homosexuality" (11), and his efforts to include documents about women and Native Americans. No doubt Katz would use different language today.

Just as significant, I think, are the ways that *Gay American History* imagined homosexuality in the future. The great secret of historical scholarship, of course, is that historians do not write (only) about the past; we write about the future. As Katz asserted in his introduction, "The study of homosexual history suggests a new basis for a radical critique of American society" (14). The introduction concluded by linking gay historical scholarship to "a much larger struggle by Gay people and others for power and control over those social institutions which most affect our lives," for "radical social change," and for "democracy" (14–15). Katz also had a more specific vision for the future, one in which "a team of Lesbian and Gay male researchers" would "work cooperatively to actually discover and disseminate our forgotten history." "Perhaps,"

Katz wrote with modesty and humility, "this book will contribute to the realization of that dream" (14).

In the year I first read *Gay American History,* my own personal dream was fulfilled several weeks after I committed suicide, when I first had sex with a man.

Katz's dream has yet to be fully realized, but no book has done more to create a future for gay, lesbian, bisexual, transgender, and queer history.

CHAPTER 2

Memories of the 1987 March on Washington

The 1987 March on Washington [for Lesbian and Gay Rights] was an incredibly important episode in my intensifying involvement in the gay and lesbian movement and my efforts to link my sexuality and my politics. From 1981 to 1985, I had been a mostly straight student at Wesleyan University in Connecticut, where I had participated in abortion rights, anti-apartheid, antiracist, antiwar, feminist, gay/lesbian, and student activism. After I graduated in 1985, I spent most of the next year working and travelling with my girlfriend in Europe and Israel. In 1986, after my girlfriend and I broke up, I moved to Boston and began working for the Institute for Defense and Disarmament Studies. Around this time I also began volunteering at *Gay Community News*, first helping with the weekly mailing of the paper on Friday nights, then assisting with layout and proofreading on Thursday nights, later joining the Board of Directors, and finally becoming the newspaper's coordinating editor in 1988 and 1989. Michael Bronski, one of *GCN*'s most active contributing writers, mentored me at *GCN*; he and several others introduced me to the gay and lesbian world, which was quite new to me.

Shortly after I began volunteering at *GCN*, I started attending meetings and demonstrations organized by the Gay and Lesbian Defense

This essay was published originally on OutHistory, Aug. 2013, http://outhistory.org /exhibits/show/march-on-washington/exhibit/by-marc-stein.

Committee, which was campaigning against Governor Michael Duka-kis's policies against placing children with gay and lesbian foster parents. Through *GCN* and GLDC I got involved with a social and political network of about two dozen gay and lesbian activists, several of whom were editors of the journal *Radical America*, which was in the process of putting out two special issues on AIDS. Within this network I became friends with two young gay men who had graduated from the Rhode Island School of Design—Fred Gorman and Gregory Gazaway—and we were taken under the wings of a group of older lesbian activists, including Margaret Cerullo and Marla Erlien, both of whom were *Radical America* editors, along with Jade McGlaughlin, Nancy Wechsler, Ann Holder, Judy Andler, and Susan Levene. Eventually, though I can't remember whether this occurred before or after the march, several of us formed the core of MASS ACT OUT, which was inspired by the work of ACT UP New York and predated the formation of ACT UP Boston.

If AIDS was one of the focal points of my developing gay and lesbian political consciousness in this period, the Supreme Court's 1986 decision in *Bowers v. Hardwick*, which upheld state sodomy laws, was the other. The Supreme Court's ruling was announced just a few months after I moved to Boston; I remember reading the decision in the *New York Times* and feeling a combination of anger, fury, rage, and disappointment. I distinctly remember going to a demonstration at Boston University to protest a speech by William Rehnquist, who joined the conservative majority in *Bowers* and was appointed Chief Justice later that year.

At some point in this period, probably in the first half of 1987, I began attending meetings of the New England Organizing Committee for the March on Washington, which I think was led by Judy Andler and operated, at least for a time, out of *GCN*'s offices. The work involved publicizing the upcoming march, distributing flyers in the bars, using buttons, stickers, and posters to recruit participants, organizing fundraisers, and participating in discussions about march demands and strategies. At Wesleyan, I had participated in campus organizing for two marches on Washington to protest cutbacks in education funding and student aid, so this type of political work was familiar to me. I experienced the organizing process for the 1987 march as very grassroots; it seemed to me that the national organizers very much involved local activists in the process. And in Boston and New England, the local organizing was led by radical gay and lesbian activists with progressive class, gender, race, and sexual politics. In fact, many of the same people who were involved with GLDC, *GCN*, *Radical America*, and MASS ACT OUT were active on the New England Organizing Committee.

I don't remember much about traveling to the march and I don't remember many details about the march itself; I attended approximately ten marches on Washington in the 1980s and 1990s and it's difficult for me to remember anything specific about each one. I remember that the 1987 march felt huge; we were so pleased and proud about the attendance. I visited the NAMES Project Quilt, which was very moving, but I think my radical friends and allies were somewhat ambivalent about its politics. We understood the emotional and political work of the quilt, but favored more aggressive, militant, and radical forms of political activism. It was either at the march or at a gay pride parade in New York or Boston that I first witnessed the impressive and inspiring spectacle of a large number of ACT UP activists marching together and chanting "Act Up, Fight Back, Fight AIDS."

What I remember more distinctly was the civil disobedience action at the U.S. Supreme Court on the day after the march [actually it was two days after the march]. At some point in the organizing process we had learned that on the day after the march activists were planning to engage in nonviolent civil disobedience at the Supreme Court building to protest the decision in Bowers. Several of us formed an affinity group and decided to participate together; I think it included Margaret, Marla, Fred, Jade, Ann, and a few others; I think we were a group of ten or twelve people. I had never done civil disobedience, but was very excited about the prospect. I think one member of our group agreed to serve as a witness in case there were troubles with the police; this was based on advice from activists who were experienced in nonviolent civil disobedience. Several of us attended an evening planning session that featured trainings in nonviolent civil disobedience. On the day of the action, the scene at the Supreme Court was intense, chaotic, and full of energy. Our group met up and joined the large crowd massing, marching, and shouting in front of the building. The police had set up barricades and they were stationed at various points around the building. We had been told in advance that they would likely be wearing plastic yellow gloves because of AIDS hysteria; sure enough they were. We had purchased plastic yellow gloves of our own and had painted them to look like we had purple nail polish; we wanted to mock the police. I saved those gloves for many years (until they fell apart)!

At some point we noticed that the police had created a small opening in their barricades, large enough for a single file line of activists to walk through. We watched as a line of activists walked through the barricades and were led directly onto a set of school buses that were positioned in a parking lot, presumably to take us to jail. At this point, I think our group had a sense of ourselves as falling somewhere in the middle of the spectrum of activists who were there that day. Some protesters were content to follow the procedures set up by the police and walk peacefully to the buses. Some were determined to break through the barricades, run as far as possible toward the building, refuse to move when confronted by the police, and act in other aggressive ways. We wanted to do more than the first group but not go as far as the second. At some point someone encouraged us to run to the back of the Supreme Court building, where apparently the police were relying on shrubs to block access. We joined several other affinity groups and rushed through an opening in the shrubs, where apparently no police officers were stationed.

I recall running with our group toward the Supreme Court building. The feeling was exhilarating; there was something about challenging authority in the way we were doing that felt incredible. I think we ran a few hundred feet and then several police appeared. Someone cried out, reminding us of our plan—sit down, link arms, and begin chanting. We did just that. I remember my heart was pounding. Soon other activists poured through the opening in the shrubs and the officers guarding us ran off to block their access to the building. At some point we realized that no one was guarding us and that we could get up and begin running toward the building again, which we did. After another few hundred feet, the police again blocked our way; this time they didn't leave us unguarded. At some point I think someone in authority came over to us and explained that we could walk ourselves to the buses or we would be physically carried. We decided to walk ourselves, which we did. I think it was at this point that Fred and I were separated from the women in our group. At some point someone in authority came onto the bus and told us that they were going to handcuff us with plastic cuffs (really plastic ties). I think we had been advised during the civil disobedience training about how to hold our wrists so that the cuffs would not be too tight. Sure enough, mine were so loose that I quickly was able to free my hands and discreetly showed Fred that, if need be, I could free myself again.

We were taken somewhere to be processed; I think it was a school gymnasium. I remember sitting for hours and talking with Fred. I remember feeling totally bored. We had been warned in advance that we might be issued a ticket and fined or we might end up spending the night in jail. We had been confident enough about this to plan our return trip to Boston that day or the next, but we also knew it was possible that we wouldn't be released in time. None of us knew exactly what would happen and there were all sorts of rumors that circulated in the gym about what the police were doing. Eventually, it was our turn to be processed. I could be wrong about this and I could be exaggerating, but I think Fred and I were fined $200 each. Having been warned to expect this, we had brought enough cash to cover the fines. I don't remember anything else about leaving the gym, meeting back up with our friends, or returning to Boston.

I remember the civil disobedience action at the Supreme Court with great pride and pleasure. There was something about the collective nature of the experience—collective in the sense of the way I participated with my friends and allies from Boston and collective in the sense of joining with hundreds of others to engage in civil disobedience at the Supreme Court—that made it feel very special. There was something about my willingness to put my body on the line—we didn't know what to expect and whether the police would respond violently—that signalled my deepening commitment to the gay and lesbian movement specifically and political activism more generally. There was something about our emotions and our politics at that particular moment in time—after the Supreme Court rejected us in *Bowers* and as the U.S. government continued to reject us in the AIDS crisis—that had a deep and lasting influence. In retrospect, I can see that the 1987 March on Washington played a role in my decisions to deepen my involvement in gay/lesbian and AIDS activism, apply for a job at *Gay Community News* in 1988, and go to graduate school to study gay and lesbian history in 1989. And the politics of the march—its class, gender, racial, and sexual politics and its radical politics—influenced how I did all of those things in the next several years.

PART TWO

Discipline, Punish, and Protest

In 1989, I left my job at *Gay Community News* in Boston to begin my new life as a PhD student at the University of Pennsylvania. This was a momentous year in world history. On the global stage, political revolutions in Eastern Europe overthrew communist regimes; Germans began destroying the Berlin Wall and ending the Cold War division of Europe; and Brazil held its first presidential election in nearly thirty years. In the United States, Republican George H. W. Bush was inaugurated as U.S. president, marking the first time in decades that one political party maintained control of the White House for more than eight years. Several weeks after I moved to Philadelphia, the National Commission on AIDS met for the first time; this was eight years after the first reports on the pandemic were published. That year, the number of reported AIDS cases in the United States reached one hundred thousand. Oral sex, anal sex, and same-sex sex were illegal in approximately half the states. Same-sex partnerships and marriages were not legally recognized anywhere. Discrimination based on sexual orientation was legal in forty-seven states; discrimination based on gender identity and expression was legal in all fifty.

In August and September 1989, my primary focus was transitioning from newspaper editor in Boston to graduate student in Philadelphia. In the midst of so much change, I failed to plan in advance for the inevitable questions from Penn faculty and classmates about what I had been doing since graduating from college and what I hoped to study. Within the first few minutes of the orientation program for my cohort of eighteen students, I was out as gay. It helped that one of my classmates was another former *GCN* staffer; several students in classes ahead of mine also were interested in queer history; and there were four LGBT faculty in my program.

The University of Pennsylvania proved to be a good place for me to become a U.S. historian and an LGBT historian, notwithstanding occasional moments of homophobia and frequent encounters with heterosexism. Carroll Smith-Rosenberg, Mary Frances Berry, and Evelyn Brooks Higginbotham taught illuminating courses on the history of gender, sexuality, and race. Larry Gross (a professor in the Annenberg School of Communications) and Bob Schoenberg (who led Penn's LGB Center) organized an exciting schedule of speakers through the Philadelphia Lesbian and Gay Academic Union. Most of my other professors and classmates, in courses on colonial, cultural, legal, political, social, African American, and women's history, responded positively to my interests in queer studies. Other than Smith-Rosenberg, the faculty did not assign much LGBT history, but I wrote most of my papers on sexuality and gender.

I also took a set of interdisciplinary and theoretical courses on gender, sexuality, and race, taught by professors in history, French, and English, including literary critics Lynda Hart and Joan Dejean. These helped me understand that the discipline of history was no longer in the forefront of LGBT studies, as it had been in the 1970s and 1980s. In interdisciplinary LGBT studies contexts, everyone still read the work of historian Michel Foucault, but the new scholarship that seemed to be capturing everyone's attention was by philosopher Judith Butler, film studies scholar Teresa de Lauretis, and literary critic Eve Kosofsky Sedgwick. It also became apparent to me that for a variety of reasons, it was now expected that faculty and students in other humanities fields, including English literature and cultural studies, familiarize themselves with LGBT issues, but this was not the case in history. In a 1995 essay, Lisa Duggan, who completed her PhD at Penn several years before I did, discussed this in her analysis of "the discipline problem," pointing to the isolation of LGBT historians in relation to the discipline of history and interdisciplinary LGBT studies.[1]

There was another problem that loomed large for me. I enjoyed academic work and saw what I was doing as political, but much of it seemed self-centered and self-indulgent. I felt this way in particular during my second year in graduate school, when I learned that an ex-boyfriend, an African American leader of the AIDS Action Committee's Multicultural Concerns Committee in Boston, had died of AIDS.[2] Profoundly upset about this, I took incompletes in two of my three classes, finishing up the deferred papers a few months later. More generally, I identified strongly as an activist and was committed to a set of progressive movements. I believed it was important to study the history of social change, but also wanted to make a difference in the here and now. Some of my *GCN* comrades had seen my decision to begin graduate studies as selling out, an abandonment of work in the trenches of movement politics in favor of financial security, professional status, and the rarefied life of the mind. I disagreed and was determined to continue participating in struggles for social justice.

One way I did so during my graduate school years (1989–1994) was by treating the university itself as a target of political activism, which I first had done as a Wesleyan undergraduate. Sometimes this meant speaking up about LGBT issues in my classes. Sometimes it meant speaking up for myself. In one incident, I found the courage to speak to a professor for whom I was working as a teaching assistant after he joked to our two-hundred-person class about the fact that most of the students I had asked to see after his lecture were male; I do not think his intentions were malevolent (he was poking fun at the fact that the students "in trouble" were men), but he failed to anticipate how his comment might be perceived by undergraduates with a gay teaching assistant. In another incident, I wrote to a dean about the nasty comment directed my way, at a reception, after I answered a question from a university overseer about the subject of my research. "Now I really need a drink," he muttered as he walked away.[3]

I also worked in more organized and collective ways. As president of the Graduate History Students Association at Penn, I successfully lobbied our department to reduce the number of undergraduates assigned to each teaching assistant. I also convinced my fellow graduate students to replace the AIDS education posters that were torn down three times after I put them up in our lounge. Less successfully, we urged the faculty to hire a lesbian visiting professor for a tenure-track position. Beyond the department, I helped lead a failed effort to unionize Penn's teaching assistants (though I still think the name we selected for our group—COGS, Coalition of Graduate Students—was clever).[4] More successfully, when the university's main student newspaper published an advertisement for a local restaurant that was offering a Valentine's Day special for "opposite-sex couples only," I organized the Valentine's

Day Coalition, which included faculty, staff, and students. After filing an antidiscrimination complaint with the Philadelphia Commission on Human Relations, we negotiated a settlement with the restaurant and newspaper.[5] Beyond the university, I participated occasionally in ACT UP Philadelphia demonstrations and helped found and name Queer Action, which was loosely affiliated with the Queer Nation movement.[6] I also began publishing short articles, drawn from my academic research, in LGBT periodicals such as *GCN* and *Philadelphia Gay News*.

With the help of a Mellon Foundation fellowship and the first Ken Dawson Award, funded by the Center for Lesbian and Gay Studies at the City University of New York and named for a Wesleyan alum who had died of AIDS in 1992, I finished my PhD in 1994. Although I had told myself years before that specializing in LGBT history would decrease the likelihood of finding work as a professor, by the time I finished my degree I was invested in having an academic career. The years that followed were full of disappointments in my search for a secure job, though I was sustained by good short-term positions. In 1994–95, I taught part-time at the University of Pennsylvania. For 1995–96 I won postdoctoral fellowships at Ohio State University (thanks to queer historian Leila Rupp) and Bryn Mawr College (thanks to queer historian Sharon Ullman); choosing the latter allowed me to remain in Philadelphia. In 1996, I was hired for a one-year visiting assistant professorship (later extended for a second year) in U.S. women's history at Colby College in Maine.

One of the striking things about my struggles on the academic job market was the contrast with my successes in scholarly publishing. Other LGBT historians of my generation had similar experiences, but in 1995 the academic magazine *Lingua Franca* featured me in an article titled "Robbing the Cradle." The piece began by hyperbolically referencing the "modest sensation" caused by my conference presentations on gay and lesbian history and then explained that I had done "what more than few in-demand professors do: he hooked up with a topflight New York literary agent." After noting that the agent had negotiated on my behalf with eight university presses and secured a contract with the University of Chicago Press, the article observed, "The thing is, Stein wasn't a professor. He was a fourth year graduate student . . . with the end of his dissertation only barely in sight. And therein lies a tale. In an age of financial pressures and glittering superstores, university presses are more keen on pushing crossover blockbusters than ever before. And they've hit on gay and lesbian history as the Garth Brooks of academic discourses; rare among scholarly genres, it sells equally well to professional and lay readerships." The article cautioned, however, that "no matter how many book deals they garner, those grad students still face arid job prospects." Niko Pfund, then an editor at New York University Press, was quoted as saying, "There must be tremendous cognitive dissonance among students in the history of sexuality. On one hand you have all these publishers handing you their business cards, and then there are no jobs teaching the history of sexuality."[7]

In contrast to some of my queer history peers, I was fortunate in landing short-term positions at Bryn Mawr and Colby. While working at the latter, I had my hands full with course development, teaching responsibilities, job applications, and the process of turning my dissertation into a book, not to mention a new relationship with a tenured professor of Latin American literature, still my partner twenty-five years later. Nevertheless, I could not avoid political activism completely. Once again, the primary target was my own educational institution, which probably was not a smart strategic move if my goal was longer-term employment. On learning that Colby had failed to follow through on a set of LGBT policy recommendations that the college's president had endorsed years earlier (including the hiring of LGBT studies faculty), I convened a group of queer faculty and allies that we termed the Fabulous Faculty Fifteen, which advocated for implementation of the recommendations. I also helped revive Colby's chapter of the American Association of University Professors and worked to challenge the college's unfair labor practices. None of this directly aided my pursuit of a secure job, notwithstanding the fact that Colby had never hired a specialist in LGBT studies for a tenure-track job or the fact that Colby's faculty included more than ten straight couples. But I remain proud of our collective efforts at Colby and, because my partner remained there until he retired in 2019, I saw some of what we fought for come to fruition.[8]

In 1998, I finally landed a tenure-track job as an assistant professor of U.S. political history at York University in Toronto. Two years later, the University of Chicago Press published my first book. That same year I began a three-year term as chair of the Committee on Lesbian and Gay History, an affiliated society of the American Historical Association. During my term, we established a governing board to democratize organizational leadership and boosted the committee's national and international membership. We also improved the representation of LGBT history on the AHA annual convention programs, advocated for LGBT historians on the academic job market, created an organizational website, produced a bibliography of LGBT history dissertations, initiated a LGBT history syllabi exchange, and supported efforts to have the National Park Service list the Stonewall Inn as a National Historic Landmark.

I later continued working with others to improve the status of LGBT historians. In 2009, I was appointed to the AHA's LGBTQ Historians Task Force. In its first year, the task force advocated for improvements in the organization's handling of a boycott of the anti-union and anti-gay San Diego hotel where the AHA convention was scheduled to take place. In 2015, the task force completed a wide-ranging report that led to the creation of the AHA's Committee on LGBTQ Status in the Profession. In 2013, I was invited to serve as the first chair of the Organization of American Historians Committee on the Status of LGBTQ Historians and Histories. We worked successfully to improve the representation of LGBT history on OAH convention programs, revise several OAH diversity policies, establish the John D'Emilio LGBTQ History Dissertation Award, and advocate for LGBT historians in OAH elections, which contributed to the election of Joanne Meyerowitz as OAH president.

Part 2 reprints four essays that critique the politics of disciplinary history and academic humanities. Because they challenged powerful decision-makers, I do not believe I would have dared to publish them before receiving tenure in 2001, but I thought then and think now that LGBT historians who gain job security have a responsibility to speak out about the collective troubles we experience in higher education. This belief has only increased as I have watched many bright and talented historians abandon the search for academic employment because of higher education's anti-LGBT animus. As works of scholarly activism that targeted the institutional power of history departments, the funding power of the National Endowment for the Humanities, and the disciplinary power of political history specialists, these essays were written to challenge bias, prejudice, and discrimination in history and the humanities.

Chapter 3, "Committee on Lesbian and Gay History Survey on LGBTQ History Careers," reprints a short version of a quantitative study completed in 2001 for the CLGH; it focuses on the graduate school and job market experiences of U.S. and Canadian LGBT historians. This version was published in *Perspectives*, the monthly publication of the AHA, which has approximately twelve thousand members. The longer study was published on the CLGH website. Quantitative methods are not very popular in history or other humanities fields, but they can be valuable. In this case, the quantitative data provided useful information to prospective graduate students and helped show that the job market difficulties experienced by LGBT historians were not individual and atypical; they were collective and systemic. I believe the quantitative evidence also contributed to sympathetic public reactions in the discipline of history, interdisciplinary LGBT studies, and the larger higher education world. For example, the study's positive coverage in *The Chronicle of Higher Education*, essentially the *New York Times* of U.S. colleges and universities, was likely influenced by the quantitative methods used.[9]

All of that said, I also was keen to share my personal stories, which I did in the second essay reprinted here, "Crossing Borders: Memories, Dreams, Fantasies, and Nightmares of the History Job Market." Published in 2004 by *Left History*, a peer-reviewed journal based at York University, the essay is based on my 1999 keynote address at York's annual graduate student history conference. For my conference presentation, I thought the audience might be interested in hearing about my job market experiences—they would learn about troubles I experienced, strategies I used, and reasons to persevere. *Left History* was an obvious choice when I later decided to publish a revised version, not only because it was based at York. Like *Radical History Review*, which published my first scholarly essay in 1994, *Left History* has a strong record of publishing work on LGBT history, which is not the case with most historical journals.

When I wrote the first version of this essay in 1999, I think there were only two people—John D'Emilio and George Chauncey—who had been hired in tenure-track positions by U.S. history departments on the basis of U.S. LGBT history dissertations. There were a few others who had written dissertations with a chapter or two on LGBT topics, a few LGBT history specialists who had been hired in interdisciplinary programs, and a few who had been hired by history departments in other countries. Thirty years later, the situation is better, though bias, prejudice, and discrimination continue to damage the academic careers of many LGBT historians. It also is more obvious today that LGBT historians in the 1970s, 1980s, and 1990s were canaries in the discipline's coal mine. As higher education budgets have been slashed by anti-government and tax-cutting conservatives, there have been declines in tenure-track faculty positions and increases in the number of part-time and poorly compensated instructors. This shift has had negative consequences for students, for the "adjunct" faculty themselves, and for tenure-track and tenured faculty. The troubles of LGBT historians, however, are rarely considered in discussions about the academic job market.

When I first began to hear more and more straight, white, and male historians complain about the challenges they were experiencing in finding good academic jobs, I was sympathetic, but wondered about where their predecessors had been during the decades in which the vast majority of history departments would not hire LGBT history specialists or specialists in the history of women or racial minorities. Many straight white men in previous generations had been hired in positions that were closed to historians of sexuality, gender, and race. Today, when the discipline devotes a great deal of time and energy to thinking about "alternate" career paths, I rarely see LGBT historians asked for their perspectives, even though they sadly have the wisdom of experience in dealing with job market challenges. Given their successes in reaching large public audiences, some of that wisdom could be helpful for other historians.

Chapter 5, "Post-Tenure Lavender Blues," moves forward a few years and shifts the focus from faculty hiring by history departments to research fellowships by the National Endowment for the Humanities. This essay describes my experiences of being recommended unanimously, through a scholarly peer-review process, for a prestigious NEH research fellowship, only to have that recommendation vetoed by the NEH's presidentially appointed chair. I presented a shorter version at the 2006 AHA convention on a session sponsored by the AHA Professional Division, the CLGH, and the Coordinating Council for Women in History; the version reprinted here was published the same week by the *History News Network*. Within days of my presentation, *Inside Higher Ed*, an online publication founded in 2004 as an alternative to *The Chronicle of Higher Education*, featured it in a story about bias allegations against the NEH. A few months later, AHA president Linda Kerber referenced it in her monthly column in *Perspectives*. My complaints also led the AHA to adopt a "Statement on Peer Review for Historical Research," which critiqued political interference with peer review. In retrospect, I am pleased that my work contributed to a collective and multiyear effort to expose and condemn conservative political bias at the NEH.[10]

Chapter 6, "Political History and the History of Sexuality," was another effort to critique anti-LGBT bias in higher education. In this case, my targets were self-appointed spokesmen for the subfield of political history, historians who wrote a 2016 *New York Times* column that bemoaned the decline of political history and did so in ways that contributed to the erasure of historical scholarship on sexuality. My essay, published in *Perspectives* in 2017 with a response by the authors, generated many appreciative comments from likeminded scholars (and approximately two thousand eight hundred views), but also a critical note (sent privately by an acquaintance) about my erasure of scholarship on sexuality and race. While the critique was overstated and missed the scholars of color referenced in my essay, it made valid points; if I could rewrite the essay today, I would do more to highlight political history scholarship that addresses sexuality and race.

CHAPTER 3

Committee on Lesbian and Gay History Survey on LGBTQ History Careers

Members of the Committee on Lesbian and Gay History (CLGH) have long been concerned about the graduate school and job market experiences of those who complete PhD dissertations on lesbian, gay, bisexual, transgender, and queer (lgbtq) history topics. Collectively, these individuals have been responsible for much of the research and teaching advances that lgbtq history has enjoyed in the last 30 years, but they are also the people who, along with independent scholars, have often been most vulnerable to institutional, professional, and departmental discrimination. A recent survey of 44 scholars who have completed or are completing PhD dissertations that deal with lgbtq history, in graduate programs based in the United States and Canada, highlights the difficulties faced by many in the field.[1]

Overall, the data suggests that despite a significant increase in the number of lgbtq history PhDs produced over the past decade, U.S. history departments have not made a commensurate increase in hiring such scholars to tenure-track positions. Unless change occurs, only about half of those completing PhDs in lgbtq history can expect to meet with success in gaining tenure-track or equivalent (TTE) employment.[2] The rest are likely to find themselves working in part-time or

This essay was published in *Perspectives on History* 39, no. 5 (May 2001): 29–31. A longer version was published in June 2001 on the Committee on Lesbian and Gay History website: http://clgbthistory.org/resources/reports/lgbtq-history-careers.

TABLE 1   CURRENT POSITIONS BY RANK, SECTOR, AND SEX

Professor	2	(5%)	(2M/0F)
Assoc. professor	6	(14%)	(2M/4F)
Asst. professor/lecturer	10	(23%)	(6M/4F)
Visiting professor/fellow	2	(5%)	(2M/0F)
Part-time lecturer/adjunct*	3	(7%)	(2M/1F)
Graduate student*	12	(27%)	(7M/5F)
Academic administration*	1	(2%)	(0M/1F)
Public history/library*	4	(9%)	(3M/1F)
Nonacademic/nonpublic	4	(9%)	(2M/2F)
Total	44	(100%)	(26M/18F)
Completed PhDs	32		(19M/13F)
Completed PhDs in tenure-Track/equivalent appointments	18		(10M/8F)

*Graduate students, academic administrators, and public historians/librarians who also work as part-time lecturers or adjuncts have been counted as graduate students, academic administrators, and public historians/librarians and not as part-time lecturers or adjuncts.

temporary academic positions, in educational administration, in libraries and archives, in public history, or in other non-academic jobs. Of the TTE positions obtained, more than half will be in history departments outside of the United States, in women's studies/gender studies units, in American Studies units, or in other nonhistory units. The evidence of two decades thus suggests that, unless things change, the majority of people completing PhDs with dissertations on lgbtq history will not meet with success in gaining tenure-track primary appointments in U.S. history departments.

Of the 44 scholars whose survey responses were analyzed, 59 percent are male, 41 percent are female, 82 percent live in the United States, 14 percent live in Canada, and 5 percent live in the U.K.[3] As the figures in Table 1 indicate, 32 respondents (73 percent) have completed their PhDs. Of these 32, 18 (56 percent) are in TTE positions. When four additional non-respondents who are known to have completed lgbtq history dissertations are included, 18 of 36 people with completed PhDs (50 percent) are in TTE positions.

The 44 respondents earned or are earning their PhDs in 31 programs at 29 universities in the United States and Canada. Eleven programs (at Duke Univ., NYU, Queen's Univ., Rutgers Univ., Stanford Univ., UCLA, Univ. of California at Santa Cruz, Univ. of Chicago, Univ. of Minnesota, Univ. of Pennsylvania, and Univ. of Wisconsin at Madison) each account for more than one respondent. These 11 schools account

TABLE 2   FIRST AND FINAL YEARS IN GRADUATE SCHOOL

	First Year	Final Year
1970–74	1 (1M/0F)	
1975–79	2 (1M/1F)	
1980–84	4 (1M/3F)	1 (1M/0F)
1985–89	13 (10M/3F)	1 (1M/0F)
1990–94	21 (12M/9F)	9 (5M/4F)
1995–99	*3 (1M/2F)	15 (8M/7F)
2000		6 (4M/2F)
Not completed		12 (7M/5F)

*There are likely more people who began graduate school in 1995–99
than is suggested by this number.

for a majority of the respondents. Over 80 percent of all respondents, respondents with completed PhDs, and respondents in TTE positions earned or are earning their PhDs in history programs.[4] (The remainder were or are in American studies or liberal arts.) All 32 respondents with completed PhDs earned their PhDs at universities in the United States.

As the figures in Table 2 reveal, there has been a sharp increase in the number of graduate students working on lgbtq history since the 1970s. Three respondents began graduate studies in the 1970s; 17 began in the 1980s; 24 began in the 1990s. Two respondents finished their PhDs in the 1980s; 24 finished in the 1990s. The majority of respondents (70 percent) are working or worked on U.S. topics.[5] The remainder are working or worked on Europe (9 percent), Canada (7 percent), Asia (5 percent), historiography (5 percent), Latin America (2 percent), and US/Canada (2 percent). Almost half of the respondents (48 percent) indicate that 100 percent of their dissertation deals with lgbtq history; 27 percent indicate that 50–90 percent of their dissertation deals with lgbtq history; 25 percent indicate that 5–35 percent of their dissertation deals with lgbtq history. The average length of time it has taken respondents to complete their PhDs is 7.8 years.[6] More than three-quarters of those who have finished did so in 6–9 years.

Thirty-one respondents have applied for some type of faculty position; 29 have applied for TTE positions. In line with the growing production of PhDs in lgbtq history, more than six times as many respondents with finished PhDs first began applying for faculty positions in the 1990s as had first begun applying for faculty positions in the 1980s.

Most respondents with completed PhDs (84 percent) have been hired as faculty (TTE, part-time, or temporary). There was a significant increase in the hiring of respondents in the 1990s: 11 times as many respondents were hired as faculty in the 1990s (22) as were hired as faculty in the 1980s (2). (Three more were hired in 2000.) On average, these 27 respondents were hired one year after first applying for faculty positions and six months before completing their PhDs.

Respondents report finding part-time and temporary employment in a wide range of fields and academic units. Of the 72 part-time and temporary positions that have been or are currently held by respondents, 28 percent were in lgbtq and/or sexuality studies, 35 percent were in women's and/or gender studies, 40 percent were in other fields of history; and 15 percent were in other disciplines. Most of these appointments, 60 percent, were in history departments or centers, but 14 percent were in women's/gender studies units, 7 percent were in American studies/civilization units, and 6 percent were in English, literature, or writing units.

Of the 32 respondents with completed PhDs, 18 (56 percent) have been hired as TTE faculty. Of the 29 respondents who completed PhDs and applied for TTE positions, 62 percent (18) have been hired as TTE faculty. Fifteen times as many respondents (15) were hired in TTE positions in the 1990s as were hired in the 1980s (1). (Two more were hired in 2000.) On average, these 18 respondents were hired 2.8 years after first applying for TTE positions and 1.5 years after completing their PhDs. On average, these 18 respondents were hired after six AHA convention interviews and six campus interviews.

Twenty schools (16 in the United States, two in Canada, and two in the U.K.) have hired respondents in TTE positions. No school has hired more than one respondent. Of the 18 respondents who have been hired in TTE positions, 11 (61 percent) were first hired to teach U.S. history/American studies, two (11 percent) to teach lgbtq studies, two (11 percent) to teach Asian history, one (6 percent) to teach History/European Studies, one (6 percent) to teach Latin American history, and one (6 percent) to teach public history. Of the 11 first hired to teach U.S. history/American studies, five were hired to teach post-1945, 20th century, or 19th/20th century U.S. history; three to teach U.S. women's history; one to teach U.S. political history; one to teach U.S. women's and U.S. political history; and one to teach American Studies. (See Table 3 for a breakdown of current positions by primary discipline.)

Those who completed PhDs in history were significantly more likely to find TTE positions (62 percent held TTE positions, as compared to 33

TABLE 3   CURRENT POSITIONS BY PRIMARY DISCIPLINE/DEPARTMENT

	All	Completed PhDs	Tenure-Track Equivalent
History	25 (57%)	13 (41%)	*11 (61%)
History and Gender/Women's Studies	2 (5%)	2 (6%)	2 (11%)
American Studies	2 (5%)	2 (6%)	2 (11%)
Women's Studies	1 (2%)	1 (3%)	1 (6%)
East Asian Languages and Cultures	1 (2%)	1 (3%)	1 (6%)
Chicano Studies/LGBT Studies	1 (2%)	1 (3%)	
Liberal Arts	1 (2%)	1 (3%)	
Psychiatry	1 (2%)	1 (3%)	
Continuing Education	1 (2%)	1 (3%)	*1 (6%)
Academic Administration	1 (2%)	1 (3%)	
Public History/Library	4 (9%)	4 (13%)	
Nonacademic/Nonpublic	4 (9%)	4 (13%)	

*Two of the eleven history positions are held in Canada; one of the eleven history positions is held in the United Kingdom; the Continuing Education position is held in the United Kingdom.

percent with PhDs in American studies or liberal arts). However, there is a net outflow of lgbtq historians from history departments to other types of academic units and from the United States to other countries. While 86 percent of respondents earned or are earning their PhDs in history departments, 63 percent of respondents, 47 percent of respondents with completed PhDs, and 72 percent of respondents with TTE appointments currently have primary or joint affiliations with history departments. Less than one-half of respondents (44 percent) with TTE jobs have exclusive appointments in U.S. history departments. Just under one-quarter of respondents (22 percent) with TTE appointments work in Canada or the U.K., one-sixth (18 percent) work in gender/women's studies units or have joint appointments in gender/women's studies units, one-ninth (11 percent) have primary appointments in American studies units. Of the 8 scholars who have exclusive appointments in U.S. history departments, two did dissertations described as 100 percent lgbtq in contents; the other six describe their dissertations as 10–30 percent lgbtq in contents. Thus, with only two exceptions, respondents who have completed history dissertations that are more than one-third lgbtq in contents are not currently employed in TTE positions in which U.S. history departments acted as the primary hiring units.

CHAPTER 4

Crossing Borders

Memories, Dreams, Fantasies, and
Nightmares of the History Job Market

In August 1998, I moved from the United States to Canada to begin my new job as a tenure-track assistant professor of US history at York University in Toronto. As a US citizen, I entered Canada on a temporary work permit but soon filed an application for permanent residency and landed immigrant status. In February 1999, I received a letter and a sealed envelope from Citizenship and Immigration Canada. The letter indicated that I needed to take the sealed envelope to the doctor who had conducted the medical examination that was a standard part of the permanent residency application process. Further tests were necessary, the letter informed me. When I called my doctor's office the next morning, I was given a same-day appointment. I asked on the telephone whether I was permitted to open the sealed envelope. The answer was no. Later that day, after the doctor opened the envelope and read the letter inside, he indicated that he was surprised. So sure was he, the doctor told me, that the additional tests would be psychiatric in nature (presumably because of gay-related information that I had supplied during my initial medical examination) that he had already started making telephone calls to find another doctor who could handle this type of case. But instead of requiring psychiatric tests, the letter indicated that an HIV test would be necessary.

This essay, drafted in 1999, was published originally in *Left History* 9, no. 2 (Spring/ Summer 2004): 119–139.

I told the doctor that this is what I had suspected. Later I learned that until 1991 Canada officially regarded people with HIV/AIDS as a danger to public health and rejected most applications for permanent residency by people known to have HIV/AIDS. In 1991 a new policy was adopted that excluded most categories of people with HIV if they were expected to place an "excessive burden" on public health and social services. From 1991 to 2000 HIV antibody testing of permanent residency applicants was selective and could be ordered if the test seemed to be clinically indicated. In 2000 a new policy was announced under which HIV antibody testing for permanent residency applicants fifteen years of age or older became mandatory. Canada retained the "excessive burden" exclusion, which applied if the estimated financial burden was greater than that of the average Canadian, and interpreted this to require the exclusion of most people with HIV who were taking antiretroviral medications and most people with HIV in poor health.[1]

I did not tell the doctor that I had spent the day wondering whether I should refuse to consent to the test. It's not that I had much uncertainty about the results. I had been tested on three previous occasions and the results had been the same (negative) each time. I had not engaged in any unsafe sexual or intravenous needle practices since my last HIV test. While my aches and pains had increased that year, I suspected that this was more attributable to turning 35 than to anything more dire than that. But I had never had a non-confidential HIV test and the thought of having one gave me the creeps.

I have spent most of my life living in the United States, a country where the chances of obtaining health insurance after a non-confidential positive HIV test have often been as small as the chances of getting a same-day appointment with a doctor. Given the fact that most US Americans obtain health insurance through their places of work, this is a particularly significant problem for anyone with an erratic employment history, which was certainly the case for me after I began graduate school in 1989. Most of my friends have had HIV tests at one time or another; none, as far as I know, has ever had it done non-confidentially.

Moreover, once upon a time in the late 1980s, at a very different moment in the AIDS crisis, I had written a column titled "Why I Choose Not to Be HIV Tested" for *Gay Community News*, the Boston-based lesbian and gay newspaper that I edited before I began graduate school. While times had certainly changed and I would not take this position today (most significantly, there are now more effective medical interventions than there were in 1988), some of the political concerns that motivated the position that I took in 1988, concerns related to confidentiality, insurance, and access to health care, remained alive and well in 1999.

I was troubled also because I resented the implication that if I were HIV positive, I would not be granted permanent residency. It's not that I failed to understand the reluctance of the Canadian government to assume the health-related costs of a US American who entered the country with HIV, particularly when the United States required HIV tests for everyone applying for permanent residency and particularly when the US health care system was (and is) so incredibly retrograde. It's not that I was not grateful that York was willing to hire a US American when US schools so rarely hire Canadians (particularly in a field like history, where US departments almost never hire scholars who specialize in Canadian history). But recognizing the realities of national borders did not lessen my resentment as a global citizen.

I also resented the fact that something in my permanent residency application or my initial medical examination apparently had placed me in a suspect class. Could it have been the many organizational memberships that I was required to list that included the words lesbian, gay, or AIDS? Could it have been the minor medical problems (some of which are often associated with gay men) that I had reported? Whatever had placed me in this suspect class presumably made all sorts of assumptions about these organizations and these problems and simultaneously made all sorts of assumptions about the non-suspect nature of other classes of applicants, assumptions that on a global level continue to threaten millions of lives.

Most of all, after a five-year academic job search that involved approximately 150 applications, 25 interviews, four offers of one-year positions, and three temporary jobs in two US states, a job search that only ended after I decided to migrate transnationally, I resented the fact that I might lose my semi-secure employment. It may seem to some that I would have had greater things to worry about if I had tested HIV positive than losing a semi-secure job, but I am not so sure about that. Given relatively long life expectancies and high health care costs for people who are HIV positive, losing semi-secure employment would certainly rank up there as a source of anxiety if I ever tested positive.

In any case, there was another reason, admittedly more perverse, that led me to think about refusing to take the HIV test. I knew that the story of refusing, being denied permanent residency, and losing my tenure-track job at York as a result would make a great introduction to my second book. That book, tentatively titled *The US Supreme Court's Sexual*

Revolution?, will feature an analysis of a 1967 ruling, *Boutilier v. the Immigration and Naturalization Service*. In this case, the US Supreme Court decided that the United States could deport a Canadian gay man because his character and conduct as a "homosexual" made him excludable under the psychopathic personality provisions of US immigration statutes.[2] Making the story even better, this is the case that formed the basis of the lecture that I gave during my job interview at York. What better way to begin my next book, I found myself thinking, than to tell the story of my being excluded from Canada more than 30 years after Boutilier was ruled excludable from the United States. It did not matter that I possibly could have continued working at York on a temporary work permit; just the thought of being able to use this melodramatic story tempted me.

Months before this thought occurred to me, a comparably perverse one had come to mind. One of the things required as part of my permanent residency application was a letter from the US Federal Bureau of Investigation indicating whether I had a police record in the United States. I had waited anxiously for this letter, not sure about what the FBI would say. In 1987, I participated in one of the largest civil disobedience actions ever organized in the United States. Along with hundreds of others, I tried nonviolently to gain access to the US Supreme Court building in Washington, DC, after the Court issued its infamous ruling in *Bowers v. Hardwick*, a 1986 decision that upheld state sodomy laws. I remember many things about that day in the US capital. I remember the yellow gloves that the police wore to protect themselves from contagious elements. In fact I still have the parodic yellow gloves that we wore, complete with purple nail polish on each fingertip. I remember running toward the building with a group of friends; being stopped by police; sitting down and locking arms; and getting up and making a second run after the police had moved on to deal with other protestors. I remember that the police then ushered my affinity group onto buses, took us to a school gymnasium, and required that we pay fines to be released. I actually remember it as one of the proudest days of my life. But I do not remember whether, technically speaking, I was arrested. Years later, when the FBI letter arrived with a stamp that indicated that I did not have a police record, I was both relieved and disappointed: relieved because I would not have this particular problem with my residency application, disappointed because something that was a source of pride to me (and that could also have been used in my book's introduction) had been diminished by not showing up in the FBI's files.

In the end, I went ahead with the HIV test, waited two weeks, and then got the same results that I had gotten the other three times that I had been tested. And within a few months, I was a permanent resident of Canada.

Years later, I still wonder why I consented to the HIV test. I think it was a sign of many things. Maybe I did not have time to think through my choices. Maybe I had grown more conservative. Maybe I thought that I had a great deal to lose. Maybe I felt more vulnerable to state authority in a country where I am not a citizen. Maybe the ex-patriot expatriate in me thought that Canada's more advanced health care system should not have to take care of those who would not be cared for in the United States. Maybe I wanted to confirm my HIV status. Maybe I felt that there were other ways that I could express my solidarity with people who are HIV positive and people who have AIDS. Maybe that's why I am sharing this story now.

One point that this story illustrates is that when it comes to the academic job market, "it ain't over" even when it seems to be over. But this story also illustrates the main point that I want to make in this essay—that understanding the academic job search process cannot be isolated from understanding the politics of identity and the political economies that operate within our societies and cultures today. Over the course of my five years on the history job market, I promised myself hundreds of times that if and when I achieved semi-secure employment, I would write and speak about my experiences as one small way of contributing to change. Now that I am tenured and can take greater advantage of so-called "academic freedom," I hope you will indulge me as I review these years.

YEAR ONE (1993–94)

I am in my fifth year of graduate studies at the University of Pennsylvania and decide to take my first shot at the history job market. Drawn back to school in the late 1980s in part by reports about the impending national shortage of academics, I have since learned that more than 50 percent of college and university courses in the United States are now being taught by part-time and temporary teachers. The general job outlook is bleak and I have told myself many times that doing a lesbian and gay history dissertation might doom my chances. Despite all of this, I have trouble controlling my hopefulness. I have done well in my graduate classes, have taught general survey courses in US history, have received excellent student evaluations, and have been elected president of my University's Graduate History Association. I have also begun to give several conference papers a year, have an article coming out in a good journal (*Radical History Review*), have an impressive set of advisors (Carroll Smith-Rosenberg, Michael Katz, and Mary Frances Berry) in a good graduate program, and have made substantial progress on my dissertation, which focuses on the history of relations between lesbians and gay men in Philadelphia from the 1940s to the 1970s. In fact, I have won the first graduate fellowship in lesbian and gay history offered in the United States (the Ken Dawson Award, given by the Center for Lesbian and Gay Studies at the City University of New York Graduate Center), as well as Mellon fellowships offered by Penn. In my work, I am making strong efforts to link my case study in lesbian and gay history to so-called "larger" themes in social, cultural, political, and urban history, as well as the history of sex, gender, and sexuality. I am on my way to becoming one of the first ten people to complete a PhD dissertation that focuses primarily on US lesbian and gay history.[3] Three of my most accomplished predecessors (John D'Emilio, George Chauncey, and Lisa Duggan), all very talented, have each taken three or more years to get tenure-track jobs and I figure that I had better start the process sooner rather than later.[4]

I apply to about 40 jobs in various fields, mostly in twentieth-century US history, post-1865 US history, and US political, social, cultural, urban, and women's history. Of all of the fields covered by history departments in the United States, twentieth-century US history has the most job openings and the most job applicants. There are no listings in lesbian and gay history or the history of sexuality. While I only apply to jobs in the United States, I otherwise do not restrict myself in terms of location, quality of school, or teaching load. In most cases, I am competing with about 200 applicants, although in some cases the number is more like 100 and in others it is as high as 500.

My advisors and I are very pleased with the set of American Historical Association (AHA) convention interviews that I obtain. Most history departments in the United States interview ten to fifteen candidates at the AHA convention in January and then invite two to four finalists for campus interviews. Of the AHA interviews that I am offered in my first year on the job market, the most exciting to me are with the University of Massachusetts at Amherst and the College of William and Mary, but I am also pleased to be interviewing with Florida International University and Virginia Commonwealth University. At the convention itself,

I am offered a last-minute interview with the University of Northern Colorado. As I prepare for the interviews, I spend more than a thousand US dollars (more than the monthly stipend that I receive as a teaching assistant) on the suits, ties, dress shirts, and long winter coat that I need. I take advantage of the practice interviews that my department schedules, which are very helpful (particularly for improving my answer to the question of why I would want to live in Williamsburg, Virginia). I also talk with my dissertation supervisor (Smith-Rosenberg) about my glasses, which I fear are too eccentrically stylish for conservative historians, my two earrings, which are not particularly stylish but which I fear may still freak out historians, and my hair, which is long enough to wear in a ponytail. She tells me to cut the hair, but says that I should not sacrifice all sense of style for the profession and encourages me to keep the earrings and glasses. Of course we also talk about matters of substance.

The interviews with UMass, William and Mary, and Florida International go well. Logistically confusing instructions involving two hotel rooms lead me to the wrong place for my interview with Virginia Commonwealth; by the time I figure out the mistake I am quite late and the interview suffers as a result. In one or two of the interviews, I get the distinct feeling that I am being considered only so that the department or search committee can congratulate itself on being open-minded enough to interview a candidate working on lesbian and gay history. My first overtly troubling moment comes when the interviewer from Northern Colorado asks me why I think my subject of research is best studied in history as opposed to psychology or anthropology. As I answer respectfully, discussing the roots of lesbian and gay studies in the disciplines of psychology and medicine, I say to myself that if these types of questions continue I will have to walk out or be confrontational. Florida International asks me the same question, but prefaces it more carefully by indicating that the committee is interested in hearing how I would answer such a question if someone ever posed it to me (as if the questioner has not just posed it). Later I am told that I did well enough with William and Mary and Florida International to make me an alternate for campus interviews. William and Mary hires a historian whose dissertation includes substantial lesbian content and Florida International hires one of my closest friends at Penn. I learn later that a senior member of the department at Florida International argues that my research is "politics, not history," and that this damages my chances there insofar as there are no comparable objections to my highly qualified friend from Penn. This will not be the only time in a highly competitive job market when one faculty member's objection dooms my candidacy.[5]

UMass invites me, along with three other candidates, to campus. In planning for the interview, I think about whether, if asked in the informal conversations that invariably take place during campus visits, I should reveal the fact that I have had a girlfriend for two years. I fear that either this will confuse the department because of assumptions made about who does lesbian and gay history, why we do it, and what it means to be lesbian or gay, or that I will lose the support of those who want to hire me precisely because they assume that I am gay and that they know what this means. In the end, although a member of the search committee initiates with me a very personal discussion about the sexual assumptions that are often made about a straight son's intimate friendship with a man who had recently died (I knew both the son and the friend as acquaintances when we all were undergraduate students at the same university), I manage to avoid the subject of my relationships. I enjoy my time at UMass and leave with high hopes. When the bad news comes, it is not entirely depressing. I rank third out of four; I am considered strong enough so that if the first two candidates turn down the job it will be offered to me; and I am told that the two candidates ranked ahead of me have finished dissertations and several years of full-time teaching behind them. Several weeks later, I check in with the chair of the search committee and learn that the first candidate has turned down the job. The chair expects the second candidate to accept the offer but cannot be sure. That's the last I hear from UMass. Years later a friend and I are talking about the many places that interviewed us but never sent official rejection letters. I joke that maybe I should write to UMass and say that after years of waiting I need to have an answer so that I can consider my other options. Meanwhile, my first year's search is over. Several of my classmates have gotten tenure-track jobs; I am very happy for them but it's hard not to feel envious. Penn offers me a position teaching three courses for the following year and I get back to work on my dissertation.

YEAR TWO (1994–95)

After the close calls with UMass, Florida International, and William and Mary, I decide that to strengthen my marketability I should finish my dissertation and teach more courses. The dissertation is done and accepted by the end of 1994. While dissertation writing is not a race, I am pleased to be the second person in my class to finish my degree. I add courses in US women's history and the history of sexuality to my teaching portfolio. I also decide that since eight publishers have approached me about signing a book contract, I should pursue this. There is something unreal about this, but other lesbian and gay historians have told me that while we are all experiencing difficulties obtaining tenure-track jobs, publishers have recognized what history departments have not—that there is substantial public interest in (and a substantial market for) our work. And sure enough, editors begin to court me, taking me out for lunches and dinners and even travelling to Philadelphia to try to clinch deals. Martin Duberman, probably the most well-known gay historian in the United States, offers to put in a good word with his New York literary agent and she agrees to take me on as a client. This is definitely unreal. My agent negotiates for me a good book deal with the University of Chicago Press that not only will place my book in a great series and guarantee me money and space for dozens of illustrations, but will also provide me with a royalties advance (enough to support me for a summer) and the means to do a small publicity tour when the book comes out. In the fall of 1994, I sign the contract, teach a full course load for the first time, finish my dissertation, and watch my relationship break up. Mourning the end of the relationship, I tell myself that at least I will not have to worry about how to avoid mentioning my girlfriend in my interviews.

I again apply to about 40 jobs and the results are strikingly different from those of my first year. I am offered only two AHA convention interviews—with Xavier University (a Catholic institution in Cincinnati) and the College of Staten Island. At the convention, I also am offered an interview with Bemidji State in northern Minnesota. Although I am told that it's futile to figure out why the job market works the way that it does, it seems telling that the jobs at Xavier and Staten Island are in women's history (whereas in the previous year I had no interviews in this field). I look back at my letters of application and see that this year I highlighted the fact that I am currently teaching women's history at Penn. I suspect that because I identified myself as a women's historian, I hurt my chances for other positions. At the convention, during one of my interviews, the chair of the search committee informs me, quite out of the blue, that s/he is gay. I wonder whether this is why I am being interviewed and how I am supposed to respond, but we quickly move on to other topics. Although I learn later that I am an alternate for a campus interview at Xavier, none of the schools ends up bringing me to campus.

Fortunately, I have applied for several postdoctoral fellowships. Friends have told me that fellowship-granting agencies, like publishers, have identified lesbian and gay studies as an area that they would like to cultivate. In fact at one point Philadelphia alone is home to five post-doctoral fellows in lesbian and gay studies. Across many humanities and social science disciplines, lesbian and gay studies scholars are winning postdoctoral fellowships and one-year faculty positions but not longer-term ones. Cynics conclude that departments like to have us around to spice things up and increase course enrollments but do not want to commit to working with us on a more long-term basis. In any case, I am tremendously relieved when I win two fellowships, one at Ohio State University, which I decline, and one at Bryn Mawr College, which I accept. In both cases, lesbian historians who specialize in the history of sexuality play prominent roles in my selection. In the spring of 1995, despite the job market problems, I am pleased to be graduating and moving on to Bryn Mawr and I am happy that several more of my classmates have gotten tenure-track jobs. My spirits are further lifted when *Lingua Franca* features me in an article called "Robbing the Cradle," which focuses on the new phenomenon of publishers pursuing book contracts with graduate students who have not finished their dissertations.[6] Maybe, I figure, this kind of media attention will help my job market chances.

On the down side, I have a disturbing encounter with another student in my graduate program, who, like me, has not obtained a tenure-track job. In passing, he says to me that he guesses that we must be of the wrong sex and race to get jobs these days. I am offended on many levels. First, his situation and mine are not comparable since he is not dealing with historically powerful prejudices against his identities and research interests. Second, what he says is inaccurate; AHA statistics demonstrate clearly that the majority of jobs in history in the United States continue to go to Euro-American men. And third, as a long-time supporter of programs to increase the abysmal representation of women and people of color in history departments, I find what he says reprehensible. I challenge him, but not nearly as strongly as I should, and I worry about whether my job market troubles are poisoning my politics.

YEAR THREE (1995–96)

As a postdoctoral fellow at Bryn Mawr, I am teaching fourth-year seminars in urban history and social movement history. I embark on new research to strengthen my manuscript until November arrives, when it's time to turn my attention again to the job season. By this time, I have a second article accepted for publication (in a Routledge anthology) and am beginning to speak not only as a panelist at several conferences a year but also as an invited guest lecturer at such schools as the University of Chicago and Johns Hopkins University. I have also purchased more conservative glasses. After applying again for approximately 40 jobs, I obtain my best set of AHA convention interviews. The jackpot is an interview for a tenure-track job at the University of California, Berkeley, but I am also very pleased about interviews for a tenure-track job at the University of Miami and shorter-term positions at Duke University and Colby College. The interviews with Berkeley, Miami, and Colby go well. (With Duke, I find it difficult to navigate through what appears to be a major conflict between search committee members, one of whom seems to object to me primarily because someone else on the committee seems to support me.) Shortly after the convention, Berkeley and Colby invite me to campus. Miami, whose position is in urban history, does not. Later I learn that I am one of three alternates for a campus interview there and that the two candidates brought to campus are considered stronger because they do "just urban history" whereas the three alternates do urban history as well as things like race, gender, and sexuality. I joke to friends about the new field of "just urban history" and the new *Journal of Just Urban History*, a journal that must include only narrowly conceived essays on architectural and environmental history since all work that directly involves people is apparently excluded.

The campus interview at Colby goes well. The job is a one-year sabbatical replacement for a US women's historian. Within days, Colby offers me the position. Unfortunately, however, Colby gives me a deadline that will coincide with my campus interview at Berkeley. Further complicating matters is the fact that on my first evening at Berkeley, I call home and learn that I have been offered a campus interview for another position. For what I believe is the second time in the United States ever, there has been a job advertised in lesbian and gay studies for which historians will be considered. The job is at Emory University.

Now I have a difficult situation to negotiate. Having been told that there's nothing more likely to increase one's academic desirability than to announce that another department finds one desirable (a phenomenon that it's easy for a historian of sexuality to recognize), I decide to speak to the chair at Berkeley, reveal my offer of a non-tenure-track job at Colby, and make clear that I will turn down the job offer at Colby if accepting it will jeopardize my chances at Berkeley. The chair tells me that Colby is behaving badly by imposing a deadline for a one-year job offer in the midst of the tenure-track job season. There are hints that Berkeley will not object if I accept Colby's offer and then either defer beginning at Berkeley for a year or find a way out of my Colby contract. Meanwhile, all of this is hypothetical since I have not been offered a position by Berkeley, which is interviewing five candidates. My interview goes well, though two troubling incidents stand out. One is with a member of the department who asks me about the courses that I have taught at Bryn Mawr. When I describe my social movements course, mentioning at first that we cover African American, women's, and lesbian/gay movements in the first three-quarters of the course, this professor interrupts and asks why I do not consider movements from the other side of the political spectrum. I finish my sentence by describing the conservative movements that I teach in the last quarter.

Far more disturbing is what happens during the research lecture that I have been asked to deliver. I have been told by multiple sources that several prominent members of the Berkeley department are very supportive of my candidacy. Partly because of this, the audience for my lecture is so large that the room has to be changed at the last minute to accommodate everyone. After I conclude my lecture, the first hand to go up belongs to a member of the department who, I have been told, is the one member of the search committee who has problems with my candidacy. The question this person asks is whether my research deals at all with pedophilia. As my stomach turns over, I pretend to have not heard the question and ask her to repeat it. On the one hand, this professor is writing a book on a related topic and can claim a personal interest in the subject. On the other hand, I have not talked about pedophilia at all, have not thought about it in relation to my work, and take the question for what it is—an inflammatory and horrific question that presumes links between lesbian and gay history and the history of pedophilia. This has been a favored rhetorical strategy used by social conservatives to attack lesbian and gay phenomena for decades. Although parallels like the one I am about to make are often dangerous and misguided, the question seems akin to asking an African American historian who has lectured about the history of slavery to comment on the subject of black men raping white women. Responding to the question as best I can, I first, without knowing where I am going, draw a political and ethical distinction between "pedophilia" involving post-pubescent youth and "pedophilia" involving pre-pubescent youth. Having set up this framework, I then figure out where to go: I say that the more moderate gay activists discussed in my lecture imposed age restrictions of eighteen on their memberships while the more radical activists, also discussed in my lecture, welcomed post-pubescent minors into their organizations. The remainder of the questions passes in a blur and I am soon back in Philadelphia. The interview for the lesbian and gay studies job at Emory goes well and now I await news.

Impatient about its one-year position, Colby demands an answer. I solicit advice from many quarters about what to do. In particular, I go to one of my teachers at Penn, who is known for offering the following comment when graduate students have confronted similar situations in the past: "Slavery was abolished in the United States in 1865." Sure enough that's precisely what this teacher says to me. After receiving advice from about a dozen professors, I accept Colby's job orally, though delay accepting in writing. Meanwhile, Berkeley calls to let me know that one candidate has been ruled out, four are still in the running, and the department would now like to see my entire manuscript. A short time later, Berkeley calls to say that another candidate has been ruled out and the department now would like to see the readers' reports submitted to my publisher. More time goes by and Berkeley calls to say that there are now two remaining finalists and the department would like the names of four scholars not affiliated with my graduate program who can comment on my work. No one I know has ever heard about a process like this for a junior hire.

Soon I find out that I have placed second for Emory's job. That position has been offered to a well-known sociologist who is an assistant professor elsewhere and has published two influential books on AIDS. While I hear that the sociologist is asking to be given the job with tenure, in the end this person accepts it without. Meanwhile, when the news comes from Berkeley I am devastated. The other candidate is chosen. I hear later that the dean at Berkeley had indicated that if there was overwhelming sentiment for a second candidate then the department could offer positions to both of us. I hear that I received a majority, but not an overwhelming majority, of votes for a second position. I also am told (without clarifying details) that things were said in departmental meetings at Berkeley that provide grounds for me to file a discrimination suit, but I choose not to pursue this. I have a difficult time getting over Berkeley's rejection, particularly because members of the department begin referring undergraduate and graduate students to me for assistance, since no one in the department is an expert in US lesbian and gay history. I help the students but privately award Berkeley with the tackiest post-search behavior prize. Notwithstanding all of this, I try to remember that I do have a good job, if a short-term one, at Colby. In the summer of 1996, I leave Philadelphia and move to rural Maine, going into what I melodramatically call "exile." I have never, as an adult, lived outside of a large metropolitan area, and the only person I know in the entire state of Maine is an ex-lover who lives 90 minutes away from Waterville, where Colby is located. Soon after arriving in Maine, I meet another exile, a Cuban American man who teaches at Colby, and we become involved. Friends tell me that it's now clear that there was "a reason" that I did not get the other jobs. This annoys me to no end but I enjoy my new role as poster-boy for single faculty who move from big cities to rural regions and find love, and I am happy beyond words for my life's surprising new direction.

YEAR FOUR (1996–97)

In the fall of 1996, my partner and I decide that I should approach my chair and dean to let them know that I am interested in remaining at Colby should a position become available. With evidence that my teaching and research are strong and deal with subjects not otherwise covered by the college faculty, and with knowledge that I have a partner who is a respected and well-liked full professor with an endowed chair and who chairs the Spanish Department and the Latin American Studies Program, Colby should have various reasons to try to keep me. By November, I have an offer for a second one-year position at Colby and several months to give my response. With an offer that will keep me working for the next eighteen months, this is the most job security that I have had since beginning graduate school in 1989. Meanwhile, I become active in the revival of a Colby chapter of the American Association of University Professors (AAUP), which quickly becomes a leading advocate for faculty interests. As a United Parcel Service strike focusing on part-time and temporary work issues disrupts business as usual on campus, I encourage our AAUP chapter to focus attention on the problems of part-time and temporary faculty, including inadequate office space, disenfranchisement in college governance, and ambiguous and discriminatory policies concerning grants and benefits.

While this is happening, I apply again for jobs, this time pursuing only tenure-track positions and only positions that seem particularly attractive. Instead of applying for 40 jobs, I apply for 25. Five schools offer me AHA convention interviews. I am most excited about the University of Oregon, but also have interviews with the University of South Florida, the University of Alabama-Birmingham, Depaul University, and Eastern Connecticut State University. All of the interviews seem to go well. I learn later that I am an alternate for a campus interview at Oregon. South Florida and Alabama-Birmingham invite me to campus shortly after the convention.

Hoping to minimize the disruption to my teaching, I schedule these interviews back-to-back during Colby's one-week break between its January and spring terms. I prepare for these interviews with feelings of dread, ambivalent about getting a job that will force me to leave my partner in Maine and not particularly excited about these schools after close calls with UMass, Berkeley, and Emory. A week before I leave for South Florida, my neck pretty much stops rotating but several days later it regains mobility. I arrive in Tampa in the evening and go directly to my hotel. In the middle of the night I wake up soaking wet. Thinking that I must be anxious or that I must be having trouble adjusting to Florida's warm climate, I change my clothes and go back to sleep. An hour later, I am soaking wet again. As it turns out, I have the worst flu of my life. The South Florida interview is a blur, but incredibly I learn later that I somehow did well enough to place second out of three for this job. Then I fly to Boston for a night, a ridiculous detour on my way from Florida to Alabama but one made necessary by what I am told is the need to avoid revealing information about other interviews to schools that are interested in me. I consider cancelling the Birmingham interview but in the end decide to go ahead with it. By the time my lecture arrives, I can barely speak and need to sip water after each sentence of my presentation. I am so out of it that I do not realize what members of the department apologetically tell me later: that one of their senior colleagues, hostile to the idea of hiring someone who does lesbian and gay history, reads his mail and journals during my lecture. Several weeks after I return to Colby, Eastern Connecticut offers me a campus interview but its process will take months and will require the active approval of the search committee, the department, the dean, and the president. Meanwhile, Colby wants an answer, which I provide in the affirmative.

YEAR FIVE (1997–98)

I have moved in with my partner. I have won a "best dissertation chapter" award. I have spent thousands of dollars on travel and accommodations related to interviewing. I have lost what I estimate to be about a year's work on my book because of the demands of applying, interviewing, and moving for jobs, but the book is now nearly finished. I have given 20 conference papers and have given invited lectures at, among other institutions, Harvard and Wesleyan. I begin to joke that I have given so many talks and have interviewed for so many jobs that I have hurt the market for my book. I am serving on the boards of two history journals. My job applications have been strong enough to get me multiple AHA convention interviews; my convention interviews have been strong enough to get me multiple campus interviews; and my campus interviews have been strong enough to get me multiple post-doctoral fellowships and one-year positions. Everyone in my graduate cohort at Penn who has finished a dissertation and done a national job search has been hired for a tenure-track job; several are already going through the standard six-semester review that is the first step toward tenure in many US schools. They express outrage at my job problems, but I begin to fear that this is just because they are my friends. I have been living what has felt like a temporary life for nine years. I have had enough.

I joke about becoming a traditional faculty spouse in the United States, taking French classes, teaching piano, and hosting teas. I think that maybe Colby will offer me occasional courses. I begin to look into alternative careers in publishing, journalism, and non-profit management. I fantasize that since my first book contract supported me for a few months, perhaps a second could support me for a longer period of time. Fearing unemployment, I have not spent much of the money that I have earned while living in the low-cost state of Maine and I figure that I can live on my savings for a year while I plan a new career.

There are now (in 1997–98) more than 30 people who have finished dissertations that are fully or partially about US lesbian, gay, bisexual, transgender, or queer (LGBTQ) history. Of those who have completed history dissertations that are primarily LGBTQ in content, I know of only three who have been hired in tenure-track positions by US history departments. Of the remainder, I am one of the lucky ones, with an Ivy League degree, various convention and campus interviews, and various temporary and part-time job offers. I sense that the dozen or so graduate students who are writing dissertations on LGBTQ history are anxiously watching those of us who have finished our degrees to see what they can expect and to see with whom they might be competing down the road. I fear that I am letting them down.

After the experiences with South Florida and Alabama, where my ambivalences probably contributed to my illness, I decide that I will only apply to jobs about which I can be genuinely enthusiastic. I am outraged when several fellowship advertisements indicate that I am ineligible because my 1994 PhD is now too old. In all, I apply for only six positions, including York's. I plan to go to the AHA convention in Seattle but cancel after I obtain no interviews. Soon thereafter, Colby offers me another one-year position but I am not sure that it will be good for me to accept and continue living a temporary life. As Colby's deadline approaches, York calls to offer an interview. By this time, campus interviews have become routine and I do not prepare for the interview very aggressively. To demonstrate that I am an experienced and successful teacher, I make sure to supply York with copies of recent teaching evaluations and a dozen syllabi that I have prepared over the years. To present myself as an accomplished and advanced scholar, I lecture about my new work on *Boutilier v. the Immigration and Naturalization Service*, rather than my older work on Philadelphia lesbian and gay history. (This has the added advantage of featuring a slice of US history that relates directly to Canada.) The campus visit goes well, I think, but then again I have thought the same thing about most of the others. During the day that I spend in Toronto, half a dozen members of the department tell me, one at a time, that York prohibits faculty from asking prospective job candidates about their personal lives. The question is repeated so often that I begin to assume that it betrays great interest in the subject, so I decide to volunteer information about my relationship over dinner. I figure that withholding personal information has not worked in previous interviews so perhaps volunteering it will help me here. I also think to myself that, to the extent that gay men are sometimes seen as "dangerous" teachers of young male students, perhaps mentioning my stable relationship with a man a few years older than I will make me seem less threatening. In any case, after the interview I return home and wait impatiently for York to turn me down. Meanwhile, Yale calls to say that I am an alternate for a one-year position in lesbian and gay studies, Bates offers me an interview for a visiting position, and Colby sets a firm deadline for me to accept its offer. After the good news comes from York, I put down the telephone and cry.

Undoubtedly concerned about retaining my partner and apparently pleased with my work, Colby indicates that it may be able to offer me a two-year position instead of a one-year one but I make clear that this will not be enough to keep me. Around this time, Maine holds a referendum that, for the first time anywhere in the United States, overturns a state statute that prohibits discrimination on the basis of sexual orientation. Canada, I soon learn, officially prohibits this type of discrimination everywhere, at least for its citizens. Soon I learn that a friend with a completed dissertation on US lesbian and gay history, who has also been looking for a tenure-track position, has been hired in a tenure-track equivalent position by the University of York, but his York is in England. We joke that the United States is exporting PhD's in lesbian and gay history as fast as it produces us. When mutual friends mistakenly express surprise that York has hired two gay historians, I allow myself to fantasize that perhaps my York will not treat me as a token and will consider hiring other historians of sexuality. My decision is not a difficult one. I am excited about living in multicultural and dynamic Toronto, about working at an institution with graduate students, and about being part of an intellectually serious and politically progressive department. I accept York's offer and believe that my job search is over.

At Colby, I was wary of becoming the poster-boy for single academics who move to Maine (or similar types of places) and find love. At York, I am wary of becoming the poster-boy for perseverance on the academic job market. According to a survey I completed in 2000 as chair of the Committee on Lesbian and Gay History, an affiliated society of the AHA, of 32 respondents who had completed PhD dissertations on LGBTQ history in graduate programs in the United States and Canada, only eighteen had secured tenure-track or equivalent positions. The other fourteen were working in part-time or temporary academic positions, in educational administration, in libraries and archives, in public history, or in other non-academic jobs. A majority of the eighteen tenure-track or equivalent positions were in history departments outside of the United States, in women's studies/gender studies units, in American Studies units, or in other non-history units. Of the eight tenure-track or equivalent respondents who had exclusive appointments in US history departments, two did dissertations described as 100 percent LGBTQ in contents; the other six did dissertations described as 10–30 percent LGBTQ in contents. Thus, with only two exceptions, respondents who completed history dissertations that were more than one-third LGBTQ in contents were not employed in tenure-track or equivalent positions in which US history departments acted as the primary hiring units.[7] In other words, I consider myself very fortunate and the general situation remains bleak.

We each have to make very personal decisions about how much of the horrors of academic job searches we want to put ourselves through.

We each have to make very personal decisions about when enough is enough. But I do think that there are several collective things, beyond the activities of the Committee on Lesbian and Gay History and the Canadian Committee on the History of Sexuality, that can be done to deal with some of the problems described here.

First, those concerned about the future of academic LGBTQ history can be more open and communicative about job searches, share information about how they work, demystify the process, train graduate students on matters of style and substance, lend support and provide information to job applicants, and hold departments accountable for their practices. At all times we should remember that confidentiality is a policy adopted by search committees, programs, and departments, not by job candidates.

Second, we can encourage academic search committees, departments, schools, and professional associations to develop more creative and more aggressive anti-discrimination and affirmative action programs. Colleges and universities are not doing a good enough job in this area and they need to do more if we are going to promote excellence in education. While hiring LGBTQ historians should certainly not be equated with hiring historians who themselves identify as LGBTQ, movement on the latter could help movement on the former, and vice versa. Those of us who are advantaged in terms of ability, class, ethnicity, gender, language, race, religion, sex, and sexuality can acknowledge these advantages, not allow localized and personalized exceptions to mislead us about general patterns, and lend our support to anti-discrimination and affirmative action struggles, even when they seem to work against our personal interests.

Third, we can build alliances, in and beyond job market contexts, between different communities of academics concerned about boundaries and hierarchies of ability, class, ethnicity, gender, language, race, religion, sex, and sexuality. When I review the interviews that I have had, I see a majority of search committees chaired by women, women's historians, African Americans, and/or African American historians. I do not think that this is an accident. And LGBTQ historians can build productive alliances with LGBTQ scholars in other disciplines.

Fourth, we can encourage history departments to be more imaginative with job categories, turning away from traditional job categories defined primarily by geography and chronology and turning toward thematic job descriptions that include references to the history of sexuality and/or LGBTQ history.

Fifth, we can help promote the development of LGBTQ history and history of sexuality courses, as well as the use of LGBTQ history and history of sexuality readings, assignments, and units in other history courses. All of this has the potential to improve the status of LGBTQ history within the discipline of history, which could have enormously positive implications for the LGBTQ history job market.

Sixth, we can use our classrooms more effectively to teach the citizens of today and tomorrow about the values of education, the hard work and long hours involved in teaching and research, and the need to pour public resources into education. We also need to fight our governments and our administrators for increased funding for faculties and students. Until we do this, we will continue to struggle over a shrinking instead of an expanding pie.

And finally, we can recognize more fully, and here I admit that I rarely achieved this during my five-year search, that there is a politics to our everyday lives in academia, a politics with effects that we rarely can see or know in the short term. When I acknowledge that my road has been paved by the graduate school applications, seminar discussions, research papers, conference presentations, job applications, and job interviews of earlier LGBTQ historians, I begin to see that a graduate program that rejected me for admission might admit the next student who indicates that they want to study LGBTQ history. A professor who had doubts about LGBTQ history before reading my work may be more optimistic the next time a student chooses to work in this area. A classmate who learned about LGBTQ history because I talked about it in our graduate seminars may someday offer a lecture, supervise a research project, or hire a candidate working on this topic. A conference that rejected my proposal for a paper on LGBTQ history may not do so the next time a proposal in this area is submitted. A search committee that rejected me might give the next candidate in LGBTQ history more of a chance. And while I have been using LGBTQ history as my example, I hope that what I have written about the everyday politics of academia, the academic politics of identity, and the political economies of higher education has resonance for scholars working in other areas.

EPILOGUE (2004)

Returning to this essay almost five years after I wrote it is certainly a strange experience. Happily for me, some of the personal anger, angst, and anxiety that motivated it have dissipated, especially since I was tenured and promoted in 2001. And with tenure-track hires of LGBTQ historians in the past few years by history departments at Albright College, Brown University, Carleton University, Simon Fraser University, the University of Manitoba, the University of Minnesota, and Tulane University, I sometimes allow myself to feel cautiously optimistic. That said, I continue to hear numerous reports of homophobia and heterosexism experienced by others on the history job market; many highly talented, extremely bright, and very accomplished LGBTQ history scholars have continued to experience job market frustration and some have left the profession because of job market obstacles; and I now have witnessed, as a member of search committees and as a participant in discussions about hiring priorities and affirmative action policies, the operations of homophobia, heterosexism, transphobia, racism, and sexism and the intensity of resistance to efforts designed to promote nondiscriminatory standards of excellence in higher education. Moreover, the political climate in the United States and Canada continues to contribute to the underfunding of public colleges and universities (and the public sector more generally), which in turn limits the ability of these institutions to come up with creative and innovative solutions to the problems of inequality in the academic workplace. I remain convinced that organizing, mobilizing, and building strong antidiscrimination and affirmative action coalitions offer us our best hopes.

CHAPTER 5

Post-Tenure Lavender Blues

In 2000–01, I conducted a survey for the Committee on Lesbian and Gay History (CLGH), an affiliated society of the American Historical Association (AHA), on the graduate school and job market experiences of 44 people who had completed or were in the process of completing Ph.D. dissertations on lesbian, gay, bisexual, transgender, and queer topics (LGBTQ) in graduate history and history-related programs in the United States and Canada. At the time, I was a survivor of five difficult years on the academic job market, the chair of the CLGH, and on the verge of receiving tenure at York University in Toronto, so for a variety of reasons it seemed like a timely project. From my perspective, the results were profoundly depressing, revealing that almost without exception U.S. history departments were not hiring job candidates who had completed LGBTQ history dissertations.[1]

Because there has been confusion about what the CLGH survey examined, and because that confusion is revealing, I want to highlight what the survey did not discuss. This was not a study of historians who necessarily identified as lesbian, gay, bisexual, transgender, or queer. It was not a study of historians trained outside the United States or Canada. Nor was the study restricted to those who worked on U.S. and Canadian topics. This was not a study of scholars trained in fields other

This essay was published originally by History News Network, 7 Jan. 2006, http://hnn.us/articles/19941.html.

than history or American studies. And the study did not examine those who research and teach LGBTQ history but who did not write dissertations on such topics. What the CLGH study examined was a self-selected group of people who had completed or were in the process of completing dissertations on LGBTQ topics in graduate history and American studies programs in the United States and Canada.

For today's AHA convention panel titled "Out There or in Here? The Chilly Climate Revisited," sponsored by the AHA Professional Division, the CLGH, and the Coordinating Council for Women in History, I was tempted to update my 2001 study. Anecdotally, I know of several hires by U.S. history departments in the past few years that suggest some small signs of improvement. I still may produce an update, but for a variety of reasons decided not to do so for this session. I was also tempted to discuss my own experiences of antigay prejudice and discrimination on the job market. Last year, however, I published a painfully detailed account of these experiences in the journal *Left History*, and I decided not to repeat that performance here.[2] Instead I am taking this opportunity to reflect on a related set of troubles. I am doing this from a position of privilege, as one of the few queer historians to have been hired and granted tenure by a history department in North America, and it is likely this privilege that emboldens me to address these topics openly. I have been troubled by inequities in spousal hiring policies and practices at many colleges and universities; by resistance to thinking through the politics of affirmative action with respect to queer scholars; by the types of tokenism that lead some departments to conclude that one queer historian is enough; and by the failure of countless history textbooks, courses, journals, and conventions to address queer topics. I have been troubled by what sometimes seems to be an entire generation of scholars who pride themselves on their detailed knowledge of queer history, which it turns out is limited to knowledge of one or two gay history books. I could say more about all of these troubles, but today I have decided to go public about another type of trouble.

In 2003, I applied for a National Endowment for the Humanities (NEH) grant with a proposal titled "The U.S. Supreme Court's Sexual Revolution? 1965–1973." The project examines five well-known liberalizing decisions on birth control, obscenity, interracial marriage, and abortion, along with an often-forgotten conservative decision on gay immigration, and it does so by analyzing the doctrines developed by the Court, the advocates who influenced the Court's rulings, and the public reception that transformed the meanings of the decisions. Essentially, the argument challenges the conventional wisdom about the liberalism of the Warren and early Burger Court's sex rulings, demonstrating that the justices developed a doctrine of heteronormative supremacy that extended special rights and privileges to heterosexual, marital, monogamous, and reproductive forms of sexual expression.[3] Having been awarded a major three-year grant for the project by the Social Sciences and Humanities Research Council of Canada, I had some hopes of a positive outcome, but knew better than to count on anything.

In December 2003, I received a letter from NEH Division of Research Acting Director Kenneth Kolson, informing me that my application had not been approved and noting that I could request copies of the expert panelists' written evaluations of my proposal. Disappointed but not devastated, I submitted the request, and shortly thereafter received a letter from Senior Program Officer Daniel Jones, who informed me that the NEH had received 1,289 applications and made 180 awards. "The competition was very keen," he observed, "and only the highest-rated proposals could be funded." Jones then described the decision-making process: peer review panels were organized by discipline or discipline-cluster; panelists rated the proposals in their area; and the results were forwarded to the presidentially appointed NEH National Council and to Bruce Cole, the presidentially-appointed NEH Chairman, "who by law is responsible for the final decisions on funding."

The next sentences came as a pleasant and unpleasant surprise: "You will see that your proposal received five ratings of excellent from the panelists. At a later stage in the process, however, your proposal was read by members of the National Council and the Chairman, and in the end the Chairman did not approve support." Enclosed were the five evaluations, and these proved quite affirming. One panelist stated, "The argument is very compelling and sounds right on target." Another described the project as "ambitious" and "authoritative." A third said the topic was "timely" and the proposal offered an "ideal combination of solid research and a topic that has a broad appeal." The fourth stated that the project "seems truly revisionary and significant." According to the fifth, "the project will change the way we think about the sexual revolution of the 1960s and 1970s; about the Warren Court; and about the culture wars." In addition, "it will be of tremendous interest to a general public." As for the author, he "has a strong track record and is well-regarded" with "an outstanding reputation as a scholar of sexuality" and a first book that is "bold and important." "This one will be even more so," s/he declared.[4]

There were, to be sure, a few critical comments. One suggested that I add a substantive conclusion on post-1973 developments. Another asked, "Does it matter that he lives and teaches in Canada?" A third wondered "if the author will be able to complete the research." Handwritten supplementary notes on this evaluation, however, stated: "conversation convinced me that this project's research plan is feasible and that Stein is the right person for this project."

Disappointed in the outcome, I was cheered up by the evaluations. The competition must have been fierce, I thought, imagining I was one of many who had received these ratings but had not been funded. Intending to revise and resubmit, I telephoned Mr. Jones to see what I could learn. Jones informed me that my proposal had been reviewed by the American History/American Studies panel, the members of which were Leslie Brown, Yong Chen, Sandra Gustafson, Alexis McGrossen, and Carla Peterson.[5] Of the 45 proposals reviewed by this panel, five received five ratings of excellent, and these five and one other were recommended for funding. The final decision by the NEH, however, had been to fund three of the top five, plus the sixth. So I was one of two applicants in this group of 45 to be recommended for funding by the expert panel but rejected by the NEH Chair. The earlier claim that "only the highest-rated proposals could be funded" was apparently false.[6] Jones recalled that the chief concerns were that my claims were too bold; the project might not be do-able; and the argument was whiggish. When I asked what was meant by the latter, he said the analysis was influenced by "hindsight."[7]

Now my disappointment began to be displaced by another set of emotions. Around this time, I shared my story with a senior historian whose opinion I trust. "Seems pretty simple," was the reply. "Bruce Cole and the Republicans don't want any work on homosexuality funded by the NEH." This historian also called my attention to a story about the NEH that had just appeared in the *Chronicle of Higher Education*, which reported on allegations that the NEH was "flagging" applications that dealt with sexuality, race, or gender.[8] In January 2004, I wrote a letter about my situation to AHA Executive Director Arnita Jones, which I asked her to forward to the AHA's president and two other officers. I sent a copy of the letter to CLGH chair Leisa Meyer, who immediately responded with a supportive and helpful letter, but more than a week went by without a response from Ms. Jones. After I prompted her with another message, she replied,

As a matter of fact your communication has started a substantial discussion. As to your own particular case, the practice of "flagging" is perfectly legal. The NEH chair is by statute the individual who decides on which applications get funded. Everything else is advisory to him. Of course, whether this is good practice is another matter. And, of course, it weakens badly the whole notion of peer review. What the AHA officers are discussing right now is whether or not the AHA . . . ought to develop a statement that explains why peer review is important. And we also want to encourage our members to do what you did—get the reviews and the names of panelists. If most applicants did this I think it would affect behavior. At the very least it would offer the possibility of tracing funding patterns during different administrations there and elsewhere. Most applicants do not do what you did; yours is really the only communication of its kind I have had in my five years here. We are still trying to figure out how to proceed. I'll be back with more later.

Despite this promise, I did not hear again from Ms. Jones or the AHA until I wrote again about a year later, although I later learned independently that in 2005 the AHA Council adopted a "Statement on Peer Review" that "strongly supports the peer review process for research and publication" funded by the NEH. The AHA statement opposes "political interference with the peer review process" and declares that "projects endorsed by peer review panels composed of competent, qualified, and unbiased reviewers . . . should not be denied funding because of political, religious, or other biases of political appointees in the funding agencies." Significantly, the AHA statement did not specifically condemn sexual, gender, or racial bias, the three types highlighted in the media.[9]

Meanwhile, in February 2004 I wrote to the *Chronicle* reporter, off the record, about my story. The reporter replied, "Your story is very interesting, and not dissimilar from what I've been hearing from other folks. During the Cheney era (and as you may have learned from my story, there are many people who were around during her tenure who are there now—both in the Chairman's office and on the council), this was very common. They did not seem inclined to finance projects dealing with sexuality, let alone homosexuality. I think this issue could become even more important as the terms of the last of Clinton scholars expire. Then, the conservatives on the council will be even more powerful. I would suggest that you talk with Bruce Craig at the Coalition for History. . . . He and John Hammer [the director of the National Humanities Alliance] are very plugged in to the NEH. During the Cheney years, John really took the NEH to task on this. However, he doesn't seem to be fighting back on this issue now, and I think it could be for two reasons. One, more scholars aren't coming forward. And two, humanities advocates are so happy to finally see an increase in the agency's budget that they're afraid to make waves."

Taking up the reporter's suggestion, I soon thereafter wrote to Bruce Craig, who replied, "I am very interested in your case and would love to talk to you about it. Many of us have been waiting for a case like yours to surface. . . . When can we talk?" Several helpful conversations followed, and at Craig's suggestion I wrote another letter to Daniel Jones asking him to confirm the information he had shared on the telephone; provide the names of the members of the NEH Council who had reviewed my proposal and the nature of their comments; and indicate the subjects of the six American History/American Studies proposals recommended for funding by the panel. When Jones replied, he declined to respond to most of my questions, though he did supply me with the names of the NEH Council members who had reviewed the proposals (Elizabeth Fox-Genovese, Andrew Ladis, Thomas Mallon, Stephen McKnight, and Jeffrey Wallin) and the names of the four applicants who had received funding in my group.[10] A short time later, at Craig's suggestion I asked Jones if he would read a draft of the revised proposal I intended to submit in the next funding cycle. According to Craig, NEH staff had been willing to do this in the past, but now Jones indicated that this would not be possible.

Pessimistic about my chances, I submitted a revised proposal in the spring of 2004, this time changing the title to "Inventing Rights and Wrongs: Sexuality and the Supreme Court."[11] In December 2004, I received a letter from Acting Director Kolson, informing me that in this round 14% of the proposals were funded and mine was not. Although this year's letter did not invite requests for copies of the panel evaluations, an omission that Bruce Craig subsequently challenged, I asked for them. Later in the month I received a letter from the NEH's Russell Wyland, who wrote that in this round the success rate had been 13%. (The minor discrepancy was never explained.) According to Wyland, "As the ratings and comments suggest, NEH panelists were favorably impressed with your project. One panelist, however, raised concerns that the context for your work was not fully developed and worried that the analysis might not be objective. Other reviewers also expressed these concerns and, noting another panelist's comment about your lack of legal training, observed that the topic might not get the full development it deserved." Wyland also sent copies of the evaluations, three of which rated my proposal as excellent/very good and two of which rated the proposal as excellent.

In this round, one panelist described the proposal as "well written and intellectually significant" and said the author was "in an excellent position to take the project in interesting directions." Another wrote, "This is a highly significant project due both to its thought-provoking thesis and its innovative organization and research," adding that "Stein's contention that while there are many good accounts on the sexual revolution, none has provided deep analysis of the Court's role, appears correct." This panelist also wrote that "given his previous work, the NEH can expect that he will produce a highly readable, original book that will provoke a great deal of discussion among those interested in the histories of the Court, social reform, and sexuality." According to a third panelist, "This fellow would seem to be a major figure in the field, with an excellent publication record.... This essay features an unusually clear statement of what this proposal is attempting.... This certainly looks distinctive and important, and what he says about the historiography sounds right to me. It certainly seems that he has something important to say about the courts and sexuality in the crucial sixties and seventies. He certainly is right that this material is of considerable contemporary interest. His approach encompassing the social history of the law and legal activists looks interesting too, as is the whole issue of public misperceptions of court decisions. I'd be more comfortable if this fellow was himself a lawyer, given the study he is undertaking, but he certainly seems well-situated enough in the field." The fourth panelist wrote, "Stein's study of the Warren Court's decisions concerning sexuality promises to be a revisionist and possibly controversial work of scholarship. With a well-conceived and logically-organized project outline, he seems well on his way to completing the study. 'Inventing Rights and Wrongs' should contribute to knowledge in several areas–as legal scholarship and cultural history, for example. His research plan and chapter outline provide a clear indication of where the project is headed." The fifth panelist rated the project as excellent/very good, but the written comments declared succinctly, "The applicant is likely to complete the project. The proposal seems to ignore the longer history and context and to be driven by a specific personal agenda."[12]

Initially holding off on responding to the issue of my personal agenda, I sent a set of additional questions to Wyland. About a month later, having not heard back from Wyland, I re-sent my message, which this time elicited an apology about an earlier "screw-up" involving my email address. According to this letter, my proposal had been reviewed by an American History panel and the five panelists were Elaine Abelson,

Roger Biles, Edith Blumhofer, Michael Fitzgerald, and Holly Mayer.[13] Wyland indicated that, with respect to my proposal, NEH Chair Bruce Cole "decided that the negative concerns outweighed the positive." A short time later, I wrote again to Wyland, asking him to clarify the meaning of the comments about my personal agenda and objectivity:

> What is the personal agenda invoked here? Does it refer to the fact that I am a permanent resident of Canada and that this means I have an agenda with respect to U.S. history? That I am the grandchild of immigrants and that this might affect my interpretation of the history of sexual exclusions at the border? Did the panelist infer (correctly) that I have used birth control and have had interracial sex, which could affect my interpretations of Supreme Court rulings on these matters? I don't believe my proposal had anything to say about my "personal" life, so I find this terribly confusing. I also wonder if you might help me understand the criticism about my lack of legal training. . . . There is an entire field of legal history populated by historians without law degrees, which I know in part because I have twice attended the annual convention of the Association for the Study of Legal History. I'm sure many practitioners would find this comment troubling. I actually studied legal history while a graduate student at the University of Pennsylvania (with a well-known chair of the U.S. Civil Rights Commission) and have presented my work at the American Bar Foundation and the University of Missouri Law School, among other locations. And I have a forthcoming article in *Law and History Review*.
>
> Should I advise all legal historians without law degrees to assume that their NEH applications will be rejected? Should social historians have degrees in sociology? Should political historians have degrees in political science? What I also find puzzling about these criticisms is that they were not made by last year's panelists. When informed by NEH staff about the minor criticisms that were made of my earlier proposal (which had received five excellent ratings), I took steps to address these criticisms, and sure enough those criticisms were not repeated this year. But now I find criticisms that were not made last year, despite the fact that the proposal is largely unchanged. Could it be that the panelists were not objective, to use the term contained within your letter to me? Can you assure me that proposals dealing with sexuality studies and proposals dealing with gay, lesbian, bisexual, and transgender studies will receive fair and equal consideration by the NEH? Or should scholars in these fields not apply for funding?"[14]

A few weeks later, I received a mass electronic mailing from Arnita Jones, who on behalf of the AHA invited me to participate in Humanities Advocacy Day in Washington, D.C. The letter described this as "an annual event that gives grassroots advocates the opportunity to educate Members of Congress and encourage federal support for research, education, preservation, and public programs in the humanities." In my response to Jones, I wrote:

I'm prompted to write by today's invitation from you to participate in 2005 Humanities Advocacy Day (which I realize was sent to a large mailing list). The message led me to review our correspondence from last year about my encounters with the NEH; among the letters I found was . . . one . . . which promised a follow-up from the AHA that never materialized. . . . I'm concerned about what, if anything, the AHA is doing to address the concerns I raised, which have only increased since the results of this year's NEH fellowship competition were announced (a few weeks ago). Can you let me know to whom I should address my concerns? I'm willing to share information about my encounters with the NEH this year, but only if the AHA has a genuine interest in dealing with this matter. I understand the AHA's interest in promoting increased funding for the NEH, but if the AHA has reasons to believe that NEH funding practices violate AHA principles (perhaps including the new statement on professional standards [which notes that "practicing history with integrity does not mean being neutral or having no point of view"]), what will the AHA do? Is the AHA investigating? I plan at some point to ask your counterparts with the OAH [Organization of American Historians] similar questions related to the column by the NEH Chair that is published in the OAH newsletter. Meanwhile, I certainly cannot support advocating for increased NEH funding if the NEH has decided against supporting LGBT history (regardless of the quality of the proposals or the external expert evaluations of the proposals).[15]

After not hearing back from Jones for several weeks, I sent another email, and in March 2005 received a reply: "We have not forgotten you. We are looking into various allegations of flagging from different quarters of the NEH while the Research Division has been working on the more general issue of peer review, because we do not think this is simply an NEH problem. We hope that by working with other disciplines that relate to other federal agencies we might have a better chance of affecting policy. NEH's chair, of course, points out correctly that flagging is not illegal and continues to defend this practice when queried in person, as one of our officers did in a meeting just a couple of weeks ago. We are encouraging our members and others, though, to take full advantage of their rights to reviewer/panelists comments and we can hold NEH's feet to the fire if they refuse to share information they are legally obliged to provide." Jones did not express interest in learning about my experiences in the 2004 round of competition; nor did anyone else at the AHA.

Meanwhile, I heard from NEH Acting Director Kolson, who observed that "we relay panelists' comments as written and cannot offer further interpretation."[16] Kolson wrote as well, "It is not surprising that the panelists' substantive criticism of your proposal are not entirely consistent with the work of last year's panel, since our policy calls for 100% turnover of NEH Fellowships panelists from one year to the next. One of the reasons for this policy is to ensure that revised and resubmitted proposals are reviewed without prejudice."[17]

Shortly thereafter, I wrote to Wyland, noting that I had received Kolson's recent letter, "which purported to respond" to my questions. Specifically, I noted,

> There was no answer to my questions about (1) the members of the NEH Council assigned to the subcommittee; (2) how the ratings I received compared to the ratings given to the proposals that were funded; (3) how many proposals in the American History group were funded . . . ; (4) which of the funded proposals were considered by the panel that considered my proposal. I received answers to comparable questions last year, so in the absence of responses this year should I assume that the NEH has changed its policy or practice with respect to compliance with the Freedom of Information Act? In addition, I am confused by Mr. Kolson's claim that the NEH staff "relay panelists' comments as written and cannot offer further interpretation." I believe that one of your letters to me interpreted the comments of the panelists and now I am not certain about whether the words you used represented the words of the panelists or your interpretation of their words. Also, is this a new policy, as last year NEH staff offered their interpretation of the comments of the panelists? Finally, Mr. Kolson only indirectly replied to my question about whether proposals dealing with sexuality studies and proposals dealing with lesbian, gay, bisexual, and transgender studies will receive fair and equal consideration by the NEH. Should I assume from his response that if such proposals meet all of the other standards and criteria used by the NEH they will be funded?

My final communication from the NEH came in the form of an April letter from Acting Director Kolson. On the issue of which members of the NEH Council had reviewed the grant proposals, he indicated that the names should have been supplied to me earlier and now he provided them: Jewel Spears Brooker, Nathan Hatch, Andrew Ladis, Wilfred McClay, and Stephan Thernstrom.[18] As for my questions about panel ratings and funded proposals, Kolson wrote that "the NEH does not compile or synthesize such information." In response to my final questions, Kolson advised me that "there are no new policies with regard to the interpretation of panelist comments that are provided to applicants who request them" and insisted that "all proposals to the NEH receive fair and equal consideration."

CHAPTER 6

Political History and the History of Sexuality

In my little corner of the world, there was quite a ruckus in August 2016 when Fredrik Logevall and Kenneth Osgood complained in the *New York Times* about "the end of political history."[1] I will not repeat the strong arguments that various historians made about the column's flaws—the false claims about the number of job advertisements in political history, the failure to recognize the field's vitality (even narrowly defined), and the constrained definition of politics.[2] Similarly valid responses could focus on the centrality of political history in survey courses and textbooks. Here I want to offer a perspective rooted in my little corner of the world, which is filled with historians of sexuality who work on politics and historians of politics who work on sexuality.

I have had the great fortune of working as a professor at York University (in Toronto) and San Francisco State University. I was hired at the former as a US political historian and at the latter as a historian of US constitutional law. My first book was a study of Philadelphia gay and lesbian politics from 1945 to 1972. My second examined US Supreme Court decisions on sex, marriage, and reproduction from 1965 to 1973. My third was a synthetic account of the US gay and lesbian movement from 1950 to 1990. I have taught many courses on the history of gender and sexuality, many on the history of politics and law, and some

This essay was published originally in *Perspectives on History*, Jan. 2017, 17–21, with a response by Fredrik Logevall and Kenneth Osgood.

that address all four. Imagine my surprise when I read one of Logevall and Osgood's explanations for the "disappearance" of political history: "The movements of the 1960s and 1970s by African-Americans, Latinos, women, homosexuals, and environmental activists brought a new emphasis on history from the bottom up, spotlighting the role of social movements in shaping the nation's past."

"Homosexuals"? I was not the only historian to notice the outdated reference. But the use of old-fashioned and scientific language was not the only indication of trouble.[3] More problematic, from the perspective of my little corner of the world, was the fact that their formulation erased the work so many have done to integrate political history with the history of social movements and the history of race, gender, and sexuality.

My library is filled with books and articles that address political history (narrowly defined) in relation to the history of sexuality, not to mention political history in relation to the histories of gender and race. These include works by Thomas Foster and Martha Hodes on the late 18th and 19th centuries; Peter Boag, David Langum, Kevin Murphy, and Ruth Rosen on the Progressive Era; George Chauncey, Blanche Wiesen Cook, Andrea Friedman, and Daniel Hurewitz on the early 20th century; Allan Bérubé, Leisa Meyer, and Michael Sherry on World War II and the military; Douglas Charles, David Johnson, and Claire Potter on the Red and Lavender Scares; Christopher Agee, Martin Duberman, Marcia Gallo, David Garrow, and Whitney Strub on the 1950s, 1960s, and 1970s; and Jennifer Brier, Finn Enke, Gillian Frank, Christina Hanhardt, and Emily Hobson on the 1970s and 1980s. Then there are works that cover multiple periods, including books by Nan Alamilla Boyd, Allan Brandt, Margot Canaday, John D'Emilio, Lisa Duggan, William Eskridge, Estelle Freedman, Linda Gordon, John Howard, Kevin Mumford, Peggy Pascoe, Leslie Reagan, Robert Self, Timothy Stewart-Winter, and Leigh Ann Wheeler.

Many historians noticed Logevall and Osgood's erasure of this work, but so far I have not seen any commentary in print that relates this problem to one that was evident in another *New York Times* column, published just a day before Logevall and Osgood's. Journalist Kevin Baker's "Living in L.B.J.'s America" seems to represent the kind of political history that Logevall and Osgood favor—it focuses on a US president and his legislative achievements.[4] In discussing the 1965 Immigration and Nationality Act, Baker quotes Lyndon Johnson's 1964 State of the Union address, which declared: "We must . . . lift by legislation the bars of discrimination against those who seek entry into our country, particularly those who have much needed skills and those joining their families. In establishing preferences, a nation that was built by the immigrants of all lands can ask those who now seek admission: 'What can you do for our country?' But we should not be asking: 'In what country were you born?'"

Praising Johnson for his political success in achieving this major reform (and ignoring the advocates who insisted that the legislation would not fundamentally change the racial composition of the United States), Baker writes, "Immigrants would finally be admitted to the United States without consideration of their race, ethnicity or country of origin." This is not quite true and Baker knows it; he acknowledges that the 1965 law imposed a cap of 120,000 immigrants a year from the Western Hemisphere. Nevertheless, he quickly returns to his main point: "The greater principle was established." As for what that principle was, Baker turns to the words of LBJ historian Randall Woods, who has written that the law "did nothing less than ensure that America remained a land of diversity whose identity rested on a set of political principles rather than blood and soil nationalism."

Except this is not quite true either. And here is where I want to return to the problem of creating artificial distinctions between political history and the history of sexuality. The 1965 Immigration and Nationality Act removed the restrictive national origins system that had been in place for more than four decades, but it also was the first US immigration law that explicitly barred people with "sexual deviations." To be sure, "sexual deviates" had been excluded under other statutory provisions: various laws barred individuals who were likely to become public charges, those who had committed crimes of "moral turpitude," and those who were "afflicted with psychopathic personality." But the 1965 law—passed in the wake of the 1964 resignation of LBJ aide Walter Jenkins after he was caught having sex with a man in a public bathroom—more overtly declared that individuals classified as having "sexual deviations," generally understood to include "homosexuals," were to be excluded.

In 1967, the Supreme Court read this intention back into the earlier "psychopathic personality" provisions of immigration law when it upheld the deportation of Clive Boutilier, a Canadian "homosexual" who had been living as a legal resident in New York for many years. And it's not as though the sexual politics of the 1965 immigration legislation are now an obscure footnote: they have been discussed by at least four US political historians—Margot Canaday, Martha Gardner, William

Turner, and me—and analyzed by scholars in legal studies, American studies, and ethnic studies, including William Eskridge, Eithne Luibhéid, Shannon Minter, Susana Peña, and Siobhan Somerville.

There's more. Political historians generally describe the 1965 law as replacing a system that restricted immigration based on national origins with one that gave preference to family members of US citizens and legal residents, along with individuals who had professional and specialized skills needed by the United States. Unless they are also historians of gender and sexuality, however, political historians do not generally comment on the gender and sexual implications of a system that granted preferences to spouses and other family members. (We might refer to this as a system of "blood nationalism.") In a world that denied legal marriage to same-sex couples and placed an array of obstacles in the paths of individuals who did not have or were estranged from or in conflict with politically recognized spouses or politically recognized families, the implications were potentially grave.

The 1965 immigration law was a major piece of legislation that accomplished many positive and important things. But in my little corner of the world, which includes a large number of US political historians, this law was also a political manifestation of larger dynamics that established, maintained, and strengthened the supremacy of family, heterosexuality, and marriage in the United States. And if we cannot recognize that this is and was political, the future of political history is dire indeed.

PART THREE

Histories of Queer Activism

In 1993, as I continued to work on my PhD dissertation and prepared to teach my first college-level courses, Bill Clinton was inaugurated as president of the United States. I turned thirty years old, and this was the first time in my life that I had cast a ballot for the successful presidential candidate, the first time in my adult life that the United States had a Democratic president, and the first time in my adult life that my mayor, governor, and president were Democrats. Clinton ended a twelve-year period of presidential rule by conservative Republicans, an era that included some of the most tragic and terrible times in LGBT history. Four years later, I was so disappointed by Clinton that I voted for a third-party candidate; I did not again vote for a winning presidential nominee until 2008.

Clinton has long been praised and criticized for his "third-way" pragmatism, which rejected liberal and conservative politics in favor of centrist policies. "The era of big government is over," Clinton famously declared, as he also promised to "end welfare as we know it." With respect to LGBT issues, 1993 was the year when Clinton attempted to triangulate by adopting the "don't ask, don't tell" policy for "gays in the military." While he was praised by centrists for coming up with a compromise that relaxed without abandoning the military's ban on gay and lesbian military service members, Clinton was attacked by the right and left. Since 1993, the queer movement has watched policy makers negotiate similarly centrist compromises on same-sex marriage, antidiscrimination law, parenting rights, trans equality, and more. While many activists have supported these moves as realistic reforms, queer and trans radicals have challenged them as intolerant and intolerable. Many also have asked what ever happened to the revolutionary politics of LGBT liberation and how could a movement committed to radical social transformation become focused on inclusion in marriage, the military, and the mainstream.

As I worked on my Philadelphia dissertation (1994), first journal articles and book chapters (1994, 1997, and 2001), and first book (2000), I was influenced by LGBT politics during the Bush and Clinton eras, most notably by radical queer criticisms of mainstream conservatism and liberalism.[1] Informed by the feminist politics that I had learned at Wesleyan and *GCN*, I decided that my project would analyze relationships between gay men and lesbian women. Curious about connections and disconnections between "the community" and "the movement," I made this my secondary focus. Situated in the complicated geography of Philadelphia and living in a predominantly working-class African American neighborhood, I emphasized class and race as powerful influences on LGBT activism. My work also was informed by the rise of queer theory and queer nationalism, which challenged more moderate LGBT politics and priorities in the early 1990s. My first article and first book offered critically queer perspectives on gay and lesbian activism; my first chapter in an edited anthology critiqued homonationalism. The latter was influenced by the arguments I had made several years earlier to call ourselves "Queer Action" rather than "Queer Nation" in Philadelphia. More generally, the goals of my work were to inform and educate, but also provoke and push, primarily by challenging racism, nationalism, sexism, and sexual conservatism in LGBT communities.

This meant questioning the notion that LGBT history began with the 1969 Stonewall Riots, so most of my work focused on the 1940s, 1950s, and 1960s. It meant critiquing the idea that the pre-Stonewall movement was invariably small, ineffective, and accommodationist and refuting the belief that pre-Stonewall LGBT activists were monolithically white, middle class, male, cisgender, and gay. In geographic terms, it meant broadening out beyond the "gay ghetto" of Center City to highlight the significance of other Philadelphia neighborhoods. With respect to diversity, it meant not accepting claims that lesbians were invariably invisible, people of color were always closeted, trans people did not exist, and Jewish leadership was unimportant. My work critiqued LGBT conservatism and liberalism, but also highlighted more radical forms of queer activism. While much of my research was community-based, I saw myself not as a community spokesperson but as a critical interpreter of the LGBT past.

As I moved toward finishing my 708-page dissertation, I was excited to begin sharing shorter samples with public audiences. When I did so, I turned primarily to community-based publications, including the 1993 Philadelphia Pride Program and LGBT newspapers in and beyond Philadelphia. I also presented my work at the gay-oriented Giovanni's Room bookstore in Philadelphia in 1993, the Lesbian/Gay Library and Archives of Philadelphia in 1993 and 1995, and an event organized by the LGBT graduate student group at the University of Pennsylvania in 1994. One of the pleasures of these publications and presentations was that, compared to the process of finishing a scholarly book, which took nearly a decade, these were the academic's version of instant gratification. I could write a short newspaper article or prepare a public presentation in a few days; when I was done, large numbers of people engaged with my work. While this bypassed the constructive criticisms that come with scholarly peer review, I actively solicited comments from friends and colleagues before submitting my work to community-based periodicals and the editors of these publications generally offered helpful recommendations.

Orienting myself to LGBT audiences made sense because of the primary publics that I wanted to inform, educate, and provoke, but also reflected the mainstream public's ongoing disinterest in queer history. Longtime lesbian journalist Victoria Brownworth featured my research in *Philadelphia Gay News* in 1993 and fellow Penn graduate student Jeaninne DeLombard interviewed me for *Philadelphia City Paper* in 1995, but there was little mainstream media interest in my work through the 1990s.[2] This changed after the University of Chicago Press published *City of Sisterly and Brotherly Loves* in 2000. By then I was no longer living in Philadelphia, but the book was highlighted in the *Camden Courier-Post*, *Philadelphia Gay News*, *Philadelphia Inquirer*, and *Philadelphia Weekly*. My work also was featured on radio programs and at community events in Philadelphia. Beyond the local scene, the book was reviewed in one mainstream periodical (*Times Literary Supplement*) and five LGBT publications (*Lambda Book Report*, *Xtra!*, *Gay & Lesbian Review*, *Lesbian News*, and *TWN*).[3] In 2001, Glenn Holsten's documentary film *Gay Pioneers*, which focuses on the Annual Reminder demonstrations at Independence Hall from 1965 to 1969, featured me as a "talking head."[4] More generally, I was pleased by the positive reception of my book in academic and nonacademic contexts.

Notwithstanding these signs of success and the evidence I supplied of faculty who were assigning the book in courses, the University of Chicago Press declined to publish a paperback edition, which was unusual for a work with respectable hardcover sales of approximately twelve hundred. The reasons were never fully explained to me, though occasionally my editor, Doug Mitchell, mentioned the large quantity of unsold copies, which reflected inflated prepublication expectations. I had my suspicions about what was really going on but was pleased when the publisher agreed to relinquish its rights to publish a paperback edition. By this time I had approached Temple University Press, which had expressed interest years earlier and was willing to work out the contractual complications. When the paperback came out in 2004, there was another wave of local interest, including media interviews, bookstore readings, and a blogger's commendation for "best dedication ever." In retrospect, I am glad I did not give up on the idea of a more affordable paperback edition. I cringe a little when other scholars use the later publication date, but the 2004 book has been cited more frequently than the 2000 one. As of 2021 it has sold approximately one thousand copies.[5]

My Philadelphia book was part of a wave of local LGBT historical studies that generated significant public interest, especially in their geographic domains. In the seven years before my book was published there were studies of Buffalo, Cherry Grove, New York, San Francisco, Memphis, Boston, and Mississippi. In the next several years these were followed by studies of Los Angeles, Portland (OR), San Francisco, Seattle, Provincetown, and New York. The authors of these books have continued to enjoy special relationships with the cities, states, and regions studied. My work on Philadelphia, for example, has been referenced in dozens of local newspaper stories, radio and television programs, and documentary films, and I have been invited back to Philadelphia to talk about local LGBT history on multiple occasions.[6] I have written letters of support for the successful nominations of several Philadelphia LGBT historical sites for local, state, and national recognition. I also have completed new historical essays on Greater Philadelphia LGBT history and plan to write more in the future.[7]

Most of us who have produced local LGBT historical studies have not found academic positions in the cities, states, or regions we initially studied. There is something unfortunate about this; we would have had more opportunities to draw on our local expertise and connect with local audiences if colleges and universities in those regions had put us to work. I think about this when remembering a moment a few years ago when I was out for lunch with Bryn Mawr College historian Sharon Ullman at a Philadelphia restaurant. We must have said something to the waiter about being queer historians and college professors, because he started regaling us with stories about Philadelphia LGBT history, which he had learned from the book he was reading for an article he was writing for a local newspaper. After winking at me and urging him to continue with his spontaneous and flattering book review, Ullman interrupted to introduce me by name, which he quickly recognized as the author of the book he was praising. We all had a good laugh, and I enjoyed my brief moment of local fame.

When I think about the essays reprinted here, all drawn from my Philadelphia research, I am proud of my accomplishments, but disappointed that I have not had more success in changing the ways that people think about LGBT history. Like John D'Emilio before me, my work challenged the notion that the LGBT movement began with the Stonewall Riots, but this myth continues to be repeated. My scholarship highlighted the sexual radicalism of some pre-Stonewall activists, but public discourse continues to erase this tradition. My research demonstrated that *Drum* magazine, based in Philadelphia, was the country's most widely circulating LGBT movement publication in the second half of the 1960s, but *ONE*, *Mattachine Review*, and *The Ladder*, based in California, continue to be invoked as the most important pre-Stonewall LGBT periodicals. My work highlighted the importance of people of color in queer movements, but LGBT activism in this era continues to be depicted as homogenously white. Neither my lengthy scholarly works nor my short public history projects have displaced preexisting narratives about LGBT history. At best, I can point to modest successes in offering alternative arguments and helping to put Philadelphia on the map of queer history.[8]

Chapter 7, "Coming Out and Going Public: A History of Lesbians and Gay Men Taking to Queer Street, Philadelphia, USA," was published originally in Philadelphia's 1993 gay pride program. I do not recall who invited me to write this essay, but I remember seeing the program everywhere I went on the day of the pride parade. I wrote this approximately eighteen months before finishing my PhD, but it captures many of the significant individuals and developments discussed in my dissertation and illustrates my interest in highlighting the contributions of lesbians, people of color, and trans people. This was written for a celebratory public event in a city often overlooked, so it is marked by the types of urban boosterism and civic cheerleading that make some scholars wince. At the same time, it emphasized some of the more multicultural, radical, and transgressive moments in Philadelphia's LGBT history, which served my purposes by challenging more mainstream, moderate, and respectable tendencies in LGBT politics.

Chapter 8, "Approaching Stonewall from the City of Sisterly and Brotherly Loves," was published in *Gay Community News* in June 1994, when millions were commemorating the twenty-fifth anniversary of the Stonewall Riots. I began to write historical articles for *GCN* in the late 1980s, when community-based newspapers were among the most important platforms for LGBT public history. In the late 1980s, when I was the paper's coordinating editor, *GCN* had approximately three thousand subscribers and a weekly print-run of seventy-five hundred, but by 1994 it was only publishing occasional issues. "Approaching Stonewall" appeared in a special gay pride issue that was timed to coincide with Stonewall's twenty-fifth anniversary; it later was reprinted in *Au Courant*, a Philadelphia-based LGBT newspaper. My goal was to honor Stonewall, but decenter it by showcasing important developments that preceded and followed the 1969 rebellion.

Chapter 9, "Recalling Dewey's Sit-In," was published in *Philadelphia Gay News* in 2005 and reprinted shortly thereafter as "The First Gay Sit-In" on the *History News Network*. This was one of several instances in which I decided to use a historical anniversary—in this case the sit-in's fortieth—to pique public interest in a long-forgotten episode in LGBT history. I also wanted to intervene in misguided local gay efforts to present the Annual Reminder demonstrations at Independence Hall as the birthplace of the gay civil rights movement. The Dewey's sit-in not only occurred before the first Annual Reminder but also was more inclusive by challenging discrimination against trans people as well as "homosexuals."[9] My earliest work on Dewey's was published in 1993 and I discussed it in my 2000 book, but it was not until several years later, when trans historian Susan Stryker began referencing my scholarship, that the protest began to receive more national attention. That has been gratifying, but also has led to unfortunate myth making. In 2007, for example, the *Transgriot* blog inaccurately reported that my work had shown that the Dewey's protesters were African American. To this day I have seen no evidence indicating that they were or were not. I see this misrepresentation as symptomatic of two larger problems in LGBT public history—we collectively have not done enough to showcase queer histories of people of color and we collectively have not done enough to emphasize the importance of primary sources as the foundations of strong historical interpretations.[10] Ten years later, I marked the fiftieth anniversary of the Dewey's sit-in with an article in the *Bay Area Reporter* and a primary source exhibit on the OutHistory website.[11] I subsequently was pleased to learn that my research was used when the Pennsylvania Historical and Museum Commission erected a historical marker at the site of the sit-in in 2018. I was not pleased to learn that the marker references "homosexuals" but not trans people, which engendered justifiable criticism and controversy in Philadelphia.[12]

Chapter 10, "Fifty Years of LGBT Movement Activism in Philadelphia," was published by *Philadelphia Gay News* in 2010. This essay, like the previous one, made use of a significant anniversary to revive interest in a long-forgotten episode, the 1960 Radnor Raid, which launched the organized LGBT movement in Greater Philadelphia. Here, too, I tried to combine my interests in the politics of memory with my investments in new political debates. By highlighting the importance of pornography in the event that launched the local LGBT movement and by challenging the politics of sexual respectability in historical memory, I joined others in critiquing the desexualization of LGBT activism that was evident in the gay marriage movement.[13]

Chapter 11, "Heterosexuality in America: Fifty Years and Counting," was published on the *Notches* history of sexuality blog in 2014. *Notches* was established that year by a new generation of historians; it describes itself as "a peer-reviewed, collaborative and international history of sexuality blog that aims to get people inside and outside the academy thinking about sexuality in the past and in the present."[14] *Notches* founder Justin Bengry tells me that he no longer has access to viewership figures from 2014, but my essay has been viewed approximately thirteen hundred times since 2015. The two museum exhibits that led me to write this essay show that I was not the only queer historian who used significant anniversaries to revisit historical episodes. Both exhibits focused on *Life* magazine's 1964 exposé "Homosexuality in America," and I was amused when they opened within months of one another in the city I was leaving—Toronto—and the city to which I was moving—San Francisco. I appreciated the Toronto exhibit but was disappointed to discover that it failed to showcase the parodic "Heterosexuality in America" essay published by *Drum* magazine in 1964. My *Notches* essay tried to rectify this mistake and in so doing attempted to present a more complicated portrait of the pre-Stonewall movement.

Unfortunately, this piece also highlights one of the potential pitfalls of public history work. After moving to San Francisco in 2014, I discovered that *Drum*'s parody was preceded by (and possibly plagiarized from) a similarly titled article in *Citizens News*, a San Francisco-based gay periodical. I discuss both in *Heterosexual Histories*, a 2021 collection of essays edited by Rebecca Davis and Michele Mitchell. In my defense, I would describe the *Notches* essay as more incomplete than inaccurate, and I partially would blame the rush to publish that is more typical in public history than in academic scholarship.[15]

Coming Out and Going Public

A History of Lesbians and Gay Men Taking to Queer Street, Philadelphia, USA

Twenty-one years ago, somewhere between 2,500 and 10,000 coura-geous and excited lesbians, gay men, and their supporters assembled on Rittenhouse Square to take part in Philadelphia's first "gay pride" march. Barbara Gittings, who in 1972 had already been a leading national "homophile" activist for 15 years, helped energize her home-city crowd with a pre-march speech. And then the parade began its route down Chestnut Street to Old City, where an open-air dance was held on Independence Mall.

Many lesbian and gay Philadelphians think the 1972 march was the first public affirmation of its kind in their city, and in many ways they're right. Never before had so many people in the "City of Brotherly Love" so triumphantly proclaimed their lesbian and gay pride in such a col-lective demonstration of solidarity and strength. But Pride 1972 was hardly the first time the "Private City" had gone public with one of its best-kept secrets. And the 1972 parade wasn't the first time queer Phila-delphians had taken to the streets. Still caught up in the aftermath of New York's Stonewall Riots in 1969, with three years of unprecedented activity by Philly's local Gay Liberation Front and Gay Activists Alli-ance behind them, and just beginning to experience the dynamic hey-day of lesbian-feminism, activists in 1972 were denied the history and

This essay was published originally in *Pride '93 Program* (Philadelphia: Lesbian, Gay and Bisexual Pride of the Delaware Valley, 1993), 11–19.

education they deserved. They in turn left buried the earlier history of public demonstrations in Philadelphia.

But if the streets of Philadelphia could speak, what stories they would tell!

The streets around Independence Hall, where the 1972 marchers danced the day away, were hardly unfamiliar with the feel of lesbian/gay activists' feet. Every July 4th, from 1965 through 1969, "homophile" activists from around the country had gathered in the "cradle of liberty" for the "Annual Reminder," a series of groundbreaking demonstrations intended to highlight discrimination faced by lesbians and gay men and the failure of American democracy to accord its lesbian and gay citizens equal rights. In fact, it was only after the June 1969 Stonewall Riots and the Annual Reminder the following month that the Eastern Regional Conference of Homophile Organizations decided to switch its major annual demonstration from July 4th in Philadelphia to the anniversary of the Riots in New York. In a sense, the origins of the Christopher Street Liberation Day parade in New York lie in the Annual Reminders in Philadelphia, not the first time in history that Philadelphia has lost its pride of place.

The home of the Liberty Bell wasn't the only Philadelphia site rich in patriotic symbols to enjoy public lesbian/gay presence and protest in the 1960s. The streets around the Philadelphia Navy Yard may have been used to marching, but on Armed Forces Day in 1966, the marching feet were those of lesbian and gay activists associated with Philly's premier gay political organization of that era, the Janus Society, which distributed 5,000 brochures to sailors and visitors. Protesting discrimination against lesbians and gay men by the federal government in general and the military in particular, these activists were themselves criticized by many in the lesbian/gay community for failing to oppose the Vietnam War and for fighting to gain entry in an objectionable military system. Sounds familiar in this year of "gays in the military."

If the Annual Reminders and the Armed Forces Day protest took aim at the government, other 1960s demonstrations focused on discrimination by business. Occasionally, in the tradition of other civil rights movements, lesbians and gay men before Pride '72 decided that sitting down could serve as a more effective public demonstration of protest than taking to the streets. Back in 1965, Dewey's, which had all-night restaurants on 13th and 17th Streets at Chancellor, refused to serve a large number of lesbians and gay men (many of whom were in drag, cross-dressed, or were gender-benders). When three teenagers refused to leave, police moved in and arrested the trio. As the Janus Society leader, Clark Polak, offered to help the three get a lawyer, he too was arrested. Janus then mobilized five days of protest demonstrations, distributed 1500 pieces of literature, and conducted a successful sit-in that resulted in a change of restaurant policy. Not the only time that drag queens, cross-dressers, and gender-benders have been in the forefront of lesbian/ gay struggles.

In fact, there may be good historical reasons to credit drag queens for the first "gay pride" parades in Philadelphia. Long before 1972 Pride, drag queens had taken to the streets every Halloween night to parade themselves before large audiences. This longstanding tradition, called "Bitches Christmas" by some, was curtailed by then-Police Captain Frank Rizzo, who threatened bar owners with loss of license if they served "female impersonators" on Halloween. Rizzo used the "near-riot" violence by homophobic spectators to justify permanently ending the parade in 1962. Many older Philadelphians recall that the Halloween parade stretched back for decades. And it seems that the parade, which was located on different streets in different years, was divided along racial lines, with whites usually marching along Locust Street and Blacks marching along South Street. Not the last time that racial segregation and separation divided lesbians and gay men.

The Annual Reminders at Independence Hall, the Armed Forces Day protest, the Dewey's sit-in, and the drag queen parades were only the largest and most concentrated public demonstrations by lesbian and gay Philadelphians before Pride 1972. But the streets of Philadelphia have a much more extensive history of supporting public affirmations of lesbian and gay liberation. Philly's streets carried an impressive group of individual lesbian and gay activists on their routes; served as distribution networks for an important group of lesbian and gay newsletters, magazines, and books; and brought countless lesbians and gay men to the businesses that became key public institutions of lesbian and gay life.

Philadelphia's streets started Barbara Gittings on her route to New York City, where she founded the lesbian Daughters of Bilitis (DOB) chapter in 1958. These same streets carried her and her partner "Kay Tobin" as they delivered the originals of the lesbian publication *The Ladder*, which Gittings edited between 1963 and 1966 and whose covers were graced with many photos by "Tobin." After helping to organize the Annual Reminders, but still before 1972 Pride, Gittings became more of a locally focused activist through the Homophile Action League, which forcefully presented a case for lesbian/gay rights to the state Democratic and Republican platform committees in 1970.

While Gittings was using the city's streets on her travels to New York, Mel Heifetz was using them on his way to court, where he was bringing suit against Rizzo for closing down Philly's new queer-positive beat/bohemian coffeehouses in 1959. Philly's streets were home to Marge McCann and "Joan Fraser," who were leading national activists in the 1960s and helped organize a series of "gay conferences" sponsored by the East Coast Homophile Organizations, the first of which was held in 1963 at the Drake Hotel in Philadelphia.

Clark Polak grew up, lived, and worked on Philly's streets as he transformed the Janus Society from a small outpost of the early 1960s homophile movement into one of the most militant gay organizations of the 1960s. Janus sponsored a series of public lectures on homosexuality held in major city hotels (many attended by hundreds); published DRUM magazine, which had the largest circulation of all lesbian/gay publications combined; and supported several major court cases, one of which reached the New Jersey Supreme Court and established the right of "well-behaved" homosexuals to assemble in bars and another of which was the first gay immigration case to reach the U.S. Supreme Court. Polak did all of this, in part, with the money he earned running one of the largest gay pornography businesses of the 1960s, Philly's very own Trojan Book Service.

Ada Bello arrived on Philly's streets from Cuba (via the Deep South), and she was instrumental in establishing Philly's first DOB chapter in 1967 (which developed partly in response to sexism in the Janus Society). After a major raid on Philly's favorite lesbian bar of the '60s, Rusty's, Bello helped transform the local DOB into the Homophile Action League, which sponsored Philly's first major public gay dances and fought for gay rights and against police harassment and media discrimination.

Rounding out this short list of early local activists is Kiyoshi Kuromiya, who had been born and imprisoned in a U.S. concentration camp for Japanese Americans in World War II and had participated in some of the major events of the civil rights and anti-war movements in the early 1960s. In 1969, after Stonewall, Kuromiya helped get Philadelphia's Gay Liberation Front off the ground and participated in the Male Homosexual Workshop at the Black Panther's People's Revolutionary Constitutional Convention held in Philadelphia in 1970.

Philly's streets carried not only individual activists but an impressive array of lesbian/gay publications before 1972. Even before lesbians and

FIGURE 2. Philadelphia activist Kiyoshi Kuromiya was honored with a bronze sidewalk plaque (designed by Carlos Casuso) on the Rainbow Honor Walk (RHW) in San Francisco. Created in 2008, the RHW features thirty-six plaques in 2021. Photograph by Marc Stein (2021).

gay men began producing this material, local firm W. B. Saunders Company made queer history by publishing Alfred Kinsey's *Sexual Behavior in the Human Male* in 1948 and *Sexual Behavior in the Human Female* in 1953. Later in the 1950s, the ELL Club, based at the Lark Hotel in Bridgeport, Pennsylvania, began producing *The Lark News*. DRUM magazine, published from 1964 to 1969 by the Janus Society, featured hard-hitting news coverage from around the country, book reviews, comics, and male physique photography.

Three local writers had been widely published in the national lesbian/gay press by the end of the 1960s—"Joan Fraser," whose short stories and poems appeared in *The Ladder*; Jody Shotwell, whose short stories appeared in *ONE* magazine and *The Ladder*; and Adrian Stanford, whose "Remembrance of Rittenhouse Square" appeared in *ONE* and whose other poems from this period were later collected in *Black and Queer* in 1977. In 1972, the year of the first pride march in Philadelphia, long-time local activist "Kay Tobin" co-authored *The Gay Crusaders*, which provided "in-depth interviews with 15 homosexuals—men and women who are shaping America's newest sexual revolution." Also before 1972 pride, some of the pieces that local writer Anita Cornwell would later publish in her collection *Black Lesbian in White America* had appeared, challenging the African American community to confront homophobia, the women's community to confront racism, and the gay community to confront sexism.

Individual activists and community publications were joined by a variety of local businesses in publicly demonstrating the strengths (and the vulnerabilities) of lesbian and gay life in Philadelphia. If a map of pre-1972 Philadelphia was dotted with every lesbian/gay bar, bathhouse, bookstore, coffeehouse, community center, cruising area, political office, and restaurant, and if this map was then dotted with every lesbian/gay household, home, and workplace, it would become perfectly clear that every street in Philadelphia could have been called Queer Street, U.S.A.

Unfortunately, however, for most lesbians and gay men, Philly's streets served not only as public thoroughfares but as public spaces of potential danger and hostility. The same streets walked on by Barbara Gittings carried Frank Rizzo. Movement publications were distributed on Philly's streets, but so were academic journals that celebrated the achievements of Penn psychiatrist Samuel Hadden, who pioneered group psychotherapeutic treatment of homosexuals in the 1940s, and Temple psychiatrist Joseph Wolpe, who continued to treat his gay patients with electroshock "aversion" therapy into the 1970s. The same streets that carried customers to lesbian/gay bars and bookstores carried the police, the morals squad, and liquor license regulators to extort money from owners and arrest and harass customers. The very streets walked on by countless lesbian and gay parents were stalked by those who challenged their custody rights. Lesbians and gay men could express their affection for one another publicly on some city streets and in some city parks, but these were also scenes of the most brutal violence. And the streets that should have carried police vans to protect lesbian and gay men instead were sites where consensual sex between those being transported to and from jail and prison was brutally repressed while sexual assaults and rapes in these same vehicles were carelessly ignored (an issue that exploded in Philadelphia in 1968).

As much as they would like to do so, the enemies of Philadelphia's lesbians and gay men will never make the city's streets queer-free. These streets will continue to carry lesbians and gay men to and from work, home, and play. In fact, after a long and now-forgotten battle, one of the most well-travelled streets in and out of Philadelphia was named for a figure we now claim as one of our own. Nearly 20 years before Philadelphia's first gay pride march and nearly 40 years ago now, the Delaware River Port Authority decided in 1954–55 to name its new bridge for Walt Whitman. Led by two Catholic clergymen with ties to the South Jersey media and the national Holy Name Society, opponents of Whitman challenged this decision in a widely publicized, but ultimately unsuccessful campaign that called into question both the poet's artistic achievements and the way in which he "boasted of his immoralities and published immorality as a personal experience." While this victory was hardly won on the most gay-positive terms (most of Whitman's defenders denied his homoeroticism), we can now claim one of Philadelphia's most important public monuments as our own.

If Philly's streets could speak, they would be able to tell us stories of oppression and resistance; of injustice and pride; of absorbing pain and fighting back. We would hear stories of lesbian and gay communities divided along lines of race, class, sex, gender, age, and health and bodily status, and we would hear stories of a community united within itself and allied with supporters outside. In other words, we would learn how our communities have come to be the way they are today.

And finally, we would understand that everyday acts of building homes together, working together, expressing affection together, caring for the unwell together, and experiencing pleasure together are as important as participating in mass demonstrations together and are among the most important ways that lesbians and gay men have publicly demonstrated pride. And as is the case with the history of these demonstrations, we have much more to learn about the history of everyday life and everyday resistance in the city of brotherly loves.

CHAPTER 8

Approaching Stonewall from the City of Sisterly and Brotherly Loves

"It may well be the case that years from now, when social historians write their accounts of the homophile movement, June 28, 1969, will be viewed as a turning point in the fight for equality for homosexuals." This was the prescient declaration of Philadelphians Carole Friedman and Ada Bello, writing in the *Homophile Action League Newsletter* shortly after the Stonewall riots.

In 1994, however, as we mark the 25th anniversary of Stonewall, the rebellion is rarely characterized as a *turning point* in the homophile movement. Instead, it is most often depicted as the first act of lesbian/ gay political resistance *ever*. While younger African American, student, peace, and women's movement activists in the 1960s either critiqued or dismissed the value of earlier activism, perhaps in no movement was a prior tradition of political organizing so completely denied.

Uncovering the resistance of lesbians and gay men in the years leading up to Stonewall helps us to understand the making of social movements. By decentering the location of lesbian/gay activism to the many cities engaged in what we now view as movement building, we can better understand that Stonewall was not the beginning, the first act, but a crucial moment that was taken up as a symbol of resistance by activists

This essay was originally published in *Gay Community News*, June 1994, 14–15, 30, and later as "Modern History: Before Stonewall, Philadelphia Was a Leading Center of Queer Activism," *Au Courant*, Oct. 1995, 11, 18, 21.

around the world. The history of lesbians and gay men in Philadelphia in the years before and just after the Stonewall rebellion, for example, reveals a complicated and complicating picture of homophile and liberationist activism.

THE JANUS SOCIETY AND *DRUM* MAGAZINE

Organized "homophile" activism began in Greater Philadelphia in 1960 with an unprecedented police raid on a meeting called to establish a chapter of the national Mattachine Society, the group founded in Los Angeles in 1950. In 1962, after Mattachine's headquarters severed ties to local chapters, Philadelphians founded the Janus Society, named for the two-faced Roman god. Like Mattachine Philadelphia, and unlike most Mattachine chapters elsewhere, Janus was initially led by a lesbian president and featured mixed-sex leadership and membership.

Philadelphia's unique mixed-sex political organizing changed after Clark Polak became Janus president in late 1963 and the group began publishing *DRUM* magazine in 1964. Edited by Polak and named for Henry David Thoreau's "different drummer," *DRUM* combined hard-hitting news and features, the raw, risqué, and campy comic strip "Harry Chess," and male physique photography. Reviled by much of the more "respectable" homophile movement, *DRUM* attempted to politicize gay men seeking pleasure and "pleasurize" gay men practicing politics. Located somewhere between respectable homophile publications such as *Mattachine Review*, *ONE*, and *The Ladder* on one side and male physique magazines on the other, *DRUM*'s sexual liberationism in the pre-Stonewall era challenges students of lesbian/gay history to think more critically about what exactly makes Stonewall the turning point that it was.

Just seven weeks before the riots, *DRUM* ceased publication. More than 10 years later, after filing a Freedom of Information Act (FOIA) request, Polak would learn the details of the coordinated campaign of repression that had been waged against him, Janus, and *DRUM*, as well as the pornographic Trojan and Beaver Book Services and bookstores that he owned. Beginning in 1964, Polak, Janus, and *DRUM* were targeted by U.S. Customs, the Post Office, and federal, state, and local law enforcement officials, including then Philadelphia District Attorney, now U.S. Senator Arlen Specter.

In the name of fighting so-called obscenity, government agencies conducted an ongoing campaign of surveillance against not only Janus activists in Philadelphia but also readers of *DRUM* around the country. Richard Schlegel, the founder of a Janus chapter in Harrisburg, lost his high-level job as the Pennsylvania Department of Highway's Director of Finance in 1965 after the results of postal monitoring of his mail were revealed to his superiors. Beginning in 1966, the Post Office examined Polak's outgoing mail, used test purchases with the cooperation of various bookstores, newsstands, and individuals, and examined the contents of "broken" packages mailed by Polak around the country.

While the federal government was monitoring Polak's activities, local law enforcement officials proceeded apace. Philadelphia police, routinely using faulty search warrants and conducting unconstitutional seizures of Polak's and Janus's property, in one case found approximately 75,000 "homosexual oriented books and periodicals" and a mailing list "conservatively estimated to contain over 100,000 names." Arrested time and time again, and facing increased harassment, Polak announced in a letter to Janus members and *DRUM* subscribers dated May 5, 1969, "There will be no further issues of *DRUM*." Ultimately, Polak would face two sets of indictments on federal obscenity charges. In 1972, Polak agreed to a plea bargain arrangement under which he was fined $5,000 and placed on probation for five years with the condition that he no longer engage in the business of mailing "non-mailable matter."

Returning to the controversies that swirled around *DRUM* in the 1960s makes it quite clear that gay activists did not wait for Stonewall to join the sexual revolution. Nor did lesbians and gay men engage in their first full-fledged sex war in the 1970s. Finally, the federal campaign against *DRUM* demonstrates that the police raid on the Stonewall Inn was not necessarily the worst example of legal repression faced by lesbians and gay men in the spring and summer of 1969.

JULY 4, 1969

Philadelphia's first homophile demonstration was a successful May 1965 sit-in at Dewey's restaurant, organized by the Janus Society to protest the denial of service to cross-dressers. Several weeks later, as part of the homophile movement's turn to direct action, activists organized their first picket at Independence Hall. Distancing themselves from Janus's Dewey's sit-in, and conforming to conventional sex-gender norms, the leaders of the Annual Reminder required female participants to wear dresses and male participants to wear jackets and ties.

FIGURE 3. In 2005, the Pennsylvania Historical and Museum Commission installed a historical marker near Philadelphia's Independence Hall to commemorate the July Fourth Annual Reminder demonstrations (1965–69). Photograph by Ranger Michael Doveton, courtesy of Independence National Historical Park, National Park Service.

Local participants in the 1965 and 1966 Reminders, in addition to Janus members, included members of a revived Mattachine-Philadelphia chapter, which was founded by lesbians opposed to Polak. In 1967, lesbian members of a new Philadelphia chapter of the Daughters of Bilitis (DOB), the women's group founded in San Francisco in 1955, joined in. After a March 1968 police raid on Rusty's, the most popular lesbian bar in Philadelphia, members of the local DOB chapter voted unanimously to regroup and form a more militant and a mixed-sex organization, which they called the Homophile Action League (HAL). Members of HAL participated in the 1968 and 1969 Annual Reminders.

As forms of lesbian/gay political action, the contrast between drag queens and bar patrons rioting in Greenwich Village and well-dressed lesbians and gay men peacefully picketing in Philadelphia couldn't have been greater. As had been the case in previous years, demonstration planners in 1969, including Philadelphia's Barbara Gittings, the founder of New York's DOB chapter (1958), the former editor of *The Ladder* (1963–66), and a member of HAL, spoke a language of patriotic respectability. Gittings told a reporter from *The Philadelphia Tribune*, an African American newspaper, that "We are here today to remind the American public that in its homosexual citizens, it has one large minority who are still not benefitting from the high ideals proclaimed for all on July 4, 1776."

Judging by *The HAL Newsletter*'s, *The Tribune*'s, and *The Ladder*'s coverage, the demonstrators were a unified group of lesbians and gay men. But Philadelphia's leftist *Distant Drummer* reported on a "dispute" that "arose between the marchers themselves—over the issue of holding hands on the picket line." Pitted against the older lesbian-gay alliance that had been responsible for the July 4th pickets since 1965 was a younger group of lesbians and gay men much affected by events at Stonewall. *The Distant Drummer* reporter explained that while he was talking to demonstration leaders, a "breathless young man came running up to tell them that two girls had been ordered not to hold hands while marching."

Organizers backed the order. "His face puffy with indignation and yelling," historian Martin Duberman reports, Washington's Frank Kameny told the couple "'None of that! None of that!' and angrily broke their hands apart." Gittings explained, "There is a time and a place for holding hands. . . . On a picket line—no." New York's Craig Rodwell objected: "Our message is that homosexual love is good. Holding hands is not inappropriate. . . . If you don't change, you're going to be left behind. . . . There's a generation gap among homosexuals, too." *The Distant Drummer* reported that Rodwell and his lover then began "defiantly marching hand in hand." Soon two young lesbian couples did likewise.

It is tempting to regard the generational conflict that erupted at the 1969 Annual Reminder as proof that the Stonewall riots, in and of themselves, were a watershed. But it may be more valuable to focus on what happened in the months after Stonewall to understand how the riots came to be understood as a turning point. New Yorkers returning home from the Annual Reminder joined together with other leftists, counterculturalists, drag queens, and women's liberationists to create the Gay Liberation Front (GLF) in New York. In the immediate post-Stonewall era, homophile activists and gay liberationists across the country worked to harness the political energies released by the Stonewall riots, beginning the process through which Stonewall has come to be regarded as a revolution.

FROM THE ANNUAL REMINDER TO LESBIAN/GAY PRIDE

When the Eastern Regional Conference of Homophile Organizations (ERCHO) met in Philadelphia, November 1-2, 1969, the new movement for "gay liberation" had not yet found an institutional vehicle in Philadelphia. So when radical gay liberationists clashed with homophile activists, Philadelphians, who had been on the radical cutting edge of their movement for at least half a decade, found themselves attacked as conservative.

From the start, the meeting was marked by conflict. In one instance, for example, GLF-NY opposed the reading of a letter addressed to the conference from Police Commissioner Frank Rizzo, who "commended the homosexuals on their conduct during the annual fourth of July demonstration in front of Independence Hall," praise that undoubtedly infuriated radicals. Extended debate focused on three issues: the Annual Reminder, participation in the upcoming anti-Vietnam war mobilizations, and a series of radical resolutions.

Craig Rodwell and Ellen Broidy proposed "that the Annual Reminder, in order to be more relevant, reach a greater number of people and encompass the ideas and ideals of the larger struggle in which we are engaged—that of our fundamental human rights—be moved both in time and location." This demonstration would have "no dress or age regulations." Broidy proposed replacing the July 4th pickets with an annual Christopher Street Liberation Day to commemorate the Stonewall riots, an idea that seems to have originated with Rodwell. On this proposal, radicals won the day, winning a unanimous vote with one abstention. This early demonstration of the symbolic power of Stonewall could not have been clearer: the lesbian/gay movement's largest annual demonstrations would no longer be held on the nation's birthday in the nation's birthplace, but would instead mark "gay liberation's birthday" in its "birthplace."

Radicals were less successful with their antiwar resolutions. The conference approved 54–6 a resolution urging lesbians and gay men to take part in the November 15 antiwar mobilization in Washington and "to do so as homosexuals." But a second resolution calling for ERCHO to endorse the mobilization was defeated 27–35.

On a third set of resolutions, the radicals won a victory. As amended, the resolutions declared that "inalienable human rights" included (1) "Dominion over one's own body" through "sexual freedom without regard to orientation" and "freedom to use birth control and abortion," (2) "Freedom from society's attempts to define and limit human sexuality," and (3) "Freedom from political and social persecution of all minority groups," which was said to include "freedom and the right of self-determination of all oppressed minority groups."

In the wake of the ERCHO conference, Philadelphia lesbian and gay activists had an opportunity to reflect on the issues that divided them from radical gay liberationists. By early 1970, HAL was describing that what had seemed like ERCHO's "marriage" with the left was "perhaps little more than an impulsive flirtation." The newsletter reported that HAL, along with five other groups represented at the ERCHO conference, had taken advantage of rules allowing member organizations to dissociate themselves from ERCHO decisions.

In the coming years, as the Stonewall riots came to be seen as the founding event of the lesbian/gay movement, the Annual Reminders would often be forgotten. Few of the millions who would march in New York's annual "pride" parade commemorating the riots would be aware that the origins of their celebration lay in a small band of respectable lesbians and gay men who marched in front of Independence Hall on the fourth of July for five consecutive years. Ironically, today, when lesbian/gay pride parades mark the anniversary of Stonewall around the country, Philadelphia's celebration remains among the smallest of those held in large U.S. cities.

TOWARD THE 25TH ANNIVERSARY OF GAY LIBERATION AND RADICALESBIANISM IN PHILADELPHIA

When a GLF formed in Philadelphia in June 1970, three characteristics distinguished the group from its predecessors in GLF-NY. First, as founding member Kiyoshi Kuromiya has explained, GLF-Philadelphia rejected the idea that gay liberation was "a political struggle of an oppressed minority," believing instead that *all people* should come out as lesbian or gay. Building on the Radicalesbians-New York (RL-NY) position paper, "The Woman-Identified Woman," GLF-Philadelphia's statement of purpose proclaimed that "homosexual love is the most complete form of expression between two members of the same sex."

Second, GLF-Philadelphia was truly multiracial. Hundreds of African American lesbians and gay men attended HAL and GLF's 1970 dances on the campuses of the University of Pennsylvania and Temple University. And to the extent that GLF-Philadelphia had a leader, that person was Kuromiya, a Japanese-American human rights activist.

Third, GLF-Philadelphia conceived of gay liberation as a male movement parallel to lesbian feminism, which had erupted with the May 1970 Lavender Menace zap at the Congress to Unite Women in New

York. Influenced by lesbian feminism, GLF-Philadelphia identified sexism as the primary source of homophobia and gay oppression. These are the principles and practices that won applause when Kuromiya presented the demands of the "Male Homosexual Workshop" to the thousands of people gathered in Philadelphia for the Black Panther–sponsored Revolutionary People's Constitutional Convention (RPCC) in September 1970.

While the Stonewall riots have come to be regarded as the revolutionary moment that led to the gay liberation movement, much less attention has focused on the closest thing to a revolutionary moment that can be identified in the history of lesbian-feminism—the Lavender Menace zap in 1970. Lesbian feminism erupted in Philadelphia in the aftermath of the Panther convention. While the multiracial gay male liberationists were applauded at the RPCC, the predominantly white Lesbian Workshop walked out of the Convention, angry at a series of incidents they perceived as sexist and the Panthers perceived as racist. Several months later, in early 1971, male members of GLF-Philadelphia helped an isolated lesbian member form RL-Philadelphia. While predominantly white, RL-Philadelphia provided an environment in which Anita Cornwell produced the essays that would later form *Black Lesbian in White America* (1983), a vital early expression of African American lesbian feminism.

The 25th anniversary of Stonewall offers lesbians and gay men, and all those interested in historical and present-day lesbian and gay life, an opportunity to explore not only a particular event that occurred in one time and place, but a long series of developments in a variety of locations that have shaped the world in which we now live. Such histories honor the movement-building work of lesbians and gay men before and after Stonewall, reveal the myth-making process that turned the riots into a revolution, and provide us with new lessons from the past as we continue to struggle today.

Recalling Dewey's Sit-In

Forty years ago, three teenagers in Philadelphia took an extraordinary step by refusing to take a step. Their sit-in began on Sunday, April 25, 1965, at Dewey's restaurant near Rittenhouse Square in Center City. According to an account provided several months later by Clark Polak, a gay-rights leader in Philadelphia, "the action was a result of Dewey's refusal to serve a large number of homosexuals and persons wearing non-conformist clothing."

On the day of the sit-in, more than 150 people were reportedly denied service. When the teenagers, one female and two male, refused to leave, the police were called, and the three were taken into custody and arrested. Polak, who rushed to the scene and offered to help the three protesters obtain a lawyer, was also arrested. All four were soon found guilty of disorderly conduct.

Over the next week, gay-rights activists affiliated with the Janus Society of America distributed 1,500 leaflets outside of Dewey's, while gay movement leaders negotiated with representatives of the restaurant and local authorities. According to a report published in 1965 in the Janus Society newsletter, "No one was further denied service on the basis of appearance or suspected affiliations."

This essay was published originally in *Philadelphia Gay News*, 29 Apr. 2005, 10, 22–23, and reprinted as "The First Gay Sit-In," *History News Network*, 9 May 2005, http://hnn .us/articles/11652.html.

On May, 2, 1965, one week after the original action, three people conducted a second sit-in at Dewey's. When they refused to leave, Dewey's contacted the police, who spoke with the protesters, declined to take further action, and departed.

Polak's 1965 account indicates that the police told him that "we could stay in there as long as we wanted as the police had no authority to ask us to leave."

One hour later, the protesters declared victory and left the restaurant.

The Janus Society took pride in what it had accomplished. *Drum* magazine, which was published by Janus, noted that "to our knowledge, this is the first sit-in of its kind in the history of the United States."

The Janus newsletter reported success in its four objectives: "(1) to bring about an immediate cessation to all indiscriminate denials of service, (2) to prevent additional arrests, (3) to assure the homosexual community that (a) we were concerned with the day-to-day problems and (b) we were prepared to intercede in helping to solve these problems, (4) to create publicity for the organization and our objectives."

The newsletter also offered revealing comments about the gender and sexual politics of the protest: "All too often, there is a tendency to be concerned with the rights of homosexuals as long as they somehow appear to be heterosexual, whatever that is. The masculine woman and the feminine man often are looked down upon by the official policy of homophile organizations, but the Janus Society is concerned with the worth of an individual and the manner in which she or he comports himself. What is offensive today we have seen become the style of tomorrow, and even if what is offensive today remains offensive tomorrow to some persons, there is no reason to penalize such non-conformist behavior unless there is direct anti-social behavior connected with it."

HISTORICAL CONTEXT

Not much more is known about the Dewey's sit-in. When I was researching the incident for my book *City of Sisterly and Brotherly Loves*, I found the Janus newsletter and *Drum* magazine accounts discussed above, a subsequent letter to the editor published in *Drum*, a letter about the protest written by a Philadelphia lesbian activist to a New York gay leader, and the flier distributed outside of Dewey's. I also spoke with two Philadelphians who remember the Dewey's sit-in and who corroborated some of the information contained within the Janus and *Drum* accounts. Apparently a local television channel reported on the protest on a news program on April 30, but I was not able to identify the station or find a tape of the broadcast. I never learned the names of the original three teenage protesters, and Polak, the other person who probably knew the most about what happened at Dewey's, died in the 1980s.

The Dewey's sit-in can be placed within several significant historical contexts. First, there's the larger context of political protest in the 1960s, and especially the black freedom struggle, New Left student and youth rebellion, and anti-war mobilization. The anti-racist sit-in movement that began in 1960 at a Woolworth's lunch counter in Greensboro, N.C., may have been a particularly inspirational example for the Dewey's protesters.

Second, there's the larger context of what was known at the time as the "homophile" movement, which was founded in the early 1950s in California and which began to embrace militant, direct action tactics in the mid-1960s. In September 1964, the Homosexual League of New York and the League for Sexual Freedom organized a demonstration in New York to protest anti-gay military policies. Just days before the Dewey's sit-in, homophile activists organized gay rights demonstrations at the White House and the United Nations.

And about two months after the Dewey's sit-in, a few dozen activists staged an Independence Day gay rights demonstration at Independence Hall. Repeated on the Fourth of July over the next four years, these five "Annual Reminders" are being remembered at fortieth-anniversary celebrations during this year's Equality Forum. The fact that the U.S. homophile movement was much smaller in the 1960s than it would later become does not mean that the early movement did not deal with some of the same internal conflicts that we continue to see today. For example, while the Dewey's protesters focused on the needs of what they called "masculine women," "feminine men" and "non-conformists," the leaders of the Annual Reminders insisted that male picketers wear jackets and ties and that female picketers wear dresses or skirts.

Another example: While the Janus Society and *Drum* magazine enthusiastically promoted the sexual revolution, Frank Kameny, one of the organizers of the Annual Reminder, declared at a national homophile conference in 1966, "This is the homophile movement—we are not fighting for sexual freedom."

Third, there's the larger context of urban geography and the politics of space. Like many other U.S. cities, Philadelphia at mid-century was experiencing anxieties and tensions associated with urban redevelopment and urban gentrification projects. Competing visions of urban downtown cores—encompassing who should live, work, and play there; what businesses should be encouraged and discouraged; and how the built and natural environments should be developed—clashed when police in the 1950s and 1960s raided local establishments and harassed users of public space.

In this sense, denials of service at Dewey's in 1965 can be linked with police raids on nearby Philadelphia coffeehouses in 1959 and the harassment of gender and sexual nonconformists in Rittenhouse Square through the 1950s and 1960s. And protests against these denials of service can be linked to the long history of lesbian, gay, bisexual, and transgender efforts to resist oppression by fighting for physical and cultural space.

Fourth and finally, there's the larger context of capitalism, consumerism, and the economy. Historians of the black freedom struggle have encouraged us to think about the symbolic significance of some of the primary targets of their movement, which in the 1950s and early 1960s included public schools, public busses, and lunch counters. In the case of the latter, they have urged us to consider why the right to purchase hamburgers and sodas (and, more generally, the rights of consumers) took on such political significance at that moment in time. We can ask similar questions about the symbolic significance of Dewey's restaurant and how it differed from the symbolic significance of other targets of protest, including the White House, the United Nations, and Independence Hall.

POLITICS OF MEMORY

Now that Equality Forum [a Philadelphia-based LGBT organization that sponsors an annual civil rights summit and LGBT History Month projects] has asked us to recognize the Independence Hall demonstrations as the birthplace of the modern gay rights movement, there's another context to consider: the politics of memory.

In the last several weeks, Equality Forum has been criticized by various commentators for failing to recognize earlier gay, lesbian, bisexual, and transgender rights protests and for ignoring the longer history of the U.S. homophile movement. There is much at stake in these debates, and it is far more than the historical accuracy or inaccuracy of Equality Forum's claims.

Debates about the past are always debates about the present. The effort to mark the fortieth anniversary of the Independence Hall

FIGURE 4. In 2018, the Pennsylvania Historical and Museum Commission installed a historical marker near the site of the 1965 Dewey's sit-in in Philadelphia (219 S. Seventeenth St.). Activists staged the sit-in to defend the rights of "homosexuals," "masculine women," "feminine men," and "persons wearing non-conformist clothing." Photograph courtesy of Equality Forum.

demonstrations reflects an impulse to remember the protests of the past, but also to promote local gay tourism in the present. The anniversary celebrations are proud efforts to recognize Philadelphia's historical significance, but also defensive moves on the part of civic boosters who expose their insecurities when they challenge their better-known counterparts in New York City and California.

The desire to present the Fourth of July protests as the birthplace of the modern gay movement reflects commendable interest in history, but also troubling disinterest in the links between sexual protest and gender nonconformity that were more evident in incidents such as the Dewey's sit-in. The focus on patriotic protests at the birthplace of the nation reflects the politics of those who believe in fundamental U.S. values, but not the politics of those who see the United States as fundamentally unequal, undemocratic, and unfree.

Finally, the selection of the Annual Reminder demonstrations as worthy of remembering reflects the tenacious activism of homophile leaders such as Frank Kameny and Barbara Gittings, who 40 years later, continue to educate us about their importance, but contributes to historical amnesia about the evanescent actions of three teenagers who initiated a sit-in at Dewey's more than two months before the first homophile pickets at Independence Hall.

Fifty Years of LGBT Movement Activism in Philadelphia

This past August marked the 50th anniversary of LGBT movement activism in Philadelphia. As I recounted in my book *City of Sisterly and Brotherly Loves: Lesbian and Gay Philadelphia, 1945–1972* (originally published in 2000), the "Radnor Raid" launched the gay and lesbian movement in the region. In this extraordinary incident, Main Line police and postal officials raided a meeting held to discuss forming a gay and lesbian rights group for Greater Philadelphia. Apparently tipped off by publicity fliers about the meeting, the police arrested more than 80 people, including Jack Adair, who had arranged for the use of the Main Line estate where the meeting took place, and "Albert J. De Dion," a New York activist who led that city's chapter of the Mattachine Society, a national "homophile" group. Eventually everyone arrested in the Radnor Raid was released, the charges were dropped, and, in the coming months, Greater Philadelphians founded their own Mattachine chapter, initiating local LGBT movement advocacy.

Historical memory is often more complicated than it may seem, and the uses we make of the past can vary greatly. When I first learned of the Radnor Raid, I regarded it as an important example and symbol of the political repression experienced by LGBT people and LGBT rights advocates then and now. I also thought it significant that the raid took place

This essay was published originally in *Philadelphia Gay News*, 30 Sep. 2010.

in the suburbs, which haven't received much attention as sites of significant developments in LGBT history. Most of all, I thought the story of the Radnor Raid was important as a story of resistance, of LGBT people struggling against oppression in ways small and substantial.

In the 10 years since my book was published, I haven't changed my mind about any of these aspects of the history of the Radnor Raid. But to mark the raid's 50th anniversary, I'd like to add another layer to the story, which centers on how I came to learn about some of the episode's most revealing details.

I can't remember exactly how I first learned about the Radnor Raid, but I know that very early in my research, I read contemporary reports about it in the gay press and in local newspapers. I was particularly struck by the language used in the first newsletter of the Philadelphia Mattachine Society, which declared that there was "no reason to believe" that such a raid "need ever occur again." The newsletter continued: "This was the first time the police have ever disrupted any Mattachine meeting, and we have confidence it will be the last." I also took note of a report by the New York activists who had been helping to organize the Philadelphia group: "Due to a misunderstanding, we were visited by the local police, who, under the misapprehension that we were showing obscene films, took the entire crowd to the police station for questioning."

Was it the defensive tone of the New York report—the insistence that the meeting did not feature the showing of obscene films—that caught my critical eye? I can't recall now, but I know my suspicions increased when I began to hear rather formulaic and defensive language about pornography in the oral interviews I conducted with activists who remembered being at the raid or hearing about it around the time it occurred. At least five people made a point of emphasizing to me that there was nothing obscene about the movies and other materials shown at the organizing meeting in Radnor.

Now of course I knew it was possible the reason they all took pains to mention this to me was that the police had tried to justify the raid on obscenity-based grounds. And it made a certain sense that the police would emphasize this rationale for the raid; otherwise, there might have been constitutional problems with denying LGBT people's rights of speech and assembly. But those of us who are professional historians are trained and encouraged to look critically at all of our sources of information. This is typically easier to do when reading a government report, a newspaper account, or a court transcript than when listening to a set of courageous activists generously sharing their memories with a younger member of their community. Nevertheless, I found something suspicious about the stories I was hearing, and began wondering if the accounts were based on strategic narratives activists constructed to defend their actions to themselves, to their friends and allies, and to potentially hostile public authorities. There's also the possibility that people are remembering the memories, rather than the events that served as the basis for the memories. Many of us have to admit that when we have told a particular story about our lives over and over, we remember the story more than the experiences that first led us to construct the story. I wondered if this was happening with the Radnor Raid.

Several years after I first learned about the raid, I caught a lucky break. While doing research in the extraordinary collection of gay movement materials housed at the New York Public Library, I came across an exchange of correspondence in 1960 and 1961 between Mattachine New York leaders and Thomas Brandon of Brandon Films. In one of the letters, Brandon emphasized that he and his company were "opposed to government censorship" and the actions of the Radnor police. Nevertheless, he would hold Mattachine responsible for misusing a film booked for a showing in New York and failing to notify the company immediately about its seizure. Mattachine responded with relief that since the district attorney had finally returned all the films seized in the raid, Brandon's film could now be returned to its rightful owners. Fortunately for me, Mattachine's response named the film: "Muscle Beach."

I remember chuckling when reading the name of the movie, and later I identified the film as a 1950 amateur short by Joseph Strick, described in one source as "a satire on the 'labors of relaxation' of exercise devotees." I also knew that one of the other films shown at the Radnor Raid was Kenneth Anger's homoerotic avant-garde "Fireworks" (1947), which an oral-history narrator took pains to emphasize was "a film about homosexuality which had previously been cleared by the courts."

What was significant to me was not the question of whether "Muscle Beach" or "Fireworks" was obscene, but why the written accounts and the oral-history testimonies emphasized, over and over again, that they were not. No one suggested that sexually provocative, risqué, or erotic materials might have been strategically useful for attracting an audience at the Mattachine organizing meeting. No one argued that the movement had sexual aims and that, in this context, sexual films were entirely appropriate to show at an organizing meeting. No one argued that sexual films were understood to be a tool that could stimulate erotic bonds and passions, which in turn could motivate political activism.

For my book, my thoughts about this became the foundation of an argument I made about the politics of respectability in the homophile, gay liberation, and lesbian feminist movements of the 1960s and '70s.

Denying the sexual content of the films that inspired the Radnor Raid was in keeping with the politics of respectability adopted by many (though certainly not all) activists in this period. At the same time, the very fact that activists planned to show sexual films on the night they launched the local homophile movement reminds us there has always been more to queer politics than the politics of respectability.

Fast-forward 50 years to our ongoing discussions about the politics of same-sex marriage. Same-sex marriage is a complicated and con-tested issue in LGBT communities, as it should be. Here I only want to use the story of the Radnor Raid to make one small point. When I hear proponents of same-sex marriage insist there is nothing sexual about their agenda, that marriage is about rights and not sex and that the legalization of same-sex marriage will not affect the politics of sex in general and the politics of sex education in particular, I hear echoes of the stories about the Radnor Raid. Without a doubt, these stories are strategically smart in political environments marked by hostility toward LGBT sexual expression. But it's worth thinking more about what we lose when we tell and listen to these stories and what happens when we forget about or deny the importance of sex in our movement and our society.

CHAPTER II

Heterosexuality in America

Fifty Years and Counting

This month, the GLBT History Museum in San Francisco is marking the fiftieth anniversary of *Life* magazine's influential photographic essay "Homosexuality in America." The essay, which appeared in a weekly periodical that was read by millions of U.S. Americans, is featured in an exhibit curated by community historian Paul Gabriel. According to the museum's website, the exhibit, titled "1964: The Year San Francisco Came Out," addresses "an infamous *LIFE* magazine article that catapulted San Francisco into national consciousness as the 'gay capital' of America." In highlighting the historical significance of "Homosexuality in America," the GLBT History Museum joins the Ryerson Image Centre in Toronto, which is featuring the *Life* magazine essay in "What It Means to Be Seen: Photography and Queer Visibility." Curated by Sophie Hackett, the associate curator of photography at the Art Gallery of Ontario, this exhibit was part of the recently concluded WorldPride 2014 festivities in Toronto.

Discussing "Homosexuality in America" on *Huffington Post*, Hackett writes that the article in *Life* was "one of the first depictions of gay life in a mainstream magazine." Hackett is right to say that it was "one of the first"; for example, in December 1962 *Philadelphia Magazine*

This essay was published originally on *Notches: (Re)marks on the History of Sexuality*, 22 July 2014, http://notchesblog.com/2014/07/22/heterosexuality-in-america-fifty-years -and-counting/.

FIGURE 5. The GLBT Historical Society, founded in 1985 as the San Francisco Bay Area Gay and Lesbian Historical Society, operates an archive and a museum. The museum, pictured here during previews in 2010, opened in 2011 in San Francisco's Castro neighborhood. Photograph by Gerard Koskovich (2010).

published "The Furtive Fraternity," a lengthy exposé on gay life by journalist Gaeton Fonzi. As is so often the case in the history of mainstream media, "national" media stories were preceded and anticipated by "local" ones.

In October 1964, two years after "The Furtive Fraternity" was "exposed," one of the most interesting and revealing responses to "Homosexuality in America" also was published in Philadelphia. The first issue of *Drum*, the self-described "gay Playboy" that quickly became the most popular gay movement magazine in North America, featured "Heterosexuality in America," an essay by the internationally acclaimed writer "P. Arody." Arody's campy name and the politics of "Heterosexuality in America" were consistent with the magazine's first advertisement, which declared: "*Drum* presents news for 'queers,' and fiction for 'perverts.' Photo essays for 'fairies,' and laughs for 'faggots.'" Over the next five years, *Drum* charted a new direction for the homophile movement and led the way in calling for gay rights advocates to join the sexual revolution.

This was not the first time that American heterosexuality became the butt of a queer joke in a U.S. periodical that celebrated sexual freedom. In 1955, Hugh Hefner's *Playboy* magazine had published Charles Beaumont's short story "The Crooked Man," which presented the revealing story of a straight man struggling against persecution in a fantastical dystopian society dominated by homosexuals.

The politics of *Drum*'s essay, however, were quite different from those that were featured in Beaumont's short story. According to Arody, who inverted and revised much of the language found in the *Life* magazine essay, "Heterosexuality shears across the spectrum of America life—the professions, the arts, business and labor. It always has. But today, especially in big cities, heterosexuals are openly admitting, even flaunting, their deviation." The essay depicted "the heterosexual world" as "sad and often sordid" and emphasized that "for every obvious heterosexual, there are probably nine nearly impossible to detect." Later in the essay, Arody noted, "It is estimated that 95% of all heterosexual men are sex criminals and . . . the overwhelming majority of heterosexual marrieds also consistently violate the law." This was because "jail sentences that may range to life imprisonment and unlimited fines can be set against married heterosexuals who do anything other than direct sexual intercourse" and "anal and oral contacts between marrieds are strictly prohibited by law." The concluding paragraph declared that heterosexuals "form a separate and distinct class of persons in many respects and they have adopted customs which seem perverse and sometimes even sinister to the average homosexual." Nevertheless, Arody argued for tolerance and compassion: "The mainstream of heterosexual life is not much different from the mainstream of homosexual life" and "differences which seem extreme at first lose most of the emotionally laden values once a close and human appreciation is applied."

Drum's response to *Life* was not limited to the essay by Arody. Immediately following "Heterosexuality in America," the magazine published a letter to *Life* by Clark Polak, the editor of *Drum* and the president of its publisher, the Janus Society, which was a Philadelphia-based homophile group. Polak wrote:

> As an individual who is homosexual and as the President of the Janus Society, I must protest your treatment of homosexuals and homosexuality. I would like to call your attention to some of the inconsistencies in your story: 1) While your photographs rivet attention on the 15% of homosexuals who

are obvious, little effort is made to show the other 85% who are unidentifiable in society. 2) You reduce the evidence of Drs. Hooker, van den Haag, and Kinsey to secondary positions while emphasizing the opinions of Dr. Bieber in addition to dwelling on the more sensational aspects of the new 'Kinsey' report. 3) You fail to explain how the majority of homosexuals . . . are in your quotes "emotionally disturbed" while they still function successfully in their respective occupations. 4) You fail to take a stand for law reform when the preponderance of the evidence is pointing forcefully in that direction. 5) Entrapment is both illegal and undesirable procedure, but your comments on the Officer-Jerry dialogue fail to call attention to this fact.

It is our position that until such time as there is clear cut evidence to contradict our stand, homosexuality per se is not a significant factor in determining military or civilian fitness for employment, psychological maturity, social desirability, or public and private acceptance.

Each individual must be judged on his or her own merits and cannot properly be accepted or rejected because of homosexuality.

Drum then published a response to Polak's letter by "Patricia Hines for the Editors" of *Life*:

Naturally we regret your disappointment in *LIFE*'s June 26 report, "Homosexuality in America." It was our intention to present a balanced and fair account of the problems surrounding homosexuality, and I believe we made clear the difficulties caused homosexuals by law enforcement procedures as they are practiced in a city such as San Francisco. We stated clearly in the article that the large majority of homosexuals are unidentifiable in society. Within the framework of our report, however, where we chose to treat the growing openness of homosexual society, we focused attention primarily upon the identifiable minority. As for our treatment of present-day scientific views, we believe we gave a fair account. As you know, the findings of many researchers such as Kinsey have been widely critized [*sic*] from a methodological viewpoint, while the opinion voiced by Dr. Bieber is representative of widely held views of psychologists and psychiatrists. We did not, however, present either approach as a final word on the subject.

Although space limitations did not permit us to publish your letter in our Letters Column, we hope you'll have a chance to see the sampling of reader response to the article—pro and con—in our July 17 issue.

Over the next five years, *Drum* championed sexual liberation, political militancy, and gay-affirmative sensibilities within the homophile movement, contributing greatly to an under-studied tradition within the early gay and lesbian movement in the United States. As we mark the fiftieth anniversary of *LIFE* magazine's essay "Homosexuality in America," let's also mark the fiftieth anniversary of the founding of *Drum*, the radicalization of gay and lesbian resistance to oppression, and the call for new ways of thinking about "Heterosexuality in America."

PART FOUR

Queer Historical Interventions

After five years of college and university teaching in positions with no long-term prospects (1993–1998), I was hired as a tenure-track assistant professor of US political history by York University in Toronto. Two years later, my book on Philadelphia was published and I was elected chair of the Committee on Lesbian and Gay History, an affiliated society of the American Historical Association. In 2001, I was tenured, promoted to associate professor, and appointed director of undergraduate studies for one of the largest history programs in North America, with more than one thousand history majors. I do not think it is an accident that it was in this period, when I first could enjoy the privileges and benefits of improved job security and greater professional status, that I began to supplement the public history work I had been doing for LGBT readers with queer historical scholarship aimed at broader audiences. One opportunity came in 2000, when several of my York colleagues organized a conference titled "Historians and Their Audiences: Mobilizing History for the Millennium."[1] A few years later, I began writing short essays for History News Network, founded by Rick Shenkman in 2000 to "help put current events into historical perspective." As Shenkman later noted in reflecting on the genesis of HNN, "It seemed obvious to me that historians should have a national platform to help journalists and the public make sense of the news."[2]

Every US historian who teaches in Canada, as I did from 1998 to 2014, has to think about "historians and their audiences." Most history professors who teach in the United States can assume that one of their primary audiences—their students—have some familiarity with US history, but this is not necessarily true in Canada. Canadian students generally know far more about the United States than US students know about Canada, but this is not saying very much given how little most US students know about their northern neighbor. Canadian students also have different relationships to US history—sometimes more celebratory, often more critical, typically less personally implicated—than their US counterparts. As a specialist in US LGBT history teaching in Canada, I sometimes felt marginalized in both countries, but most of my Canadian colleagues and students responded with interest to my work and I occasionally shared my scholarship with broader Canadian audiences. In 2000 and 2002, I joined the steering committees of the Bent on Change conferences in Toronto, which brought together academics and activists to discuss "queer issues on campus and in communities."[3] In 2007, while serving as the director of my university's new Sexuality Studies Program, I organized a symposium titled "Sex Talk: Sexuality Studies Research at York."[4] In the same year, *Academic Matters*, a higher education magazine in Canada, published my critical response to an attack on women's studies, queer studies, native studies, and cultural studies for practicing "advocacy scholarship." A few years later, my partner and I were featured in an article about commuting academic couples in the Canadian magazine *University Affairs*.[5] These publications and projects were directed primarily to Canadians. For reaching US audiences, I increasingly turned to online platforms.

Relationships between historians and their audiences, whether online or not, were influenced by shifts in national politics in the early twenty-first century. Divided government in the United States makes it difficult to capture this, but US and Canadian politics have rarely been aligned in the last several decades, meaning that political influences on historical scholarship were different in the two countries. When I moved to Canada in 1998, the United States was governed by a Democratic president and a Republican Congress, whereas Canada was governed by the Liberal Party. Two years later, the US Electoral College selected Republican George W. Bush to serve as president and for most of the next six years the Republican Party controlled the US Congress, meaning that US national politics were considerably more conservative than their Canadian counterparts. From 2006 to 2015, however, political winds in the two countries shifted: Canada was governed by the Conservative Party, whereas the United States was governed by Democratic president Barack Obama and a Democratic Congress from 2008 to 2010 and then by Obama and a divided Congress from 2010 to 2016. When I returned to the United States in 2014, I left a country with a Conservative prime minister and entered one with a Democratic president, but after national elections in 2015 and 2016, Canada was led by Liberal Justin Trudeau and the United States by Republican Donald Trump. Four years later, the politics of the two countries experienced a rare convergence, with Canadian Liberals and US Democrats leading their respective national governments. As the essays reprinted in this section make clear, changes in national politics prompted responses by public historians.

This was certainly the case for queer history. Multiple historians of sexuality, for example, responded to new possibilities for legal reform in the early twenty-first century, playing vital roles in the US Supreme Court's 2003 decision to invalidate state sodomy laws and its 2013 and 2015 rulings on same-sex marriage. I addressed the sexual politics of President Clinton's 1998 impeachment at the 2000 York conference. Over the next several years, I wrote several History News Network essays about sexual politics during the Bush and Obama presidencies. As a mid-career queer historian who wanted to communicate with larger audiences, I was pleased to find new public interest in LGBT history.

HNN proved to be an outstanding platform for reaching broader public audiences. My HNN essays have been shared more than one thousand times and many thousands more have read these articles. That said, I have not always been happy about the changes HNN made to my proposed titles. My discussions about this with HNN's editor illustrate some of the complications that can arise when academic scholars try to write for public audiences. I may have been sensitive about this because I had written hundreds of headlines for the *Wesleyan Argus* and *GCN*, so thought of myself as knowledgeable and experienced in this area. The first conflict occurred in 2003, when I suggested "Alienated Affections: Remembering Clive Michael Boutilier (1933–2003)" for an essay reprinted in part 5. HNN initially used a headline (now lost) that I criticized for emphasizing that gay activists had neglected the case, which was not my point. HNN editor Rick Shenkman responded, "On the Internet you can't be subtle. Titles have to tell people what they're getting. Otherwise, they won't bother with it." He nevertheless agreed to change the headline to "Forgetting and Remembering a Deported Alien." In 2004, "In My Wildest Dreams: Advice for George Bush" became "Mr. President, I Am Glad You Called." When

I expressed concern about removing the reference to queer writer Oscar Wilde, whose voice I was attempting to channel, Shenkman responded, "My title will draw more readers. Yes, it's less literary but on the Internet titles that work best are those that hit the reader over the head with an idea. Can't be too subtle." In 2005, "Recalling Dewey's Sit-In" (reprinted in part 3) became "The First Gay Sit-In." In this case, I complained that while one of my sources had referred to the Dewey's protest as the "first" gay sit-in, I had avoided endorsing this, "because claims about 'firsts' are always subject to criticism when new research uncovers new evidence." I also noted that "the headline was especially awkward because around the same time I was quoted in some Philly newspapers as challenging the claims of Philly Pridefest organizers who were claiming that the Independence Hall pickets were 'firsts,' and the piece itself criticized the type of urban boosterism that leads to hyperbolic claims about 'firsts.'"

My conversations with HNN about titles continued over the next several years. In 2005, I suggested three titles for an essay about Supreme Court Justice Abe Fortas: "Find the Fortas File!" or "Queer Eye for the FBI" or "Queer Eye for the Supreme Court Filibuster." Shenkman responded, "I like titles to be plain, meaning that they tell the reader what they are going to find out." He added, "My experience has given me a pretty good feel for titles that work on the Internet. Most writers want titles like they see in the *Atlantic*, which don't work on the Internet." In the end, he titled my essay (reprinted in part 6) "Did the FBI Try to Blackmail Supreme Court Justice Abe Fortas?" In 2014, "From the Glorious Strike to Obama's New Executive Order" became "The Long Struggle to Stop Employment Discrimination against LGBT People Is Even Longer Than You Think." In this case, Shenkman's original title used "gays" instead of "LGBT people," but he relented after I explained, "Saying 'gays' is problematic here given intense sensitivities about including trans people. After all, the exec order is careful to include gender identity along with sexual orientation." In 2015, "Constitution Day Loyalty" became "Did You Know California Requires Professors to Sign a Loyalty Oath?" In 2016, "In My Mind I'm (Not) Going to Carolina," which referenced a popular song by James Taylor, became "North Carolina's Brutal Tradition of Sexual and Gender Discrimination." In 2017, "Defectives of the World, Unite!" became "50 Years Ago the US Supreme Court Upheld the Deportation of 'Homosexuals' as 'Psychopaths.'"

In 2017, Shenkman and I had an extended conversation about language after he proposed titles referencing immigrant Clive Boutilier as "gay" or "homosexual." At one point, I wrote,

> Yours is a news network that works to bridge the academic/public divide. That's why I love it. Isn't one of the points to figure out how to translate complex academic scholarship for more public audiences? I try to do that in the pieces I submit. . . . We don't know that he *was* gay. We know that he engaged in same-sex sex and the government labelled him "homosexual" and "afflicted with psychopathic personality." Names matter. I've been very careful in my work about Boutilier in terms of referring to him as gay. When I'm talking about how the government labelled him, I use homosexual and I generally put it in quotation marks to mark my distance from an outdated and offensive term. But note that one of the options I offered used gay differently: 50 Years Ago the US Supreme Court Upheld Anti-Gay Immigration Restriction. That solves the problem by not calling him gay but referring to the law as antigay. You might regard that as semantic or pedantic, but it's a meaningful distinction.

My 2017 dialogue with Shenkman was particularly complicated because at some point in the previous fifteen years, he had revealed to me that he is gay. He would be the first to admit that he is not a specialist in LGBT history, but in our exchanges, he drew upon the authority of personal experience in emphasizing that he does not mind being called a "homosexual." Ultimately Shenkman's headline for the 2017 essay used "homosexual," but put it in quotation marks. More generally, I think our conflicts about headlines point to some of the possibilities and pitfalls of packaging and promoting academic scholarship for broader public audiences.

Three years later, when I wrote to Shenkman to request permission to identify him as gay and quote from our correspondence in this book, I asked him about whether he saw a relationship between his gay identity and his work as a public historian. He responded that he did, explaining that being gay gave him "an outsider's perspective," which "affected everything" he did, "including history." Taught by a mentor who had emphasized the "value in addressing issues of public concern from a historical perspective," Shenkman came to view public history as a "perfect marriage" of his "two great intellectual loves, history and journalism." As for being gay, he observed, "It shaped what I looked for anytime I examined a subject. Being gay made me acutely aware of the difference between how we as humans present ourselves in public and how we behave in private. I knew many gay men, for example, who passed for straight: the young gay seminarian preparing for the priesthood, the gay actor playing Jesus in plays put on by the Mormons. This knowledge shaped the lens through which I looked at people. It made me skeptical. I always wondered when I met people what secrets they might be hiding." Shenkman specifically referenced his work on political history: "When I wrote about presidents I assumed there is a great deal of difference between how they appeared in public and what they must be like in private. When, for example, it was reported that Bill Clinton was a less than faithful husband, I wasn't surprised. I don't think any gay man was. Gay men know by experience how often many people stray and how powerful the lure of sex outside marriage is." In more general terms, he added, "Being gay enlarged my expectations about human behavior. Humans are complicated. They don't conform to stereotypes." Shenkman's reflections raise the provocative possibility that historians who identify as LGBT, whether or not they study the queer past, might have distinct relationships to public history.

Chapter 12, "Monica, Bill, History, and Sex," explores this possibility by imagining what historians of sexuality might have said had journalists asked for their perspectives on the presidential sex scandal. Originally presented at the "Historians and Their Audiences" conference in 2000, it was published in 2015 on Active History, which describes itself as "a website that connects the work of historians with the wider public and the importance of the past to current events." Founded in 2008, the website declares, "We define active history variously as history that listens and is responsive; history that will make a tangible difference in people's lives; history that makes an intervention and is transformative to both practitioners and communities. We seek a practice of history that emphasizes collegiality, builds community among active historians and other members of communities, and recognizes the public responsibilities of the historian."[6]

Chapter 13, "In My Wildest Dreams: Advice for George Bush," was published by HNN in 2004. This essay, like others I presented on HNN, relied on a campy voice that I had used in columns written for the *Graduate Perspective* at the University of Pennsylvania.[7] Prompted by the sexual hypocrisy of social conservatives in the run-up to the 2004 presidential election, the essay used media stories I was collecting for my book *Sexual Injustice* (2010). These stories showed that while the Supreme Court had invalidated state sodomy laws in 2003, local officials were still using laws against cohabitation, fornication, and obscenity to police sex. In a sense, my goal was to recruit straight people into the struggle for sexual freedom, since they, too, were vulnerable to legal punishment for engaging in popular activities such as living together outside of wedlock, having sex "before" marriage, and using vibrators and other sex toys.

Chapter 14, "In My Wildest Dreams: The Marriage That Dare Not Speak Its Name," was published by HNN in 2010. Influenced by the intensification of same-sex marriage debates in the Obama era, this essay challenged conservative invocations of "traditional marriage," which were at odds with historical realities. The essay also was prompted by my ambivalence about same-sex marriage. I have long opposed the concept of state-sanctioned marriage, but also believe that if the state grants special rights and privileges to cross-sex marriages, it should do the same for same-sex ones. Several months after this essay was published, my partner and I married in Canada; one reason was our expectation that this would be necessary for my partner to migrate to Canada legally after he retired. A short time later we celebrated our marriage with a party for several dozen friends and family near our home in Maine, which at the time did not recognize same-sex marriages. In 2009, Maine's legislature had passed a statute providing for the recognition of same-sex marriages, but later that year the state's voters rejected the legislation in a referendum. Three years later, Maine's voters revisited the issue, this time authorizing the legal recognition of same-sex marriages.

Chapter 15, "From the Glorious Strike to Obama's New Executive Order," was published by HNN in 2014. This essay was prompted by Obama's decision to sign an executive order requiring most companies that have US government contracts to pledge that they do not practice employment discrimination based on sexual orientation and gender identity. Obama did this because of the refusal of the Republican-dominated US Congress to pass the Employment Non-Discrimination Act. I was pleased by Obama's move, but troubled by its limitations and disturbed by false claims about the origins of this struggle in the 1970s, when I knew it had begun in the 1950s and 1960s. I decided to illustrate this by reviving a 1968 April Fool's joke about the "glorious strike" of "homosexuals" against employment discrimination.[8]

Chapter 16, "In My Mind I'm (Not) Going to Carolina," was published by HNN in 2016. This essay responded to a new North Carolina law that limited the ability of local communities to adopt and enforce antidiscrimination laws and limited the ability of trans people to use bathrooms designated for their genders. Later that year my essay was cited in an amicus brief by trans studies scholars in a Fourth Circuit

Court challenge to the law.[9] California responded to the statute by banning state-funded travel to states with anti-LGBT laws. While this was well-intentioned, it ironically hinders the type of research travel that was required to complete my essay. The ban currently applies to eighteen states, including North Carolina. In 2021, I persuaded the Committee on LGBT History and the American Historical Association to recommend amendments to California's law so that faculty and students at state-funded colleges and universities can use state funds to travel to these states for educational and research projects that support LGBT and other struggles for social justice. I recently wrote an essay about this for the *Public Seminar* blog, but so far California legislators have not responded.[10]

Monica, Bill, History, and Sex

Twenty years ago this month, U.S. Democratic President Bill Clinton began having sex with White House intern Monica Lewinsky. More than two years later, during testimony in a sexual harassment lawsuit filed by Paula Jones, Clinton denied that he was having a sexual relationship with Lewinsky. Several months later, Independent Counsel Kenneth Starr reported to the U.S. Congress that Clinton had committed perjury and obstruction of justice in his testimony about Lewinsky and related actions in the Jones litigation. The U.S. House of Representatives, controlled by the Republican Party, impeached Clinton in December 1998. In January and February 1999, the Republican-controlled U.S. Senate tried Clinton, but the president was acquitted when the Senate failed to meet the constitutional requirement of a two-thirds vote for conviction.

This essay was originally written in 2000 for "Historians and Their Audiences: Mobilizing History for the Millennium," a conference sponsored by the York University History Department. My goal was to address the privileging of traditional political historians over historians of sexuality in mainstream public discussions about the Clinton/ Lewinsky scandal, but I also wanted to use my presentation to consider the place of humor, satire, and parody in the work of historians. If the opening parody of both *The McLaughlin Group* (a long-running

This essay, parts of which were drafted in 2000, was revised and published on *Active History*, 13 Nov. 2015, http://activehistory.ca/2015/11/monica-bill-history-and-sex/.

public affairs television program) and historical scholarship in sexuality studies seems excessively reliant on inside jokes that only historians of sexuality of a certain generation might understand, my hope was (and is) that this, too, might contribute to new ways of thinking about historians and their audiences.

For the most part, I have avoided editing or revising the essay, wanting it to stand as a reflection of my thinking about these issues in 2000, but some of the parodied names have been changed to protect the innocent and prevent further litigation.

. . .

Welcome to this edition of *The McLaughlinstein Group*, hosted by me, Marc McLaughlinstein. Today's topic: Monica, Bill, Sex, and History. Our regular guests, Doris Kearns Johnson, Michael Wilentz, and Sean Beschloss, were unable to join us today, so instead our program will feature widely acclaimed historians Mary Contrary Daly, Carroll Rosen-Smithberg, John-Boy Howard, George Chancy, Lilliana Faderwoman, and Steve Edgwick.

Question: Monica and Bill—did they or didn't they? What do the historians say? Professor Mary Contrary Daly? Would you like to begin?

"Not really, but I will. Bill Clinton sexually harassed, assaulted, and raped Monica Lewinsky. But even more significant is the fact that all of this occurred in the Oval Office. And the oval, as all womyn know, is a spiritually, metaphysically, and herstorically feminine shape. Originally, men were not meant to exist inside the Oval Office. The rape of Monica and the rape of all women began on the day that men first began entering womyn's oval offices."

Professor Carroll Rosen-Smithberg? Did they or didn't they?

"What I think we have here is a White House world of love and ritual, and it would be wrong for us to transpose the sexual values of the world outside the White House to the world inside the White House. Monica and Bill touched, they were intimate, they were physically with each other, but did they have a sexual relationship? Bill certainly was exploiting Monica for sex. But Monica was not a passive victim. She resisted. She had sexual agency and sexual subjectivity."

What do you think, Professor John-Boy Howard?

"So far all of the panelists have missed the critical issue: the distinctive regional, spatial, and generational sexual cultures that shaped this series of sexual encounters. Bill was a Baby Boomer from the rural South. Monica was a member of Generation X from suburban California. As long as we keep using a northeastern and urban framework for understanding this relationship, we won't get anywhere."

Yes, Professor George Chancy. I see that you'd like to say something.

"I'd just like to add that, if it's true that Monica performed oral and manual sex on Bill and that he did not reciprocate, Bill resembles some of the men I discussed in my book *Gay York*. I'm thinking of the straight men whose masculine identities were not threatened by having sex with men, as long as they played the 'masculine' role in sex. Similarly, Bill's identity as a devoted husband was not threatened by having sex with Monica, as long as he received but did not give pleasure."

You've been awfully quiet, Professor Lilliana Faderwoman. Would you like to respond?

"For me, the most significant relationship here was not Bill and Monica's, but the one between Monica and her confidant Linda Tripp. Before Linda betrayed Monica, this was a classic romantic friendship. These two women exchanged confidences and talked intimately. Their love surpassed the love of men. Sex was not the issue at all."

And what do you think, Professor Steve Edgwick?

"Well I agree that Monica and Linda's relationship was significant, but we have to remember that this homosocial relationship was triangulated via their heterosocial relationships with Bill. And even more significantly, Bill's homosocial relationship with presidential advisor Vernon Jordan was acted out on the body of Monica. Come to think of it, Monica and Hillary's homosocial relationship was acted out on the body of Bill. And Bill and Kenneth Starr's relationship was acted out on the body of Monica. So what we have here are complex triangulations, rather than simple pairings."

Well that just about completes our show. Thank you to our special guests and thank you to our audience for joining *The McLaughlinstein Group*.

. . .

The impeachment and trial of U.S. President William Jefferson Clinton in 1998–1999 were fascinating political episodes witnessed by worldwide audiences of millions. For those of us who are professional historians, one of the most intriguing aspects of this extravaganza was the prominent role played by some of our colleagues. Presidential historians Doris Kearns Goodwin and Michael Beschloss were featured regularly on television news programs, initially commenting on the impeachment of President Andrew Johnson more than a hundred years ago and then offering historically informed commentary on the proceedings concerning President Clinton. Princeton historian Sean Wilentz testified before Congress, famously warning the Republicans that future historians would not look favourably upon their actions. Dozens of other historians commented publicly on the impeachment and trial on radio and television programs and in newspaper and magazine articles. Perhaps never before have historians reached a larger public audience on a matter of contemporary political significance.

As a historian of politics I was fascinated by all of this. But as a historian of sexuality, I was troubled. Where were historians of sexuality in the parade of experts called upon to comment on historical issues related to the presidential crisis? During this period, the North American public was exposed to an unprecedented education in U.S. constitutional, legal, presidential, and congressional history, and an unprecedented discussion of political sex. Yet somehow the relationship between history and sexuality was never consummated, this despite the fact that the whole controversy turned on the question not of what "is" is (as Clinton famously asserted) but of what "sex" is. While historians may not have been able to answer this question, they could have shed light on the related question of what "sex" has been.

Sexual questions were at the heart of the national impeachment drama. Did Clinton have a history of extramarital sexual experiences before he entered the White House? Were these experiences consensual, quasi-consensual, or non-consensual? Did Clinton continue to have such experiences after he became President? What sexual acts did Clinton engage in outside of marriage? Oral sex? Mutual or non-mutual masturbation? Penis-in-vagina, vagina-around-penis sex? Did Clinton and his partners regard each of these sexual acts as sex? Did they regard each of these sexual acts as sexual intercourse? How did Clinton and his partners define a "sexual relationship," as opposed to just "sex"? Did Clinton's wife Hillary Rodham Clinton know about her husband's extramarital sexual experiences? If so, when and how did she find out and did she talk about them with her husband? Did Hillary have her own sexual experiences, with men and/or with women, outside of marriage? What kind of marriage and what kind of sexual understanding did Bill and Hillary have? What, if anything, did Bill's sexual experiences and sexual values reveal about his character? Was there a relationship between his "private" life and his "public" life? Each of these questions could also be reframed to focus on the sexual experiences, relationships, and values of Clinton's supporters, Clinton's opponents, and the American public as a whole. While some might claim that the central impeachment issues involved lying under oath and obstructing justice, rather than having extramarital sex, determining whether and in what ways Clinton lied under oath and obstructed justice arguably turns on how one answers these and other sexual questions.

Despite the fact that sexual questions were central in Clinton's impeachment and trial, I saw no evidence that mainstream politicians, political advisors, judges, lawyers, or journalists were interested in what historians of sexuality, or for that matter any scholars in sexuality studies, might contribute to the public debate or the legal proceedings, this despite the virtually unprecedented interest in the contributions of traditional political historians. As I began to think about this, I called to mind a number of historians of sexuality and imagined what they might have had to say if asked to comment. I thought first of John Howard, whose work deals with sexualities in the American South. Howard argues against the inappropriate use of northern and urban sexual frameworks, insisting that southern sexualities be understood in different terms. Howard, I imagine, would have encouraged us to think about distinctive southern sexual traditions and how these traditions may have played a role in shaping Clinton's sexual values and behaviours. Continuing along this regional train of thought, I began to imagine what historians of sexuality in Chicago, including Joanne Meyerowitz and Leslie Reagan, might have had to say about the Chicago or Midwestern roots of Hillary's sexuality, and what historians of sexuality in California, including Peggy Pascoe, Susan Johnson, and Nan Boyd, might have had to say about the California or Western roots of Monica's sexuality. Were the sexual encounters that did or did not occur between Bill and Monica, Bill and Hillary, Bill and the courts, and Bill and the American public shaped by distinctive regional sexual histories?

Historians of sexuality might also have commented on relevant generational continuities and discontinuities. Bill and Monica encountered one another, after all, not only as an Arkansan and a Californian, but also as a Baby Boomer and a Generation Xer. And they encountered one another in the Age of AIDS. What would John D'Emilio and Estelle Freedman, for example, or the authors of various recent sex surveys have said about the significance of generational change in values, discourses, and practices associated with oral sex, masturbation, marital sex, non-marital sex, and marriage? Were Bill, Monica, and Hillary in step or out of step with their respective generational cohorts, with subgroups within generational cohorts, and with American society as a whole? And how did this shape the Clinton-Lewinsky scandal?

In addition to exploring regional and generational differences, historians of sexuality might also have had much to say about sex and gender differences. One tradition of feminist scholarship, exemplified by the very different perspectives of Susan Brownmiller, Andrea Dworkin, and Karen Dubinsky, could have helped us understand the history of men's sexual exploitation of women, setting Bill and Monica's sexual encounter in the context of changing practices and changing conceptions of sex in the workplace, sex between older men and younger women, and sex between empowered men and disempowered women. Another tradition of feminist scholarship, exemplified by the work of Marybeth Hamilton Arnold, Ruth Rosen, and Lisa Duggan, might have encouraged us to focus on Monica's sexual agency, exploring Monica's use of her sexuality to gain particular things that she wanted. And George Chauncey might have urged us to consider the relationship between gender identity and sexuality, focusing, for example, on the ways in which Bill used a masculine discourse of non-reciprocal sex in his attempt to deny that he had had "sex" or a sexual "relationship" with Monica. After all, some of Bill's testimony suggested strongly that while Monica may have had sex with Bill, Bill did not have sex with Monica. All of these traditions might have helped us to set the Clinton-Lewinsky scandal in the context of the history of sex and gender.

And the list could go on. Historians of sexuality could have set Bill's, Hillary's, and Monica's families and Bill and Hillary's marriage in the context of the history of marriage, the history of the family, and the history of relationships between marriage, family, and sexuality. They could have set the public discussion of Bill's, Hillary's, and Monica's sexual "problems" in the context of the history of sexual sin, crime, and disease. They could have explored the history of the commercialization of sex and how this shaped the national political drama. They could have pursued Eve Sedgwick's theories of triangulated homosocial, heterosocial, homosexual, and heterosexual relationships. They could have explored historical intersections between class, race, and sexuality, helping to contextualize, for example, representations of presidential secretary Betty Currie as a sexually respectable African American woman, depictions of Bill Clinton's interracial friendship with presidential advisor Vernon Jordan, and suggestions that at some level Bill had become the country's first Black president. And finally, perhaps most interesting of all, historians of sexuality could have commented on the history of sex panics and sex scandals in the United States, setting the Christian Right's and Republican Party's use of sexual politics within the context of a long history of right-wing sexual campaigns.

In other words, historians of sexuality might have made important contributions to the public debate and legal proceedings surrounding Clinton's impeachment and trial. And yet they did not. It's not difficult, I think, to account for this. Unlike politics, sexuality continues to be viewed by most people as a transhistorical, essential, and unchanging phenomenon, a form of experience without history. Politics may change, according to this view, but sexuality does not. Moreover, whereas politics is seen as an arena in which expertise matters, sexuality is seen as an arena of general expertise. Who, after all, is willing to admit lack of knowledge and expertise in matters of sex? And finally, despite the unprecedented level of public discussion of sex during the impeachment scandal, most of that discussion remained incredibly superficial. In the end, who could imagine television journalists Sam Donaldson and Cokie Roberts, not to mention Doris Kearns Goodwin or Michael Beschloss, talking about the history of oral sex and masturbation, the history of what counts as "sex" or a sexual "relationship," or the history of extramarital sex? And so even in a period in which traditional political historians claim that their work is undervalued, they effectively maintained a monopoly on the mainstream public's interest in history.

Rather than simply bemoan this fact, I want instead to juxtapose the absence of historians of sexuality in the developments just discussed with the astonishing successes that historians of sexuality have had in reaching large, though not necessarily mainstream, public audiences. In a period in which many academic historians have become quite anxious about a perceived crisis in getting scholarly work published, maintaining large student enrollments, and reaching large public audiences, historians of sexuality are sought after and fought over by academic and trade presses alike, they attract large numbers of students, and they sell books. Just to take one index of this, graduate students in the United States and Canada who are working on topics in the history of sexuality are often approached by academic and trade publishers long before their dissertations are completed. In fact, it is not uncommon for graduate students working in the history of sexuality to have literary agents who succeed in obtaining royalties advances for their clients. While I would like to think that this reflects the high quality of work being produced (and indeed much of this work is of very high quality), it also obviously reflects market-driven considerations and the perception by publishers that books on the history of sexuality sell. Whatever the reason, clearly publishers perceive this field as having a track record and a future promise of reaching large public audiences.

And relationships between historians of sexuality and their public audiences are not purely commercial. To take the specific case of lesbian and gay history, there is now a 25-year history of productive and organic relationships between lesbian and gay historians and lesbian and gay communities. Many lesbian and gay historians develop community-based oral history projects, they work with community-based libraries and archives, they publish their work in community-based media, and they share their work at community-based events. Even more than is the case for lesbian and gay studies scholars in other disciplines, lesbian and gay historians have a highly productive and mutually beneficial relationship with their large public audiences. Perhaps, then, the issue here is not just that historians of sexuality have been excluded from mainstream public debate but that such historians have chosen to work in dialogue with different publics.

Having juxtaposed the absence of historians of sexuality in the mainstream public sphere and the successes of historians of sexuality in reaching large alternative publics, I want to turn finally to the place of historians of sexuality within academic history departments. Here, the unfortunate truth is that public and student interest in the history of sexuality has not been matched by interest on the part of academic history departments in hiring faculty who do this work. (York of course is an exception here.) To take the specific case of U.S. lesbian and gay history, of the dozen or so people who have now completed dissertations in this field, two have primary appointments in women's studies units, two have primary appointments in American Studies units, and one has a primary appointment in an African American Studies unit. Two of us have left the United States for appointments in history departments in other countries. The majority are unemployed or under-employed. As far as I know, only one person who has completed a dissertation on U.S. lesbian and gay history has a primary appointment in a U.S. history department.

And so what we have here seems to be an alignment on the one side of American political elites, mainstream media pundits, and academic historians, who collectively demonstrate little interest in the history of sexuality, and on the other side of American historians of sexuality, members of sexual "minorities," book publishers, university students, and the reading public, who collectively demonstrate great interest in the history of sexuality.

I certainly don't mean to suggest that political, media, and academic elites should pander to public interest in sexual matters, or, for that matter, in nonsexual matters. But nor should such elites ignore the enduring significance of sexuality in the past, present, and future.

In My Wildest Dreams

Advice for George Bush

My good friend George W. gets up early in the morning, so I should not have been surprised when the telephone rang at six a.m. "I've been thinking about announcing a cabinet shakeup before my second term and want to get some advice from my favorite historian. Who could help me mobilize my base?"

It just so happens that I had spent years clipping newspaper articles in anticipation of the day I would be asked this question. Now was my chance.

"Mr. President," I declared. "I have just the person for Heterosexual Health and Human Spousal Services. Her name is Vickie Avants, and in 2000 she caused quite a stir in a state you need to win, New Mexico. According to the *New York Times* and the *Albuquerque Journal*, Mrs. Avants arranged for Richard Pitcher, one of her several ex-husbands, to be charged with violating New Mexico's statute against unlawful cohabitation. Charges were filed against Pitcher's fiancée, too. Seems that Mrs. Avants had once cohabited with Mr. Pitcher herself (before they got married), but after she became a born-again Christian she decided that she did not want her daughter exposed to a 'nonfamily environment.'"

"Now there's a woman who believes in good old-fashioned marriage," George replied. "Good for her. She's the perfect person to lead

This essay was published originally as "Mr. President, I'm Glad You Called," by History News Network on 8 March 2004, http://hnn.us/articles/3969.html.

my new marriage promotion programs. I don't understand why it's so difficult for people to understand that we want gay people to stop marrying and straight people to stop living together. Shouldn't be so hard to keep that straight."

As George chuckled at his own pun, I continued: "And you should give her two assistants. According to the same *Times* article, a state legislative committee chairman in Arizona helped convince that state to keep its 80-year-old cohabitation law by calling the statute a bulwark against the 'decaying fabric of society.' Let's get him. Meanwhile, in 2003, also according to the *Times*, North Dakota state senator John Andrist helped convince his state legislature to keep its law prohibiting a man and woman from living together 'openly and notoriously.' Andrist was quoted as saying that the law 'stands as a reminder that there is right and there is wrong.'"

"Or a right and a left, as we like to say in Texas," George joked.

"What about someone for Attorney Gender?"

Here I had just the person. "I know Laura reads the papers for you, Mr. President, but did she tell you about the article in the *Charlotte Observer* in 2001 about North Carolina federal judge Carl Horn? Get this: Horn's been invoking a state law banning fornication in cases involving straight defendants who acknowledge they're living with their girlfriends or boyfriends. Horn keeps saying that he will not release a criminal defendant on bail knowing that he or she will break the law. So he tells defendants who are cohabiting that they won't be freed on bond until they agree to get married, move out of the house or have their partner leave. One lawyer complained that this had been happening to his clients five to ten times a year and in about half of the cases the clients agreed to get married immediately. In one instance, the boyfriend of a female defendant raised his hand in court and told the judge that he had been planning to ask his girlfriend to marry him on her birthday. Instead, the judge asked the defendant if she would marry the man and the two were then married several weeks later. According to the *Observer*, since 1993, dozens of defendants in this situation had gotten married."

"Laura and I just love a good wedding. Not one of those San Francisco types, but a good old-fashioned wedding with a judge who upholds all of the law. And maybe this Horn can help with the proposed constitutional amendment banning sex outside of heterosexual marriage."

"I have one more suggestion, Mr. President. You might want someone over at the Clean Commerce Department who knows the difference between making money and making whoopie. Last month I read an article in the *Times* that says that Joanne Webb, a sales representative of Passion Parties, a sex toy company that uses 'Tupperware-style marketing,' was arrested in Johnson County, Texas, for violating a state law that prohibits the sale of obscene devices, defined as materials 'designed or marketed as useful primarily for the stimulation of human genital organs.' This is a married, forty-three-year-old woman with three children! You should find out who the prosecutor was and put him (or her) in the cabinet."

"I knew I could count on you," the president declared. "This is going to be an election about values, and if we can win the votes of everyone who agrees with strict laws against adultery, cohabitation, divorce, fornication, homosexuality, and obscenity, we may see the biggest electoral realignment in history."

"You have that right, Mr. President. With your type of campaign, everyone will understand the difference between right and wrong."

In My Wildest Dreams

The Marriage That Dare
Not Speak Its Name

Living in Maine for much of the successful recent campaign to overturn the state's legalization of same-sex marriage, I grew increasingly confused about what people mean when they refer to traditional marriage. I'm a historian, so usually I pretend to understand the concept of "tradition," but in this case I could not figure it out. So I decided to visit my friend Oscar Wilde and ask for his help. Oscar's very good with words and he's also very smart, so I thought I could count on him.

"Oscar, I'm confused. Opponents of same-sex marriage extol the virtues of traditional marriage, but what do they mean by traditional marriage?"

Oscar paused for a moment and then declared, "Well, if they're Old Testament traditionalists, they obviously are referring to polygamous marriages. Those old patriarchs really knew how to uphold traditional marriage. I also really like those old rules that oblige a man to marry his dead brother's widow. I can't wait to tell my wife, my brother, and my sister-in-law about the revival of traditional marriage!"

"I don't think that's what they mean, Oscar," I replied. "Maine is overwhelmingly Christian and I don't think the Old Testament is their

This essay was published originally by History News Network, 4 Jan. 2010, https://history newsnetwork.org/article/121810. It was reprinted shortly thereafter by *LA Progressive*, https://www.laprogressive.com/in-my-wildest-dreams-the-marriage-that-dare-not-speak-its -name/.

point of reference. For the same reason, I don't think they're referring to the marriage traditions of Africa, Asia, Latin America, or Native America. Mainers, like other people in the United States, might celebrate the history of immigration, champion ethnic diversity, and express regret for the treatment of Native Americans, but that doesn't mean they want the United States to treat other traditions with equal respect."

"Oh, well then it's obvious they must mean the type of traditional marriage most Christians enjoyed in the first millennium after Jesus Christ: marriages performed by religious officials without any involvement by the state. I can't wait to tell my priest about how much more autonomy he's going to have when the Church is freed from government control. And imagine how much shorter the standard wedding ceremony is going to be when they don't have to say, 'By the power vested in me by the state.'"

"No, I can't imagine that's what they mean," I demurred. "Traditional marriage supporters seem to favor big government involvement in personal relationships. They like it when governments tell people who can marry and who can't. I know some of them go on and on about reducing the size of government, but have you noticed how much they favor a big military and fight for increases in spending on immigration control, prison construction, corporate bailouts, and drug law enforcement? I don't think they want a reduced role for the state in marriage."

"Hmmm. I'm beginning to see why you're confused. But I bet we can figure this out. Maybe traditional marriage refers to marriage in the early days of the U.S. republic: marriages with highly restricted access to divorce, marriages that frequently followed premarital sex and pregnancy, frontier marriages not sanctioned by church or state, marriages that produced an average of seven children. And of course traditional marriage was mostly for whites, since most African Americans were enslaved and slave marriages were not recognized by the state."

"Somehow I don't think you've captured what traditional marriage proponents mean by traditional marriage, Oscar. Most traditional marriage proponents I know wouldn't endorse most of these things. They must mean something different; I just can't figure out what they mean."

"I see your problem. Maybe these traditional marriage activists are referring to more recent traditions. What about traditional marriages through much of the nineteenth century, when women surrendered most of their property rights when they married and when marital rape was not a recognized crime?"

"No, no, no, Oscar. Some of these traditional marriage proponents seem pretty conservative about women's roles, but most of them don't seem to favor that kind of traditional marriage. Maybe we're going to have to give up."

"Now that would be no fun," Oscar replied. He always enjoys the pleasures of a good mystery. "Hmmmm. What could they mean? I'm sure they know that traditional marriage in many parts of the United States did not allow for interracial marriages involving whites until the last decades of the twentieth century. Could that be what they mean?"

I didn't think so and I was just about ready to abandon my quest when Oscar shouted, "Wait: I've got it! I can't believe it took us this long to figure this out! They mean heterosexual marriage! That's what they mean by traditional marriage."

"But Oscar, the word 'heterosexuality' didn't even exist until the late nineteenth century, so how could that be what they mean? How traditional could heterosexual marriage be if there was no word for heterosexuality through most of recorded history. And besides, if they mean heterosexual marriage why don't they just say so instead of calling it traditional marriage?"

Oscar laughed. "Why of course they can't call it heterosexual marriage! That would make them appear like bigots. They would sound as if they endorse discrimination. They would seem prejudiced. They would be saying openly that they think heterosexuality is superior to homosexuality. And besides, if they called it 'heterosexual' marriage it would be too easy to ask questions about why the state has to confer so many special rights and privileges on heterosexual marriages in order to get people to marry heterosexually. Better to call it 'traditional' marriage and avoid those salacious allegations and dangerous implications."

I had to admit that Oscar, as usual, had a point.

From the Glorious Strike to Obama's New Executive Order

President Obama apparently will soon sign an executive order requiring most companies that have contracts with the U.S. federal government to pledge that they do not practice employment discrimination based on sexual orientation and gender identity. Media reports indicate that he is doing so because it is highly unlikely that the Republican-led U.S. House of Representatives will pass the Employment Non-Discrimination Act, which would provide a limited national ban on sexual orientation and gender identity discrimination in the workplace. Many commentators have presented these developments as the culmination of a struggle that began 40 years ago, in 1974, when U.S. Representative Bella Abzug introduced legislation that would have added sexual and affectional preference as prohibited grounds of discrimination to the 1964 Civil Rights Act. In fact, there is a longer history to this struggle, which began in the 1950s and accelerated after the passage of the groundbreaking 1964 legislation.

One of the more dramatic episodes in this struggle occurred in 1968, when the Philadelphia chapter of the Daughters of Bilitis (DOB), a national lesbian organization, reported in its monthly newsletter on the "glorious strike" of homosexuals that was wreaking havoc on the

This essay was published originally as "The Long Struggle to Stop Employment Discrimination against LGBT People Is Even Longer Than You Think" by History News Network, 23 Jun. 2014, http://hnn.us/article/156103.

U.S. economy and U.S. politics. According to the newsletter, "President Johnson appeared on network television last night—pre-empting 'The Flying Nun'—to urge the 10 million striking homosexuals to return to work. Justifying his concessions to the strikers, the President said, 'Our department store windows lie bare; our gym teaching force has been decimated; and Lady Bird can't get her hair done.' Noting that the lack of a quorum in the Senate was also a problem, the President pledged to end by Executive Order all federal discriminatory practices against homosexuals."

In case its readers missed the joke, the DOB Philadelphia newsletter helpfully pointed out that this was its April Fools' issue. In April 1969, however, after the DOB chapter had changed its name to the Homophile Action League (HAL), the new group's newsletter reported that the Eastern Regional Conference of Homophile Organizations had entrusted the local group to carry out its "Employment Discrimination Survey." Shortly thereafter, HAL wrote to 500 large corporations to ask about their policies. In March 1970, HAL reported on the results in an editorial titled "On Economic Independence for Gays." According to HAL, only twenty companies had replied to the survey and only one, Bantam Books, "answered unequivocally that the sexual orientation of applicants and employees was completely irrelevant to their suitability for employment and promotion." Several said that "they would employ homosexuals as long as no one knew they were homosexuals." One said that it would employ homosexuals but requested that HAL not publicize this fact.

According to HAL, the survey results demonstrated that gays and lesbians needed employment counselors more than psychiatrists and fair employment laws more than mental health policies: "The one overriding problem we homosexuals face is economic, not emotional, for most of us are financially secure only to the degree that we hide our sexual orientation from our employers." Looking toward the future and influenced by the African American freedom struggle, HAL recommended two strategies for achieving the "emancipation of homosexuals from economic dependence." One was to promote "gay capitalism," which would involve "encouraging gay businessmen to hire gays" and "gay consumers to support them." The other was to challenge "laws and customs which deny us equal employment opportunities."

We have certainly witnessed the growth of "gay capitalism" over the last four decades, though it is equally clear that this has not resulted in the "emancipation of homosexuals from economic dependence."

Millions of LGBT workers continue to experience sexual and gender discrimination; many LGBT people continue to struggle economically; and economic inequality within the LGBT world reflects and contributes to the problems of economic inequality in the United States more generally. As for fair employment laws, the absence of these mean that in the majority of U.S. states it is perfectly legal in a variety of circumstances to practice employment discrimination on the basis of sexual orientation and gender identity.

Obama's executive order is an important step, though a limited one. It will likely exempt small businesses; it may exclude religious organizations; and it will not directly challenge employment discrimination by companies that do not have contracts with the federal government. Some of the largest corporations that could be affected by Obama's executive order will be Exxon-Mobil, Berkshire Hathaway, and Valero Energy. According to the Human Rights Campaign Foundation's "Corporate Equality Index 2014," these three companies—all in the top twenty Fortune-ranked corporations in the United States—lack basic anti-discrimination protections for LGBT workers.

One company—Bantam Books—was singled out for praise in HAL's 1970 employment discrimination survey. More than 300 major businesses earned the Human Rights Campaign's top employment equity score in 2014. This represents an extraordinary transformation and is the result of the efforts of countless activists and advocates. Obama's executive order will be another important achievement. It should not, however, be seen as a sign that the struggle for sexual equality in the workplace is over or that the United States has decided to address, in any serious way, the fundamental problems of economic inequality. For that, we just may need another "glorious strike."

"In My Mind I'm (Not) Going to Carolina"

On April Fool's Day, North Carolina's new anti-anti-discrimination law—preempting and superseding local anti-discrimination statutes on grounds other than race, religion, color, national origin, age, or biological sex—went into effect. The new law covers discrimination in employment (for employers with fifteen or more regular workers) and public accommodations. Curiously the law includes "handicap" as a prohibited basis of discrimination in employment but not public accommodations and it overrides local laws that restrict discrimination based on marital or veteran status. The new statute also requires public schools and agencies in the state to designate every multiple occupancy bathroom or changing room as appropriate for use by either males or females, with an individual's "biological sex" to be determined by the information listed on their birth certificate.

In keeping with the spirit of April Fool's Day, it might be appropriate to point out that it is now legal everywhere in North Carolina to discriminate against straight people on the basis of their sexual orientation. After all, the local ordinances "trumped" by the new state law did not just prohibit discrimination against sexual minorities; they prohibited discrimination on the basis of sexual orientation. Along similar

This essay was published originally as "North Carolina's Brutal Tradition of Sexual and Gender Discrimination" by History News Network on 4 April 2016, https://historynewsnetwork.org/article/162473.

lines, while the state now bans discrimination against males and females based on their biological sex, it is legal under state law to discriminate against men and women based on their gender identity. As far as state law is concerned, it's also legal to discriminate against married people on the basis of their marital status.

More seriously, North Carolina has a long and harrowing history of opposition to sexual and gender freedom. In the eighteenth century, North Carolina followed the lead of England and England's other North American colonies in criminalizing buggery, which was generally understood to refer to anal intercourse; the maximum punishment was death. After the Revolutionary War, most northern states abolished the death penalty for sodomy and buggery, but in 1837 North Carolina reaffirmed its commitment to capital punishment for "the abominable and detestable crime against nature," which was also understood to refer to anal sex. Three decades later, North Carolina was among the last few states to eliminate capital punishment for this heinous crime. This occurred in 1868, during Reconstruction, when the U.S. federal government forced rebellious southern states to radically restructure their governments and laws. Reforms enacted by North Carolina's newly multiracial state legislature—controlled by the Republican Party—eliminated the death penalty for a variety of crimes, including the crime against nature. Notwithstanding the significance of this reform, the state's criminalization of sex remained harshly punitive. The new penalty for crimes against nature was 20–60 years in prison; one year later the minimum was reduced to 5 years, but the maximum remained at 60, one of the most severe punishments for crimes against nature in the nation.

There wasn't much sexual progress in North Carolina during the Progressive Era. In the 1910s, several cities in the state banned cross-dressing, lewd and indecent dress, indecent behavior, lewd solicitation, obscene publications, and immoral plays; the state enacted a sterilization law for institutionalized individuals whose "moral condition" would improve as a result of the operation. In 1914 and 1917, the North Carolina Supreme Court broadened the scope of the state's existing crimes against nature law in a set of cases that addressed oral sex. So much for judicial restraint. This was part of a national transformation in the legal regulation of sex in the late nineteenth and early twentieth centuries, when laws against sodomy, buggery, and crimes against nature were revised, reinterpreted, and supplemented to cover a wider range of sexual offenses. Decades later, in 1961, the North Carolina Supreme Court re-affirmed this reinterpretation of the state's crimes against nature law in the case of a man with cerebral palsy who allegedly had engaged in cross-sex oral sex.

Many of these developments escaped national notice, but in the 1960s North Carolina's strident opposition to gender and sexual freedom suddenly came to broader public attention. By this time the state's maximum penalty for a crime against nature, which was still 60 years, was among the most severe in the nation. In 1962, Maxine Doyle Perkins, who was referred to in the court and media as a "homosexual," a "transvestite," a "female impersonator," and a man ("Max") who dressed like a woman, was arrested and convicted for engaging in oral sex with Robert McCorkle in Charlotte. (Perkins apparently had an extensive record of arrests for assault, disorderly conduct, drunkenness, solicitation, and prostitution.) Having pleaded not guilty to the charges in 1962, Perkins was sentenced to 20–30 years in prison, while McCorkle, who did not contest the charges, was sentenced to 5–7 years and released after 17 months. Two years later, federal district judge James Craven (who later served on the Fourth Circuit Court of Appeals) ruled that Perkins had not received a fair trial and ordered the state to release "him" or grant a new trial. Citing the U.S. Supreme Court's decision in *Powell v. Alabama* (the "Scottsboro Boys" case), Craven argued that the lawyer appointed by the court for Perkins had not been given sufficient time to interview witnesses or prepare for trial. He had been assigned to Perkins at 4:00 p.m. and the trial had begun at 9:00 a.m. the next day, leaving him insufficient time to interview witnesses or prepare a strong defense.

Judge Craven's ruling prodded North Carolina legislators by asking, "Is it not time to redraft a criminal statute first enacted in 1533?" He specifically referenced a recent proposal by the American Law Institute to "punish only those 'deviate sexual relations' which involve force, imposition, or corruption of the young." The ruling in favor of Perkins, however, was not exactly a shining example of gender or sexual enlightenment. After noting that "putting Perkins into the North Carolina prison system is a little like throwing Brer Rabbit into the briarpatch" since the "prison environment . . . provides an outlet for the gratification of sexually-deviate desires," Craven asked, "cannot the criminal law draftsman be helped by those better informed on the subject—medical doctors—in attempting to classify offenders?"

Perkins's case and Craven's ruling received significant coverage in local newspapers such as the *Charlotte Observer* and the *Carolina Israelite*, national magazines such as *Time* and the *New Republic*, and gay periodicals such as *Drum, Eastern Mattachine Magazine*, and the *Mattachine Society of New York Newsletter*. In subsequent decades the case and ruling have been researched by New York historian Martin Duberman, Greensboro lawyer John Boddie, and Charlotte journalist Bruce Henderson. In 1965, influenced by the unfavorable local and national attention, North Carolina reduced its penalty for crimes against nature to a minimum of 4 months and a maximum of 10 years. Over the next few decades more North Carolinians were arrested, charged, convicted, and imprisoned for consensual crimes against nature (same-sex and cross-sex). Although there were a significant number of court challenges, the state's law remained valid until 2003, when the Supreme Court overturned sodomy laws in *Lawrence v. Texas*.

As for Perkins, she was acquitted in a new trial, though only after doing her best to dress, look, and act like a man in court. This must have been difficult to do for a person who had spent so many years fiercely defying society's gender and sexual conventions. Perhaps she took solace (if she was not bothered by the pronouns) in an editorial published in *Drum*, the country's most popular gay movement magazine in the 1960s, which declared, "Max Doyle . . . is not the kind of client lawyers prize as 'good case' material. Not only is he a queen, but he is a drag queen to boot. And not only is he a drag queen, but he has served time for being a hooker. When, three years ago, he was convicted for giving it away, the town heaved a sigh of relief and the trial judge awarded him 20–30 years in the hoose-gow. Whereupon his counsel appealed and Maxie is now, as it were, walking the streets of North Carolina again. Doyle's case brings home the need for appeals of sodomy convictions as one of the most effective methods for bringing our legal chaos to an abrupt end."

Fifty years later, North Carolina is once again making national news for its strident opposition to gender and sexual freedom. Once again the state is receiving extensive negative media attention for violating basic principles of equality and justice. And once again brave and courageous individuals, assisted by progressive legal and political advocates, are going to court to defend their rights and ours.

PART FIVE

Queer Immigration

In 2010, ten years after my first book came out, the University of North Carolina Press published my second, *Sexual Injustice: Supreme Court Decisions from* Griswold *to* Roe. The genesis of *Sexual Injustice* stretched back to the early 1990s, when I wrote a graduate seminar paper on *Boutilier v. Immigration and Naturalization Service* (1967). This was a US Supreme Court decision upholding the deportation of a "homosexual" immigrant from Canada on the basis of a 1952 law that applied to "aliens" with "psychopathic personality." I first learned about *Boutilier* while doing research for my dissertation on Philadelphia. Clive Boutilier had lived in New York, but his litigation was funded, supported, and publicized by the Philadelphia-based Homosexual Law Reform Society. I wrote my seminar paper on *Boutilier* for a legal history class taught by Mary Frances Berry, a University of Pennsylvania professor and member (later chair) of the US Civil Rights Commission. In the early 1990s, I never could have imagined that more than twenty years later my work on *Boutilier* would lead to my hiring as a specialist in US constitutional law by San Francisco State University.

While focusing on my Philadelphia research in the 1990s, I set aside work on *Boutilier*, but I returned to it in the early 2000s. In part, this was because of my 1998 move to Canada, which heightened my interest in transnational migration. This was also a period when the US Supreme Court loomed large in LGBT struggles. In 2003, the *Lawrence* decision struck down state sodomy laws. In the early 2000s, struggles were underway that would culminate in the Court's favorable rulings on same-sex marriage in *Windsor* (2013) and *Obergefell* (2015). I was influenced as well by new developments in immigration politics. After the 9/11 attacks of 2001, which killed approximately three thousand people in New York, Pennsylvania, and Washington, D.C., the United States launched a "War on Terror," which killed hundreds of thousands of people in Asia. The 9/11 attacks and the War on Terror prompted major changes in US immigration policies and significant increases in nativism, which later contributed to the 2016 election of nationalist Donald Trump as US president. All of these developments inspired a new wave of scholarship on the queer history of immigration.[1]

When I first wrote about *Boutilier* in the 1990s, I situated it primarily in the context of LGBT history. I focused on the history of anti-homosexual immigration laws, gay social movements, queer legal advocacy, and US Supreme Court rulings on LGBT rights. By the time I returned to *Boutilier* in the 2000s, I had grown increasingly concerned about the ghettoization of LGBT history. The field was now regularly represented on the annual convention programs of the American Historical Association and Organization of American Historians, for example, but almost always in sessions on LGBT history; queer historians were not generally included on other types of sessions. In 2004 and 2009, I wrote to the editors of *Reviews in American History* to criticize the journal's decade-long failure to review books on LGBT history. In 2006, I coauthored a letter to *Perspectives* that criticized the AHA's fifty-page annual convention supplement, which addressed multiple aspects of Philadelphia history but ignored women's history and LGBT history.[2] LGBT historical scholarship was thriving, but this was rarely reflected in general US history textbooks or courses. In my teaching, I resisted ghettoization by developing courses on the history of sexuality and gender, not LGBT history, and by incorporating LGBT history into my courses on constitutional law and social movements. In helping to found and lead York University's Sexuality Studies Program, which quickly became one of the largest of its kind in North America, I similarly worked to position LGBT history within broad frameworks that were intersectional, transnational, and interdisciplinary.

My concerns about ghettoization led me to produce a book that situated *Boutilier* in relation to better-known Supreme Court decisions on abortion, birth control, interracial marriage, and obscenity. The book's subtitle, which referenced the period from *Griswold* to *Roe*, tried to take advantage of popular interest in these major decisions on reproductive rights. The same concerns encouraged me to emphasize links to better-known social movements. My Philadelphia book had highlighted the multiple ways that African American and feminist activism influenced LGBT movements; now I became fascinated by legal coalitions in court cases about sex, marriage, and reproduction. The *Boutilier* litigation was funded by the LGBT movement, for example, but immigration advocates and civil libertarians played key roles. The arguments developed by Boutilier's lawyers were influenced by their earlier work defending immigrants, leftists, and people with disabilities. Rather than presenting the LGBT movement as isolated, I portrayed it as deeply connected to other social movements.

Publishing *Sexual Injustice* required patience, resiliency, and tenacity. In 2001, I was awarded a major three-year grant by the Social Sciences and Humanities Research Council of Canada, but I later was told that this only happened because a feminist scholar, supported by a senior male historian, fought for me against antigay critics in the peer review process. In 2003, I was unanimously recommended by five peer reviewers for an NEH fellowship, only to have that recommendation vetoed by the NEH's chair. In the same year, the *Journal of American History* responded with a pessimistic "revise and resubmit" to an essay I had written on *Boutilier*, though *Law and History Review* later published it. In 2005, my book proposal was rejected for a university press series on modern US history; the editors told me they did not want their first book on queer history to be so critical of LGBT activists and advocates. In 2006, I withdrew my solicited chapter for an anthology on the history of the 1970s because of the editors' inappropriate and unacceptable editorial comments (this after I had to explain to them why they needed a separate essay on women's history). In 2008, a senior law professor who had peer reviewed my *Journal of American History* submission and my book manuscript preempted my work, without permission, by using and citing my drafts in a book they published. (The evidence of this is undeniable, as they cite the book's working title, which was not *Sexual Injustice*.) All of these episodes were discouraging and disappointing, but my identity as a scholarly activist and the support I received from other queer historians encouraged me to persist.

While I worked on *Sexual Injustice* and finished a related set of scholarly essays published in *Law and History Review* (2005), *torquere* (2005), *Journal of American Ethnic History* (2010), *Understanding and Teaching U.S. LGBT History* (2014), and *Connexions* (2016), I continued to look for opportunities to share my work in the broader public sphere.[3] When doing so, I favored media outlets that would resist the ghettoization of LGBT history. These included the History News Network and *OAH Magazine of History*. In 2017, I marked the fiftieth anniversary of the *Boutilier* decision with an OutHistory exhibit, a pair of essays published by the *University of North Carolina Press Blog* and HNN (see chapters 19 and 20), and a roundtable on the *Notches* blog.[4] In all of these works, I linked *Boutilier* to other topics, including immigration and immigration restriction; race and class; communism and the left; disability and disease; and abortion, birth control, interracial marriage, and obscenity.

There were other factors at play, beyond my determination to resist ghettoization, in the decision to shift from a local study of lesbian and gay Philadelphia to a national study of Supreme Court decisions on sex, marriage, and reproduction. I was proud of my Philadelphia book, but there were moments when I felt that no matter how good the work might be, it had little chance of "competing" with LGBT histories of New York and San Francisco. Philadelphia may have been one of the country's largest cities and an urban center with distinct importance for US history, but it was not generally seen as one of the nation's queer capitals. A national study of Supreme Court decisions on sex, marriage, and reproduction seemed like it might reach a broader public audience than a book about lesbian and gay Philadelphia.

I also wanted to challenge the tendency to link LGBT history exclusively to social and cultural history rather than political or legal history. If social history is defined as the study of ordinary people and everyday life, it made sense to treat the LGBT past as an aspect of social history. If cultural history is defined as the study of elite culture, popular culture, and a broad range of cultural discourses, narratives, and representations, it made sense to treat LGBT topics as aspects of cultural history. As a new generation of political and legal historians developed more expansive ways of thinking about politics and law, I thought LGBT issues should be considered within political and legal history as well. And yet there was resistance to doing so. Sure enough, while I was hired at York for a position in political history, I was asked to teach my department's large introduction to social and cultural history ("Life, Labor, and Love: Ordinary People in a Changing World") rather than our large introduction to political history ("War, Revolution, and Society"). Beyond the classroom, I resisted the tendency to conflate LGBT history with social and cultural history by describing my research as examining the social and cultural foundations of politics and law. I also argued for a capacious conception of political history that incorporated everyday resistance, organized movements, partisan politics, and state governance. I hoped that thinking about politics in these ways would help resist the ghettoization and marginalization of LGBT history.

My concerns about ghettoization coexisted with worries about the politics of rejecting the ghetto (ghetto shame). In queer contexts, there have been growing concerns about whether mainstream tolerance and acceptance have come at the expense of LGBT businesses, institutions, neighborhoods, organizations, and publications.[5] Historians of class, race, and gender had taught me about the problems that can occur when working-class people, people of color, and women prioritize inclusion and acceptance in worlds made and controlled by elite white men. Was I turning my back on LGBT communities by pursuing platforms oriented to broader audiences? Was I minimizing the intrinsic importance of LGBT history by emphasizing its connections to topics and themes commonly recognized as significant? I hoped not, and in my public history work I tried to strike a good balance between orienting myself to LGBT communities and working on projects that reached broader audiences.

In any case, we know what happens to the best laid plans. My work on *Boutilier* was well received in academic contexts. My 2005 *Law and History Review* essay won the Committee on Gay and Lesbian History's Audre Lorde prize for best essay on LGBT history; it continues to be one of my most frequently cited articles. *Sexual Injustice* received excellent reviews in scholarly journals, the best in my career, and it was selected as an "Outstanding Academic Title" by *Choice*. My legal history work convinced San Francisco State to hire me as a specialist in constitutional law. But the book failed to gain the larger public audience that I hoped it would reach. The publisher has sold approximately one thousand copies, which is a respectable number for a scholarly publication, but the weakest of my four books. While the reviews were positive in academic journals, the book received almost no attention in LGBT publications, mainstream periodicals, or other media platforms. All of this may reflect resistance to, disagreement with, or disinterest in the book's main arguments, but it is also possible that the book was perceived as "too academic" or "too scholarly." For LGBT audiences, perhaps my anti-marginalization strategies, exemplified by a subtitle that referenced *Griswold* and *Roe*, backfired by creating the impression that the book did not focus sufficiently on queer issues. Regardless of the reasons, the public history essays reprinted in this section reached larger audiences than *Sexual Injustice* did, demonstrating again that historians who are interested in communicating with broader audiences may need to supplement their academic publications with works of public history.

Chapter 17, "Alienated Affections: Remembering Clive Michael Boutilier (1933–2003)," was published by HNN in 2003. The essay was prompted by Boutilier's death, which received no attention in the LGBT or non-LGBT press. My first paragraph intentionally disguised the reasons for Boutilier's deportation; I wanted readers to see his story in more universal terms—as the story of an immigrant who had moved to the United States in search of new opportunities, only to find his path blocked by bias, prejudice, and discrimination. This was one of the reasons I fought hard against an alternative headline that would have "outed" Boutilier prematurely. Written in a post-9/11 moment when anti-immigrant attitudes—especially against Muslims and Arabs—were growing in the United States, I wanted to use Boutilier's story to highlight the importance of broad-based coalitions in struggles against new nativist and nationalist politics. This essay and the next one provide additional examples of errors that probably are more common in public history essays written in days or weeks as compared to scholarly books written in years or decades: I claim in these essays that Boutilier attempted suicide after the Supreme Court ruled against him, but later research (captured in chapter 20) revealed that this family narrative was at odds with the timing of Boutilier's catastrophic traffic accident.[6]

Chapter 18, "The Supreme Court's Sexual Counter-Revolution," was published in 2006 in a special issue of the *OAH Magazine of History*. Focused on the history of sexuality, the issue was guest edited by Leisa Meyer, who had succeeded me as chair of the Committee on Lesbian and Gay History. The *Magazine of History*, published from 1985 to 2013, presented short topical essays, lesson plans, and teaching resources; it was aimed at a broader audience of historians and educators than the OAH's *Journal of American History*, which publishes lengthy scholarly essays and reviews. My contribution, which distilled the first two chapters of *Sexual Injustice*, argued that the Supreme Court's decisions on abortion, birth control, homosexuality, interracial marriage, and obscenity in the late 1960s and early 1970s were based on a doctrine of heteronormative supremacy.

Chapter 19, "Immigration Is a Queer Issue: From *Fleuti* to *Trump*," was published on the *UNC Press Blog* in 2017. I began presenting short legal history essays on this blog in 2010, the year that UNC Press published *Sexual Injustice*. I hoped that this would be a good way to

promote my book, though readership of my posts has been small, ranging from 185 to 300. In 2017, as the fiftieth anniversary of the *Boutilier*
decision approached, I began to think about using the anniversary for
educational and political purposes. After President Trump began issu-
ing racist and Islamophobic executive orders that banned immigration
and travel from countries with Muslim majorities, I decided to revisit
some of the issues I had raised in my 2003 HNN essay. My opportunity
came when the Ninth Circuit Court referenced a 1963 gay immigration
case, *Rosenberg v. Fleuti*, in a procedural decision against Trump. As the
title of my essay indicates, my primary goal was to remind readers that
"immigration is a queer issue."

Chapter 20, "Defectives of the World, Unite!," was published by
HNN (with a different headline) on the fiftieth anniversary of the
Boutilier decision. My suggested headline, which riffed on the *Communist Manifesto*'s call for workers of the world to unite, introduced the
point of the essay, which was to situate *Boutilier* in the context of the
history of immigration restrictions based on diseases and disabilities.
As *Sexual Injustice* had emphasized, much of the LGBT movement has
worked hard to reject scientific and medical models that treat homosexuality and transgenderism as illnesses, diseases, or defects, but they
often have done so in ways that disrespect and demean people with disabilities. My essay called on the LGBT movement to reject the politics
of dis-identification with disabilities and challenge multiple forms of
disability-based discrimination in immigration law.

Alienated Affections

Remembering Clive Michael Boutilier
(1933–2003)

As far as we know, he came to the United States with his family from an economically troubled region of a U.S. ally, hoping for a better life. But he arrived at a time when the U.S. government was targeting a variety of imagined domestic and foreign enemies and was waging cold and hot wars at home and abroad. He was 21 years old when he became a permanent resident of the United States and over the next decade he worked, lived, bowled, and prayed in New York. There he eventually came to share an apartment with a friend in the same Brooklyn building where his mother and stepfather lived. Two of his brothers served in the U.S. military; several of his siblings settled in the United States, married, and had children. He spoke English. As his lawyers would later make sure to emphasize, in many respects he was a model U.S. immigrant when evaluated according to dominant U.S. values. A few years after coming to the United States he was arrested for a sexual offense with a 17-year-old, but when the complainant refused to cooperate with the authorities the charges were dismissed. The more significant troubles began when he applied for citizenship and mentioned the arrest.

His name was Clive Michael Boutilier, born in Nova Scotia in 1933, and in 1967 six of nine members of the U.S. Supreme Court upheld his deportation back to Canada on the grounds that he had been excludable

This essay was published originally as "Forgetting and Remembering a Deported Alien" by History News Network, 3 Nov. 2003, http://hnn.us/articles/1769.html.

FIGURE 6. Clive Boutilier, second from right, lost his appeal to the US Supreme Court in 1967 and was deported to Canada in 1968. The Court ruled that the 1952 Immigration and Nationality Act provided for the exclusion of people "afflicted with psychopathic personalities," which included "homosexuals." In the early 1960s Boutilier was photographed in New York City with his brother Andrew, Andrew's wife Joyce, and Boutilier's partner Eugene O'Rourke. Photograph courtesy of Anita Shunamon and the estate of Joyce Taylor.

at the time of his original entry. According to the Court, Congress intended to exclude homosexuals under the psychopathic personality provisions of the 1952 Immigration and Nationality Act, and the Immigration and Naturalization Service (INS) was not violating Boutilier's rights by deporting him. As Justice Tom Clark stated for the majority, "Congress used the phrase 'psychopathic personality' . . . to effectuate its purpose to exclude from entry all homosexuals and other sex perverts." In dissent, Justice William O. Douglas replied, "The term 'psychopathic personality' is a treacherous one like 'communist' or in an earlier day 'Bolshevik.' A label of this kind when freely used may mean only an unpopular person."

According to one of his relatives, Boutilier died of complications related to a heart condition on 12 April 2003. More than six months have passed and there has yet to be an obituary in the U.S. or Canadian press (including the gay press). His death occurred about eight weeks before an appeals court in Ontario ruled that current Canadian marriage laws discriminate against homosexuals and about 11 weeks before the U.S. Supreme Court (in *Lawrence v. Texas*) issued a ruling striking down state sodomy laws as unconstitutional.

Boutilier apparently had a very difficult life after the Supreme Court ruled against him. Presumably distraught about the Court's decision in 1967, Boutilier attempted suicide before leaving New York, survived a month-long coma that left him brain-damaged with permanent disabilities, and moved to southern Ontario with his parents, who took on the task of caring for him for more than 20 years.

In his final decade he resided in group homes for the disabled, reportedly remembering his former "lifestyle." "I am sure," writes a member of his family, "that [his mother] drummed it into his head that what happened was to never be brought into the light of day ever again." U.S. historians have apparently shared that agenda with Boutilier's mother, ignoring one of the Supreme Court's first major gay rights rulings and an important immigration rights ruling as well. Instead, when looking at this period in U.S. history, scholars have generally highlighted the Court's sexually "liberalizing" rulings in birth control, obscenity, interracial marriage, and abortion cases and the Congress's racially "liberalizing" immigration reforms.

In the context of litigation concerning the 1952 immigration act's provisions, Congress tried to clarify its intentions in 1965, when it specifically excluded immigrants with "sexual deviations" along with those afflicted with "psychopathic personalities." These restrictions remained on the books until 1990, when they were eliminated at the same time that new procedures allowed the INS to exclude people with HIV and/or AIDS.

As the United States experiences another period in which immigrants and aliens are particularly vulnerable to the racial, religious, linguistic, class, gender, and sexual prejudices of U.S. policymakers and government officials, there is much to be learned by studying the alliances and arguments that formed around Boutilier more than 35 years ago. Among the leading figures who opposed Boutilier were 2nd Circuit Court of Appeals Judge Irving Kaufman, who had sentenced Julius and Ethel Rosenberg to death in the 1950s and who wrote his court's majority opinion against Boutilier in 1966; Solicitor General Thurgood Marshall, who betrayed his civil rights credentials by signing the government's brief against Boutilier; and Justice Clark, who had presided over the internment of Japanese American and other citizens and aliens during World War Two.

Boutilier was supported by the Philadelphia-based Homosexual Law Reform Society, a long-forgotten organization that funded his appeal and submitted a brief to the Supreme Court (the Society was

later destroyed in a campaign of state repression against the gay movement), the American Civil Liberties Union, which also submitted a
brief, and his lawyer Blanch Freedman, who was affiliated with the
American Committee for the Protection of the Foreign Born and was
the law partner of Gloria Agrin, who had worked on the Rosenbergs'
defense team and on the post-execution custody cases involving the
Rosenbergs' two sons.

These advocates, in making arguments about Boutilier's respectable
characteristics, risked winning the kind of limited second-class victory
that was recently achieved in *Lawrence*. For example, Boutilier's supporters, by emphasizing the limited extent of Boutilier's sexual experiences, the fact that he had also had heterosexual sex, and the private
nature of his sexual encounters, might have worsened the situation for
people with extensive same-sex sexual experiences, those who were
exclusively homosexual, and those who engaged in public displays of
same-sex affection. Gay-supportive critics of *Lawrence* have begun to
express similar concerns about that ruling, in which Justice Anthony
Kennedy emphasized the rights of adult homosexuals in relationships
to have sex with their partners in their private homes. This reasoning
could be used to argue against forms of public sexual equality and types
of sexual activity that exceed the bounds of committed relationships.

Nevertheless, the alliances that formed between civil libertarians,
sexual rights activists, and immigrant advocates in *Boutilier* offered
an important challenge to the unjust policing of U.S. borders in the
1960s. Remembering *Boutilier* today should remind various consti-
tuencies, including gay, lesbian, bisexual, and transgendered people;
women; immigrants; ethnic, linguistic, racial, and religious minorities;
and disabled people that their causes and interests are linked. Only
a strong coalition of political forces has the potential to stop today's
unjust exclusions, detentions, and deportations, which are raising the
level of national insecurity in the United States to new heights.

CHAPTER 18

The Supreme Court's Sexual Counter-Revolution

In a series of controversial rulings during the post–World War II "sexual revolution," the U.S. Supreme Court redefined relationships between law and sex in the United States.[1] Decades later, some of these decisions continue to attract intense public interest, though most Americans have never read them. *Griswold v. Connecticut*, the 1965 decision that struck down state laws banning the use of birth control by married couples, is often denounced by conservatives and celebrated by liberals, in both cases because *Griswold* is seen as affirming a constitutional right of sexual privacy. *Loving v. Virginia*, the 1967 decision that overturned state laws against interracial marriage, is invoked by opposing sides in recent debates about same-sex marriage. Perhaps the Court's best-known ruling after *Brown v. Board of Education* is *Roe v. Wade*, the 1973 decision that overruled various state restrictions on abortions. *Roe* may well be the Court's most passionately defended and passionately attacked case of the twentieth century.[2]

While less well-known today, other "liberalizing" Supreme Court rulings from the same period are studied and taught by specialists in legal history. In 1966, *Fanny Hill v. Massachusetts* established the principle that only sexual materials "utterly without redeeming social value" could be restricted by federal, state, or local authorities. Three

This essay was published originally in the *OAH Magazine of History* 20, no. 2 (Mar. 2006): 21–25 (reprinted with the permission of Oxford University Press).

years later, *Stanley v. Georgia* struck down laws that criminalized the possession of obscene materials in one's home. In 1972, *Eisenstadt v. Baird* extended the *Griswold* ruling to cover the use of birth control by the unmarried. These decisions are not as well known as *Griswold, Loving*, and *Roe*, but they, too, are invoked as evidence of legal and sexual liberalization during the late 1960s and early 1970s.[3]

The conventional view today is that *Roe* was the culmination of a process of legal and sexual liberalization that began with *Griswold*. After *Roe*, the story goes, the Court, like the country in general, became more conservative. In 1973, the Court adopted a more conservative obscenity doctrine. Later in the 1970s, the Court upheld laws that restricted public funding of abortions. In the 1980s, it accepted more and more anti-abortion regulations, while in 1986 the *Bowers v. Hardwick* ruling declared that state laws against same-sex sex were constitutional. According to the conventional view, the liberal court presided over by Chief Justice Earl Warren in the 1960s was replaced by the more conservative court presided over by Chief Justice Warren Burger in the 1970s, and the Court's rulings on sexual issues reflected that shift.[4]

This essay highlights two significant problems with the conventional view. The first is that it depends on highly selective readings of the Court's "liberalizing" rulings. If the decisions in *Griswold, Fanny Hill, Loving, Eisenstadt,* and *Roe* are read with care, it is difficult to escape the conclusion that a majority of the justices rejected a libertarian and egalitarian doctrine of sexual freedom.[5] Instead, the evidence suggests that the majority endorsed a doctrine of heteronormative supremacy, granting special rights, privileges, and protections to heterosexual, marital, and reproductive forms of sexual expression. Conservatives have more reasons to praise these rulings, and liberals more reasons to criticize them, than is generally believed today.

The second problem with the conventional view is it requires that we ignore, dismiss, or set aside a set of profoundly conservative decisions made by the Court in the *Griswold* to *Roe* era. *Ginzburg v. United States* (1966) and *Mishkin v. New York* (1966), for example, upheld obscenity convictions on the very same day that the Court ruled in favor of *Fanny Hill*. In *Ginzburg*, the Court ruled against a publisher who engaged in "pandering" when he advertised materials containing representations of female promiscuity and interracial sex and when he tried to mail his publications from towns named Intercourse, Blue Ball, and Middlesex. In *Mishkin*, which concerned representations of fetishism, homosexuality, and sadomasochism, the Court ruled that materials aimed at a "clearly defined deviant sexual group" could be judged by standards different from the ones used for other materials. In several other obscenity decisions, including *Landau v. Fording* (1967) and *G.I. Distributors v. New York* (1967), the Court affirmed convictions in cases involving homoerotic and sadomasochistic materials.[6]

Boutilier v. Immigration and Naturalization Service (1967) also challenges the notion that the Court adopted a sexually libertarian or sexually egalitarian doctrine in the *Griswold* to *Roe* era. In this case, the Court upheld a provision in the 1952 Immigration and Nationality Act that mandated the exclusion and deportation of aliens "afflicted with psychopathic personality," which the Court and the Immigration and Naturalization Service (INS) understood to refer to "homosexuals." While the specific details of this case concerned a Canadian-born man who was deported from the United States after more than a decade of legal residency, the ruling suggested that U.S. authorities could classify all homosexuals as "psychopaths," with potential implications that included disenfranchisement, incarceration, and institutionalization.[7]

It is tempting to view these conservative rulings as anomalies, or as exceptions, or as evidence of the Court's hypocrisy or inconsistency during the 1960s and 1970s. If, however, we acknowledge the Court's doctrine of heteronormative supremacy, *Boutilier* and the Court's other sexually conservative decisions seem perfectly consistent with what the Court was doing in its "liberalizing" rulings. At a minimum, this observation suggests the need to revise our sense of the Supreme Court's role in the history of the sexual revolution. If "sexual revolution" is a useful way of conceptualizing a set of important post–World War II developments, the Court's role may best be described as counter-revolutionary. Beyond this conclusion, if so many commentators have exaggerated or misrepresented the nature of the Court's sexual liberalism in the late 1960s and early 1970s, perhaps we need to revise the way we think about sexual liberalism and the sexual revolution more generally.

LIBERALISM'S LIMITS

The primary basis for the claim that the Court developed a doctrine of heteronormative supremacy in the late 1960s and early 1970s is the texts of the decisions themselves. In *Griswold*, for instance, the majority opinion by Justice William O. Douglas referred repeatedly to the right of "marital" privacy and not once to the right of "sexual" privacy. With dramatic rhetorical flourish, Douglas wrote: "Would we allow the police to search the sacred precincts of marital bedrooms for telltale signs of the use of contraceptives? The very idea is repulsive to the notions of privacy surrounding the marriage relationship." In a concurring opinion joined by Earl Warren and William Brennan, Arthur Goldberg also emphasized that the state birth control law violated the rights of married couples. According to Goldberg's opinion, laws against adultery, fornication, and homosexuality were constitutional, but laws that interfered with the privacy rights of married couples were not. In separate concurrences, John Harlan and Byron White also distinguished between laws that regulated nonmarital sex, which they said were constitutional, and those that interfered with the rights of married couples, which they said were not. *Griswold* has often been seen as a decision that endorsed a right of sexual privacy because increased access to birth control made it more possible to engage in sex without reproductive consequences, but most of the justices who decided *Griswold* made it clear that they did not believe there was a constitutional right to sexual privacy.

In *Fanny Hill*, the majority of the justices rejected the libertarian positions adopted by Douglas and Hugo Black, who wanted to extend the protection of the First Amendment to obscene speech. Instead, the plurality position (endorsed by Brennan, Warren, and Abe Fortas) asked "whether to the average person, applying contemporary community standards, the dominant theme of the material taken as a whole appeals to prurient interest."[8] Only materials "utterly without redeeming social value" could be classified as obscene. By this definition, if the "average person" believed that "contemporary community standards" judged homosexuality more negatively than it judged heterosexuality, or if the "average person" believed that heterosexuality had more "social value" than did homosexuality, it was perfectly constitutional to judge homosexual and heterosexual representations by unequal standards.

In *Loving*, a unanimous Court struck down laws against interracial marriage, primarily because they violated the Fourteenth Amendment's equal protection clause. *Loving* was not a sex case per se, but most states criminalized nonmarital sex, so laws that regulated who could legally marry whom also regulated who could legally have sex with whom. By custom, states did not knowingly permit same-sex marriage, so a ruling in favor of interracial marriage expanded the range of legal heterosexual partners while retaining prohibitions on homosexual sex and marriage. *Loving* did not comment directly on state laws against nonmarital sex, but in three instances the Court cited the precedent of *McLaughlin v. Florida*. In this 1964 ruling, the Court overturned a law that treated unmarried interracial cohabitants more harshly than it did unmarried intraracial cohabitants. White's majority opinion in *McLaughlin* affirmed the constitutionality of Florida's "general" and "neutral" laws against adultery, cohabitation, fornication, and premarital sex, but rejected the differential treatment of interracial and intraracial cohabitation.[9] Nothing in *Loving* challenged this conclusion. Moreover, Warren's majority opinion in *Loving* declared, "The freedom to marry has long been recognized as one of the vital personal rights essential to the orderly pursuit of happiness by free men. Marriage is one of the 'basic civil rights of man,' fundamental to our very existence and survival." Marriage, of course, is only necessary for human existence and survival within a conceptual framework that imagines that reproduction cannot occur outside of marriage. In other words, Warren's opinion was based on a narrowly procreative and heterosexual conception of marriage and a narrowly marital and heterosexual conception of procreation.

Reproduction was also central to the Court's ruling in *Eisenstadt*, which overturned a state ban on the distribution of birth control to the unmarried. Only seven justices participated in the Court's decision in this case, and only four joined the majority opinion by Brennan. (Two justices concurred because there was no evidence that the woman given birth control in this case was unmarried.) Like Griswold, *Eisenstadt* never mentioned sexual privacy, but while Griswold invoked a right of marital privacy, *Eisenstadt* invoked one of reproductive privacy. In several passages, Brennan's opinion suggested that laws against premarital and extramarital sex were constitutional, but challenged the claim that the ban on distributing contraceptives to the unmarried had a rational relationship to the goal of discouraging nonmarital sex. Such a ban, the majority argued, did nothing to prevent married people from having sex with people other than their spouses. Moreover, the state did not ban the distribution of disease-prevention devices, which also could be used to prevent pregnancy. In the end, the ruling in *Eisenstadt* affirmed the privileged status of potentially reproductive forms of sexual expression, which were given special privacy protections.

Like *Eisenstadt*, *Roe* concerned reproductive rights. *Roe* has been demonized by conservatives, but in several important respects the ruling was far more conservative than is generally believed. First, it did not endorse "abortion on demand"; the Court's trimester framework permitted significant restrictions on abortion in the second and third trimesters, and the ruling did not require state and federal programs to fund abortions. Second, the ruling emphasized the rights of doctors, not the rights of women seeking abortions. As for the right of privacy endorsed by the Court, Harry Blackmun's majority opinion noted that earlier Court decisions had extended the right of privacy to activities related to "marriage," "procreation," "contraception," "family relationships," and "child rearing and education." Now the Court was extending the right to encompass abortion, but Blackmun emphasized, "It is not clear to us that the claim asserted by some amici that one has an unlimited right to do with one's body as one pleases bears a close relationship to the right of privacy previously articulated in the Court's decisions. The Court has refused to recognize an unlimited right of this kind in the past." A few months later, Burger wrote for the majority in *Paris Adult Theatre I v. Slaton* (1973): "For us to say that our Constitution incorporates the proposition that conduct involving consenting adults only is always beyond state regulation is a step we are unable to take." The accompanying footnote listed various types of statutes that were "constitutionally unchallenged," including laws against adultery, bigamy, fornication, and prostitution.[10]

The conservative elements of the Court's rulings in *Griswold, Fanny Hill, Loving, Eisenstadt,* and *Roe* are often missed in the rush to denounce or celebrate their accomplishments. If we actually read the opinions of the justices, however, it begins to look like the Court was attempting to set limits on the dynamics of legal and sexual liberalization. In a rare comment on the sexual revolution, Burger's majority opinion in *Miller v. California* (1973) declared, "One can concede that the 'sexual revolution' of recent years may have had useful byproducts in striking layers of prudery from a subject long irrationally kept from needed ventilation. But it does not follow that no regulation of patently offensive 'hard core' materials is needed or permissible; civilized people do not allow unregulated access to heroin because it is a derivative of medicinal morphine." In Burger's complex analogy, the sexual revolution was like medicinal morphine, but sexual excess (in the form of hardcore pornography) was like heroin. The Court, Burger seemed to imply, would extend constitutional protection to those aspects of the sexual revolution that were like medicinal morphine, but not to those that were like heroin.[11]

CONSERVATIVE CONSISTENCY

If one problem with the conventional view of the "liberalizing" rulings from *Griswold* to *Roe* is that it fails to acknowledge the Court's doctrine of heteronormative supremacy, a second problem is that it ignores a set of conservative rulings that make the Court's opposition to sexual freedom and sexual equality even more evident. As mentioned above, in several cases the Court upheld obscenity convictions when the target audiences were "clearly defined deviant sexual groups." These rulings were substantively conservative, but they also suggested that the Court would feel free to revise its existing rules for determining if a text was obscene if the rules did not yield the Court's desired results, as was the case when Mishkin's lawyers argued that materials aimed at "deviant sexual groups" did not appeal to the "prurient" interests of "average" people. The conventional view also ignores *Boutilier*, in which the Court ruled that under the 1952 Immigration and Nationality Act, the INS could exclude and deport homosexual aliens because by definition they were "afflicted with psychopathic personality."

Just as social and cultural historians of sexuality challenge the popular misconception that lesbian, gay, bisexual, and transgender (LGBT) history began with New York City's Stonewall Riots of 1969, legal historians of sexuality must struggle against the popular misconception that the Supreme Court's first LGBT rights decisions took place in the post-Stonewall era. In fact, the pre-Stonewall "homophile" movement registered its first significant Supreme Court victory in 1958, when the Court, without comment, overturned a lower court obscenity ruling against *ONE* magazine. *ONE* was among the most respectable gay publications in existence, featuring neither erotic prose nor sexual photographs, and in the absence of majority and minority opinions the reasons for the Court's ruling remained unclear. The Supreme Court also struck down a gay-related obscenity conviction in *Manual Enterprise v. Day* (1962) and a gay-related deportation order in *Rosenberg v. Fleuti* (1963), but both of these cases turned on legal technicalities, so their implications for LGBT rights were not clear. Meanwhile, in *Womack v. United States* (1961) and *Darnell v. United States* (1963) the Court upheld gay-related obscenity convictions, which left the meaning of the victory in *ONE* even more uncertain. All of these cases were decided in the pre-*Griswold* era, and in none of them did the Court make a clear statement about the rights of "homosexuals." *Boutilier* thus stands as the Supreme Court's most significant comment on LGBT rights in the period when the Court was announcing its "liberalizing" rulings on birth control, obscenity, interracial marriage, and abortion.[12]

Born in Nova Scotia, Canada, Clive Michael Boutilier migrated to the United States as a permanent resident in the 1950s, around the same time that his mother, stepfather, and several siblings also took up legal residence there. In the early 1960s, Boutilier applied for U.S. citizenship, revealing in the process that he had once been arrested in New York on a sodomy charge. When the other party failed to appear in court, the charge had been dropped, but Boutilier's admission set in motion an interrogation process that yielded information about his occasional same-sex sexual experiences before and after his entry into the United States and his long-term cohabitation with a "homosexual" man in New York. Based on this information, the Immigration and Naturalization Service ordered Boutilier deported on the grounds that he had been afflicted with psychopathic personality when he entered the United States. Two private psychiatrists testified that Boutilier was not a psychopath, but the INS disregarded this evidence, insisting that Congress, when it passed the Immigration and Nationality Act in 1952, intended to classify all "homosexual" aliens as "afflicted with psychopathic personality."

Three sets of legal advocates defended Boutilier. His primary lawyer, Blanch Freedman, was a leftist immigration specialist affiliated with the American Committee for the Protection of the Foreign Born. Friend of the Court briefs were filed by the Philadelphia-based Homosexual Law Reform Society (HLRS) and the American and New York Civil Liberties Unions. Meanwhile, HLRS and the National Legal Defense Fund, a San Francisco-based homophile organization, raised funds to support the litigation. This is not the place for an in-depth discussion of the homophile movement's turn to constitutional litigation in the 1960s, but the depth and breadth of the movement's commitment to court-based strategies belies the popular misconception that the LGBT movement did not pursue this path to social change in the pre-Stonewall era.

Boutilier's lawyers offered several different arguments in defense of their client. The "psychopathic personality" statute was unconstitutionally vague, they declared, which failed to warn Boutilier about conduct that might make him vulnerable to deportation. Homosexuality was not necessarily psychopathological, they insisted, submitting statements by dozens of scientific experts in support of this position. Neither did the legislative history support the firm conclusion that Congress wanted to exclude and deport all homosexual aliens, they pointed out. Boutilier's lawyers also claimed that the INS had failed to follow proper procedures by relying on evidence of post-entry conduct to establish a pre-entry condition, failing to have the Public Health Service conduct a medical examination of Boutilier (which was required under the law), and not advising Boutilier of his right to counsel when he was interrogated.

Unfortunately for Boutilier, six of the nine justices accepted the government's arguments. Citing the precedent of the *Chinese Exclusion Cases* from the 1880s, the Court affirmed that Congress had the power to order the exclusion and deportation of aliens with specified "characteristics." The timing of this argument is striking. Congress had repealed the Chinese Exclusion Act in 1943 and abandoned the national origins immigration system in 1965, yet in *Boutilier* the Court affirmed that Congress retained the power to exclude immigrants on the basis of characteristics such as race, nationality, and sexual orientation. The timing is also striking because by this time the Court regarded laws and practices that classified U.S. citizens on the basis of race as "suspect," requiring the Court's "strict scrutiny." *Boutilier*, however, did not concern the rights of a citizen, and while the Court found it helpful to make an analogy between a group defined by racial/national characteristics and a group defined by sexual ones, in other cases it distinguished between classifications (such as race) that were subject to "strict scrutiny" and classifications (such as sexual orientation) that were not. Having determined that Congress had the power to exclude and deport homosexual aliens, the Court concluded that the congressional intent to exclude homosexuals was clear, the evidence convincingly demonstrated that Boutilier was homosexual, and Congress had the power to classify homosexuals as psychopathic personalities, regardless of what scientific experts might say. All of the other arguments offered by Boutilier's lawyers were dismissed as irrelevant.

After *Boutilier* was decided in 1967, the Supreme Court did not accept another LGBT rights case for argument until the mid-1980s. As for Boutilier himself, presumably distraught because of what was happening to him, he attempted suicide shortly after the Court's ruling. After surviving a month-long coma that left him with permanent disabilities, Boutilier moved back to Canada with his mother and stepfather, who cared for him for many years. Forgotten by the country that deported him in the 1960s, Boutilier died in Ontario, Canada, in 2003.

CONCLUSION

Boutilier received minimal attention in the U.S. press in 1967, and subsequently the case has been ignored by most scholars in legal history, immigration history, and the history of sexuality. There are many reasons for this historical amnesia, but one reason is that *Boutilier* does not fit easily into the stories that scholars often tell about the Supreme

Court and the sexual revolution in the late 1960s and early 1970s. This is seen as the era of *Griswold*, *Loving*, and *Roe*. Liberals celebrate and conservatives condemn the rights of sexual freedom they associate with the Supreme Court's rulings in this period, but *Boutilier* challenges the stories told by both liberals and conservatives about the Court's sexual revolution. Looking at *Boutilier* alongside *Griswold*, *Loving*, *Roe*, and the other cases discussed in this essay would make more transparent the legal doctrine of heteronormative supremacy that operates in the United States. This in turn might force people to acknowledge the special rights, privileges, and protections that are extended to heterosexual, marital, and reproductive forms of sexual expression. It might also force Americans to confront the uncomfortable fact that most adults in the U.S. in the last decades of the twentieth century were unconvicted sexual criminals who had violated various laws against nonmarital sex. And it might lead them to recognize the special vulnerabilities of the millions of U.S. residents who are subject to the unjust policing of the country's sexual and national borders.

CHAPTER 19

Immigration Is a Queer Issue

From Fleuti *to* Trump

Earlier this month, after a three-judge panel of the Ninth Circuit Court of Appeals rejected the Trump administration's motion to stay a temporary restraining order for Executive Order 13769, a number of observers noticed that the ruling cited a major gay rights case as an important precedent. The case was *Rosenberg v. Fleuti*, decided by the U.S. Supreme Court in 1963. Thanks to the broad and deep education that most of us now receive in the history of LGBT rights and freedoms, few knowledgeable commentators could have missed the reference.

OK, that last part was fake; few of us receive much of an education in LGBT history. And the number of people who noticed the reference to *Fleuti* was probably quite low. Truth be told, the decision in *Washington v. Trump*, which addressed the 90-day ban on the entry of Muslims from seven Middle Eastern and African countries, only makes passing reference to *Fleuti*. It's not even clear that *Fleuti* was a major gay rights victory; I myself did not single it out in a 2014 essay I wrote about teaching the U.S. Supreme Court's greatest gay and lesbian hits.[1]

Still, it's worth taking the opportunity to revisit *Fleuti*, which the Ninth Circuit panel quoted as saying that "the returning resident alien is entitled as a matter of due process to a hearing on the charges underlying any attempt to exclude him."

This essay was published originally on the *University of North Carolina Press Blog*, 24 Feb. 2017, http://uncpressblog.com/2017/02/24/marc-stein-immigration-is-a-queer-issue/.

Rosenberg v. Fleuti was a strange case in many ways. According to the facts presented in the Supreme Court's decision, George Fleuti was a Swiss national who had been legally admitted as a U.S. permanent resident in October 1952 and had remained in the United States continuously except for a short day-trip to Ensenada, Mexico, in August 1956. For reasons that are unclear, in 1959 the Immigration and Naturalization Service attempted to deport Fleuti, claiming that when he re-entered the United States in 1956, he was excludable because he had been convicted of a crime of "moral turpitude" between his original entry in 1952 and his re-entry in 1956.

Unfortunately for the INS, it soon became clear that the minor same-sex sex offenses for which Fleuti had been convicted did not meet the definition of a crime of moral turpitude. Unfortunately for Fleuti, the INS had recourse to another law: in June 1952 Congress had passed a new immigration statute that provided for the deportation of aliens "afflicted with psychopathic personality." The INS had begun to use this provision against "homosexual" aliens and that's what it tried to use against Fleuti. Relying primarily on his prior convictions, the INS claimed that Fleuti had been afflicted with psychopathic personality when he re-entered the United States after his trip to Ensenada. (It could not make a similar claim about his original entry because the 1952 law did not take effect until December.) Fleuti's lawyer Hiram Kwan argued in response that the psychopathic personality law was unconstitutionally vague.

Research in the papers of the justices reveals that initially the Supreme Court voted 5–4 against Fleuti, with the senior justice in the majority, Tom Clark, selecting the newest justice, Arthur Goldberg, to write the Court's main opinion. Goldberg, however, changed his mind and he ended up writing a 5–4 decision in favor of Fleuti. The majority opinion did not address the constitutionality of the psychopathic personality law, a choice that had negative consequences for the Supreme Court's 1967 decision in *Boutilier v. INS*, which upheld the law. Instead, Goldberg concluded that Fleuti's return from Mexico after a short day-trip did not constitute "entry" under the terms of the law. Drawing on the statutory language that defined "entry" and two 1952 Supreme Court precedents, Goldberg wrote that an alien's return to the United States after an "innocent, casual, and brief" trip outside the United States did not meet the legal definition of "entry." (One of the precedents addressed an alien who had entered and exited Canada while on an overnight train from Buffalo to Detroit; the other concerned an alien who had spent a week in Cuba while recovering from injuries sustained when his merchant ship was torpedoed in the Caribbean during World War Two.) On this basis, the Supreme Court remanded the case to the lower court to determine whether Fleuti was excludable given the guidance provided by the Court. In the end, it was determined that Fleuti was not excludable.

On the one hand, the Supreme Court's decision in *Rosenberg v. Fleuti* is disturbing in the way it came close to implying that the legal borders of the United States extend well beyond its literal borders. Whether the cases concerned Canada, Cuba, or Mexico, all of which have directly experienced U.S. military interventions, there's something deeply troubling about the Supreme Court's reluctance to treat a visit to a U.S. neighbor as a visit to a U.S. neighbor.

It's also disturbing to think about the possibility that Fleuti only won his case because he was white, male, employed, gender-normative, and respectable. To take the best available counter-example, the outcome was less favorable in *Quiroz v. Neely*, a 1961 Second Circuit decision that upheld the deportation of a female U.S. permanent resident from Mexico. She, too, had encountered trouble when returning from a short trip to Mexico (one of many she took) and she, too, was labelled a "psychopathic personality" based on allegations about homosexuality. Unlike Fleuti, Quiroz lost her appeal.

On the other hand, it's significant that Fleuti won his case and it's significant that the Ninth Circuit panel invoked the *Fleuti* ruling in *Trump v. Washington*. U.S. federal courts have long relied on precedents that demonstrate that the histories of racialized, gendered, and sexualized groups in U.S. society are interconnected. In the late nineteenth century, when the justices upheld the Chinese Exclusion Acts (in violation of treaties that the United States had signed with China), they invoked prior decisions in which the Court had permitted Congress to override pre-existing treaties with Native Americans. In *Boutilier v. INS*, the 1967 decision that upheld the exclusion and deportation of "homosexuals," the Court cited the Chinese Exclusion cases as key precedents that affirmed the power of Congress to exclude aliens with specific "characteristics." Now in *Trump v. Washington*, the Ninth Circuit panel has used a decision in a "gay rights" case as a precedent for a decision in a "Muslim rights" one.

Justice Goldberg wrote in *Fleuti* that "Congress unquestionably has the power to exclude all classes of undesirable aliens from this country, and the courts are charged with enforcing such exclusion when Congress has directed it." This was before Congress dramatically changed U.S. immigration law in 1965; before Congress removed the ban on people "afflicted with psychopathic personality" in 1990; before Congress passed the Illegal Immigration Reform and Immigrant Responsibility Act of 1996; and before the courts developed new methods of evaluating laws that discriminate based on race, religion, nationality, and other factors. Goldberg also was addressing actions taken by Congress, not the President, and his comments referred to the exclusion of "undesirable aliens," not entire classes of aliens based on their nationality and religion. *Fleuti* and other gay rights rulings may or may not be useful in upcoming legal struggles about policing the border, but they remind us that immigration is a queer issue.

CHAPTER 20

Defectives of the World, Unite!

Today, May 22, is the fiftieth anniversary of the U.S. Supreme Court's decision in *Clive Michael Boutilier v. the Immigration and Naturalization Service* (1967), a long-forgotten ruling that upheld the deportation of a legal resident from Canada who was classified by the U.S. government as having a "mental or physical defect." According to the INS's *Annual Report for 1967*, the United States excluded or deported more than 100,000 people on this basis from 1892 to 1967, but this represented a small fraction of the total number of foreign "defectives" rejected by the United States for immigration, residency, and citizenship.

Historian Douglas Baynton's book *Defectives in the Land* (2016) explains that in the late nineteenth and early twentieth centuries U.S. immigration law barred the entry of lunatics, idiots, epileptics, imbeciles, feeble-minded people, constitutional psychopathic inferiors, and anyone likely to become a public charge. Physical "defects" that were grounds for exclusion and deportation included arthritis, asthma, blindness, bunions, deafness, deformities, flat feet, heart disease, hernia, spinal curvature, and varicose veins. Influenced by eugenics, nativism, and racism, policymakers were determined to promote their (limited) vision of national strength.

This essay was published originally as "50 Years Ago the US Supreme Court Upheld the Deportation of 'Homosexuals' as 'Psychopaths,'" by History News Network, 22 May 2017, http://historynewsnetwork.org/article/165958.

Boutilier's deportation was based on a provision of the 1952 Immigration and Nationality Act that applied to aliens "afflicted with psychopathic personality." During oral arguments in the Boutilier case, Associate Justice Potter Stewart asked the U.S. government's lawyer about the types of people classified by the INS as afflicted with psychopathic personality. He could not answer, but one day later Solicitor General Thurgood Marshall forwarded to the Supreme Court a memorandum prepared by INS General Counsel Charles Gordon. According to Gordon, INS statistics did not break down the mental or physical defectives category. He noted that there were multiple conditions that could lead the INS to classify an individual as psychopathic, including compulsive, paranoid, passive-aggressive, and schizoid personality disorders, but "our general impression is that sexual perversion is the critical consideration in the preponderance of cases where the 'psychopathic personality' charge has been used."

"Sexual perversion" was the "critical consideration" for Boutilier. Born in 1933, he had moved from Nova Scotia to New York in 1955. By the time he applied for U.S. citizenship in 1963, his mother and most of his siblings also lived in the United States and he was working as a building maintenance man; ironically, he had earlier worked as an attendant for a man who was mentally ill. Boutilier's immigration troubles began when he noted on his citizenship application that in 1959 he had been arrested, but not convicted, on a sodomy charge in New York. This prompted an interrogation by the INS in which Boutilier revealed that he had engaged in sex with men and women before entering the United States and that he had continued to engage in same-sex sex, with his partner Eugene O'Rourke and with other men, after moving to New York. Based on this information, the INS rejected his citizenship application and ordered him deported as a "psychopathic personality."

Boutilier's lawyers, affiliated with the American Committee for the Protection of the Foreign Born, the American Civil Liberties Union, and the Homosexual Law Reform Society, challenged his deportation with multiple arguments. They submitted medical affidavits indicating that Boutilier was not a psychopathic personality. They raised procedural objections because the Public Health Service had not examined Boutilier. They offered expert testimony that challenged the government's claim that homosexuality was psychopathic. They questioned whether the intent of Congress was to exclude and deport all homosexual aliens. They argued that even if it was, the law was unconstitutionally vague because the average person would not know that the government regarded homosexuality as evidence of psychopathic personality.

Boutilier's lawyers had reasons to be hopeful. In its 1958 ruling in *ONE v. Olesen*, the Supreme Court had rejected the Post Office's censorship of a gay magazine. In its 1963 ruling in *Rosenberg v. Fleuti*, the justices had used a legal technicality to prevent the deportation of a Swiss gay immigrant. In *McLaughlin v. Florida* (1964) and *Griswold v. Connecticut* (1965), the Supreme Court had rejected state laws that criminalized interracial cohabitation and contraception for married people. And less than three weeks after deciding *Boutilier*, the justices unanimously struck down state restrictions on interracial marriage in *Loving v. Virginia*.

The Supreme Court, however, ruled 6–3 against Boutilier. Justice Tom Clark's majority opinion rejected much of the medical testimony by noting that "Congress used the phrase 'psychopathic personality' not in the clinical sense, but to effectuate its purpose to exclude from entry all homosexuals and other sex perverts." As for whether Congress had the constitutional power to do so, Clark cited the 1882 *Chinese Exclusion Cases* to support the majority's determination that "Congress has plenary power to make rules for the admission of aliens and to exclude those who possess those characteristics which Congress has forbidden."

Sadly, Boutilier was in no condition to understand the ruling against him. Twelve days earlier, he had been hit by a car in New York and suffered traumatic head injuries, leaving him in a coma that lasted for several weeks. Some members of his family believe this was a suicide attempt. A few months later, one of his doctors reported, with no apparent irony, that he was suffering from "post-traumatic psychosis." Meanwhile, Boutilier's lawyer asked the INS for a compassionate deferral of his deportation. This was granted until November 1968, when Boutilier was sufficiently recovered to return to Canada. His mother, a nurse, accompanied him, first to Nova Scotia and later to Ontario. The American Psychiatric Association declassified homosexuality as a mental illness in 1973, but Congress did not eliminate the "psychopathic personality" provision in U.S. immigration law until 1990. Boutilier died in a home for people with disabilities in 2003, two months before the U.S. Supreme Court overturned state sodomy laws in *Lawrence v. Texas*.

As we remember *Boutilier v. the INS* on its fiftieth anniversary, there are good reasons to be angry and upset about the historical mistreatment of "homosexuals" and other gender and sexual "deviates" in the U.S. immigration system. In this context, we have options about how we choose to remember. We can disavow the historical connections between homosexuality and disability, insisting that the primary injustice in *Boutilier* lies in the mischaracterization of "homosexuals" as psychopaths. We also can consider what it might mean to recognize and explore these connections, which might be a better starting place for thinking about our ongoing struggles against immigration restriction. Defectives of the world, unite!

PART SIX

Sex, Law, and the Supreme Court

In 2014, San Francisco State University offered me a job as a tenured full professor of U.S. history. The position was for a specialist in constitutional law and came with an endowed chair. The endowment, established in 2000 thanks to a donation by a graduate of SFSU's MA history program, funded two course releases per year and provided significant research support. When offered the chair, I was pleased for myself, but also proud for the field of LGBT history: SFSU could have offered this position to a specialist in any aspect of constitutional law, but it chose an LGBT historian. My 2010 book *Sexual Injustice* presumably established my core credentials. It also must have helped that the undergraduate course I taught most frequently at York was "Constitutional Law and Equal Rights in U.S. History." In addition, my students had successfully nominated me for York's annual graduate teaching award in 2010 and Routledge had published my third book, *Rethinking the Gay and Lesbian Movement*, in 2012. Notwithstanding these conventional markers of success, it would not have surprised me if SFSU had bypassed LGBT historians. I had applied for multiple faculty positions in the United States during my sixteen years in Canada; I came close three times but was never hired. Twenty years after completing my PhD, I had my first tenure-stream job offer from a US history department.

Leaving my job at York was the most difficult professional decision I have ever made. The stress I felt in relation to this contributed to my one and only experience with fainting, at a US history conference no less; I have a scar on my forehead to remind me. I had enjoyed working at York and living in Toronto; I had fabulous friends, smart colleagues, and engaging students. But I could not figure out how to ease the burdens of supervising more than twenty graduate students at York. More and more students were interested in queer history, but my two departments (History and Gender, Sexuality, and Women's Studies) would not hire another LGBT historian of the United States or Canada, notwithstanding the fact that together they had more than fifty tenure-track faculty positions and I had not been hired to teach LGBT history. Departmental decisions about hiring priorities routinely referenced student demand, but almost no one seemed to notice or care that I was supervising more graduate students than just about anyone. Meanwhile, in the context of declining public funding for higher education, the number of US historians at York had dropped steadily—from seven in 1998 to three in 2014—meaning that I was expected to cover more and more aspects of US history. I routinely supported the hiring of more historians of the Global South, but not the destruction of our US history field.

There were other factors that contributed to my decision. In my last few years at York, I was part of a successful effort to replace our faculty union's conservative officers with more progressive leaders, but the work required to make this happen was long, hard, and divisive, and we failed to win equal voting rights for the stewards of the union's race equity, indigenous, disability, and queer caucuses. (This apparently was rectified after my departure.) Having turned fifty in 2013, I also was experiencing the academic version of a midlife crisis, which increased my excitement about embarking on new adventures. This was especially the case because my partner, still teaching in Maine, would soon be retiring and we would finally have the opportunity to live together full time. York made a generous counteroffer, but could not match the reduced teaching, research funding, and better weather promised at SFSU. I also knew that a faculty position in one of the centers of LGBT life in the United States, at a university with a long and storied history of social justice activism, would provide me with new possibilities for building on my work as a queer public historian and LGBT scholarly activist.

In hiring an LGBT historian for a position in US constitutional law, my SFSU colleagues likely were influenced by historical developments in the early twenty-first century. In 2003, the US Supreme Court not only invalidated state sodomy laws but also rejected decades of legal precedents about moral and religious justifications for infringements on personal freedom and equal rights. In 2013 and 2015, the Court invalidated federal and state statutes that denied legal recognition to same-sex marriages. The Supreme Court's 1967 decision in *Boutilier* had never been recognized as a major ruling, but in the 2010s there was no denying that LGBT issues mattered in the field of constitutional law. SFSU's commitments to social justice and ethnic studies and its opposition to the new politics of racism and nativism also may have played roles in my hiring. During my campus interview, I strategically balanced my research presentation on queer immigration law in the twentieth century with a teaching demonstration on Supreme Court decisions about African Americans, Asian Americans, Native Americans, and women in the late nineteenth century. The timing also was fortuitous in the life of the History Department; SFSU historian Barbara Loomis, who had taught courses on LGBT history and edited the *Journal of the History of Sexuality*, had retired in 2013. In 2014, SFSU's faculty included other queer historians, most notably Nan Alamilla Boyd, Amy Sueyoshi, and Clare Sears, but they taught in other departments (Women and Gender Studies, Race and Resistance Studies, and Sociology and Sexuality Studies). While it is difficult to explain the outcomes of complicated faculty hiring processes, it likely helped my cause that SFSU's History Department conducted its search at a time when LGBT legal issues were recognized as nationally significant and at a moment when the department had just lost its one tenured specialist in LGBT history.

Moving from York to SFSU shifted the emphases of my teaching and service. At York, a majority of my courses had concentrated on gender and sexuality and my most significant university service had focused on the Sexuality Studies Program. At SFSU, a majority of my courses address constitutional law and my teaching focuses more on Native Americans, African Americans, Asian Americans, women, and immigrants than it does on LGBT people. With respect to university service, since 2015 I have coordinated SFSU's annual "Rights and Wrongs" conference, which is timed to coincide with the national Constitution and Citizenship Day holiday. Over time, the conference has become a hybrid of a traditional academic conference and a public event with strong student attendance and community participation. Annual attendance exceeded one thousand from 2016 to 2019. Most of our keynote presenters have focused on race, indigeneity, immigration, gender, and class.[1] Beyond the university, I was honored to contribute to an amicus brief for *San Francisco v. Trump* (2018), a Ninth Circuit case about the president's threat to withhold federal funds from sanctuary jurisdictions that did not cooperate with US immigration enforcement.[2] As all of this suggests, since moving to SFSU, much of my teaching and service have been oriented to constitutional law.

In contrast to my teaching and service, my scholarship continues to prioritize LGBT history. In 2014, I was proud to contribute to *Making the Framework FAIR*, a report by Don Romesburg, Leila J. Rupp, and David M. Donahue that addressed California's new mandate to teach LGBT history in public schools. In 2016 and 2018, I published two synthetic essays on the history of LGBT law, one for the National Park Service's queer theme study and one for the *Routledge History of Queer America*.[3] Some of my recent public history publications have focused on queer legal history; some have addressed non-LGBT topics. While I have never wanted to turn my back on LGBT history, I also have never wanted to be ghettoized as a queer historian. Sometimes this has emboldened me to address topics far removed from LGBT history, including affirmative action, loyalty oaths, Supreme Court nominations, and voting rights.[4] On the one hand, I am proud that my public history work has resisted the ghettoization of LGBT history and pleased that my hiring as a specialist in constitutional law can be seen as signaling the rejection of this type of marginalization. On the other hand, since moving to San Francisco I have fielded dozens of media calls about LGBT history but almost none about other aspects of constitutional law or US history. In many respects, this is fine with me; I am not looking for more work. I worry, though, about whether this is symptomatic of the ongoing marginalization of queer historians in the public sphere.

Chapter 21, "Queer Eye for the FBI," was published by HNN in 2005. I wrote the essay after the FBI declined to provide me with copies of controversial archival materials containing allegations of same-sex sexual acts by Abe Fortas, an associate justice of the US Supreme Court in the 1960s. I had requested the documents under the terms of the Freedom of Information Act. The FBI's response acknowledged that the file existed, but claimed it was missing. I published the essay at a sensitive historical moment—Associate Justice Sandra Day O'Connor had recently announced her resignation and Chief Justice William Rehnquist was gravely ill. In this context, I was concerned about false public assertions about the history of Supreme Court nominations, which ignored the history of Lyndon Johnson's failed 1968 nomination of Fortas to be chief justice. I also was disturbed by the FBI's intransigence or incompetence in not providing me with the materials I requested. Sure enough, the publicity generated by my HNN essay apparently persuaded the FBI to redouble its efforts to find the missing file, copies of which were sent to me several months later. (For my interpretation of the materials, see *Sexual Injustice*, pages 11–12.) For readers too young to understand the playful title (not used by HNN), it was based on *Queer Eye for the Straight Guy*, a television reality show that aired originally from 2003 to 2007.

Chapter 22, "Gay Rights and the Supreme Court: The Early Years," was published by the *University of North Carolina Press Blog* in 2010. The timing coincided with the publication of my book *Sexual Injustice*. I hoped that this essay, presented on my publisher's blog, would help publicize the book. More substantively, I wanted to challenge ahistorical accounts of LGBT law reform, which were proliferating in the context of the struggle for legalizing same-sex marriages.

Chapter 23, "Justice Kennedy and the Future of Same-Sex Marriage," also was published by the *University of North Carolina Press Blog* in 2010. This essay attempted to predict Kennedy's vote on upcoming same-sex marriage cases by looking back to a 1989 Supreme Court decision that had rejected a man's paternity suit after he had an adulterous relationship with a woman married to a different man. I thought the opinions in this case revealed a significant philosophical conflict between Justices Kennedy and Scalia, with possible implications for the legalization of same-sex marriages.

Chapter 24, "Five Myths about *Roe v. Wade*," was published by the *University of North Carolina Press Blog* in 2013. While *Sexual Injustice* devoted four chapters to the *Boutilier* case, there were three that addressed Supreme Court decisions on birth control, obscenity, interracial marriage, and abortion. Timed to coincide with the fortieth anniversary of the abortion rights ruling in *Roe*, this essay challenged a set of myths that *Sexual Injustice* had tried to displace.

Chapter 25, "Refreshing Abominations: An Open Letter to Anthony Kennedy," was published by OutHistory in 2015. I wrote this after listening to the oral arguments in *Obergefell v. Hodges*, the 2015 Supreme Court case on same-sex marriage. While the LGBT litigation strategies in this case were successful (and I was proud to have my work cited in the briefs), I thought they relied on fundamentally ahistorical arguments. Historical research had established that same-sex marriage was not a new phenomenon; scholars had uncovered many such unions across US history. The only thing new was state recognition, and even that was not entirely new. Moreover, same-sex marriages were not the only unions that government authorities had refused to recognize or recognized belatedly; other examples included slave marriages, frontier marriages, Native American marriages, and polygamous marriages. This essay imagined different questions that the justices could have asked the lawyers, questions that might have prompted stronger historical arguments. My title played with an episode that occurred during the *Obergefell* oral arguments; after a spectator interrupted the proceedings and referred to homosexuality as an abomination, Justice Scalia reportedly responded that the man's comments were "refreshing." I thought "refreshing abominations" sounded like a great name for a cocktail.

Queer Eye for the FBI

A controversial FBI file that reportedly contains allegations of homosexual conduct by Abe Fortas, an Associate Justice of the Supreme Court in the 1960s, is missing, according to the FBI. Never proven, the allegations may have been made as a way for the FBI to threaten Fortas with exposure, encourage his resignation, or prevent his appointment as Chief Justice.

Fortas has been in the news recently because of inaccurate Republican claims about the history of the filibuster and the history of judicial appointments. In 1968 Fortas, who had served as an Associate Justice since 1965, was nominated by President Lyndon Johnson to replace Earl Warren as Chief Justice. Fortas was denied confirmation because of a Republican-led filibuster in the U.S. Senate. According to historians who have studied the episode, the filibuster was motivated in part by concerns about financial improprieties and in part by objections to Fortas's close ties to Johnson (the two reasons commonly invoked by journalists), but also by false allegations made by Senator Strom Thurmond (and others) about Fortas's roles in a set of rape and obscenity cases and by anti-Semitic objections to what would have been the nation's first Jewish Chief Justice. Because of the timing of these developments, Republican

This essay was published originally as "Did the FBI Try to Blackmail Supreme Court Justice Abe Fortas?" by History News Network, 18 July 2005, http://hnn.us/articles/13170 .html.

Richard Nixon, elected in November 1968, gained the power to appoint Warren's successor, and in 1969 the Democratic-led Senate confirmed Nixon's nominee Warren Burger. Fortas resigned from the Court in 1969 and was replaced by Harry Blackmun, also nominated by Nixon.

Several years ago, Laura Kalman, the author of *Abe Fortas: A Biography* (Yale University Press, 1990), encouraged me to look into the allegations about Fortas's homosexuality after she heard a paper I presented at the annual convention of the Organization of American Historians. Kalman's book discusses several of the reasons that may have led Fortas to resign from the Court shortly after the filibuster against his appointment as Chief Justice proved successful. (A majority, but not the needed two-thirds, of the senators present voted for cloture, thus preventing what U.S. Senate Majority Leader Bill Frist has called an "up or down vote.") Kalman writes (on page 375), "Other gossip was more startling. No one who knew of Fortas's enthusiastic heterosexuality would ever have accused him of homosexuality, but [*New York Times* reporter Fred] Graham and [*Life* magazine reporter William] Lambert were told, presumably by sources within the government who offered to 'bootleg' the information 'out of the FBI,' that the FBI had a morals file on Fortas that included allegations he had once been involved in a sexual relationship with a teenage boy. Regardless of their truth, such stories were damaging." Kalman cites as documentation a conversation with Lambert in Graham's papers at the Library of Congress.

Some years after Kalman's biography was published, J. J. Maloney published a related article in the electronic *Crime Magazine: An Encyclopedia of Crime*. (The website identifies Maloney as a convicted murderer who served 13 years in prison and then became an award-winning journalist, receiving five Pulitzer Prize nominations, the American Bar Association's Silver Gavel prize, and the American Society of Newspaper Publishers award for Best Investigative Story.) Maloney's article consists for the most part of two documents purportedly obtained from the FBI (with various words and sentences blacked out). The first, dated July 20, 1967, discusses "an active and aggressive homosexual who has been an informant of the Washington Field Office" and who "over the years has provided a great deal of reliable information." According to this document, the informant told a Washington Field Office agent that "he had 'balled' with Abe Fortas on several occasions prior to Mr. Fortas' becoming a Justice of the United States Supreme Court." The informant reportedly indicated that "to 'ball' is to have a homosexual relationship with another male."

The second document, dated July 24, 1967, is a letter from the FBI's Cartha DeLoach to the FBI's Clyde Tolson. It reads, in part, "Pursuant to the Director's instructions, I saw Justice Fortas at his home. . . . I told him we had received an allegation from a source of information reflecting participation in homosexual activities on his part. I stated that the Director wanted this matter discreetly and informally brought to his attention so that he would be aware of such an allegation. I mentioned that the FBI was taking no further action in connection with this matter and that the fact that the Director was making this available to him was strictly for his own personal protection and knowledge. Justice Fortas was handed the attached memorandum so that he could read it personally. After reading this memorandum, he told me that the charges were ridiculous and absolutely false. He stated he had never committed a homosexual act in his life and while he might be properly accused of normal sexual relations while a young man and during his married life, he most certainly had never committed homosexual acts at any time. . . . Justice Fortas expressed great appreciation for having been provided with the above facts. He asked that his thanks be extended to the Director for having handled the matter in this manner."

In 2003, Susan Braudy's book *Family Circle: The Boudins and the Aristocracy of the Left* (Knopf) made a passing reference to the allegations about Fortas. According to Braudy (page 331), "In fact, Fortas resigned because of J. Edgar Hoover's threat of blackmail: an FBI agent had visited Fortas in 1968 to inform him of Hoover's 'concern' that Fortas had been seen at a homosexual bar. It was left to President Nixon to appoint Fortas's successor as well as the chief justice. Thus did Hoover deliver a history-changing coup de grace to the liberal Supreme Court."

Braudy cites the FBI's file on Fortas, adding in her footnotes (page 431), "It would be many years before a hint of more complicated factors leading to Fortas's resignation surfaced. According to a document from the FBI files, an FBI agent had visited Fortas and politely explained that on Director Hoover's orders, he was alerting Fortas to the dismaying fact that an informant had seen Fortas at a homosexual club. Abe Fortas thanked his visitor and resigned from the Supreme Court." I have written to Braudy via her publisher, but have not received a response.

In late 2004, I contacted the FBI to request an appointment to see the pertinent Fortas file during a planned research trip to Washington, D.C. I had determined that I was looking for O&C Files, Abe Fortas Folder 71, which was listed on the FBI's website as available in the FBI's public reading room. Having previously filed Freedom of Information

Act requests and having previously worked with materials in the FBI's public reading room, I expected that I would have to go to the reading room to see the file, but when I telephoned I was told that the file contained just six pages and these materials could be photocopied and sent to me. In February, however, I received a letter about my request signed by David Hardy, the section chief of the Record/Information Dissemination Section of the FBI's Records Management Division. According to the letter, "Information which might relate to your FOIA request in our Reading Room is unavailable at this time. The original and blacked out copy are missing at this time. When this information becomes available, it will be provided to you."

Shortly thereafter I called the FBI's Records Management Division and spoke with a staff member named Debbie Beatty, who explained that the documents "existed at one time" but apparently had been "misplaced." No further information was forthcoming, but I asked if I might send to the FBI a copy of the *Crime Magazine* materials so that the FBI might let me know whether or not they were (or appeared to be) authentic. Ms. Beatty agreed to see what she could do. On March 15, I received a second letter from Mr. Hardy, who wrote, "After a thorough search, we are unable to locate the files pertaining to Abe Fortas, therefore, we cannot confirm that the document is in fact an FBI document. From the appearance of the document, it is very similar to the way the FBI processes documents."

What are the likely explanations for the recent FBI responses to my query? The consensus of the scholars I have consulted is that there are three possibilities. One is that the materials are missing because of administrative mistakes or administrative incompetence. A second is that the materials were stolen by someone who had access to them in the FBI reading room. A third is that the materials are being withheld as a result of a decision made by someone at the FBI, the Justice Department, the White House, or another government agency with authority over the documents.

If the primary documents discussed by Kalman, Maloney, and Braudy are authentic (by which I mean that they exist, not that they are necessarily accurate), what are the implications for historical interpretation? To begin with, it is important to acknowledge that while all of the documents refer to allegations about same-sex sexual conduct by Fortas, their claims differ in important respects. For instance, if the Maloney documents are the basis for the accounts given by Kalman's and Braudy's sources, the references in the latter to a "teenage boy," a "homosexual bar," and a "homosexual club" may have been elaborations or inventions, since they do not appear in the Maloney materials. The comment about a "teenage boy" is particularly inflammatory, and here it is important to note that the phrase could refer as readily to a 19-year-old as it could to a 13-year-old, and the allegation does not indicate Fortas's age when this incident occurred. More generally, this episode may have much to teach us about the history of sexual gossip, rumor, shame, and pride, all of which have emerged as topics of significant interest to the public and the profession.

Whether or not the allegations about Fortas were true (by which I mean that they provided truthful accounts of Fortas's sexual conduct), they will likely be of interest to historians of sexual behavior, sexual identity, and the relationship between the two. They also have the potential for influencing our understanding of national politics and sexual politics during this period, and especially the history of the FBI, the Senate, and the White House during the Johnson and Nixon administrations. As for the history of the Supreme Court, Fortas played an important role in several sex-related rulings in the 1960s, and we may want to understand the rulings and the allegations in relation to one another. In 1966 Fortas voted with narrow majorities in three obscenity rulings (*Fanny Hill*, *Ginzburg*, and *Mishkin*). In *Ginzburg* and *Mishkin* (which dealt in part with materials produced for the gay market), the Court upheld obscenity convictions, though Fortas later expressed regret about his votes. Then in 1967 Fortas was one of three dissenters in one of the Court's first gay rights cases, *Boutilier v. the INS*, which upheld the deportation of a Canadian "homosexual" on the grounds that under U.S. immigration law homosexuals were excludable and deportable because they were "afflicted with psychopathic personality." In the oral arguments on *Boutilier*, Fortas aggressively questioned the government lawyer on the INS claim that homosexuality was intrinsically psychopathological. Two months after the Court announced its ruling in *Boutilier*, the FBI's DeLoach reportedly visited Fortas (if the Maloney documents are to be believed). Did Fortas's sexual history influence his votes? Can the same be said of the other justices, many of whom extolled the virtues of family, heterosexuality, marriage, and procreation in decisions about birth control, obscenity, and interracial marriage in this period? Did Fortas's votes in these and other cases lead to the FBI's visit and to the FBI's implied threats?

If authentic, these documents may also influence our understanding of Johnson's failed nomination of Fortas as Chief Justice, Fortas's subsequent resignation, and the role that the FBI and the Senate played in both. The failed nomination and the resignation, in turn, are linked to the subsequent history of the Supreme Court, which ended up with Warren Burger as Chief Justice and Harry Blackmun as Associate Justice.

In any event, it is unfortunate that the public's right to know about a relevant episode in the history of the U.S. Supreme Court is blocked at a moment when the president of the United States will be nominating a new Associate Justice, and possibly a new Chief Justice, and when the U.S. Senate will be advising the president on the nomination and deciding whether to consent.

Gay Rights and the Supreme Court

The Early Years

As the new U.S. Supreme Court term begins and as the California same-sex marriage case continues to make its way through the courts, it's a good moment to consider the early years of the gay and lesbian movement's efforts to achieve legal reform through appeals to the Supreme Court. In an August 2005 *New Yorker* article on the nomination of John G. Roberts to a position on the Supreme Court, Jeffrey Toobin, who is often a perceptive and astute commentator on legal matters, wrote that "systematic legal efforts on behalf of gays began only in the nineteen-seventies, and the Justices didn't address the issue in a sub-stantive way until the eighties." Toobin's view is all too common, and it reflects the weak state of popular knowledge about the history of sexuality in the United States. In fact, these efforts began in the 1950s and 1960s, and while the Supreme Court refused to consider gay and lesbian rights appeals from the late 1960s through the early 1980s, in an earlier period the justices decided several significant cases with impor-tant implications for gay and lesbian rights.

As those who have studied U.S. gay and lesbian history know, "homo-phile" activists began challenging discriminatory policies and practices in the courts in the 1950s. Influenced by the successes of the civil rights movement, most notably in *Brown v. Board of Education* (1954), gay

This essay was published originally on the *University of North Carolina Press Blog*, 4 Oct. 2010, http://uncpressblog.com/2010/10/04/gay-rights-and-the-supreme-court/.

advocates soon began to pin their hopes on the Supreme Court. In 1957, for example, a Brooklyn, New York, man suggested in a letter to the editor of the California-based gay magazine *ONE* that activists should support taking a gay rights case "all the way up to the Supreme Court." In his view, "the benefits of this action would be inestimable," in part because "for the first time in U.S. history the American citizen would know just where he stands on the subject of individual sexual rights." Implicitly placing his faith in the Supreme Court, he wrote that in adopting this course of action homosexuals would "no longer be at the mercy of hysterical state legislatures and the whims of the local constabulary." Three years later, after a series of gay bar raids in New York, a *ONE* columnist asked, "Will the tavern owners have the guts to fight for their rights (all the way to the high courts if need be) and for the rights of their customers?" A few months later, the same columnist noted, "There are two approaches to law reform: through legislative bodies or thru the courts. Appeal to the courts to test the legitimacy of an unfair law may be the faster and sounder way."

Emboldened by victories at the Supreme Court in two gay-related obscenity cases (*ONE* in 1958 and *Manual* in 1962) and one gay immigration case (*Rosenberg* in 1963), some gay rights advocates began arguing for increased use of court-based strategies. In 1963, a letter to *ONE* from a Florida man urged the movement to "study the possibility of setting up a test case which might reach the U.S. Supreme Court." More specifically, "Two adults accompanied by a friendly attorney could go and confess to committing a 'crime against nature' in the privacy of their home." In a 1964 discussion of sex law reform, Philadelphia gay rights leader Clark Polak wrote to his organization's board of directors, "Perhaps the best policy will be . . . to attempt to bring actions in several states so that the Supreme Court will be forced to make an adjudication."

That same year, Washington, D.C.–based homophile leader Frank Kameny advocated that "already existing legal channels, including the Supreme Court, be more widely used." Kameny argued at a 1964 homophile movement conference that "one good court case or court decision will go farther than a dozen radio appearances." He "urged that discriminatory laws and regulations be tested in the courts and that cases be encouraged, even rigged up if necessary." After noting that "judicial means are more practical, since legislatures are tied in too closely with the prejudices we're fighting," Kameny observed, "The Negro went to the courts and Southerners still don't like him. He nevertheless now has his basic rights. . . . The changes in attitude will accommodate themselves to what constituted authority hands down."

At the same conference, David Carliner, an attorney who had worked on important interracial marriage, immigration, and gay rights cases, urged the homophile movement to utilize court-based strategies. According to a published summary of Carliner's comments, "Arguments about morality and attempts to influence votes are fruitless tactics for homophile groups. . . . We must distinguish between what the courts will do and what Congress will do. . . . The courts . . . are very sensitive to demands for rights in the due process field. One way of getting to the Supreme Court is through conflicting decisions obtained in the various circuit courts. Most landmark cases in the Supreme Court have been the result of deliberate strategy." Three lawyers on a panel with Carliner agreed. According to one, "Brick by brick, and stone by stone, the law is built. The homosexual is consigned to slow and piecemeal progress. Start with the easiest inroad: change in and enlargement of procedural rights in cases of dismissal for homosexuality." According to the second panelist, "Attitudes in the courts toward homosexuality are now more realistic and civilized, and the prognosis for change is favourable." The third lawyer noted, "Only recently have enlightened and courageous defendants been willing to give their lawyers the opportunity to push the courts into rulings which would help build a defense for the position of the homosexual. Homophile groups can lend support to these defendants."

Reacting favorably to the comments made by the three lawyers, Frank Kameny asked if they were "willing to form a board to look into the possibility of a coordinated, multi-attorney approach to planned legal strategy." After a positive response, Carliner noted that "the NAACP has raised a legal defense fund" and Kameny "proposed that such a plan be the first order of business for the new Board." Sure enough, in the second half of the 1960s the National Legal Defense Fund in San Francisco and the Homosexual Law Reform Society in Philadelphia were established to pursue gay rights law reform through the courts, while homophile groups around the country pursued similar strategies to challenge employment discrimination, immigration restriction, police harassment, sodomy law enforcement, and sexual censorship.

Over time, court-based strategies gained more support in the movement. Toward the end of 1965, an article in *ONE* highlighted the importance of the magazine's victory in an earlier Supreme Court obscenity case: "A U.S. Supreme Court decision creates 'case law' which is binding upon the Courts of all the States. It is as if all of the legislatures had in that particular matter acted favourably." At a 1965 conference, psychoanalyst Ernest van den Haag "urged the homophile organizations to do what Negro groups have done successfully—they should get test cases in the courts and try to get the laws against homosexual acts invalidated." Shortly thereafter, Clark Polak wrote in a gay magazine that the Supreme Court's decision in the *Griswold* birth control case had bolstered his confidence and shifted his focus: "Law reform will not be effectuated through the State Legislatures" since "few elected legislators are willing to risk a brand as one who advocates perversion." Polak wrote that for this and other reasons, "We see the solution within the Federal Court system, with the Supreme Court as the final voice. The Connecticut birth control decision points the way—invasion of privacy. Clear appreciation of the value of Church-State separation is another." In 1966, Ernestine Eckstein, an African American member of the NAACP and several homophile organizations, observed in a lesbian magazine, "I don't find in the homophile movement enough stress on courtroom action. I would like to see more test cases." Later in 1966, a lesbian conference panel concluded that "legal improvements" were "far more likely . . . to be made through judicial processes than by State legislatures" because the courts were "freer from inhibiting political pressures."

By 1968, homosexual law reform efforts were significant, visible, and noteworthy enough to merit a front-page story in the *Wall Street Journal*. The Homosexual Law Reform Society was described as "one of the more active legal aid groups" and Polak was quoted as saying, "Until recently, the only court cases we got involved in were the ones we couldn't avoid. . . . Now we are very much concerned with initiating litigation." HLRS's greatest success came in a New Jersey gay bar case in 1967. One year earlier, a gay magazine report about this case had predicted "a long drawn-out legal battle, culminating in a U.S. Supreme Court case." This was described as "unfortunate" for the bar, but "fortunate" for "the homosexual community," since "a favourable ruling by the U.S. Supreme Court . . . would firmly establish the homosexual's freedom of assembly in every state." The article also asserted that "the 'legalization' of gay bars would establish a precedent" and the case could be "as important to the homophile movement as the school-desegregation case was to the Negro rights movement." As it turns out, gay rights advocates won a qualified victory in the New Jersey Supreme Court, which effectively ended the litigation.

HLRS was less successful when it joined forces with the American Civil Liberties Union and lawyers affiliated with the American Committee for the Protection of the Foreign Born to defend a U.S. permanent resident subject to deportation. Clive Boutilier, a Canadian citizen who had lived as a legal resident in the United States since 1955, applied for U.S. citizenship in 1963. After he acknowledged that he had been arrested (though not convicted) on a sodomy charge in New York City in 1959, Boutilier was ordered deported by the Immigration and Naturalization Service. Under a U.S. law passed in the 1950s, aliens "afflicted with psychopathic personality" were excludable and deportable from the United States, and the INS interpreted this provision to apply to "homosexuals." In a 6-3 decision in 1967, the U.S. Supreme Court upheld the law and the INS's use of it, in part because Congress could classify homosexuals as psychopaths if it wished to do so and in part because Congress could order the exclusion and deportation of aliens with "characteristics" that were "forbidden."

Boutilier was by no means the gay movement's only significant setback in cases appealed to the Supreme Court in the 1960s. In various gay-related immigration, employment discrimination, obscenity, and sodomy cases, the Court either declined to accept the appeals for argument or issued summary dismissals. Meanwhile, concurring opinions in the 1965 *Griswold* birth control case referred to the ongoing legitimacy of laws against homosexuality and the majority opinion in the 1966 *Mishkin* obscenity case upheld a conviction based on materials "designed for and primarily disseminated to a clearly defined deviant sexual group." Nevertheless, the *Boutilier* decision was a uniquely devastating loss for the gay and lesbian rights movement. Not since the victory in *ONE* had the movement focused as much attention and as many resources on a Supreme Court case. Never before had the justices accepted a policy or practice that designated "homosexuals" as "psychopaths," with potentially huge ramifications for the rights of those classified as such. The setback was also a sustained one: for the next seventeen years, gay rights advocates failed to convince the Supreme Court to accept one of their cases for consideration.

In today's political context, there's much to be learned by revisiting the early years of gay and lesbian rights appeals to the Supreme Court. One lesson is the clear historical influence of the struggle for racial equality on the struggle for sexual equality. Other lessons relate to the reasons the early gay and lesbian rights movement identified the courts in general, and the Supreme Court in particular, as favored instruments of legal reform. Most movement leaders in the 1950s and 1960s did not think that their proposals for reform would be supported by popular or legislative majorities, but they viewed the courts as institutionally and politically positioned to stand up for minority rights and constitutional rights. On an institutional level, they knew that the Constitution and the Supreme Court were designed (in theory) to constrain the tyranny of popular and legislative majorities. On a political level, they knew that the Court of the 1950s and 1960s was dominated by moderates and liberals. They believed that timing was on their side. Decades later, with public support for same-sex marriage growing and with the Supreme Court still dominated (as it has been for the last forty years) by Republican appointees, it's not clear that we are in a similar moment today, though there may be reasons to be hopeful about the pivotal role that Justice Anthony Kennedy will likely play (which I plan to address in a forthcoming article).

There are other lessons to be learned about the promise and perils of seeking legal reform through Supreme Court decisions. On the one hand, gay and lesbian rights advocates were right when they argued in the 1950s and 1960s that Supreme Court decisions can be powerful instruments of legal reform, capable of nationalizing legal reforms that would otherwise face variable prospects across different state and local jurisdictions. On the other hand, the perils are painfully evident when we consider the failure of gay and lesbian rights advocates to have a case accepted for consideration by the Supreme Court for a generation after the devastating loss in the 1967 *Boutilier* case.

Justice Kennedy and the Future of Same-Sex Marriage

If and when the California same-sex marriage case (or a similar case) reaches the U.S. Supreme Court, the results may well depend on Justice Anthony Kennedy, a Californian appointed to the Court in the 1980s by Republican President (and former California Governor) Ronald Reagan. With four likely votes for and four likely votes against same-sex marriage, the Supreme Court decision may well depend on Kennedy's tiebreaking vote. If so, it will be a useful reminder that some of the divisions that threaten the unity of the Republican Party today—between moderates and conservatives, but also between social, economic, foreign policy, and libertarian conservatives—run right through the Republican majority on the Supreme Court. In fact, these divisions have been evident in the Republican majorities on the Court for more than forty years.

Predicting Justice Kennedy's vote with any degree of certainty is a risky game. Much will undoubtedly depend on the facts of the case and the litigation strategies used by the opposing sides, as well as the many other political, legal, social, and cultural factors that influence Supreme Court decisions. Kennedy's majority opinions in *Romer* (1996) and *Lawrence* (2003), while supportive of gay rights, can be read to suggest both positive and negative outcomes for proponents of same-sex

This essay was published originally on the *University of North Carolina Press Blog*, 8 Nov. 2010, http://uncpressblog.com/2010/11/08/justice-kennedy/.

marriage. But there may be useful clues in a case decided by the Court in 1989, just after Justice Kennedy was appointed.

In *Michael H.*, the Court ruled against a man seeking to establish paternity and gain the right to visit his biological daughter, whom he had fathered in an adulterous relationship with a married woman. According to the plurality opinion by Justice Antonin Scalia (and endorsed for the most part by three other justices), California law presumed that a child born to a married woman who lived with her husband was the husband's child. Noting that the only liberties protected by the Constitution were those that were "fundamental" and "traditionally protected by our society," Scalia emphasized "the historic respect—indeed, sanctity would not be too strong a term—traditionally accorded to the relationships that develop within the unitary family." A footnote explained that the "unitary family" was "typified, of course, by the marital family, but also includes the household of unmarried parents and their children."

Scalia's use of the concept of the "unitary family" and his inclusion of families made up of unmarried parents and their children are noteworthy. The origins of the term "unitary family" are not entirely clear, and Scalia did not reference any legal cases or scholarly works that discuss the concept. Historical scholarship on the social acceptance and legal rights of unmarried parents and cohabiting couples certainly might cast doubt on Scalia's claims about the traditional protections extended by society to the members of such families. At the very least, this seems a marked departure from the mode of legal reasoning commonly associated with Scalia, which as we will see defines "fundamental rights" in the narrowest possible terms. It's also seemingly at odds with the substantive decision in *Michael H.*, which emphasized marital rights. Nevertheless, four justices (including Kennedy) endorsed these conclusions, while a fifth, John Paul Stevens, concurred with the judgment because, in his view, the appellant had been given a fair opportunity to argue in court for his parental rights.

Michael H. continued a discussion that began in the 1986 *Bowers v. Hardwick* sodomy case about how the Court should identify which liberty or privacy interests were protected by the Constitution. In *Bowers*, the conservative majority had asked whether the Constitution conferred on homosexuals the fundamental right to engage in sodomy (and answered no). The dissenters had asked whether the Constitution recognized, as part of the long-recognized "right to be let alone," the right of consenting adults to make decisions about engaging in private sexual activity (and answered yes).

In *Michael H.*, all of the justices seemed to agree that it was important to consider which interests were historically protected and recognized as fundamental in the United States, but they disagreed on whether those interests should be defined in specific, narrow, and concrete terms or in general, broad, and abstract ones. Discussing *Bowers* and *Michael H.*, Scalia claimed in a footnote that "we refer to the most specific level at which a relevant tradition protecting, or denying protection to, the asserted right can be identified." For Scalia, just as the Court had asked in Bowers whether "homosexual sodomy" was traditionally protected, in *Michael H.* the Court asked whether "the rights of an adulterous natural father" were traditionally protected. Such rights were not traditionally protected, according to Scalia, and this was the basis for his decision. Significantly, only Justice William Rehnquist endorsed Scalia's footnote. Justices Sandra Day O'Connor and Anthony Kennedy agreed with all aspects of Scalia's opinion except this footnote, and they felt strongly enough about the footnote that they went to the trouble of distancing themselves from it and explaining their reasons for doing so.

Citing *Griswold v. Connecticut* (1965), *Eisenstadt v. Baird* (1972), and *Loving v. Virginia* (1967), O'Connor and Kennedy's concurring opinion argued that "on occasion the Court has characterized relevant traditions protecting asserted rights at levels of generality that might not be 'the most specific level' available." *Griswold* and *Eisenstadt* were important birth control precedents, and O'Connor and Kennedy presumably were concerned that Scalia's rule could have led to different outcomes in these two cases, but there are reasons to believe that they were even more concerned about *Loving*, the decision that overturned state bans on interracial marriage. They were apparently concerned that Scalia's reasoning could have led to a different result in *Loving*. In that case, Scalia's rule might have led the Court to ask whether the specific right to marry across racial lines, as opposed to the general right to marry, was traditionally protected in U.S. society. The answer might well have left interracial marriage bans in place.

In *Michael H.*, Justice William Brennan wrote a dissenting opinion that was endorsed by Justices Thurgood Marshall and Harry Blackmun. (Justice Byron White wrote a separate dissent.) Brennan criticized Scalia for identifying traditional rights in such narrow terms. Just as Blackmun's *Bowers* dissent had emphasized that the case concerned not the narrow issue of homosexual sodomy but the general issue of sexual privacy, Brennan argued that the core issue in *Michael H.* was not adulterous parenthood but parenthood more generally. Brennan also echoed the concerns expressed by O'Connor and Kennedy about what Scalia's reasoning would have meant for *Griswold*, *Loving*, and *Eisenstadt*.

In the same-sex marriage cases heading to the Supreme Court, both sides typically emphasize fundamental rights arguments. Supporters and opponents of same-sex marriage both invoke what they see as the fundamental right to marry, though they disagree about whether the right to marry should be conceptualized in historically specific, narrow, and concrete terms or in more general, broad, and abstract terms. For opponents of same-sex marriage, the right to marry is specifically, narrowly, and concretely heterosexual. For supporters, the right to marry is more general, broad, and abstract and it is capacious enough to permit or require the legalization of same-sex marriage. If *Michael H.* provides us with any clues about what Justice Kennedy will do when and if the Court considers California's Proposition 8 or the U.S. federal government's Defense of Marriage Act, supporters of same-sex marriage may have reasons to be hopeful.

Five Myths about *Roe v. Wade*

On 22 January 1973, the U.S. Supreme Court announced its decision in *Roe v. Wade*, the abortion rights case that culminated in one of the most controversial legal rulings in the country's history. Forty years later, numerous myths continue to circulate about the contents and meanings of *Roe*. Here are five of the most significant:

Myth #1: *Roe* endorsed abortion on demand.

The Supreme Court's majority opinion in *Roe*, authored by Justice Harry Blackmun and supported by seven of the nine justices, recognized three important interests at stake in decisions about abortion: (1) the privacy rights of the pregnant woman (often problematically called "the mother" by the Court); (2) the state's interest in the health of the pregnant woman; and (3) the state's interest in what the Court termed "potential life," which was compromise language that avoided the problems associated with other obvious choices such as "unborn child," "life," or "embryo and fetus." In some parts of the Court's opinion, the justices mentioned a fourth important interest, that of medical doctors, and in several passages the Court privileged the decision-making of doctors rather than the women under their care, but ultimately the ruling

This essay was published originally on the *University of North Carolina Press Blog*, 22 Jan. 2013, http://uncpressblog.com/2013/01/22/marc-stein-five-myths-about-roe-v-wade/.

focused on the woman's privacy rights, the state's interest in promoting public health, and the state's interest in protecting "potential life."

This became the basis for the Court's complex trimester framework, which rejected both restrictive abortion bans and liberalized abortion on demand. According to the Court, in the first trimester, when abortion procedures are relatively safe and when the "potential life" is more potential than life, the pregnant woman's reproductive rights are preeminent and therefore the states may not impose major restrictions on abortion. For the Court, the second trimester is different in that abortion procedures become somewhat more dangerous and the "potential life" is closer to "life." On this basis, the Court ruled that states may regulate but not ban second-trimester abortions (for example, by requiring that they be performed in specific types of medical facilities). According to the Court, in the third trimester, when abortion procedures become more complicated and when the fetus is often able to survive outside the pregnant woman's body, the state's interests in promoting the health of the woman and protecting the "potential life" become sufficiently compelling that more state restrictions on abortion are constitutionally permissible. Significantly, the Court ruled that even in the third trimester, abortions could not be banned when they were necessary to preserve the life or health of the pregnant woman.

The decision in *Roe* thus satisfied neither opponents of all abortions nor advocates of abortion on demand. This was a compromise ruling. To be sure, *Roe* liberalized abortion law in the United States, but U.S. Americans need only look north to Canada, which more fully decriminalized abortion in the 1980s, to understand that *Roe*, for better or for worse, did not recognize a legal right to abortion on demand.

Myth #2: *Roe* rejected traditional restrictions and religious prohibitions on abortion.

Blackmun devoted a substantial part of his Supreme Court opinion to a broad historical overview of the legal status of abortion in the West, which led him to conclude that the restrictive abortion laws under consideration by the justices were "of relatively recent vintage" and "not of ancient or even of common-law origin." They were derived, he argued, from state statutes that were first enacted in the second half of the nineteenth century. English common law, for example, did not criminalize abortions before "quickening," which effectively meant that abortions in the early months of pregnancies were legal. English common law was the basis for most U.S. state laws on abortion until the mid-nineteenth century. This led Blackmun to the conclusion that "at common law, at the time of the adoption of our Constitution, and throughout the major portion of the 19th century, abortion was viewed with less disfavor than under most American statutes currently in effect."

The Supreme Court's decision also addressed religious perspectives on abortion, noting the "wide divergence of thinking on this most sensitive and difficult question" and specifically referring to substantial Jewish and Protestant denominational support for "the view that life does not begin until live birth" and the notion that abortion is "a matter for the conscience of the individual and her family." Religious opponents of abortion, Blackmun was reminding his readers, did not have a monopoly on religious opinions. For better or for worse, *Roe* was aligned with traditional and religious support for abortion rights in the United States.

Myth #3: *Roe* was a strongly feminist decision.

For decades, Roe has been celebrated and criticized as a feminist ruling that was based on the Supreme Court's support for women's rights. Blackmun's majority opinion, however, had very little to say about women's rights (beyond abortion rights) and it avoided most of the feminist arguments made by the lawyers who litigated the case. In several passages that addressed the doctors who performed abortions, Blackmun emphasized "his" rights to practice medicine more than the rights of the pregnant woman. In one, the Court concluded that during the first trimester "the attending physician, in consultation with the patient, is free to determine, without regulation by the State, that, in his medical judgment, the patient's pregnancy should be terminated." Summarizing its findings, the Court declared that in this stage of pregnancy "the abortion decision and its effectuation must be left to the medical judgment of the pregnant woman's attending physician." In this formulation, the pregnant woman was not even given a consultative role; the decision seemed as if it were the doctor's alone to make. More generally, the Court set aside the arguments of those in *Roe* who emphasized that abortion rights were necessary to secure women's autonomy, empowerment, and equality.

In subsequent years, as *Roe* was attacked by antifeminists and as Blackmun defended his work, he depicted his majority opinion as far more feminist than it was. As journalist and biographer Linda Greenhouse has written in *Becoming Justice Blackmun*, "The reality of Roe itself, the extent to which its author's focus was on doctors rather than on women, was largely lost to myth and the mists of memory." *Roe* certainly can be interpreted as a ruling that was influenced by feminist activism and that had feminist effects. For better or for worse, however, the ruling itself was based on other types of arguments.

Myth #4: *Roe* recognized constitutional rights of sexual privacy.

Supporters and opponents of *Roe* have had good reasons to depict *Roe* as a sexual privacy decision, the former to defend it and the latter to attack it. In that context, it may come as a surprise to many that the decision in *Roe* had almost nothing to say about sexual privacy and never endorsed the concept. *Roe* was a decision about reproductive rights, not sexual rights.

In one passage, for example, Blackmun's opinion noted that the Court's precedents had made it clear that the right to privacy, which was based in part on the Constitution's references to freedom and liberty, had important applications in cases concerning marriage, procreation, contraception, family relationships, child rearing, and education. Now the Court was declaring that this right was "broad enough" to encompass abortion. Notably the majority did not include sex or sexuality on this list. Blackmun also cautioned, "It is not clear to us that the claim asserted by some amici that one has an unlimited right to do with one's body as one pleases bears a close relationship to the right of privacy previously articulated in the Court's decision." Elsewhere in the Court's opinion, Blackmun noted that Roe's lawyers had argued that the constitutional basis of the right to terminate a pregnancy was "the concept of personal 'liberty' embodied in the Fourteenth Amendment's Due Process Clause" or the "personal, marital, familial, and sexual privacy said to be protected by the Bill of Rights or its penumbras." This passage has been used by many journalists and commentators to suggest that the decision in *Roe* recognized a right of sexual privacy, but here Blackmun was describing the arguments, not announcing the Court's conclusions. When Blackmun's opinion later presented the Court's views on the nature of privacy, it referred to "marriage" and "family" but not sex.

What about the Court's conclusions about the relationship between laws on abortion and laws on sex, which in the 1970s included laws against adultery, cohabitation, fornication, and sodomy? According to Blackmun, it had been argued by some that anti-abortion laws such as the Texas statute challenged in *Roe* "were the product of a Victorian social concern to discourage illicit sexual conduct." This idea was based on the notion that legal restrictions on abortion discouraged non-marital sex by foreclosing the option of ending an unwanted pregnancy. Blackmun responded that Texas had not made this claim and "no court or commentator has taken the argument seriously." Nevertheless, he observed that Roe's lawyers and friends of the court had asserted that "this is not a proper state purpose at all" and argued that "if it were, the Texas statutes are overbroad . . . since the law fails to distinguish between married and unwed mothers." Here, too, the Court was describing arguments, not announcing conclusions. At most, the Court was suggesting that it did not see a relationship between laws against abortion and laws against sex, but it was not endorsing the notion of a constitutional right to sexual privacy. Over the course of the last forty years, the media and the public have come to believe that *Roe* was a sexual privacy decision, but the Court did not recognize a constitutional right of sexual privacy until the *Lawrence* decision of 2003.

Myth #5: *Roe* was only supported by big-government Democratic liberals, and it was invariably opposed by small-government Republican conservatives.

For decades, Republican conservatives have successfully presented themselves as opponents and Democratic liberals as supporters of big government. This has been so effective in the court of public opinion that Democrats often take great pains to emphasize that they, too, are opponents of big government. Only occasionally do dissident voices break through, as is the case with historian Steve Conn's recent book *To Promote the General Welfare: The Case for Big Government* (2012). In truth, both major political parties support big government. Most Republican conservatives support a strong role for the federal government in national defense, immigration control, and law and order. In the last several decades, most have favored substantial government restrictions on homosexuality, obscenity, and sex education. Today, most Republican conservatives support the Defense of Marriage Act, which dictates whose marriages are recognized by the U.S. federal government. Conservative Republicans who oppose *Roe* because they support major restrictions on abortion are advocates of big government.

In fact, while support for abortion rights is stronger among Democrats than Republicans, many Republicans support abortion rights. Abortion was not mentioned in the Republican Party presidential platform of 1972 and in the 1970s a significant number of Republican politicians supported abortion rights. Roe's primary author, Blackmun, was appointed by Republican President Richard Nixon. Of the seven justices who endorsed Blackmun's majority opinion in *Roe*, four were appointed by Republican presidents, three by Democratic ones. Of the two dissenters, one was appointed by a Republican, one by a Democrat. In the 1992 *Casey* decision, three Republican appointees, Justices Kennedy, O'Connor, and Souter, reaffirmed the central holding of *Roe*. From 1975 until 2009, the Supreme Court consistently had seven or eight Republican appointees and just one or two Democratic ones. For more than three decades, Republican appointees had an overwhelming majority of seats on the Supreme Court, yet the justices did not overturn *Roe*. Republicans, including some who support big government, some who criticize big government, and many who do both, have joined together with Democrats and independents to support abortion rights.

The popular press bears partial responsibility for these and many other myths about *Roe v. Wade*. In her 1992 autobiography, Sarah Weddington, the lawyer who defended abortion rights in *Roe*, recalled that in 1973 she was "disappointed that so few of the journalists described the legal arguments accurately." In 1979, Chief Justice Warren Burger expressed concern that lower court judges "might be misreading" recent decisions by the Supreme Court and suggested that the misrepresentations of Washington reporters might be responsible for this. A few days later, Justice Lewis Powell reportedly stated that the Court was "totally dependent on the media to interpret what we do" since "that's all the public knows about us." Unfortunately, he observed, "sometimes, 'under the constraint of deadlines, we find that what is written appears to bear little relationship to what we did decide.'" In 1991, Justice William Brennan told reporter Nat Hentoff that he was disappointed by press coverage of the Court and specifically by "the inaccuracy of the reporting and the placing of decisions out of context." Weddington and Brennan did not exactly see eye to eye with Burger and Powell on many issues, but they all expressed concern about how the media reported on Supreme Court decisions.

Notwithstanding the validity of these concerns, there is another useful way to think about the myths that surround *Roe*. For the last several years, an influential group of scholars has been discussing, developing, and debating the concept of popular constitutionalism, which holds that the meanings of the U.S. Constitution are generated in the public sphere and not just in the text of the Constitution or the decisions of the Supreme Court. Extending this notion, we might also say that the meanings of U.S. Supreme Court decisions are generated in the public sphere and not just in the texts of the Court's rulings or the justices' subsequent depictions of their earlier work. Instead of discounting the myths that I have discussed, we might better be served by asking questions about the purposes they serve and the effects of these myths in the past, present, and future.

Refreshing Abominations

An Open Letter to Anthony Kennedy

Dear Tony,

As I listened to the Supreme Court's oral arguments in the same-sex marriage case a few days ago, I began to worry about the questions that you and the other justices asked and the answers you received about the history of marriage over the last millennium. Most of the questions and answers began with the assumption that marriage, always and everywhere over the past 1,000 years, has only joined together men and women. In the discussions that ensued, there were many good points raised about the ways in which marriage has changed significantly over the course of history, touching especially on the legalization of interracial marriage, the prohibition of polygamous unions, and the transformation of gender hierarchies. It's good that these issues were discussed and highlighted, but I'm concerned that there were other relevant questions about the history of marriage that were not asked and answered during the oral arguments. I worry especially about some of the false assertions that were made about the essential and definitional features of marriage across centuries and centuries of human history. So I'm offering you a few questions that could and should have been asked and hoping that experts on the history of marriage might help the Supreme Court find useful answers.

This essay was published originally on OutHistory, 4 May 2015, http://outhistory.org /blog/refreshing-abominations-an-open-letter-to-anthony-kennedy/.

(1) Insofar as marriage has meaning as a legal institution, a religious practice, a community ritual, and a type of personal relationship, when, where, and why have same-sex couples married over the last millennium? When same-sex marriage has not been legally recognized, has it existed as a religious practice, a community ritual, or a type of personal relationship? To take several examples, what do we know about women who formed "Boston marriages" in the nineteenth century? Is there evidence that same-sex couples engaged in wedding rituals and marriage ceremonies in the early and middle decades of the twentieth century? Does any of this matter in your consideration of the definition of marriage?

(2) When, where, and why did marriage become a legally recognized institution? After this occurred, how did the state address marriages that were not legally recognized? When and where did the state recognize common-law marriages? How did European countries and American colonies with established religions (typically Catholic or Protestant) address marriages that were performed outside of the established church? In colonial and other contexts, how did the state address marriages that formed in the absence of recognized legal or religious authorities? How did U.S. and state laws address Native American marriages and marriages that had occurred on land that the United States conquered and claimed? How did U.S. and state laws address slave marriages before the Civil War? After slavery was abolished (except as punishment for crime), how did the United States and the states address pre–Civil War slave marriages? Why do we refer to frontier, Native American, and slave marriages as "marriages" if they were not legally recognized under U.S. and state law? Do we do so because these marriages were meaningful to the marital partners and to the communities and cultures in which they took place?

(3) When, where, and why did U.S. or state officials engage in examinations and investigations to determine that two individuals who wished to marry were "male" and "female"? How were such examinations and investigations conducted? In marriage practices, did biological males ever present themselves as women and did biological females ever present themselves as men? What happened when this occurred? Do we know how frequently this occurred? Did the couples involved think of themselves as "man" and "woman"? Did intersex people ever marry? How did the state handle their marriages?

(4) When did states first pass laws that explicitly restricted marriage to one man and one woman? Why were these laws passed? Before these

laws were passed, did the states decline to recognize same-sex marriages because of explicit legal restrictions on marriage, because of common-law definitions, or because of longstanding social and cultural assumptions about marriage?

(5) What religions have recognized same-sex unions, partnerships, and marriages? When, where, and why did they do so?

(6) What do we know about the history of same-sex marriage as a community ritual and a personal relationship? Have same-sex couples ever referred to themselves as married? Have they ever been referred to by others as married? Have U.S. subcultures ever recognized same-sex marriages? Which subcultures? Have same-sex marriages ever been recognized in meaningful ways by people inside and outside of the cultures and communities in which these marriages occurred? Why or why not?

(7) If we use the 14th Amendment's equal protection clause to invalidate state restrictions on same-sex marriage, what do we do about equal protection claims by single people who suffer from discrimination based on marital status?

I hope you find good answers to these questions, Tony. By the way, please thank Antonin for inspiring what may be generations of political groups, sports teams, drag performers, and specialty cocktails that will be named Refreshing Abominations.

PART SEVEN

Exhibiting Queer History

On 19 December 2016, 304 of the 538 presidential electors of the United States, who themselves had been elected by voters in fifty states and the District of Columbia, selected Republican Party candidate Donald J. Trump, a wealthy businessman and reality-television actor, as the next US president. The results were certified by the US Congress, with Vice President Joseph Biden presiding, on 6 January 2017. Trump had campaigned as a nationalist, nativist, and critic of scientific expertise, mainstream media, and the "deep state." Voters in thirty states apparently preferred Trump to Democratic Party candidate Hillary Clinton, a former First Lady, US senator, and secretary of state who would have been the country's first female president. Two weeks after Congress certified the results, Trump was inaugurated. One day later, on 21 January, White House Press Secretary Sean Spicer made patently false and hyperbolic claims about the number of people at Trump's inauguration. Trying to defend Spicer on NBC television's *Meet the Press* program on 22 January, Counselor to the President Kellyanne Conway responded to host Chuck Todd's aggressive questioning by noting that Spicer had not made a false statement; he had presented "alternative facts."

Since that time, the concept of "alternative facts" has been deployed by supporters and critics of Trump. In debates about the science of climate change, foreign interference in US elections, the global coronavirus pandemic, and numerous other subjects, many Trump supporters have used "alternative facts" to challenge the conclusions of experts in a broad range of fields. Meanwhile, Trump and his supporters have complained about "fake news," which apparently does not meet their standards for accuracy. Many Trump critics have responded by identifying the concept of "alternative facts" and the attacks on "fake news" as emblematic of deeply troubling developments in the Trump administration, the Republican Party, and the politics of conservatism, which they accuse of discounting, disregarding, and disrespecting science, knowledge, and truth.

All of this has created a conundrum for scholars in the humanities, social sciences, and natural sciences. In some contexts, of course, "alternative facts" are not factual at all; this was the case for Spicer's claims about Trump's inauguration and many of the president's statements about climate change, the coronavirus pandemic, and voting irregularities. In other contexts, however, the concept of "alternative facts" is compatible with commonly accepted ideas about the existence of conflicting evidence, the validity of subjective interpretation, and the possibility of multiple truths. In the Trump and post-Trump eras, many scholars have retreated to safe ground by insisting on singular facts and verifiable truths, rather than trying to defend more vulnerable terrain where alternative facts, conflicting interpretations, and multiple truths can be considered. But this risks returning us to discredited ideas about empiricism and objectivity. It additionally has the potential to privilege academic, disciplinary, professional, and university-based knowledge production over the production of knowledge in community-based settings and the broader public sphere. It also risks erasing all that we have learned about the uses and abuses of fact-based knowledge in the production of inequality and injustice.[1]

Historians routinely distinguish between facts found in primary sources (artifacts from the past) and interpretations presented in secondary texts (scholarship about the past). This can be useful, but only if it is recognized that facts in primary sources are themselves interpretive and interpretations in secondary texts often present themselves as factual. In both senses, historians have to wrestle with "alternative facts"—primary sources might contain conflicting information and secondary texts might offer conflicting interpretations. In "fact," if we revisit the contentious exchange between postmodern theorist Kellyanne Conway and scientific empiricist Chuck Todd, it is worth noting that primary sources routinely offer alternative facts about crowd size. I recall disputes about the number of people who participated in the many marches that I attended in the 1980s and 1990s, when activists routinely complained about undercounting. The problem with the formulations of Conway and her defenders is less that the notion of "alternative facts" is ridiculous and more that there was so little evidentiary basis for Trump's, Spicer's, and Conway's claims.

In scholarly publications, historians typically privilege primary sources whose facts are aligned with their interpretations, though they might also address anomalies, contradictions, exceptions, and inconsistencies found in other sources. Most historians would argue that their primary sources are aligned with their interpretations because their interpretations are based on their sources; the disciplinary ideal is not to start with an interpretation and then prove it, but rather to start with the evidence and then build an interpretation. Historians, however, typically only present short excerpts of or paraphrased summaries of primary sources; we try to strike fine balances between "showing" and "telling" our audiences what our evidence says. One of the functions of scholarly peer review in the humanities, commonly expected for university press books and scholarly journals, is to catch gaps and errors in the use of primary sources. In most historical subfields, however, peer reviewers are not expected to be familiar with the archival sources used by the researchers whose work they are reviewing. After all, one of the things most highly valued in the discipline is the discovery of unique archival materials; in contrast to scholarship in disciplines like literature, philosophy, and religion, historical scholarship rarely relies heavily on widely available and widely read canonical texts. In public history, scholarly peer review is less typically expected, which means fewer checks on the use of primary sources, but even in scholarly publications, peer review does not and cannot ensure that historians are exercising good judgment in their selection and interpretation of primary sources.

Historians do have ways to make their primary sources available to broader publics. Before the internet, there were scholarly editions of important texts, edited anthologies of primary sources, published transcripts of oral histories, and microform reproductions of historical documents. The Oral History Association mentions in its "best practices" guide that "whenever possible and/or practical, oral histories—either individual or many within a project—should be deposited in a repository such as a library or archive that has the capacity to ensure long-term and professionally managed preservation and access."[2] In the internet age, digital history projects have increased public access to primary sources, but these can be highly selective and many are not open access.[3] Moreover, when historians share their primary sources in one or more of these formats, they are taking risks. For example, their work in finding, transcribing, editing, and curating historical materials often goes uncredited. In addition, this type of work is rarely recognized and rewarded in academic contexts; it generally does not count much in decisions about hiring, tenure, and promotion. Sharing primary sources also can provide materials that others will use to critique one's work. In some senses, this is comparable to the "discovery" process in legal contexts, where the opposing sides are required to provide evidence to their antagonists. In history, we are not expected or required to share all of our evidence with our audiences, but doing so can be beneficial. Historians who share their primary sources can take pride in their discoveries, encourage readers to engage with their interpretations, incite interest in other researchers, and participate in the further democratization of historical inquiry.

None of this should be taken to imply that historians who share their primary sources are simply presenting the facts. Some facts are lost because they do not leave traces in archival artifacts. Power, politics, and factors such as citizenship, class, (dis)ability, gender, language, race, religion, and sexuality influence whose records are preserved, saved, maintained, and archived. Censorship and repression can erase and suppress some types of evidence; this is a distinctly significant problem in queer history. Moreover, historians who share their primary sources make choices about which materials to present; how to define the scopes of their projects; how to introduce and organize the materials; and how, where, and when to present them. Just as good historians are expected to work actively to interpret their primary sources, good users of primary source exhibits work actively to interpret the materials they encounter.

In LGBT studies, one of the most important digital history projects has been OutHistory, launched by Jonathan Ned Katz in 2008. As noted in the introduction to part 1, Katz established OutHistory as a digital platform that would promote active public participation in LGBTQ history research and education. Today it features hundreds of online exhibits and thousands of archival documents. In 2010, OutHistory won the inaugural Allan Bérubé Prize, presented by the Committee on LGBT History for outstanding work in public or community-based LGBTQ history. One of the hallmarks of OutHistory is its commitment to an open access philosophy, which stands in contrast to subscription- and fee-based digital history projects. Unfortunately, OutHistory's limited funding has contributed to some of its weaknesses—infrequent technological upgrades, problems with website usability, and dependence on unpaid labor by content providers.[4]

Since 2010, I have produced five digital history exhibits for Out-History; since 2017, I have been one of the website's contributing editors. The first of my exhibits provided a platform to share my Philadelphia-based oral histories (see chapter 26). Three subsequent exhibits focused on important episodes in LGBT history—the Dewey's sit-in of 1965, the Annual Reminder demonstrations of 1965–69, and *Boutilier v. Immigration and Naturalization Service* in 1967. In all three of these projects, the exhibits were timed to coincide with fiftieth-anniversary commemorations.[5] My fifth OutHistory exhibit, produced in collaboration with six York University PhD students, was titled "U.S. Homophile Internationalism"; it addressed American LGBT magazine representations of multiple global regions, primarily in the Global South, in the years from 1953 to 1964 (see chapter 27).

In my digital history work, I have been challenged by some of the distinctive aspects of projects that present primary historical materials on public history platforms. In the discipline of history, we are encouraged to offer bold, original, and strong interpretations. In projects of this nature, however, one of the goals is to encourage other people to develop their own interpretations; the primary sources require introduction and contextualization, but too much analysis by curators can discourage and influence the conclusions that others reach. This is not an entirely unique problem; museum curators regularly confront similar problems when they consider the signage to be used in their exhibits; do they want visitors to spend their time looking at the objects on display or do they want them to spend their time reading the accompanying texts? As some of my OutHistory project introductions demonstrate, I have sometimes favored a minimalist approach, but in the examples reprinted here I provided more substantial guidance.

Another challenge takes us back to the problems of "alternative facts." All of my OutHistory exhibits have included "alternative facts," "fake news," and problematic information. Some oral history narrators, for example, misdate the developments they discuss; some media articles present factually incorrect information; some primary sources include language that has changed in meaning or usage; some materials mischaracterize people's genders, races, and sexual orientations. All of these items also can be racist, sexist, and anti-LGBT. In a primary source exhibit, it is theoretically possible to "correct" or call attention to these "mistakes," but this might be at odds with the point of

presenting historical materials in formats that are as close to the original as is possible. It also can be disrespectful to oral history narrators
and disempowering to new historians. In my primary source exhibits,
I instead have tried to guide my readers by emphasizing the importance
of analysis and interpretation.

I have been pleased, disappointed, and surprised by the results of my
work on online exhibits. I am pleased that scholars, students, librarians, archivists, and journalists have used my primary sources, especially in the case of the oral histories and most frequently in the case
of Asian American gay liberationist Kiyoshi Kuromiya.[6] My digital history projects have been cited and used in historical landmark nominations, biographical studies, legal briefs, and museum exhibits. On the
more negative side, some of the materials in my exhibits have been used
without credit or citation. Some have been minimally used, especially
in the case of the homophile internationalism project. I hoped that the
exhibits would be more fully utilized for teaching high school, college,
and university students about the craft of history and the complexities
of the LGBT past, but that does not seem to have occurred. Some of the
exhibits have not reduced the frequency of historical misrepresentations
for events such as the Dewey's sit-in and the Annual Reminders. On
balance, however, I continue to see immense potential in queer history
projects that exhibit primary sources to large public audiences.

Chapter 26 reprints the introduction to my oral history project. In
1993 and 1994, I interviewed thirty-seven people for my PhD dissertation; in 1995, 1996, and 1997, I interviewed six more. In 2010, I began
to publish edited transcripts of the oral histories on OutHistory; I subsequently added more transcripts, most recently in 2021, and added visual
supplements when possible. At present, my OutHistory exhibit includes
thirty-five transcripts; I hope to publish the remainder (minus one from
a narrator who asked me not to do so) in the future. My 2010 introduction does not address two issues that I would like to highlight here.
First, there are distinct ethical issues involved in sharing oral history
interviews that were completed before most of us understood key features of the internet. In the 1990s, neither I nor my narrators knew that
my oral histories might someday be available to billions of people on a
public platform. While my narrators signed legal releases that give me
broad rights to use the interviews, ethical considerations have led me to
proceed cautiously; as of now, I only have provided transcripts for narrators who have died, have consented, or are unreachable. This relates
to a second issue. While many digital oral history projects include sound

recordings, mine does not. Partly this relates to my own technological limitations, but I also am concerned about providing sound recordings for narrators who asked me to use pseudonyms. Since voices are commonly identifiable, I thought it best to leave the audiotapes in an archive and provide transcripts online. I have donated the audiotapes to the John J. Wilcox LGBT Archives at the William Way Community Center in Philadelphia, though I retain possession of the remaining tapes awaiting final transcription and publication.

Chapter 27 reprints the introduction to my OutHistory exhibit "U.S. Homophile Internationalism," which I produced in collaboration with six York University graduate students in 2015. Funded by a grant from the Social Sciences and Humanities Research Council of Canada and focused on the 1950s and 1960s, the exhibit featured hundreds of US homophile magazine representations of Africa; Asia and the Pacific; Canada; Latin America and the Caribbean; the Middle East; and Russia, the Soviet Union, and Eastern Europe. In working on this exhibit with my collaborators, I became keenly aware of the challenges of online digital history exhibits that aim to promote active audience engagement: in our introductions, we restrained ourselves from doing too much of the interpretive work that we wanted our users to do. Because we all wanted to offer more in-depth scholarly analyses of the materials presented in our exhibit, we later worked together on a special 2017 issue of the *Journal of Homosexuality*.[7]

Chapter 28, "'Black Lesbian in White America': Interviewing Anita Cornwell," is a lightly edited transcript of my 2017 interview with Callie Hitchcock, host of the *Lesbian Testimony* podcast, a project of the Archives of Lesbian Oral Testimony (ALOT). Founded in 2010 by El Chenier at Simon Fraser University in British Columbia, Canada, ALOT describes itself as a project that "digitizes and makes available online oral histories and testimony of same-sex and same-gender attracted women, inclusive of Two Spirit, queer, bisexual, and lesbian women, transmen, and others." When ALOT approached me about doing an interview, I recommended that we focus on my 1993 oral history with Anita Cornwell, author of *Black Lesbian in White America* (1983). This was partly because she was such an interesting narrator but also because my conversation with her raises a set of useful questions about oral history methodologies and queer public histories.

Introduction to the Philadelphia LGBT History Project

In 1992, when I was a Ph.D. history student at the University of Pennsylvania, I began work on my doctoral dissertation, which I decided would focus on the history of relationships between lesbians and gay men in Philadelphia from the 1940s to the 1970s. Much of my research consisted of searching for references to same-sex sexuality in Philadelphia (and other) newspapers and magazines; reading the gay and lesbian newsletters, magazines, and newspapers that began to be published in the 1950s and 1960s; looking for references to Philadelphia gay and lesbian bars and other meeting places in old gay bar guides; and examining local, state, and federal government documents that touched on the lives of lesbians and gay men in Philadelphia. I also made use of the taped and videotaped oral histories that local activist, journalist, writer, and archivist Tommi Avicolli Mecca had given to the Philadelphia Lesbian and Gay Archives. In 1993, I began a series of oral history interviews of my own, most of which I completed before I finished my 1994 Ph.D. dissertation ("The City of Sisterly and Brotherly Loves: The Making of Lesbian and Gay Movements in Greater Philadelphia, 1945–1972"). Over the next few years, I did several more interviews before finishing *City of Sisterly and Brotherly Loves: Lesbian and Gay Philadelphia,*

This essay, which accompanied an OutHistory exhibit, was published originally in Jan. 2010; it was revised slightly in Sep. 2013 and Nov. 2014, http://outhistory.org/exhibits /show/philadelphia-lgbt-interviews/introduction.

1945–1972, published by the University of Chicago Press in 2000 and, in a second edition, by Temple University Press in 2004.

Before conducting my interviews, I learned a great deal about oral history methodology by reading scholarly books that made use of oral histories, talking with senior scholars who did interviews as part of their research, and visiting the Columbia Oral History Office, which provided me with a set of helpful articles and guides. As I note in my book, I interviewed a total of forty-three people, twenty-four of whom were men and nineteen of whom were women. One of the men and one of the women identified themselves to me as straight; I interviewed the former because he was a lawyer for a leading Philadelphia gay activist in the 1960s (who had subsequently died) and the latter because she owned and managed a gay bar. Of the forty-three, ten were born in the 1910s and 1920s, fifteen in the 1930s, and eighteen in the 1940s and early 1950s. One identified as Cuban American, one as Asian American, eight as African American or Black, and thirty-four (including the Latina) as Euro-American or white. As I observe in my book (page 20), "while 27% of Philadelphians and 16% of Greater Philadelphians were designated 'non-white' by the census of 1960, 21% of the lesbian and gay narrators would be similarly categorized."

I identified individuals willing to be interviewed in multiple ways: through gay and lesbian newspaper and newsletter articles, letters, and advertisements about my project (with contact information provided); through my work as a volunteer with the Philadelphia Gay and Lesbian Library and Archives and my involvement in various LGBT, AIDS, and queer activist groups; through my efforts to contact publicly visible gay and lesbian activists from the period I was studying; and through word of mouth and the assistance of mutual friends and acquaintances. I had particularly close connections to two of my lesbian narrators: I had lived with one in a West Philadelphia group house several years earlier and the other was the longtime partner of my Ph.D. supervisor.

My goal was to interview a broad cross-section of gay and lesbian Philadelphians, roughly approximating Philadelphia's ethnoracial demographics, aiming for equal numbers of men and women, finding members of different age and generational cohorts, including people with diverse class backgrounds and material circumstances, and ensuring good representation of both activists and non-activists. At an early stage of my work, I realized that if I interviewed the first individuals who volunteered, I would end up with a group of oral history narrators who were predominantly white middle-class gay men who became active in the gay community in the late 1960s and early 1970s. Concerned about what this would mean for my study, I began declining offers of assistance by potential oral history narrators who had these characteristics and searching more actively for other types of narrators.

There are ongoing debates and discussions by those interested in oral history about the importance and the significance of personal and political disclosure by interviewers, in both the interview process and in published work that uses oral histories. I certainly believe that my social location—as a white, gay-identified, middle-class, Jewish, Ivy League graduate student and graduate—influenced my easier access to white middle-class gay male narrators who became active in the gay community in the late 1960s and early 1970s. So did my age and generation; I was born in 1963, which meant that my youngest narrators were approximately a decade older than I was while my oldest ones were nearly forty years older. All of these factors influenced the content of the interviews as well, as did the fact that I was born and bred in New York, went to college in Connecticut, and lived for four years after graduating from college in Boston, which meant that I was a relative newcomer to Philadelphia when these interviews were conducted (having moved there in 1989). But the nature of that "influence" is not always as straightforward as it might seem. For instance, while I often felt quicker rapport with my Jewish and my activist narrators, I also often developed quicker rapport with my lesbian, as opposed to my gay, narrators, which replicated patterns in my social life.

One of the most difficult issues I faced in the interview process was how to handle disclosure about my gay identity and my sexual history. During this period of my life, I identified strongly as gay. I began to have sex with men in the early 1980s, came out as gay in the mid-1980s, worked as the coordinating editor of Boston's *Gay Community News* in the late 1980s, and intended to focus my research on gay and lesbian history when I began graduate school in 1989. All of that said, I also had a long history of having sexual relationships with women as well, and my primary (though open) relationship from 1991 to 1994 (when many of my interviews were conducted) was with a woman (who identified as "not straight"). I was quite conflicted about whether to disclose my heterosexual relationship and history to my narrators and consulted widely with oral history experts and academic colleagues, whose advice varied considerably. On the one hand, the interviews were not (primarily) about me and some of the people I asked for advice argued that my identity and my history were irrelevant. On the other hand,

I thought it was likely that most of my oral history narrators would assume that I was gay, either because they had encountered me in contexts where most people were gay or because the common assumption in the 1990s (and to some extent still today) was that straight people were not interested or would not pursue research projects in gay and lesbian history. I was concerned that some of those who assumed that I was gay (which I regarded as a correct assumption) and assumed that I only had sex with men (which was not correct) might not want to talk with me, or might talk with me differently, if they knew about my past sexual history and my current primary sexual relationship. In the end, I decided that before the taped component of the interview began, I would make it my practice to make clear that my narrators could ask me anything they wished about my personal or professional life if they wanted to do so before the taped part of the interview began. I typically repeated this offer more than once and I committed myself to revealing my heterosexual history if there was a question that even remotely related to this subject. Only rarely did my narrators ask me anything after I offered to answer their questions, and even more rarely (fewer than five times) did they ask a question that led me to reveal my history of sexual relationships with women. No one withdrew from the interview process or expressed concern about this. I did not notice a difference (which does not mean there wasn't a difference) in the contents of the interviews based on whether my heterosexual history was discussed before the taped part of the interview began.

In almost every case, I initially made arrangements via telephone for when and where the interview would take place. Most of the interviews took place in Greater Philadelphia, but one took place in central Pennsylvania, three in California, one in Greater Boston, and three in New York City. I indicated that the interview would likely last two to three hours (except for the one with Richard Schlegel, who was enthusiastic about doing a longer interview) and that I had been told that it was best to interview people in locations where they felt most comfortable, which was typically in their homes. Most of the interviews took place in the narrators' homes, but several took place elsewhere. There was only one instance in which I was concerned about my personal safety in a potential narrator's home. This was in Philadelphia and there was something about the initial telephone conversation that gave me pause. This was the only case in which I made a prior arrangement with my roommate to call her about thirty minutes after my scheduled arrival at this man's house. When I called, I happily reported that all was well, though ultimately this narrator did not agree to be interviewed on tape.

In our telephone conversation, I introduced the five or six topics that I would be interested in covering (including coming out, participation in gay/lesbian cultural life, and involvement in gay/lesbian activism) and emphasized that we could also cover other topics if they wished. I had been told that it was best to not build the interview around a detailed and long list of specific questions but rather to outline a set of broad topics and then engage in rather open-ended conversations about each of the topics. I also explained in our telephone conversation that I would be asking them to sign a standard permission form (which I produced based on a template provided by the Columbia Oral History Office) that would give us both rights to use the interview material until their death and then the rights would be mine alone. (Only one person added a condition to the permission form, stipulating that I would need to ask permission to use specific quotations from our interview in published work.) I noted as well that I intended to deposit the interview tapes after I finished my research to an appropriate library or archives (which I have not yet done). I explained that they could choose to have me use a pseudonym and that they could select the pseudonym if they wished. I also told them that my hope was to produce a complete transcript of the interview, which I then would share with them. If they wished to make any corrections or clarifications, they could do so, and I promised to deposit both the original version and their corrections and clarifications in the library/archive that I selected. I repeated much of this when we met for the interview. Then we together filled out a two-page biographical information form (with sections devoted to their family, residential, and work histories) and the permission form before the taped part of the interview began.

Over the last several years, I have come to the conclusion that my oral history interview transcripts could be a valuable internet-based resource for others interested in LGBT history. I decided to begin with narrators who have died. (This helps explain why the first several interviews that I posted were with men, since more of my male narrators had died when I began posting the interviews.) My intention for the future is to ask permission of living narrators before adding their transcripts to this site. The transcripts posted on this site are edited versions of the originals. There are several reasons for this. There are different schools of thought about how to do oral history transcripts. At one extreme, some oral history practitioners indicate every "um," "oh," sound, and pause in their transcripts. At the other extreme, some produce a heavily edited version of the original. My original transcripts fell somewhere in the middle of this spectrum, indicating each "um," "oh," and "you know," as well as laughter, sounds indicating assent, and repeated words. I learned in doing my original transcripts that most of us, in our spoken language, not only use many "ums" and "you knows" but also routinely repeat words and regularly construct long sentences in which we interrupt ourselves repeatedly and begin new sentences before we have finished the last ones. Some of my narrators were quite disturbed when I showed them my original transcripts, fearing that I would be publishing long excerpts of the unedited transcripts in my book, which was never my intention. Still, I got the strong sense from the conversations that ensued that most of my narrators would prefer that I edit the transcripts to remove "ums," "you knows," and repeated words. I have done so, and I have also occasionally edited the original transcripts for purposes of clarity and comprehension.

As you will see, each transcript is preceded by a short account of how I came to interview the particular individual and a reproduction of the biographical information that I obtained before the taped component of the interview began. I also use these brief introductions to note any other significant information that I think would be useful to readers, including information about when and how the individual died, where further information can be obtained, and whether I think there are reasons to have any concerns about the accuracy of the information conveyed in the interview. I strongly encourage readers of these transcripts to consult with other primary and secondary sources to obtain other perspectives on the stories shared in these interviews. At times, the information and interpretations conveyed are at odds with the information and interpretations presented in other sources (including other interviews, printed sources from the period under discussion, or published work by me or other scholars). All sources of historical information should be read with a critical eye; oral histories are not an exception to this rule. Readers should keep in mind that in each interview transcript they are encountering one person's interpretation at a particular moment in time, one person's memories of events that may have occurred many years earlier, and one person's way of telling a story. Some experts in oral history argue that oral histories tell us more about the period when the interview takes place than they do about the period being discussed. I certainly agree that the intervening years greatly influence how we remember the past. For example, the rise of feminist ways of thinking and speaking in the 1970s may well have influenced the stories my narrators tell about the 1950s and 1960s. For these and other reasons, I have adopted the practice of thinking of my oral history narrators as experts looking back on the past. In my published work I try to signal this understanding through the tenses that I use. For example, in my published work I might say that in our interview Barbara Gittings *notes* that in the 1950s she *went* to gay bars dressed as a boy. In any case, these interview transcripts are now available for multiple uses. I ask only that readers use these transcripts with care, consideration, and respect. I remain deeply grateful to my narrators for spending time and sharing their stories with me and I hope you will be appreciative as well.

U.S. Homophile Internationalism

Archive and Exhibit

In the last several decades, the study of U.S. history has been greatly influenced by the rise of transnational, comparative, and global history. Some subfields of U.S. history, including diplomatic history and the history of international relations, have long placed the United States within larger geographic frameworks, but until recently most tended to treat the United States in isolation, ignoring international influences, impacts, intersections, and interdependencies. Though there have been important exceptions, this has been true of most scholarship on U.S. gay, lesbian, bisexual, transgender, and queer history. Inspired in part by the groundbreaking historical work of Leila Rupp, David Churchill, and Craig Loftin on U.S. homophile internationalism, this online archive and exhibit features annotated bibliographies, digitized materials, and introductory essays on U.S. homophile magazine references to, representations of, and contributions from other parts of the world. The exhibit focuses on the years from 1953 to 1964 and it addresses three of the most important U.S. homophile magazines of the 1950s and 1960s: ONE, *Mattachine Review*, and *The Ladder*. The exhibit does not focus on all regions of the world; it highlights (1) Africa; (2) Asia and the Pacific; (3) Canada; (4) Latin America and

This introduction to an online OutHistory exhibit was published originally in Dec. 2015, http://www.outhistory.org/exhibits/show/us-homophile. Note that names and pronouns have been updated when appropriate.

the Caribbean; (5) the Middle East; and (6) Russia, the Soviet Union, and Eastern Europe.

This project originated in a 2014 Insight Grant that I received from the Social Sciences and Humanities Research Council of Canada (SSHRC), which awarded me five years of funding to support a project titled "U.S. Perspectives on Canadian Sexual Politics: Historical Case Studies." One of the proposed chapters of that project and the first that I began researching focused on references to, representations of, and contributions from Canada in the U.S. homophile press of the 1950s and 1960s. One of the broader goals of the larger project is to consider the pre-history of the recent North American perception that Canada is more sexually liberal than the United States. When I began work on the project, I hoped that by looking at the U.S. homophile periodicals of the 1950s and 1960s I would develop a sense of whether the perception that Canada is more sexually liberal than the United States pre-dated the decriminalization of homosexuality that occurred (with important exceptions) when Pierre Trudeau was Canada's prime minister in the late 1960s (more than three decades before national decriminalization was achieved in the United States). In working on this chapter, I began to realize that my analysis would be strengthened by a broader consideration of U.S. homophile references to, representations of, and contributions from other parts of the world.

In 2015, with financial support from SSHRC, I assembled an interdisciplinary team of research assistants at York University, where I was based from 1998 to 2014. All of the research assistants are Ph.D. students at York; several previously completed their M.A. degrees at York. While I was at York, I served as their M.A. and/or Ph.D. supervisor. For those who are completing their Ph.D.s in the next year or two, I am continuing to serve as their supervisor or as a member of their supervisory committee.

The research team consists of Tamara de Szegheo Lang, Sage Milo, and Healy Thompson, who are completing Ph.D.s in Gender, Feminist, and Women's Studies; Carly Simpson, who is completing a Ph.D. in History; Dasha Serykh, who is completing a Ph.D. in Social and Political Thought; and Shlomo Gleibman, who is completing a Ph.D. in Humanities. Because Tamara is working on a dissertation on LGBTQ public history in North America, I asked her to take the lead on digital photography and exhibit design and work with me on the Canada bibliography. Before beginning her Ph.D. studies, Dasha completed an M.A. Major Research Paper on U.S. LGBT magazine and newspaper representations of Russia, Eastern Europe, and the Soviet Union, so she took responsibility for that region. Healy, who is completing a dissertation on the international dimensions of U.S. reproductive and sexual politics, worked previously on Africa as a U.S.-based international AIDS activist, so she was assigned this continent. Sage, who is writing a dissertation on British feminist periodicals, has lived in the Middle East, so took responsibility for that region. Shlomo, who is working on a dissertation on representations of religion in Jewish North American LGBT cultural texts, took the lead on Latin America and the Caribbean. Carly is completing a dissertation on LGBT history in three mid-sized Ontario cities; she assumed responsibility for Asia and the Pacific.

The first major task was to produce the regional bibliographies. We did this in two complementary ways. First, each research assistant used EBSCO Publishing's *LGBT Life with Full Text*, a digitized database with partial coverage of the three homophile magazines, to identify potentially relevant items. We consulted about search terms to catch as many items as possible and then reviewed the contents to make sure that they were relevant. The search terms included the names of cities, countries, and regions; mountains, lakes, and rivers; and well-known individuals (including political leaders, writers, and artists). Second, each research assistant took responsibility for specific years and specific periodicals and skimmed printed copies of the "real" magazines (available at the Canadian Lesbian and Gay Archives and the University of Toronto Robarts Library) to identify items with relevance for any of the regional bibliographies. The results were then shared and incorporated into the regional bibliographies.

The second major task was to develop an annotation system for each item. The goal was to maximize the usefulness of the bibliographies for future researchers. After discussion, we agreed to include three types of information in each annotation: (1) item type, (2) country/city names, and (3) major or minor. Item types were identified as News, Feature, Editorial, Fiction, Poetry, Reprint, Letter, Advertisement, Review, Photograph, Art, or Miscellaneous. Country/city references were provided to allow future researchers with interests in particular cities, countries, or regions to identify relevant materials. Since many of the items we discovered contained just passing references to the relevant region, we distinguished between major and minor references, though it should be acknowledged that we made many subjective judgments about this and other researchers might disagree with our assessments.

The third major task was to photograph digitally the hundreds of items that we identified.

The fourth major task was to draft, circulate, and revise two introductory essays (one by me and one by Tamara) and the regional introductory essays (by Carly, Dasha, Healy, Sage, Shlomo, and me). I provided a template for the regional essays so each would address similar topics and issues.

The fifth major task was to upload the materials and design the Outhistory exhibit.

At the outset of the project, we hoped that we might complete the bibliographies for the period from 1953, when *ONE* magazine began publication, to 1969, which is generally recognized as the transition year between the homophile era and the era of gay liberation and lesbian feminism. It became clear, however, that we did not have sufficient time and resources to complete the full period and decided instead to concentrate on 1953 to 1964. There was a certain logic to ending the bibliographies in 1964, as this was the year when a new homophile magazine, *Drum*, began publication and quickly surpassed the others in circulation. If time and resources permit, a future extension of this project will cover the homophile press from 1964 to 1969. Because of time and resource constraints, items from 1953 to 1957 were digitized, but not items from later years; the latter will be done as part of a future extension of the project.

The selection of regions deserves some explanation. The U.S. homophile periodicals devoted significant attention to and received significant contributions from Western Europe and especially Great Britain, Germany, and Scandinavia. In part, this reflected longstanding U.S. links to Western Europe, powerful Western European influences on the United States, and the existence of strong Cold War alliances with Western European countries. It also reflected the earlier development of homophile activism and homophile periodicals in Western Europe and, at least in the case of Great Britain, the shared privileging of English language communication. Why, then, did this project not identify Western Europe as one of its regions? One reason is that we know far more about U.S. homophile relationships to Western Europe than we do about U.S. homophile relationships with other parts of the world. (One example would be the oft-cited influence of the British Wolfenden Commission on the U.S. homophile movement.) Another is that the sheer volume of references to, representations of, and contributions by Western Europe was so great that it would have been difficult to manage a

Western European annotated bibliography and digitization project. In addition, there were the positive reasons for focusing on other regions in the world and especially the opportunity to encourage research on Africa, Asia and the Pacific, Latin America and the Caribbean, and the Middle East. Canada was included in part because of the original design of my research project, in part because of the Canadian source of funding, in part because the researchers all have personal connections to Canada, and in part because Canada is often overlooked in projects attempting to internationalize the study of the United States. As for Australia and New Zealand, the research assistants began to collect relevant references midway through the research process and we hope that a future extension of this project might allow for coverage of these two countries.

We envision three primary uses of these materials. First, researchers who are interested in the history of the six regions might find useful references, representations, and sources that would point to additional research possibilities. For example, a U.S. homophile magazine reference to a film in India, a book in Cuba, a bar in China, a speech in Beirut, or a law in Nigeria might provide a research lead to scholars who are interested in studying the history of these places. In addition, letters to the editor from and other contributions by and about the six regions might tell us something about the history of these regions, their perceptions of the United States, and their perceptions of the U.S. homophile movement. Of course these materials should be used with caution: some may be idiosyncratic and non-representative, and some may tell us more about U.S. biases and prejudices than they do about the history of other countries.

Second, researchers who are interested in the United States might use these materials to consider the ways in which the United States was (or was not) influenced by other countries, the ways in which U.S. Americans conceptualized themselves and their country in relation to other regions and countries, and the influence (or lack of influence) of the United States on other countries. Insofar as the project focuses on the 1950s and 1960s, there may be particularly interesting issues to consider about how the U.S. homophile periodicals imaginatively mapped the world in relation to colonialism, postcolonialism, imperialism, Orientalism, racism, and the Cold War. Students and scholars who are interested in the history of U.S. exceptionalism—the notion that the United States is an exceptional, atypical, and special country—may also find useful materials for analysis. Here, too, the materials should be used with caution. There is no reason to assume that individuals who contributed to the U.S. homophile periodicals were representative of the much larger number of U.S. Americans who identified as gay, lesbian, bisexual, or transgender or the even larger number who engaged in same-sex sex or crossed genders. Moreover, while the homophile periodicals reached thousands or tens of thousands of readers in the United States, this was just a small fraction of the number of people who identified as LGBT, engaged in same-sex sex, or crossed genders in the United States.

Third, researchers who are interested in transnational and international communications, exchanges, and flows might use these materials to consider how homophile magazines as material objects and as conveyors of textual and visual representations circulated around the world and how material objects and textual and visual representations produced elsewhere circulated in the United States. This might lead to constructive and productive questions about the transnational and international character of homosexual, homophile, and transgender cultures in the 1950s and 1960s. Again, for the reasons highlighted above, researchers should exercise caution when using the materials for these purposes.

"U.S. Homophile Internationalism: An Online Archive and Exhibit of the 1950s and 1960s" is designed for students, scholars, and everyone interested in the history of gender and sexuality. We very much hope that it will inspire new interest in global histories of gender and sexuality and contribute to the internationalization of U.S. LGBT history.

"Black Lesbian in White America"

Interviewing Anita Cornwell

CH: I'm Callie Hitchcock and you're listening to the Lesbian Testimony Podcast for the Archives of Lesbian Oral Testimony, an online trans-inclusive open-access archive for oral testimony of same-sex or same-gender desiring women, including lesbian, queer, and two-spirit people. Each week we'll talk to a donor from the Archives about one of their donations or an oral historian about their recent work. This week we're speaking to Marc Stein about his interviews with Anita Cornwell, a seminal American lesbian author who wrote *Black Lesbian in White America* in 1983. Marc Stein is a history professor at San Francisco State University, teaching U.S. law, politics, and society, with concentrations in constitutional law, social movements, gender, race, and sexuality. His most recent book is *Rethinking the Gay and Lesbian Movement* and he was also the editor-in-chief of the *Encyclopedia of Lesbian, Gay, Bisexual, and Transgender History in America*, along with many other publications. So without further ado, hello Marc. It's great to have you here today. So can you tell us a bit about your oral history research?

This is a lightly edited transcript of Callie Hitchcock's 2017 interview with me for the *Lesbian Testimony* podcast. See *Lesbian Testimony Podcast–Episode 11*, Archives of Lesbian Oral Testimony, 6 Sep. 2017, https://alotarchives.org/2017/09/06/lesbian-testimony -podcast-episode-11. Please note that Cornwell used the n-word and out of respect for her I have retained her use of it in an excerpt of our 1993 interview.

MS: I was in graduate school at the University of Pennsylvania from 1989 to 1994 and wrote a Ph.D. dissertation on Philadelphia gay and lesbian history from the 1940s to the 1970s. As part of that I did about forty-five oral history interviews with men and women whose stories went back to the '30s and I try to trace their lives through the 1970s.

CH: Great. So can you give us some background on Anita and some context for the clip we're going to play?

MS: In doing the oral histories I tried to capture, as much as I could, gender diversity, race diversity, class diversity, generational diversity. I knew about Anita Cornwell from my preliminary research, mostly because she wrote this book, as you mentioned, *Black Lesbian in White America*, a really early groundbreaking statement about what I think we now refer to as intersectional politics. She talks a lot, autobiographically and also analytically, about intersections of race, class, gender, and sexuality in that book, and it was based on journalistic essays that she had begun writing in the 1960s and then continued in the 1970s, so actually they predate some of the works that we tend to associate with people like Audre Lorde and Barbara Smith and others of a somewhat later generation. In any case, I reached out to Anita. I had heard about her and I believe I got contact information about her from another African American woman who actually was one of my roommates during my first year of graduate school; they knew each other from Black lesbian feminist circles in Philadelphia. And she had me to her home in a section of West Philadelphia called Powelton Village. One of the things that I noticed in listening to the tape recently was that the very first words that I hear are Anita saying, "Are you warm? Are you warm enough?" before I do my introduction to the tape. I've been going back and forth about whether to include that line, because usually I like my transcripts to just begin with my introduction, but in fact I was interviewing her in October and the house was pretty cold. I don't know if it was that she hadn't yet turned on the heat for the winter. I feared that to save costs in this old Victorian house in Philadelphia that must have been very expensive to heat, she kept the heat turned way down. Over the course of the interview she asks several times if I was warm enough, she commented about how cold she was, and I think it was just an interesting way that the tape captures what might have been a level of poverty that wasn't true for most of my other oral history narrators.

CH: It's a very interesting indicator of the life and the intersections that she then goes on to explain throughout this whole interview.

FIGURE 7. Anita Cornwell, author of *Black Lesbian in White America* (1983), spoke at a "Burger Roast" protest at Philadelphia's Independence Hall in 1986. The demonstration targeted US Supreme Court Chief Justice Warren Burger, who had supported the Court's 1986 ruling in *Bowers v. Hardwick*, which upheld state sodomy laws. Photograph courtesy of the Philadelphia Gay and Lesbian Task Force Collection at the John J. Wilcox Jr. Archives at the William Way LGBT Community Center in Philadelphia.

And she also has quite a thick accent as well, so it's all painting a very descriptive picture of the scene.

MS: Yes, I think so, and I hope the tape will be comprehensible to listeners. Cornwell was born in 1923 in South Carolina, and she moved north in her teenage years with her mother and family and ended up in Philadelphia in the early 1940s. So right, she speaks with what to me, as a northern American New Yorker, sounds like a pretty heavy accent, but of course all of us have accents, and we are familiar with debates about transcribing oral histories and how to capture accents. I've chosen to not in any way really capture accent in the way I transcribe this oral history. There were a lot of positional differences, we could say, between Anita Cornwell and me. She was of course of an older generation. I was born in the '60s, so she was a good four decades older. I'm white and Jewish. She's Black and at least Christian by background. She was from the South. I was from the North. And in the clip that you're going to play, I think some of the dynamics that play out reflect those differences. I think she thought some of my questions were really either uninformed or coming out of left field. She may not have fully appreciated the extent to which I was asking open-ended questions and hoping to engender interesting responses, and sure enough she gave very interesting responses. But when I asked her questions about where she lived and why she chose the neighborhoods in which she lived, I think you'll hear in the tape that she at one point describes herself as having a very different orientation. I thought that was such an interesting word to use. And then I think you're going to play a clip that has some of her comments that are very critical of butch-fem relationships. I came of age in the '80s and '90s, in the era in which butch-fem was experiencing a revival and was being reclaimed by historians and by community members and by activists, but she was part of that older generation and that part of a radical feminist generation that was very critical of butch-fem. I think that's also one of the more interesting parts of the interview, but it raises all sorts of questions for me about how one deals as an oral historian with opinions with which one might strongly disagree and how much that should or should not become overt in the oral history process or in the analysis of the oral history transcript. Those all became very interesting questions for me.

CH: Right, and that's such an important question as an interviewer—how much of yourself are you inserting into this interaction and how much are you trying to just illuminate this person's humanness and their experience.

MS: Exactly, and I think that can happen at such a subtle level. So presumably she perceived me as male and gay. I wondered, after listening to the tape many times, about whether she perceived me as Jewish. I found myself wondering about that because there's a part of the clip that refers to her reaction to the movie *Yentl*. She would have no reason to know that I was the grandchild of Jewish immigrants from Europe, and when she talks about conflicts between African Americans and what she calls foreigners, she indirectly was referring to my own family history. And I can bring that to bear in my analysis of the interview transcript, but it remains an open question about whether she was thinking about that, consciously or unconsciously, during that part of our exchange.

CH: Did you feel like that was a tension or a clash or did you just absorb it and say, "O.K., we're still moving forward."

MS: The interview is full of laughter. I don't think that there was any negative dimension to our interactions per se. I think she had been interviewed a good number of times, so it wasn't completely unfamiliar to her to have younger researchers or younger people interested in hearing her stories. But as she says, she has very forceful opinions and she's very confident in her views and she was just putting them out there. And I certainly was trying to be respectful and engaged about what I was asking her. Another challenge in the interview was that she had written a whole book of autobiographical essays. I regret now when I listen back to the tape—it's been twenty years already; I interviewed her in 1993—not following up on some of the questions that arose from reading her work. I was thinking at the time that I had access to that work and I would make use of that published work, and so I wanted to ask her about different things, but someone looking only at the oral history tape and not the published book and her other published work might wonder why didn't I follow up on this, why didn't I follow up on that. But I think that's part of the process of analyzing any kind of oral history, to be considering the larger context.

CH: Right, and it's sort of a play of how do I document this human experience the best I can and move forward with that. So let us play the clip so everyone can catch up:

> MS: You wrote in your book in a few different places about your not being very positive about butch-fem relationships. Could you talk to me a little bit about that?
>
> AC: See I have very strong feelings about a lot of stuff and I don't mind expressing them, not to say I'm right or wrong. But I had an argument. It wasn't necessarily an argument. I don't know how the discussion came up.

And the way I see it, I mean why ape the straight world? I think there are always exceptions, mind you, but I think relationships between men and women are atrocious. You don't think so?

MS: No, I do, I do. And you thought butch-fem was the same thing?

AC: It's an aping of that world. I mean there are degrees, granted. I'm not saying you are gay or not gay because of that. I think you're gay because to some extent you're born that way. But I got into this argument with this woman. She said if you don't play roles, it's like a mockery of being gay. And I think it's just the opposite! I mean if you're going to be a fem, then go ahead and be a fem in the straight world, where at least you won't be scorned and at least you might have some kind of protection. I mean what's the difference! I think it's ridiculous! Granted, some people are more this way and that way. But I'm talking about rigid roles here now. And that's the way they were in the Black community. When I say the Black community, I mean the Black lesbian community. In fact, that's the reason I withdrew. I don't know whether I said that in the book, but I know I've written it somewhere. Because it just didn't make sense to me. It got on my nerves. And I mean don't come pushing me into any kind of pigeon hole. And it just seemed ludicrous to me, swaggering around. If that's the way you are, it's all right, but most of it was exaggeration. Like I said, sometimes that's the way you are, but don't go exaggerating and stuff. I mean just be natural. To me it doesn't make sense.

MS: Let me ask you something else. We were talking before the tape was on about neighborhoods. And you were saying something I thought was very interesting. You said you didn't think Black gay men and lesbians . . .

AC: Not men. Remember I said I don't know that much about men.

MS: OK.

AC: But I think to some extent what I say about Black women applies to Black men. Remember, don't be insulted now, but a lot of white people, when I say white people I don't mean everybody. There are some differences. But white people think, when they buy a house, they have bought the whole neighborhood. "It's our neighborhood. You stay out of our neighborhood." In fact, people who just got out of the boat and can't even speak English, "Get out of our neighborhood." See that's why there's a good deal of hostility between a lot of Black people and the foreigners. Because we have seen foreigners come here and before they could even learn a word of English, they think they can say, "Nigger, get out of my neighborhood." That's why you find that hostility. I'll tell you something. *Yentl*? That movie *Yentl*?

MS: Yeah.

AC: I saw it about twice, maybe the ending once, the beginning once, and all through once. And of course the first time it annoyed me greatly because of how a woman was treated. And the second time something else annoyed me. But the third time, when those immigrants came and saw the Statue of Liberty and I realized that they were getting off the boat and the minute they got off the boat, they're going to have more rights than I? Through with *Yentl*. Not that I'm blaming those people. And people say, "Why do Black people feel that way?" White people don't understand a thing about Black people. Like I said, there are exceptions now, but that's generally speaking.

MS: What you were saying before was that you thought Black gay women didn't move into some of those neighborhoods, that they tended to stay in their home neighborhoods, right?

AC: Well in the first place, let me say, there's a matter of money and there's a matter of "don't come in our neighborhood." So actually, in other words, Black people are just not as free to move around as white people. Plus the fact that even if we were, a lot of times we wouldn't want to move there anyhow. We want to stay with our family or friends and stuff.

MS: So was there any part of the city that you think was better for Black gay women to live in?

AC: Well see I never looked at it that way.

MS: Tell me how you looked at it. That's what I'm asking.

AC: I just looked at it. I moved where I wanted. I wasn't looking for other Black women or gay Black people to move to. I was looking for somewhere I could afford. Or when I moved to North Tower, I moved there because it was a safe place for a single woman to be. You had a door person, people you'd see walking in and out.

MS: Right.

AC: So that's why I moved there. That's why I moved back there when I didn't have a roommate.

MS: I see.

AC: Well like I said, I think partly it's because remember there's not that many Black people in the country period. So you know how many Black gay people there are. So if you go around looking for them to move somewhere, I mean it doesn't make sense.

MS: Right, OK.

AC: I guess it's a difference in orientation or something.

CH: So what's really interesting about this clip is that you can sense Anita's tension between locating what is a natural way to be and what is a performance of what she sees as harmful gender roles. And on the one hand, she's saying that butch-fem gender roles are aping the straight world, which can have negative gender relations, but then she also makes room to say that if that's what you are, that's all right, as long as you aren't exaggerating it, and it starts to become a bit confusing. What's interesting to me is that she ends by saying "just be natural," which is an interesting statement, because what is natural? I think the struggle is present today, even at the point of what is gender performance and what is intrinsic gender, and should anyone really dictate whether their gender expression is intrinsic or exaggerated? So I just wanted to get your take on this section of the interview.

MS: It's so complicated and in a sense I think to think about this we have to think about three historical moments. There's the historical moments that formed Anita, and I think the periods that most directly shaped her attitudes were the '50s and '60s, when she experienced butch-fem culture in the Black community in Philadelphia. She was part of that community, so there's that moment. Actually maybe there's four moments. Then we have the moment in the early '70s, when she became a very significant member of the lesbian feminist community in Philadelphia, participated in Philadelphia's version of the group Radicalesbians. In that context, that's when these ideas emerged that were critical of butch-fem and valorized "natural" performance, or not even performance, because I think so often in that moment it was a question of not performing, but being "natural." I actually see that as very much influenced by the counterculture or countercultural ideas, but the counterculture as it intersected with the feminist movement. Then there's the early '90s. Our interview was in 1993, so I'm in graduate school. I'm reading the newly published work of Judith Butler, informed by the earlier work of Esther Newton and others about butch-fem and drag and what we now call trans. And now there's the moment in 2017, when you and I are talking, and that of course is another couple of decades further along, when we have different ideas about gender and sexuality and what's natural and what's performative and all of that. So it allows for, I think, a real textured and layered consideration of these issues, and I'm pleased, I guess, when I listen to the tape about how I was obviously respectful of her views. I wasn't critical, I think, in my response. If I can reach back and try to remember what I was thinking, [her views] certainly would have been at odds with what I was learning and thinking and experiencing myself in graduate school in that moment, but as you said earlier, I was letting her articulate her own point of view and then was able to make use of that in my work.

CH: Right, and I've talked with some other people in this podcast about similarly looking at the waves of the women's movement, which used to be quite anti-lesbian and anti-butch-fem, and then, as you say, once we had gender performance from Butler, that switches over to a new era of thinking about gender and the natural.

MS: If I could just say, I think it really predates Butler. I think that much academic theory often picks up on dynamics that are happening earlier in the community and in the movement. So before I went to graduate school, I worked at *Gay Community News* and for a time as the coordinating editor of *Gay Community News*. I remember we once had a fundraiser where Joan Nestle, who I know did one of your other podcasts, spoke, and she performed in high fem. I think she wore a nightgown while reading some of her stories and her poems to an audience in Boston. We did that as a fundraiser. That was in the second half of the 1980s, so predating Butler's published work in the early '90s there was this community-based revival of butch-fem. And in the historical field it was really Elizabeth Kennedy and Madeline Davis in their work on the Buffalo lesbian community that was emphasizing that. They had come out of the lesbian feminist community of the earlier '70s, but they were in the forefront of reviving butch-fem, reconsidering butch-fem. Those were really vital contributions. So I don't know if we want to say that Anita remained kind of stuck in an earlier moment; that might be too easy. But in the early '90s she continued to feel very strongly about that subject.

CH: Right, and academia has echoes of historical moments, so that's definitely good to point out. That's interesting. I didn't realize that the '90s was a butch-fem revival period.

MS: Yes, I would say it started earlier, in the second half of the '80s, maybe even earlier, but it certainly was in process and before the '90s.

CH: Interesting. Yeah, I'm also reading *Female Masculinity* by Jack Halberstam, so it's interesting to look at. Once we're detaching gender from male or femaleness, I guess, we can look at masculinity and femininity as their own aesthetic objects. They get to sort of mutate and form more. I guess I prefer that way of thinking about it; that is what I'm trying to say.

MS: Right, right. And Esther Newton, who I mentioned before—her book *Mother Camp* was an even earlier academic consideration of that with respect specifically to gay drag queens. And Butler to some extent credits Newton's earlier work, but sometimes in these discussions Newton's earlier work gets lost, and as a gay man interested in lesbian history as well as gay history, I was inspired by the whole idea that Esther Newton, a butch lesbian, was really fascinated by gay male drag queens. Much of my work on Philadelphia was focused on questions about relationships between lesbians and gay men. The research process, looking at lesbian materials but then also interviewing lesbians, was really rich for thinking about those relationships in the past, which for me was the '40s, '50s, '60s, and early '70s, and then in the present, which for me was the early '90s, when I was doing much of this research.

CH: Right, and it's really cool that you get to look at all of these influencing layers and sediments. I also wanted to talk to you about the section of the clip that I thought was really interesting, about how Anita laid out more intersections of their living geography and how to outline that safety and money became a priority over racism and sexual orientation. So she's demonstrating how a lot of marginalized groups are put into these vulnerable positions because they have to fulfill certain basic needs. And I was just wondering if Anita talked about any other intersections of race, class, gender, geography, and sexual orientation in the rest of the interview that you wanted to share or maybe you want to speak on the geography part.

MS: Well I was determined to do part of my dissertation on lesbian and gay geographies and address the question of whether gay geographies and lesbian geographies overlapped or did not. There was a body of work at the time associated most clearly with a sociologist named Manuel Castells. He argued that gay men concentrated territorially in cities but that lesbians did not, that there were really no such thing as lesbian geographies, and I was determined to take him on. So all of my interviews have some section where I ask people about where they lived and how they thought about neighborhoods, and I quickly realized that my analysis had to address class and race as well. So sure enough, I did find that in Philadelphia lesbians concentrated residentially, commercially, and politically in particular neighborhoods, some of which overlapped with gay men and some of which did not. So it then became interesting in my interview with Anita to hear her insist that questions about where gay men lived, where lesbians lived, didn't matter so much for her in where she chose to live. I ended up identifying seven neighborhoods with some level of lesbian and gay concentrations in Philadelphia. If you ask people today, most gay men would just reference Center City in Philadelphia as the gay neighborhood. Lesbians often also would reference West Philadelphia and Germantown/Mt. Airy. Those were the most common responses that I got in the '90s and might be the most common responses today as well, so those three neighborhoods. Well Anita lived for a time in West Philadelphia and that's where I interviewed her, but for large portions of her life in Philadelphia, she lived in North Philadelphia, which is the neighborhood around Temple University. It's known as an African American neighborhood. It's gone through a lot of changes over the years, but during her time it was African American and increasingly African American, and so she became one of my important sources for the realization that while people of color and African Americans in particular did to some extent follow the patterns that I discerned from my white narrators, living primarily in Center City, West Philadelphia, and Germantown/Mt. Airy, there were also really important divergences. And the most important one was that often Black LGBT people stayed in Black neighborhoods.

She articulates that when she talks about wanting to stay around family and friends, and then she adds to that the issues of class, affordability, and safety as a woman, and as a lesbian, and as a lesbian of color. And the idea of living in an apartment building with a doorman was really important when she was living alone. And so I think she really helped me understand the multi-dimensional nature of lesbian and gay geographies in Philadelphia.

CH: Right, so as much as there's maybe a racial separation by neighborhood, there's also affordability and the safety context of being a woman single in the world, trying to live a life.

MS: That's absolutely right. And the larger oral history makes very clear and her published writing makes very clear that Anita thought that she had over the course of her life in the '50s, '60s, '70s distanced herself from the straight community because she was really troubled and disgusted by heterosexual relationships and male sexism. And then she separated herself from the Black lesbian community because she found it was dominated by butch-fem and she didn't like that. And she also was alienated from the Black civil rights movement and Black politics because she encountered sexism there. There's one point in the interview where she talks about certain kinds of Black male nationalists basically wanted their women to stop working for white men and instead work for them. And then she landed by the '70s in the women's movement, and while she's critical of racism in the women's movement, I think she ultimately found a more friendly and favorable home in the women's movement, the multiracial women's movement but it must be said the predominantly white women's movement. The book itself is dedicated "to the womyn of the world who have done so much for so little." And even when I spoke with her in the early 1990s, I think that was her primary affiliation—the women's movement, the feminist movement.

CH: So it looks like she's experienced a lot of sexism and in a way that informs the aversion to butch-fem dynamics.

MS: I think that's right. In another part of the tape she talks about men pawing women and how that didn't happen to her anymore now that she was an older woman—I interviewed her when she was seventy—but it had happened earlier in her life, and she couldn't stand to see men pawing women. And I think she probably found in butch-fem culture that some butches were sexually aggressive or sexually assertive in ways that reminded her of what she didn't like about straight culture or Black straight culture. I think that was just one aspect of sexism that she abhorred, and it comes through in particularly powerful ways in her autobiographical writings. Maybe she downplayed that a little bit in the interview, because after all she was doing an interview with a gay man. And maybe that's why she kept saying, "Oh of course there are exceptions to everything I'm saying about white people and men, but generally speaking." It strikes me she didn't want to let the exceptions prevent her from making generalizations that she thought were valid. She certainly, I think, did that about men, always qualifying about exceptions, and maybe she was prompted to emphasize that because her oral history interviewer was a man.

CH: Yeah, and that goes back to the positionality we were talking about earlier between interviewer and interviewee. Do you have a tip for someone interested in doing oral history interviews?

MS: Well first I think there are the technical tips. The one that I think was most valuable to me was to not go in with a list of a hundred questions and not go in completely without an agenda, but to find a happy medium. So I would typically go in and in a pre-interview phone call establish maybe six or seven areas that I wanted to touch on. I was encouraged to do that because it allows the narrator to begin thinking about what they might want to talk about in the lead-up to the actual interview, and then in the actual interview we had somewhat of an agenda. But I found the most valuable skills in doing oral histories were conversational skills, so making sure that I was being an attentive listener and making sure that I knew how to ask follow-up questions and not just let things end each time the narrator completed a sentence or a thought. So those are the technical aspects, but I think maybe the larger thing is just to have the courage to plunge in and do it. And it's one of those things that I think one learns by practice. And one changes over time in how one does interviews. I remember that even though I had been a journalist and even though I had done various kinds of interviewing before, I had to psych myself up to make the initial calls to interview my narrators, and then I always enjoyed the interviews. So I don't know why I felt shy about the cold call. Today, maybe it's more common to do that by email, but that was impossible when I was doing my interviews. I think just having the courage to dive in and start doing them and then one learns in the process about what works, what doesn't work, and sometimes things that work with one person don't work with other people. So it's really important to be attentive to the situation and the context and how people are different and converse differently. I'm, for example, going on. Every time you ask me a question I go on for a few minutes and that's like a lot of oral history narrators, but some will give one-word answers or one-sentence answers and will be very clipped. And the dynamic of an oral history is really different with that kind of narrator as compared to someone who is as loquacious as I'm being.

CH: Right, there's a ton of fluctuation, and you have to be prepared for all situations. Also, Marc has some current research that he's going to put out. Marc, do you want to tell us about that?

MS: I've been going back to my oral histories from Philadelphia over the last few years and I've started uploading transcripts of those interviews on the OutHistory website, outhistory.org, founded by gay historian Jonathan Ned Katz. So far I've uploaded about twenty transcripts. Anita's is going to be in the next batch that I'm going to upload sometime in the next few months, so people who are interested can read the whole transcript. I've debated back and forth about whether to make audio available. So far I'm not doing that, mostly because a good number of my narrators requested anonymity and voice would disclose identity in a way that I wouldn't feel comfortable doing for a good number of my narrators. What I'm uploading are lightly edited transcripts of the oral histories. And as I said, the interview with Anita will be available within a few months.

CH: OK, great. I'm really excited to hear more of these interviews. The clip was really, really interesting, so I'm excited to hear more. . . . Thank you so much, Marc, for coming to the podcast.

PART EIGHT

Stonewall, Popularity, and Publicity

Many academic historians have mixed feelings about popularity and publicity. On the one hand, it can be affirming to have fully enrolled classes, receive positive teaching evaluations, and be selected for guidance and mentorship by students. Most historians appreciate positive reviews of their books, favorable responses to their articles, and frequent citations of their work. Most are pleased by strong book sales, affirmative media attention, and enthusiastic public interest. On the other hand, popularity with students can mean more work for professors. Positive teaching evaluations can say more about sunny personalities, high grades, light workloads, political biases, and minimal critiques of student work than they do about educational effectiveness. Scholarly citations, speaking invitations, and media interviews can reflect star power rather than intellectual merit. These mixed feelings commonly come to the surface when another book on the Civil War becomes a bestseller, another presidential biographer is anointed an expert media commentator, or another scholar finds success with a commercial publisher. Some academics are suspicious about historical works that are excessively popular; surely, they must be overly simplistic, or they pander to the public, or they reinforce conventional ideas.

Public historians can have similarly mixed feelings about popular success, notwithstanding their interest in reaching large audiences. The popularity of the *New York Times Magazine* 1619 Project, for example, contributed to conservative backlash against historical projects that critique slavery, segregation, and racism. Museum directors who support blockbuster exhibits on Claude Monet, Vincent Van Gogh, Pablo Picasso, King Tut, and Tyrannosaurus Rex are sometimes criticized by those who prefer less popular exhibits on more obscure subjects. Historian Don Romesburg has highlighted a similar dynamic at the GLBT Historical Society Museum in San Francisco. According to Romesburg, "While many visitors would like a 'greatest hits' exhibition of the GLBT past, organizers understand that this is not enough." The museum "begins by giving them what they often think they came for," including artifacts from the life and times of San Francisco Supervisor Harvey Milk, who was assassinated in 1978, but then the museum "complicates matters" and "opens up new possibilities for queer recognition."[1]

In writing the introductions for this book, my own mixed feelings about popularity and publicity came to the surface. Did I really want to share sales figures for my books, readership numbers for periodical articles, and share counts for online publications? Did my critical comments about the ghettoization of LGBT history grow out of problematic feelings of gay shame and narcissistic desires for mainstream success?

Notwithstanding these mixed feelings, in the mid-2010s I began thinking about writing a book about the 1969 Stonewall Riots, the best-known event in LGBT history. I knew the fiftieth anniversary of Stonewall was approaching; a book might take several years to produce; and the anniversary commemorations would create opportunities for generating public interest in queer history. At first, I saw myself more as an advocate for a Stonewall book and not as its author. In 2015, I wrote to the European history editor of a major primary source book series; I had once taken a class with her and she was a lesbian. She referred me to the US history editor, an Ivy League historian who ignored my correspondence for the better part of a year. My letters to both editors indicated that I was an enthusiastic fan of the series, which was true; I have used many of its volumes in my courses and continue to do so. But I also wrote as a critic: the series features more than one hundred edited collections of primary sources and not one focuses on LGBT history. I suggested multiple topics, including Stonewall, and offered to recommend authors for each.

In 2016, after I re-sent my earlier message to the US history editor (this time with a copy to the European history editor), he finally responded, claiming that he had been trying to find someone to write a volume on Stonewall for years. Soon I decided I was interested in doing the book myself and submitted a proposal. A short time later the publisher's

FIGURE 8. The Stonewall National Monument, which commem-
orates the 1969 uprising at the Stonewall Inn (51–53 Christopher
Street in New York City), was established by the National Park
Service in 2016. The monument includes Christopher Park and
sculptor George Segal's work "Gay Liberation" (1980), which
features two standing men and two seated women. Photograph
by Marc Stein (2019).

acquisitions editor told me that he had obtained two enthusiastically
positive reviews of my proposal. As it turns out, however, the reviews
were never shared with me because the owner of the publishing company decided to suspend publication of new volumes in the series.
The reasons cited had to do with newly emerging uncertainties about
whether, in the internet age, primary source readers were commercially
viable. I agreed to wait for a few months, but by 2017, with a research
sabbatical approaching and the fiftieth anniversary of Stonewall coming
up, I decided it was time to pursue other options. New York University
Press, located just blocks from where the Stonewall Riots occurred and

a major publisher of high-quality books on the history of gender and sexuality, seemed like an excellent choice. The rest, as they say, is history. *The Stonewall Riots: A Documentary History* was published by New York University Press in 2019.

My decision to catch the Stonewall wave generated some of the mixed feelings described above in several professional colleagues and friends. When I shared my plans with one senior scholar in the field, for example, he responded, "Oh no!" During the spring and summer of 2019, others complained about the excessive attention that Stonewall's anniversary was receiving and the negative effects this was having on public interest in other queer historical topics. When asked about this, I emphasized two things. First, the Stonewall Riots *are* important and there is value in offering new approaches. Second, like it or not, the fiftieth anniversary commemorations were generating unprecedented public interest in LGBT history and there were important strategic choices to face about how to take advantage of the moment. My Stonewall book tried to do so in three ways. First, I extended the chronological focus from the spring and summer of 1969 to the broader history of the period from 1965 to 1973. Second, I widened the geographic lens from Greenwich Village in New York to multiple locations in the United States. Third, I presented the history of the riots not through the singular and authoritative interpretation of a historian but rather through the multiple and heterogeneous perspectives of two hundred primary sources. In this, my goals were similar to the ones discussed in part 7: to share primary sources with the public in order to promote the democratization of historical analysis.[2]

Beginning in April 2019, my Stonewall spring and summer was marked by a whirlwind of activity, far beyond anything I had experienced previously in my work as a public historian and scholarly activist.[3] I keynoted a Stonewall-themed conference in Paris and presented my work at the Rosa Luxemburg Foundation in New York, the Stonewall National Museum in Ft. Lauderdale, and Giovanni's Room bookstore in Philadelphia. Closer to home, I spoke about my work at two California State Universities, the California Historical Society in San Francisco, the Queer History Conference at San Francisco State, and the GLBT History Museum and Dog Eared Books in San Francisco's Castro district. Christian Purdy, a freelance publicist engaged by NYU Press, pitched my work to dozens of media outlets, which helped secure coverage in the *Atlantic, New York Times, San Francisco Chronicle, Slate, TIME,* and other publications; I also did more than a dozen radio, television, and podcast interviews.[4] The latter included an hour-long interview at the Stonewall National Monument for C-SPAN's *American History TV*. In its first year, the book sold approximately twenty-six hundred copies, the best first-year sales I have experienced. It also was recognized with starred reviews and included on "best" book lists by *Publishers Weekly*, *Library Journal*, the *Advocate*, and the American Library Association's GLBT Round Table. All in all, the quantity and quality of public attention were great.

The record is less clear with respect to my other goals. Many reviewers commented favorably on the value of reprinting primary sources, but some reviews were accompanied by visual images mistakenly identified as photographs from the riots. Many people who write about Stonewall continue to ignore documentary evidence, relying exclusively on oral testimonies. The Stonewall anniversary created opportunities to redirect public attention to other moments in queer history, but interest soon began to dissipate. While the book was extensively reviewed in LGBT periodicals and mainstream media, there have been few reviews in scholarly journals. This follows a pattern I first noticed after my third book was published in 2012. *Rethinking the Gay and Lesbian Movement*, more of a course textbook than a research monograph, garnered almost no reviews in scholarly journals, but with sales of approximately three thousand it is my bestselling publication and the publisher recently asked me to produce a second edition. *Rethinking* also is my second-most-cited work, exceeded only by *City of Sisterly and Brotherly Loves*. With respect to my last three books, there seems to be an inverse relationship between the number of scholarly journal reviews and the number of books sold. If this reflects the ways in which scholarly journals privilege research monographs over books like *Rethinking* and *The Stonewall Riots* when deciding which works to review, this might be worth reconsidering.

Perhaps the most puzzling review appeared in the *Times Literary Supplement*, which considered my book alongside other new works on Stonewall. Commenting on my work and Jason Baumann's *The Stonewall Reader* (which incidentally included excerpts of my oral history with Kiyoshi Kuromiya), public historian Hugh Ryan noted that both books "are resolutely anti-interpretation, resisting the urge to smooth primary sources into a cohesive narrative." After noting that my book's introduction discusses "four main theoretical approaches," Ryan added that "beyond this, readers are offered little guidance as they peruse the assembled articles." I was puzzled by this because I certainly made interpretive choices in setting the book's chronological, geographic, and thematic parameters; organizing the documents into eight chapters; selecting and editing the primary sources; and writing the introduction. Ryan was right that my approach did not rely on a singular cohesive narrative, but he seemingly missed the introduction's fifth and most original interpretive framework (see chapter 29). I trust that Ryan's intent was to praise my book for encouraging readers to develop their own interpretations, but I would not characterize it as "anti-interpretation"; I thought I was both summarizing past interpretations and offering a new one.[5] This perhaps just goes to prove a fundamental truth about public history: once we release our work into the public domain, we cannot control how it will be taken up.

Chapter 29, "Toward a Theory of the Stonewall Revolution," was published in *The Gay and Lesbian Review* in May 2019. The title I use here (rejected by the journal's editor in favor of "A Theory of Revolution for the Riots") riffed on "Toward a Theory of Revolution," an influential 1962 *American Sociological Review* essay by James C. Davies. My essay distilled one of my book's main arguments, that the Stonewall moment fit the profile of revolutionary situations discussed by Davies, when periods of improving conditions are followed by rapid reversals. *GLR* was founded in 1994 as *The Harvard Gay & Lesbian Review*; its website states that in the mid-1990s, "nowhere in Gaydom was there a publication for the literate non-specialist." Today, with nine thousand subscribers, it claims to be "widely regarded as the leading GLBT cultural and intellectual magazine in the U.S."[6] I had long been interested in publishing in *GLR* and thought it would be a better venue for this essay than a local LGBT newspaper, primarily because it was too long and scholarly for that type of publication.

Chapter 30, "Queer Rage: Police Violence and the Stonewall Rebellion of 1969," was published by the Organization of American Historians *Process* blog in June 2019. Aimed at a broad audience of historians, the essay attempted to situate the riots within broader national contexts marked by an escalation of anti-queer police violence, the rise of "law and order" politics, and an upsurge in LGBT resistance. I hoped to use the anniversary commemorations of Stonewall to shine light on long-forgotten episodes of police violence, challenge popular narratives of Stonewall exceptionalism, and highlight the intersectional politics of resistance to unjust policing in the context of the Black Lives Matter movement.

Chapter 31, "A Documentary History of Stonewall: An Interview with Marc Stein," was initiated by Katie Uva, a PhD student at the City University of New York Graduate Center. It was published by *Gotham: A Blog for Scholars of New York City History* in June 2019. I did more than twenty media interviews before, during, and after the publication of my book on Stonewall, but I thought this one was among the best; it certainly did more to situate the riots within urban history and the history of New York City. Perhaps it was successful because the interview was conducted via email, which allowed me to offer more coherent responses than is sometimes possible in interviews that rely on extemporaneous responses. More generally, published interviews are often effective venues for discussing new books—they are interactive; the format permits coverage of a broad range of issues; and the genre discourages excessive length and detail. *Gotham* is published by the Gotham Center for New York City, a research and educational center founded in 2000 and sponsored by the CUNY Graduate Center. Its mission statement emphasizes its support for "independent and professional" historians, its efforts to share knowledge with "the widest possible audience," and its orientation to research that will be "useful to actors influencing culture and policy today."[7]

Chapter 32, "Stonewall and Queens," was published by *From the Square: NYU Press Blog* in August 2019. This essay, published after the excitement generated by the fiftieth anniversary commemorations of Stonewall had begun to dissipate, attempted to catch the public's fleeting attention by revisiting another episode of anti-LGBT violence in 1969, one that generated more media attention than the Stonewall Riots did. As the essay immediately makes clear, the title's reference to "Queens" was meant to be deliberately misleading. Most readers probably assumed that I was writing about drag queens, but the essay focuses on the New York City borough of Queens, where vigilantes destroyed trees and shrubs in a crackdown on queer public sex in a community park. Here, too, my goal was to challenge narratives of Stonewall exceptionalism and use the Stonewall moment to call attention to other important episodes in queer history. I also wanted to link LGBT history to the struggle for environmental justice, the defense of public sex, and the radical sexual politics of gay liberation.[8]

Chapter 33, "Recalling Purple Hands Protests of 1969," was published by the *Bay Area Reporter* on Halloween, 31 October 2019. Much of my public speaking about the Stonewall Riots in 2019 emphasized the radicalization of Bay Area LGBT activism in the months leading up to the rebellion in New York. In this essay, which tried to evoke the spirit of Halloween, I turned to the months following Stonewall and in particular to a major LGBT protest at the *San Francisco Examiner* in October 1969, which I linked to similar protests against the *Village Voice* and *Harper's* in New York City and the *Los Angeles Times* in Los Angeles. As with much of my other writings about Stonewall, this essay addressed police violence, media bias, government inaction, LGBT diversity, and queer resistance. I also was trying to extend the Stonewall anniversary moment, broaden the geographic focus beyond Manhattan, and redirect public attention to the critical period that followed the Stonewall rebellion, when the LGBT movement mobilized, diversified, and radicalized.[9]

Toward a Theory of the Stonewall Revolution

Why did the Stonewall Riots occur when and where they did? When historians have tried to address this question, they have come up with several plausible answers. Few give much credence to the popular myth that the riots in 1969, when thousands of people protested in the streets of Greenwich Village in response to a police raid on the Stonewall Inn, were a completely spontaneous and entirely unprecedented reaction to the oppression faced by LGBT people.

With varying degrees of persuasiveness, historians have settled on essentially three alternative explanations, each of which contributes to our understanding of the rebellion. First is the argument that the uprising was the culmination of political organizing by the "homophile" movement that began in the early 1950s and radicalized in the mid-1960s. Second, there's the idea that the riots were profoundly influenced by a long tradition of bar-based oppression and resistance and the distinct factors that shaped that tradition in New York City. A third explanation stresses that the rebellion was influenced by the radicalization of other social movements in the late 1960s and inspired by the wave of urban riots that began with the Watts rebellion in Los Angeles in 1965.

This essay was published originally as "A Theory of Revolution for the Riots," *The Gay and Lesbian Review*, May 2019, 19–20. The version reprinted here corresponds to the online version of the essay; the version published in the print edition contained several editorial errors.

In *The Stonewall Riots: A Documentary History*, which will be published by NYU Press in time for the fiftieth anniversary of the uprising, I present 200 documents from 1965 to 1973 that illuminate developments before, during, and after the LGBT movement's most important turning point. The first three chapters, which address bars and policing, agendas and visions, and political protests before the riots, provide ample evidence for supporters of all three explanations. They also challenge simplistic portrayals of the pre-Stonewall era as relentlessly oppressive, as well as the widely held belief that the homophile movement was consistently small, accommodationist, and ineffective.

In the course of working on *The Stonewall Riots*, I came across an early report on the rebellion that pointed to a fourth possible interpretation of why the uprising occurred when and where it did. I discuss this interpretation (along with the others referenced above) in my book's introduction and I reprint the report in the book's fifth chapter, but my discussion of the document below serves as an excellent illustration of how I hope *The Stonewall Riots* will be used to inspire further research and analysis.

When I first read Don Jackson's "Reflections on the N.Y. Riots" in the October 1969 issue of the *Los Angeles Advocate*, I was intrigued by his discussion of the uprising's "sociological implications." Today, Jackson is perhaps best known for proposing in late 1969 that gay liberationists migrate to and take control of California's sparsely populated Alpine County. Jackson's "Stonewall Nation" project never reached fruition, but it garnered extensive national media attention and stimulated wide-ranging debates about "gay power," political separatism, and indigenous land in LGBT and other communities. (Jackson was later known as a strong advocate for LGBT inmates, prisoners, and homeless people, and as a strong opponent of affirmative action.) Jackson's report was one of the most widely circulated accounts of the Stonewall rebellion in the LGBT press. What caught my attention was this line: "Experts in group behavior say that tensions in a minority group become most acute at times when the minority group members see their status suddenly take a turn for the worse after a long period of improvement. This exactly describes the situation in New York, preceding the riots."

There were three aspects of this formulation that intrigued me. Who were Jackson's "experts in group behavior" and what other "minority groups" had they studied? What did Jackson mean when he referred to "a long period of improvement"? And what was the sudden turn for the worse that Jackson was referencing?

My search for Jackson's experts in group behavior ultimately led me to political scientist James Chowning Davies (1918–2012), who earned his doctorate at the University of California, Berkeley, in 1952, taught at the California Institute of Technology in the early 1960s, and spent much of his career at the University of Oregon. Davies's best-known publication, "Toward a Theory of Revolution," was published in the *American Sociological Review* in 1962; it was widely taught in history, political science, and sociology courses in the '60s and '70s. In a wide-ranging essay that challenged the theories of both Karl Marx and Alexis de Tocqueville, Davies used case studies of Dorr's Rebellion in 1842, the Russian Revolution of 1917, and the Egyptian Revolution of 1952 to support his "J-Curve" theory.

According to this theory, revolutions are most likely to occur not when conditions are at their worst, and not when conditions are improving at an insufficient pace, but instead when "a prolonged period of objective economic and social development is followed by a short period of sharp reversal." Influenced by the African American urban rebellions of the 1960s, Davies later elaborated on his theory in a chapter published in *The History of Violence in America*, an influential 1969 report submitted to the National Commission on the Causes and Prevention of Violence. Here Davies used case studies of the French Revolution, the U.S. Civil War, the Nazis' rise to power, and the urban riots of the 1960s to support his argument that "revolution is most likely to take place when a prolonged period of rising expectations and rising gratifications is followed by a short period of sharp reversal, during which the gap between expectations and gratifications quickly widens and becomes intolerable."

The value and validity of Davies's theory have been thoroughly debated for decades; the question for us is why Don Jackson thought it might be applicable to Stonewall. Unfortunately, he did not explain what he meant in suggesting that New York's gay community had experienced a "long period of improvement" in the years leading up to the Stonewall riots, but he might have been referring to the reforms achieved by the homophile movement in the latter half of the 1960s. In 1966 and '67, for example, Mattachine Society and other activists had convinced New York City's mayor and police commissioner to limit the use of police entrapment practices and the enforcement of sexual solicitation laws. In 1967 and '68, New York state activists had helped secure a new law that further constrained police entrapment practices and a court decision (*Matter of Kerma*) that provided increased protection to gay bars. *The New York Times Magazine* in 1967 and *The Wall Street Journal* in 1968 had published major articles that seemed to predict further advances for gay rights. Just weeks before the Stonewall Riots, the city's Civil Service Commission had agreed to end its ban on hiring homosexuals in most city government jobs.

There were also signs of improvement elsewhere. In 1967, a federal district court in Minnesota had ruled in favor of a major gay publisher in an obscenity case. In the same year, England and Wales had decriminalized private and consensual same-sex sexual activity for non-military adults over the age of 21. In the early days of 1969, the Los Angeles Police Commission dropped its prohibition on cross-gender impersonation by entertainers. In the early days of June 1969, Connecticut became the second U.S. state (after Illinois) to repeal its sodomy law. Around the same time San Francisco's Committee for Homosexual Freedom declared victory in its fight to secure the reinstatement of a fired bisexual worker at Tower Records. West Germany partially decriminalized sodomy three days before the Christopher Street riots began and Canada did so just hours before the police raided the Stonewall Inn. While they could not have known this when the riots erupted, the *San Francisco Chronicle* began a groundbreaking three-part series on lesbians on June 30th and gay activists won a major federal court ruling against employment discrimination by the U.S. Civil Service Commission on July 1st.

If all of this sustains the notion that LGBT people had reasons for perceiving major improvements in their status in the years, months, and weeks before the rebellion (and that New Yorkers had reasons for feeling frustrated because some of this did not apply to them), are there grounds for thinking that they might have seen the raid on the Stonewall as part of Jackson's "turn for the worse"? Much of the country had grown darkly pessimistic in the preceding eighteen months. In 1968, the Tet Offensive had raised the prospects of an escalation of the Vietnam War in January and February; civil rights leader Martin Luther King, Jr., was assassinated in April; Democratic presidential candidate Robert Kennedy was assassinated in June; and Chicago police violently attacked protesters at the Democratic Party convention in August. For many observers, these were bloody new chapters in the long and brutal history of American violence. In November 1968, Republican Richard Nixon was elected U.S. president on a law-and-order platform that promised to reverse the reforms of the Kennedy and Johnson administrations; he took office in January 1969.

For New Yorkers, this was the first time since 1903 that Republicans had held executive power at the local, state, and national levels. Governor Nelson Rockefeller (elected 1959) and Mayor John Lindsay (elected 1966) may have been known as liberal or moderate Republicans, but Nixon's election seemed to threaten the future of progressive reform, and Lindsay was defeated by a more conservative candidate in the Republican primary on June 17th (though he later ran and won as the candidate of the Liberal Party). Fears about the future of reform were confirmed in May, when Nixon nominated conservative Warren Burger to replace liberal Earl Warren as Chief Justice of the Supreme Court. Burger was sworn in five days before the riots began.

There were other reasons for believing that conditions were deteriorating. In the weeks and months leading up to the Stonewall Riots, a series of police raids on New York bars and bathhouses, including one on the Stonewall Inn just a few days before the riots, had inspired new anger and frustration about gender and sexual oppression. Some blamed the raids on the upcoming mayoral election, but the crackdown caught many by surprise, since LGBT people had come to expect better treatment from Mayor Lindsay. In May, local, state, and federal prosecutors used obscenity laws to force the closure of one of the country's most popular and sex-positive gay periodicals, the Philadelphia-based *Drum* magazine. In the weeks leading up to the Stonewall Riots, vigilantes in Kew Gardens (a neighborhood in Queens, one of New York City's five boroughs) initiated a campaign of harassment against men who cruised for sex in a local park; when those efforts failed, axe-wielding men chopped down several dozen of the park's trees just a few days before the riots began.

Also in June, the Mattachine Society of New York's newsletter reported on three recent killings of gay men. In New York, police had discovered the body of a man strangled to death in March; his corpse was found in the Hudson River near a popular gay cruising spot. In Los Angeles, police had violently attacked and killed Howard Efland during a March raid on a gay hotel. In the Bay Area, in April, Frank Bartley had been shot and killed by an undercover policeman who sexually entrapped him in a Berkeley cruising park. Then, on June 21st, Philip Caplan died after a public toilet beating by vice squad officers in Oakland, California.

We cannot know whether the Stonewall rioters knew about these developments, whether they were part of a larger trend of increased hate and hostility, or whether the media stories that reported on these incidents reflected or produced increased public attention to violence against LGBT people. We can only imagine what the mood was like in the bar and on the streets during and after the raid. The existing social and political conditions, however, seem to fit Davies's and Jackson's profile of a revolutionary situation, when "minority group members see their status suddenly take a turn for the worse after a long period of improvement." This is especially true if we think about the street people, trans people, and people of color who played distinctly prominent roles in the riots.

Whether or not we are persuaded by Jackson's interpretation of the Stonewall Riots, I think this example makes a persuasive case for revisiting the documentary sources from the late 1960s and early '70s that help us situate the rebellion in its historical context. Each of the documents reprinted in my book has the potential to inspire new interpretations of the Stonewall Riots, new explorations of LGBT history, and new ideas about social change.

Queer Rage

Police Violence and the Stonewall Rebellion of 1969

This summer, millions of people around the world will mark the fiftieth anniversary of the Stonewall rebellion, when thousands of people—gay, lesbian, bi, trans, queer, and straight—rioted in the streets of New York to protest an aggressive police raid on a Greenwich Village gay bar. The Stonewall uprising was a turning point in gender and sexual activism, setting in motion a wave of demonstrations, marches, and sit-ins that changed the country and the world. But contrary to what many people believe, the rebellion was not unprecedented and it was not the first time that LGBT people fought back. Historians have now documented more than thirty direct-action protests in which LGBT activists challenged their mistreatment in the years leading up to the New York riots. And this spring, we have the opportunity to commemorate the fiftieth anniversary of a series of violent episodes that contributed to the anger that fueled the summer explosion.

Anniversary commemorations of the Stonewall Riots often highlight the police raid that triggered the uprising, but they rarely reference the wave of violence against LGBT people in the months leading up to the rebellion. Reports of anti-queer police violence in particular spread via major urban newspapers including the *Los Angeles Times* and *San Francisco Chronicle*, alternative periodicals such as the *Berkeley*

This essay was published originally by *Process: A Blog for American History*, 3 June 2019, processhistory.org/stein-stonewall.

Barb, Berkeley Tribe, and *Los Angeles Free Press,* and LGBT newsletters, newspapers, and magazines, including the *Committee for Homosexual Freedom Newsletter, The Ladder,* the *Los Angeles Advocate,* the *Mattachine Society of New York Newsletter,* and *Vector.* Some of these accounts suggested that police forces around the country felt newly emboldened by the inauguration of President Richard Nixon in January 1969. The self-proclaimed leader of the "silent majority" had campaigned on a "law and order" platform and a promise to crush the radicalizing political movements that threatened the existing social order. LGBT people and people perceived to be queer suffered greatly in this context.

On March 9, for example, Los Angeles police attacked and killed Howard Efland, a 37-year-old nurse also known as Jack McCann, during an antigay vice raid on the Dover Hotel, which was popular with men who had sex with men. Multiple eyewitnesses risked public exposure and state retribution by courageously testifying about the police brutality that took Efland's life, but a local jury ruled in April that the killing was "excusable homicide" because, according to the police, the victim had resisted arrest.

On April 3, New York police discovered the body of a man, estimated to be 20–25 years of age, who apparently had been strangled to death in March. His corpse was found in the Hudson River near the Christopher Street docks, a popular gay cruising spot not far from the Stonewall Inn.

On April 17, an undercover police officer in Berkeley shot 33-year-old Frank Bartley, a local chef, when the latter tried to flee Aquatic Park, a well-known cruising area where the officer had engaged in the common police practice of sexual entrapment. Bartley died five days later. Local authorities declined to pursue charges against the killer or his partner.

On June 21, vice squad officers in Oakland, California, attacked Philip Caplan, a professor visiting family in the area, after they accused him of loitering and lewd behavior in a public toilet near Lake Merritt. Caplan, a married father who was on medication for prostate problems and sometimes needed to urinate frequently, died several days later. Local authorities again declined to pursue charges against the police. The death of Caplan, presumptively straight, exemplified the ways in which all people could be vulnerable to anti-queer violence.

We do not know whether the Stonewall rioters knew about all of these incidents, but politically organized LGBT people in New York, some of whom participated in the rebellion, were definitely concerned about police violence. Several weeks before the uprising the *Mattachine*

Society of New York Newsletter reported on the first three of these killings, informing hundreds if not thousands of local subscribers about the "grim reapings." The same newsletter reported in April 1969 that a policeman who had shot and killed two gay men on the Christopher Street docks in September 1968 was absolved of wrongdoing by a grand jury.

All of these violent episodes and countless others likely contributed to the growing sense of LGBT anger and frustration that can be found in multiple first-person accounts and oral histories of the uprising. This may help explain why the Stonewall rioters responded as they did when the police invaded their space. And the violence did not end with Stonewall. On March 8, 1970, for example, more than two hundred protesters gathered in Los Angeles to mark the anniversary of Efland's death. The crowd, estimated to include more than fifty African Americans, was horrified to learn about the latest victim of state violence: local police had killed Larry Laverne Turner, a 20-year-old African American trans sex worker, earlier that day.

In the coming months, the anniversary of Stonewall will be celebrated with parties and parades. Many of us will mark and marvel over the progress that has occurred over the last 50 years. The ongoing devaluation of LGBT lives, loves, and lusts, however, should give us pause, and our collective ignorance about these other moments in our shared history is cause for shame rather than pride.

A Documentary History of Stonewall

An Interview with Marc Stein

KU: Why is a sourcebook like this a helpful tool for understanding the Stonewall Riots?

MS: When I began working on this project, there were two excellent narrative histories of the Stonewall Riots, one by academic historian Martin Duberman and one by public historian David Carter. For the fiftieth anniversary I wanted to do something different and it occurred to me that a primary source reader could encourage renewed attention to the documentary sources that most historians use when developing their interpretations. My book begins with an introductory essay, but then I present 200 documents along with a set of maps and photographs. Most of the book's primary sources are media stories, but I also include some demonstration fliers, court decisions, song lyrics, and gay bar guide listings.

As a university-based historian, I often assign primary source readers in my classes. I love putting in the hands of my students the raw materials from which historical interpretations can be developed; it allows me to work with my students on the craft of researching and writing history. This type of primary source collection also allows readers to experience the messiness of history. There are gaps, inconsistencies, and conflicts in the accounts. If we're paying attention, it's easy to see the

This interview was conducted by Katie Uva and was published originally by *Gotham: A Blog for Scholars of New York City History*, 13 June 2019.

importance of perspective, standpoint, and viewpoint. If we're sensitive to language, we can be challenged by the complexities of translation, since the words, concepts, and categories of the past are not necessarily the words, concepts, and categories of today.

With respect to Stonewall more specifically, I think it's fascinating to compare mainstream, alternative, and LGBT media sources; to look at media stories, photographs, first-person accounts, letters, and demonstration fliers alongside one another; and to explore the dissemination, evolution, and transformation of stories about the riots. I hope my readers will be in a stronger position to criticize historical myths and misconceptions and to develop new and original interpretations.

KU: How did you decide on the geographic and temporal parameters for these documents?

MS: With respect to geography, I wanted to broaden out beyond Greenwich Village, Manhattan, and New York City, without losing a sense of the importance, impact, and influence of developments in "the city" (I grew up in the New York suburbs and my grandparents lived in the Bronx and Queens, so of course New York will always be "the city" to me, even though I've lived most of my adult life in Boston, Philadelphia, Toronto, and San Francisco). I think the more national approach I adopted actually helps underscore the broader influences on and impacts of developments in New York. I was tempted to adopt a more global approach, but I worried about the superficiality that might result—like the tourist who wants to visit everything but ends up seeing nothing. My book favors six cities—New York, Philadelphia, Washington, D.C., Chicago, San Francisco, and Los Angeles. I know I've opened myself up to criticisms about not sufficiently covering other parts of the country, but there are as many reasons to be concerned about anti-urban bias as there are to be concerned about urban bias. In the end, I made choices about geography based on impact and influence and I've certainly included documents that cover other places, including Dallas, Honolulu, Miami, Minneapolis, and New Orleans.

As for chronology, I wanted to broaden out beyond the summer of 1969, but not attempt to capture the entire history of the universe. I also was committed to covering the same number of years before and after the riots; I thought this would help situate the rebellion in historical time. I settled on the years from 1965 to 1973 for several reasons. For a long time I've believed that the second half of the 1960s, when the LGBT movement began to mobilize, radicalize, and diversify, has not received as much attention as it should; most accounts of the homophile movement seem stuck in the 1950s. By starting in 1965, I thought I could highlight the national upsurge in LGBT direct action that began in that year and the influence of other radicalizing social movements, including black power. By ending in 1973, I could cover the first four years of pride marches, address one of the great achievements of the movement in this period (the American Psychiatric Association's declassification of homosexuality as a mental illness), and capture some of the changes in LGBT politics that occurred as the energies unleashed by Stonewall began to dissipate.

KU: Does your book tell us anything new about the history of New York?

MS: I hope so! My introduction situates the riots within the larger history of New York City, including the reforms achieved by the LGBT movement in the second half of the 1960s, when John Lindsay was mayor; the police violence and state repression that seemed to be growing in 1968 and 1969; the implications of having a Republican mayor, governor, and president in the first half of 1969 (the first time in decades that this was the case for New Yorkers); and the Republican primary election defeat of Lindsay by a more conservative candidate just days before the riots began. Lindsay, perceived by many as a friend to the gay community, ended up winning the general election on a third-party ticket, but the Stonewall rioters could not have known that this was going to happen. I present all of this as consistent with a theory that says that revolutions are most likely to happen when a long period of improvement in social conditions is followed by rapid reversals.

Beyond the riots themselves, I think the post-Stonewall chapters will bring new attention to the history of LGBT activism in New York in the final months of 1969 and the early years of the 1970s.

KU: Many historians and activists have debunked the claim that Stonewall began the LGBT rights movement, but what do you think were key impacts of this specific event? What were major continuities pre- and post-Stonewall?

MS: Most queer historians, I think, are irritated and annoyed by the notion that the LGBT movement began with Stonewall; there's been a pretty clear scholarly consensus now for more than thirty years that the movement in the United States began about twenty years before Stonewall (and even earlier in Europe). Historians have now documented more than thirty pre-Stonewall LGBT protests, demonstrations, sit-ins, and riots, so even on that score there's little basis for the claim that Stonewall was "first." That said, I don't agree with those who would diminish the influence and impact of the riots. I see three primary impacts: mass mobilization, political radicalization, and social diversification. As important as the riots themselves were, developments after the riots were key in what happened next. And it was really a year later, when the first pride marches took place, that Stonewall's place in our collective imaginings of our history really strengthened.

KU: Why do you think it is that Stonewall looms so much larger in popular memory than other LGBT protests that happened in that era?

MS: Compared to earlier protests, the Stonewall rebellion involved more people; it lasted longer; and there was more violence. It also occurred in New York, which often has an advantage when it comes to recognition and remembrance. And it happened at a critical historical moment, in the aftermath of 1968, an international year of rebellion, revolution, reaction, and repression. All of that said, I think Stonewall looms so large in popular memory today because of the annual commemorations that first occurred in the spring and summer of 1970 and the history of those commemorations over the next several decades.

KU: Part 2 juxtaposes several varying press accounts of what happened during the Stonewall Riots. What are the biggest distinctions between these different contemporary accounts?

MS: Yes, my book reprints about thirty different media accounts from the mainstream, alternative, and LGBT press. I see one set of differences across these three categories and another set of differences as the accounts changed over time. I think we can ask many interesting questions about this. For example, what does it mean that the first set of mainstream media reports, published in the *New York Times*, *New York Post*, and *New York Daily News*, described the rioters as young "homosexuals" or young "homosexual men," but a week later the Post and Daily News also began depicting them as "gays," "fags," "fems," "nellies," and "queens?" What does it mean that alternative papers such as the *Village Voice* used most of the same terms, but also referenced "fairies," "swishes," "dykes," "queers," and "sex changes?" Interestingly, the *Voice* was the first to report on the key role played by a "dyke," and shortly thereafter another alternative paper, the *Berkeley Barb*, provided a similar account with a reference to a "chick."

Many readers might be surprised to discover that two significant American trans periodicals of 1969, the *Erickson Educational Foundation Newsletter* and *Transvestia*, did not cover the riots, while the gay-oriented *Mattachine Society of New York Newsletter*, which provided the most extensive coverage, consistently highlighted the presence and prominence of sissies, swishes, drags, and queens. Adding to the complications of interpretation is the fact that the words and concepts of today are not the words and concepts of 1969. Fifty years ago, for example, it was common to refer to "gay transvestites." Many genderqueer people referred to themselves as gay in 1969, but this is not necessarily how we think, speak, or write today. Unless we want to insist on the superiority of today's categories and concepts, which is a condescending way to approach the past, we need to address the challenges of translation. If we do not, we are setting a dangerous precedent for future interpreters of *our* categories and concepts, who will almost inevitably question our ways of thinking, speaking, and writing.

With respect to race, what does it mean that most of the mainstream, alternative, and LGBT media reports said nothing about race, at a time when it was common for journalists to describe urban rioters as black and brown? In an important exception, Mattachine's first report briefly mentioned a Puerto Rican queen, but otherwise did not reference race until the article's conclusion, which quoted a policeman who indicated that he preferred black riots to fairy riots because "you can't hit a sick man." Unless we want to believe that the cop's compassion extended to African American fairies, his formulation implied that he did not view the Stonewall rioters as predominantly black. In two other exceptional references to race, the author of a first-person account in the *East Village Other* described himself as white and another alternative media account in the newspaper *Rat* made a passing reference to a "hip spade," meaning an African American man. In general, however, there were few references to race in media stories about Stonewall. When I say this I do not mean to imply that the rioters were necessarily white; in fact there were few references to whites, blacks, or others in media stories about the rebellion. There may be reasons that the media did not highlight the presence and prominence of people of color in the uprising, but surely we cannot ignore the documentary evidence, including media stories, photographic images, and police reports, if we are interested in race and the riots.

KU: In recent years there has been increasing mainstream emphasis on the presence of trans and gender nonconforming people as the key actors and leaders in the Stonewall Uprising, particularly Sylvia Rivera, Marsha P. Johnson, and Storme DeLarverie. Does your research confirm or challenge their respective roles in the events at Stonewall?

MS: I'll be very interested to see what my readers do with this issue. With respect to both gender and race, I've been talking with friends and colleagues about the importance of key qualifying words, including "some," "many," "a significant number," a "substantial number," "primarily," "predominantly," and "most." I see credible and trustworthy accounts that emphasize the presence and prominence of trans and gender-queer people in the Stonewall riots. That's not the same as saying that most of the rioters were. And as I noted above, trans and gender-queer people may also have thought of themselves as gay. Just because we define these words and police these boundaries in certain ways today doesn't mean that we should define these words and police these boundaries in the same ways when we think about the past.

The documentary sources in my chapter about the riots don't single out or rule out Sylvia Rivera, Marsha P. Johnson, or Storme DeLarverie. It's important to acknowledge that they themselves presented conflicting accounts about whether they were there when the riots began. It can be condescending and patronizing to insist that they were, just as it can be problematic to insist that they played no role in the riots. My post-Stonewall chapters include documents by and about Rivera and Johnson. And the mantra of my book is that "there's always more to the story."

KU: You note your choice to focus on LGBT press, mainstream press, and organizing ephemera, and to exclude oral histories and interviews. If someone did want to seek out firsthand accounts after reading the sources in this book, where should they start?

MS: First, let me note that I very much believe in the importance of oral histories and I've done and used many oral histories in my previous work. In many cases, it can be greatly beneficial to read oral histories and documentary sources alongside one another; that's the approach I've often taken. This book does include firsthand accounts, but not oral histories; that's an important distinction. I think there are now hundreds of oral histories of the Stonewall Riots. I think it would be fascinating to focus on the ones that were done in the months and years immediately following the riots, since those were done closer in time to the events they discussed and were less influenced by subsequent developments. Another set of oral histories that I would recommend were the ones done by Eric Marcus, Martin Duberman, and David Carter. Now that more and more LGBT periodicals from the 1970s and 1980s have been digitized, it could be fruitful to search for additional firsthand accounts that haven't received attention.

KU: Implicit in your sources are questions of language—how people describe themselves often differs from how they are described by others, and there are also major changes in the language of identity over time. Additionally, there's been growing debate about referring to this event as the Stonewall Riots vs. the Stonewall Rebellion or Uprising. Why do you feel the term "Stonewall Riots" is apt?

MS: Yes, this is a familiar issue from debates and discussions about the Watts Riots or Rebellion. From what I understand, some people argue against using the term "riots" because the word carries implications of rage, anger, fury, nihilism, and purposelessness. Perhaps because I came of age politically during the first decade of the AIDS crisis and participated in AIDS activism, I appreciate and do not want to deny the emotional dimensions of activism. I think there was every reason for LGBT people to feel rage, anger, and fury when the police raided the Stonewall. Riots also can be intentional, purposeful, and political. And of course people at the time referred to the Stonewall "riots." In my book, I refer to the Stonewall riots, rebellion, and uprising. I'll confess it's also a stylistic choice; it can be boring to use the same word over and over again, especially if it's one of your key words!

KU: As you note, the Obama Administration was a turning point in the mainstream embracing of Stonewall as key to the nation's history and the long national struggle for rights and justice. What do you feel are the advantages and disadvantages of widespread recognition and memorialization of Stonewall?

MS: I raise some questions about this in my book and I hope my readers will as well. And it's a question for people beyond the United States as well, since Stonewall can be memorialized in ways that contribute to American colonialism, imperialism, and nationalism. At their worst, commemorations of Stonewall promote U.S. nationalism, corporate capitalism, white supremacy, gender conservatism, and sexual normativity. At their best, they teach us about gender and sexual injustice, intersectional oppression, state violence, capitalist exploitation, queer and trans resistance, coalition politics, and the importance of embodied direct action in the history of social change.

Stonewall and Queens

Not those queens. Not the drag queens, street queens, or radical queens who played key roles in the Stonewall Riots of 1969.

I mean Queens, one of the five boroughs of New York City, reputed birthplace of Donald Trump in the 1940s, home to the Miracle Mets of 1969, and my family's destination for monthly visits with my grandparents in the 1960s and 1970s. Queens may have been a short distance from Manhattan's Greenwich Village, where Stonewall's gay rebellion occurred, but in social, cultural, and political terms it was far, far away. According to the 1970 Census, Queens was home to two million people, well above Manhattan's 1.5 million, but it was significantly less diverse—85 percent white, as opposed to Manhattan's 71 percent. In 1969, when I turned six years old, Queens displayed little of the bohemian cosmopolitanism, left politics, or sexual diversity that I would later come to associate with Manhattan.

And yet in the summer of 1969, sexual repression and resistance in Queens received far more media attention than did the Stonewall Riots in Manhattan.

Could that possibly be true? In June, the world marked the fiftieth anniversary of Stonewall, justifiably understood as a momentous turning point in LGBT history. But as many commentators have noted, it

This essay was published originally by *From the Square: NYU Press Blog*, 9 Aug. 2019, https://www.fromthesquare.org/stonewall-and-queens/#.XVSCNehKhPY.

was only later—and especially when the riots were commemorated with marches, protests, and parades on their anniversary—that the Stonewall uprising became central to the ways that we imagine and narrate LGBT history.

The *New York Times*, for example, reported on Stonewall in three brief June and July stories that appeared on pages 33, 22, and 19. In contrast, the *Times* more extensively covered a group of antigay vigilantes in Kew Gardens, Queens, who on June 19 and 20 cut down dozens of trees in a public park frequented by men cruising for sex with men. From July to September there were at least six *Times* news stories (including a lengthy front-page news report during the week of the Stonewall rebellion), one editorial, and multiple letters to the editor about the vigilantes. On the West Coast, to take another example, the *San Francisco Chronicle* provided no coverage of Stonewall, but on July 1, while the riots were still underway, it reprinted the initial *New York Times* story about the Kew Gardens bullies.

According to these stories, a "vigilante committee" of 30–40 Kew Gardens men, who claimed that they were "concerned for the safety of the women and children," initially tried to use flashlights and patrols to harass the men who used the park for nighttime sex. In mid-June, however, after the cruisers "began to insist they had a right to be on public land," the vigilantes chopped down fifteen dogwood trees, eleven London planes, a set of wild cherry trees, and other trees and shrubs. Three eyewitnesses reported that they had contacted the police to report on the vigilantes, but after officers visited the park and chatted with the men who were cutting down the trees, they left without making any arrests.

According to the *New York Times* and *New York Post*, one neighborhood woman called the vigilante actions a "dangerous infringement of people's rights." Another questioned the stated justification for cutting down the trees, asking, "What mothers and children are out at 1 o'clock in the morning?" The Parks Department Commissioner decried the criminal vandalism, estimated that the trees would cost $15,000 to replace, and promised action after an official investigation.

The American Civil Liberties Union called on the Mayor and Police Commissioner to "make it clear to all members of the police force that homosexuals have as much right to be in the parks as heterosexuals, and are entitled to the same degree of protection by the police." The Mattachine Society of New York, a gay rights organization, described the vigilantism as "outrageous" and indicated that it was initiating a

"Trees for Queens" fundraising drive to replace the ones that had been chopped down. The *Times* opined that "it is the job of the police to uphold all laws, not to stand by while destructive elements take the law into their own hands," though its editorial sympathized with the "arboreal vandals," declaring that "there are laws against public nuisances and indecent behavior which, if warranted, could have been invoked in this case."

The mainstream press did not report on further actions taken by LGBT activists, though LGBT magazines and newsletters in California, New York, Illinois, and Washington, D.C., did. According to the Mattachine Society of New York's July newsletter, gay activists planned to "patrol the park with dogs to prevent further harassment." One month later, Mattachine announced plans to affix a metal plaque to one of its "Trees for Queens"; the plaque would describe the trees as "a gift from the homosexual people of New York to the people of Queens."

After likening the vigilantes to fascists and the Ku Klux Klan, Mattachine also reported that it had filed complaints with the Mayor, Police Commissioner, Parks Department, and Queens District Attorney. Mattachine denounced as a "farce" the official investigation, which ultimately led nowhere because of noncooperation by the police and disinterest by the District Attorney, and called for the disbarment of a lawyer who had been serving as a leader of and spokesperson for the vigilantes.

We also know from LGBT (though not from mainstream) media sources that fifty years ago, on August 10, 1969, "approximately 100 homosexuals of both sexes, and heterosexual supporters, invaded the small park where the vigilantes had cut down the trees." The demonstration, mistakenly described in some sources as having taken place on August 4, was sponsored by two gay and lesbian rights organizations that had been founded long before the Stonewall Riots: the Mattachine Society of New York and the New York chapter of the Daughters of Bilitis. Protesters wore lavender armbands, carried signs that declared "Homosexuals Have Rights—And So Do Trees," listened to speeches by gay liberationist Marty Robinson and lesbian feminist Martha Shelley, and watched a performance of Shelley's short play, "The Boys in Queens."

Now that public attention has largely moved beyond the fiftieth anniversary commemorations of the 1969 Stonewall Riots, will the mainstream and LGBT public be interested in all of the other significant fiftieth anniversaries in LGBT history that are coming up? Stonewall was transformative because it contributed to the LGBT movement's mass mobilization, political radicalization, and social diversification, not because it instantaneously changed the world. Recognizing this month's fiftieth anniversary of the 1969 Kew Gardens demonstration against antigay vigilantism would be a way of signaling our understanding that Stonewall would never have transformed the world if it had not been followed by a massive wave of LGBT protests in the weeks, months, and years that followed the riots. It also would remind us that for at least one short period of time in 1969, the public recognized Queens as central to LGBT history and politics.

Recalling Purple Hands Protests of 1969

Halloween has long been one of the queerest of holidays, but on October 31, 1969, San Francisco LGBT activists found new ways to confront their terrifying fears of media misrepresentations and police violence. In their wake, they left behind ghostly new symbols of gay liberation, purple hands, which continue to make apparitional appearances in the work of those who practice the dark arts of queer history.

The horrifying tale began on Saturday, October 25, 1969, when the *San Francisco Examiner* published journalist Robert Patterson's slashing expose on Folsom Street gay bars, clubs, and restaurants. For Patterson, these "deviate establishments" were "sad" and "dreary" sites for the "sick" ceremonies of "homosexuals," "transvestites," "drag queens," and "male prostitutes." The frightening feature was particularly hostile to those Patterson described as "semi-males," "members of the pseudo-fair sex," "women who aren't exactly women," and "hybrid blossoms."

Over the next two days, LGBT critics of Patterson and the *Examiner* attempted to speak with the beastly journalist and his monstrous editors, who refused to meet with them. On Monday, October 27, two members of the Committee for Homosexual Freedom, a radical gay liberation group that had been staging demonstrations since April, disguised themselves as human beings and entered the Examiner building

This essay was published originally by *Bay Area Reporter*, 31 Oct. 2019, 4–5, https://www.ebar.com/news/news//283715.

at 110 Fifth Street, where they reportedly were verbally and physically attacked by Patterson.

On Wednesday, October 29, CHF activists were joined by members of two new Bay Area groups, Gay Guerilla Theatre and Gay Liberation Front, for an invasion of the *Examiner*. Carrying signs and leaflets, they criticized the newspaper for its "malicious, erroneous, and irresponsible" story and called on the *Examiner* to fire the ghastly Patterson. According to one media source, newspaper workers responded by throwing activist Darwin Dias down a staircase.

At this point, CHF and GLF decided to organize a major demonstration at the *Examiner* at noon on Friday, October 31. Hoping to exorcise the building's demons, 50–100 protesters peacefully picketed outside the newspaper's building until they were viciously attacked from above. According to a CHF spokesperson, "Suddenly a plastic bag full of printers' ink was thrown from a second-floor *Examiner* office, soaking the pickets and splattering the walls of the building. Someone wiped his hands on the wall. In a few seconds, inked handprints covered the wall and windows. 'Fuck the Examiner,' was written by a finger dripping with ink. 'Gay is,' wrote a handsome young man just before he was dragged by the hair into the waiting police van."

Multiple first-person accounts indicate that after the activists began leaving purple imprints of their hands on the *Examiner* building (with some reports indicating that Stevens McClave was the first to do so), the possessed police responded by aggressively attacking the protesters. One demonstrator, Michael Carbone, suffered two broken ribs and a torn ear; Dias lost his front teeth. The police also targeted two journalists, Marcus Overseth of the *San Francisco Free Press* and Leo Laurence of the *Berkeley Tribe*. Laurence managed to toss his camera film to Larry Littlejohn, president of the Society for Individual Rights, before he was taken into custody. In all, the police arrested 12 or 13 protesters, ranging in age from 19 to 36. All were charged with misdemeanors, including disturbing the peace, malicious mischief, blocking a sidewalk, resisting arrest, using obscene language, and refusing to follow police orders. Five or six were additionally charged with battery on an officer, which was a felony.

After the police broke up the demonstration at the *Examiner*, LGBT activists regrouped at the nearby Glide Methodist Church, where they decided to march on City Hall to protest police brutality. There, at approximately 2 p.m., 15–25 activists formed a picket line outside the building; they later conducted a sit-in in the offices of Mayor Joseph

Alioto. Most of the protesters agreed to leave when the mayor's office closed for the day at 5 p.m.; the three who refused to do so (James Connolly, Larry Clarkson, and Stephen Matthews, ages 19–29) were taken into custody on charges of trespassing, unlawful assembly, and remaining at the site of a riot.

Two weeks later, eight of the activists who had been arrested at the *Examiner* pleaded no contest to the charge of refusing to obey police orders (the other charges were dropped); they were given five-day suspended sentences and six months' probation. Al Alvarez, a member of the Society for Individual Rights, refused to accept a similar deal and was acquitted after a jury trial. Media sources do not reveal what happened to the rest, though several indicate that felony charges were dropped against all but one of the activists; the exception was accused of biting the hand of Sergeant Sol Weiner during the *Examiner* demonstration.

In the aftermath of the Purple Hands protest, there was praise for the spirit of queer unity that seemed to prevail during and after Halloween. Of the 12 or 13 activists arrested at the Examiner, media reports identified one as a woman (Karen Harrick/Herrick/Hurrick); one or two used gender-ambiguous names; two had names suggesting they were Latino. The late lesbian leader Del Martin later wrote that another woman was taken into custody but not booked. According to one report about the demonstration at the Examiner, "A transvestite clunked a pig over the head with the picket sign he was carrying. The pole broke and the dazed officer looked shocked as he watched him escape running as fast as he could in his tight skirt, his high heeled shoes clicking like a typewriter as he ran down the sidewalk." With respect to the demonstration's racial politics, some may have objected to leaflet language that used the N-word to condemn society's treatment of the gay community, but the text also called on the community to "oppose the exploitation of all oppressed minorities" and "fight discrimination and racism."

Other signs of LGBT diversity and queer unity emerged after the protest at the *Examiner*. At the City Hall demonstration, a "black gay" protester "scolded" the police for nearly knocking him down as he tried to enter the building: "City Hall is a public building open to everyone." In a first-person account of his time in jail, Overseth mentioned conversations with fellow prisoners who were "united in oppression"; they included "elderly alcoholics from the Tenderloin, Blacks, Chicanos, American Indians, Heads and Gays." Multiple left and queer groups provided financial, legal, and political assistance for those who were attacked, arrested, and jailed on Halloween. A few months later, Martin provided further support for coalitional politics when she reported in a gay publication that Patterson, the offending *Examiner* journalist, had been criticized by African American activists for racist reporting in 1968 and 1969.

Subsequent developments suggest that Patterson may have been haunted by the ghosts of purple hands. In 1972, rival reporters spilled ink and spilled the beans about a recent series of *Examiner* stories by Patterson. The stories purportedly were based on a visit that Patterson had made to mainland China, except there was no evidence that he had gotten further than Hong Kong. After Patterson failed to provide any proof that he had visited the mainland, the *Examiner* fired him.

In the meantime, other U.S. newspapers and magazines may have wondered whether they might be the next victims of purple protesters. On September 12, the Gay Liberation Front in New York had staged a major demonstration at the *Village Voice* to protest the newspaper's coverage of gay issues and its refusal to accept classified advertisements with the word "gay." On November 5, just a few days after the Purple Hands protest, the Homosexual Information Center sponsored a demonstration at the *Los Angeles Times* when that newspaper refused to accept advertisements with the word "homosexual." Then on October 27, 1970, the anniversary of the first gay confrontation at the *Examiner*, New York's Gay Activists Alliance staged an all-day sit-in at *Harper's* to protest the magazine's publication of a genocidal article about homosexuality by journalist Joseph Epstein and its refusal to provide equal space for a response.

In reporting on the 1969 Purple Hands protest in the *San Francisco Free Press*, Overseth wrote that "for many of us it all changed on Halloween." Fifty years later, much has changed but some has not in the treatment of LGBT people by the press and the police. To address the ongoing demonization of queer "others" by those who exercise power in our society, it might be time to summon the ghosts of Purple Hands to spook the political reactionaries who continue to terrify and terrorize the most vulnerable among us.

Conclusion

As I reflect on the growth and development of queer public history and LGBT scholarly activism over the last several decades, it is easy to marvel about how much has changed. When I entered graduate school in 1989, there were almost no tenured historians at North American colleges and universities who had written PhD dissertations on LGBT topics. In 2021, I can name more than thirty. There has been similar growth in the number of paid staff at LGBT libraries, archives, and museums. Thirty years ago, mainstream media coverage of LGBT history was rare and exceptional; today it is far more common. In the 1980s, LGBT history was almost never taught in primary and secondary schools; today six US states mandate its inclusion. On a personal level, when I first began producing essays on queer history for public audiences, I wrote primarily for LGBT readers and relied heavily on LGBT newspapers. In the last two decades, I have continued to produce content for queer history publications and projects, including OutHistory, but also have shared my work in mainstream outlets, including History News Network and the publications of the American Historical Association and Organization of American Historians. Some of this may reflect changes in professional seniority rather than alterations in historical conditions, but there is no denying that the latter has made a difference.

No brief survey can capture the depth and breadth of exciting new work in queer public history, but the following recent examples are illustrative:

- In 2010–11, Hugh Ryan founded the Pop-Up Museum of Queer History in Brooklyn; similar exhibits, installations, and performances subsequently popped up in other locations, including Manhattan, Bloomington, and Philadelphia.[1]

- In 2011, the San Francisco-based GLBT Historical Society, which had been operating one of the country's most significant queer archives since the 1980s, opened a museum that soon welcomed tens of thousands of visitors each year.[2]

- In 2011 California became the first state to mandate the teaching of LGBT history in public schools; Colorado, Illinois, Nevada, New Jersey, and Oregon now do so as well.[3]

- In 2013, Sarah Prager founded Quist, an LGBT history app with tens of thousands of followers.[4]

- In 2013, Allyson Mitchell and Deirdre Logue launched Killjoy's Kastle, a historically informed lesbian feminist haunted house that has entertained, frightened, and provoked visitors in Toronto, Los Angeles, Philadelphia, and London.[5]

- In 2013, Chris Vargas founded the Museum of Transgender Hirstory and Art to create "a cohesive visual history of transgender culture."[6]

- In 2014, the *Transgender Studies Quarterly* began publication with a unique and uniquely transparent financial model that relied heavily on public fundraising.[7]

- In 2014 and 2015, *Radical History Review* published two special issues on "queering archives."[8]

- In 2015, Andrew Dolkart, Ken Lustbader, and Jay Shockley founded the New York City LGBT Historic Sites Project "to broaden people's knowledge of LGBT history beyond Stonewall and to place that history in a geographical context." In the same year, Mark Meinke and Megan Springate founded the Rainbow Heritage Network, "a national organization for the recognition and preservation of sites, history, and heritage associated with sexual and gender minorities in the United States."[9]

- In 2015, to commemorate the fiftieth anniversary of the Annual Reminder demonstrations at Independence Hall, Bob Skiba curated "Speaking Out for Equality: The Constitution, Gay Rights, and the Supreme Court" at the National Constitution Center in Philadelphia. The Liberty Bell Center, National

FIGURE 9. In 2015, the Liberty Bell Center at Independence National Historical Park commemorated the fiftieth anniversary of the first Annual Reminder July Fourth protests at Independence Hall with an exhibit titled "Speaking Out for Equality." The exhibit's picket signs, cut-out human figures, and police barriers were based on historical artifacts from the Annual Reminders. Photograph by Joseph E. B. Elliott, courtesy of Independence National Historical Park, National Park Service.

Museum of American Jewish History, and other local institutions organized related exhibits.[10]

- In 2016, the National Park Foundation and National Park Service published a queer theme study that inspired multiple successful efforts to recognize LGBT historical landmarks. As of 2021, one site is recognized as a national historical monument (Stonewall); seven are recognized as national historic landmarks; and twenty-two are listed on the National Register of Historic Places.[11]

More recently, in 2019 *The Public Historian* published a special issue titled "Queering Public History: The State of the Field"; one of its essays focused on Stephen Vider's 2017 exhibit "AIDS at Home: Art and Everyday Activism" at the Museum of the City of New York.[12] Also in 2019, Joseph Plaster organized "The Ballroom Experience" at the Johns Hopkins University George Peabody Library; Julio Capó Jr. curated "Queer Miami: A History of LGBTQ Communities" at the HistoryMiami Museum; and Christina Linden curated "Queer California:

Untold Stories" at the Oakland Museum of California.[13] In the last decade, blogs and podcasts such as *Lesbian Testimony, Making Gay History, Michigan LGBTQ Remember, Notches, Philadelphia Gay-borhood Guru, Queer America,* and *Sexing History* have utilized new technologies to extend the reach of queer public history.[14] The Toronto-based *LGBTQ Oral History Digital Collaboratory,* directed by Elspeth Brown, provides links for more than forty community-based oral history projects. These include the ACT UP Oral History Project, the Dragon Fruit Project (for queer Asian Americans and Pacific Island-ers), the LGBTQ Religious Archives Network Oral Histories Collec-tion, the New York City Trans Oral History Project, and the Queer Newark Oral History Project.[15] The *Lavender Legacies Guide* lists dozens of community-based archives, libraries, and history projects.[16] Recent additions to the ever-expanding world of LGBT radio, televi-sion, film, and video include historical documentaries *The Lavender Scare* (2017), *The Death and Life of Marsha P. Johnson* (2017), *Killing Patient Zero* (2019), *Cured* (2020), *Pride* (2021), and *My Name Is Pauli Murray* (2021).[17] In 2019, the fiftieth anniversary of the Stonewall Riots prompted dozens of museums, in and beyond New York, to feature exhibits, lectures, panels, and presentations on LGBT history. This is just a selective sampling, but it highlights queer public history's growth and transformation in the recent past.[18]

Notwithstanding these signs of positive change, there are reasons for concern. In higher education, more history departments are willing to consider hiring specialists in LGBT history, but they are doing so at a time when colleges and universities are increasingly reliant on short-term, low-paid, and over-worked faculty. While six states now man-date the teaching of LGBT history in public schools, forty-four do not and multiple states are considering new restrictions on LGBT history education.[19] In Missouri, Republican state leaders ordered the removal of an LGBT history exhibit from the state capitol building in Septem-ber 2021.[20] In various contexts, queer history projects face some of the same challenges that have been experienced by LGBT bars, bookstores, and other businesses: declining public support because of increasing mainstream acceptance.[21] LGBT public history projects also continue to struggle with organizational legacies that reinforce and reproduce social hierarchies based on ability, age, citizenship, class, gender, lan-guage, nationality, race, and religion.[22]

Meanwhile, multiple local queer history projects report that aca-demic historians, who were key organizational founders, collaborators, and leaders in previous decades, are now less engaged. Academics, in turn, have raised critical questions about whether the phenomenon described by Myrl Beam in *Gay, Inc.: The Nonprofitization of Queer Politics* (2018) applies to local LGBT history projects.[23] In some, board and staff positions increasingly go to people with backgrounds in nonprofit management, public relations, financial development, and business administration, not to queer studies scholars with strong connections to academic and public history. This phenomenon, which I think of as "history without historians," can be linked to the broader denigration of expertise—or the privileging of some forms of expertise over others—that we have witnessed in recent years. It also may be contributing to a reorientation of queer public history projects: many of us celebrate their recent successes in reaching new audiences through museum exhibits, public programs, and digitization initiatives, but we worry about declining access to, knowledge of, and support for the physical archives needed for historical scholarship. Meanwhile, LGBT historical digitization projects are expanding public access to primary sources, but economic, legal, and political factors (including sexual censorship) are blocking the digitization of many materials.[24]

I witnessed some of this during my time as a member of the GLBT Historical Society board (2016–2019). Many candidates for board positions, for example, were familiar with the Society's relatively new museum but not its long-standing archives. This was no surprise given organizational strategies that highlighted public programs rather than scholarly research, but there are risks associated with this shift. Before the COVID-19 pandemic, for instance, the museum was open to the public forty-seven hours per week, whereas the archives were open eighteen hours per week. The latter was reduced to six during a months-long staff transition, notwithstanding offers of help by volunteer historians, archivists, and librarians. In contrast, when I traveled to San Francisco to do research in the archives in the 1990s, the all-volunteer staff, which included working historians, understood that I was on a limited budget and made it possible for me to access the archives for several consecutive days.

When I left the GLBT Historical Society board in 2019, I was its last member with a regular faculty position and scholarly publications on LGBT history. Historians Don Romesburg, Amy Sueyoshi, and Gerard Koskovich continue to curate exhibits at the museum, but academic and public historians formerly were well-represented on the organization's board and staff; now they are not. The Society's first two executive directors, Susan Stryker and Terence Kissack, were academic and public historians; their two successors were not. As this book goes to press, San Francisco mayor London Breed has proposed to provide millions of dollars to support the GLBT Historical Society's plans for a new museum, but it is not clear that working historians will have a seat at the table when the new museum is planned and developed.[25] Meanwhile, the leader of a major New York-based LGBT history museum project with minimal ground-level participation by historians tells me that historical experts will be asked to produce exhibits when the project is launched, but this underestimates the importance of active and early engagement by academic and nonacademic historians in museum planning and development.

As if all of this were not enough, LGBT researchers confront new challenges as they try to build on past successes. I can illustrate this by asking you to imagine that instead of beginning my graduate studies at a private university in Pennsylvania in 1989, I had done so at a public university in California in 2019. Keep in mind that my younger version, Zoomer Marc, lives in what is commonly regarded as one of the most LGBT-friendly regions of one of the most LGBT-friendly states. First, Z-Marc's dissertation progress was blocked for more than a year because the GLBT Historical Society understandably restricted access to its archival collections because of the pandemic. Second, he could not travel to LGBT archives in more distant locations for similar reasons and because of health-related travel regulations. Third, his progress almost was constrained for an additional year because administrators at his university responded prematurely to cutbacks in government financing by eliminating all state-funded support for research travel (Boomer Marc's provost announced plans to do this for 2021–22 but reversed herself after federal and state funding increased). Fourth, while my younger counterpart wants to resume his research when LGBT archives re-open, it is safe to travel, and his university restores travel funding, he then faces another major challenge: in 2016, LGBT legislators in California convinced their colleagues to ban state-funded travel to states with anti-LGBT laws; as of November 2021, this applies to eighteen states.[26] Zoomer Marc supports the boycott in general, but thinks the law's seven exceptions should be modified to include travel for LGBT-affirmative education and research. ZM keeps hearing from people in other fields that surely he can complete his dissertation with online and digital materials, but such comments are based on ignorance about historical methods. If Z-Marc somehow finds a way to complete his PhD in the next few years, he then will confront a dismal academic job market in which tenure-track positions (featuring relatively high pay, reasonable job security, and possibilities for research support) continue to be replaced by short-term faculty positions (with relatively low pay, minimal job security, and no research support). Knowing what I know about Zoomer Marc, I would be very cautious about advising him to continue his PhD studies.

For another illustration, I can point to my experiences with *Queer Pasts*, an online digital history project that the publisher Alexander Street, now owned by ProQuest, launched in 2021. Just before the pandemic began, I was contacted by an Alexander Street product management director; we had worked together previously when I edited the award-winning *Encyclopedia of LGBT History in America* (2003) for Scribners/Gale. Alexander Street wanted to know if I would be willing to coedit an LGBT history platform modeled on *Women and Social Movements*, a digital database founded by Tom Dublin and Kathryn Kish Sklar and now edited by Rebecca Jo Plant and Judy Tzu-Chun Wu. I was interested and soon recruited Lisa Arellano, then a professor of women's, gender, and sexuality studies at Colby College and now at Mills College, to serve as coeditor. Together we developed a mission statement that explains,

> *Queer Pasts* is a collection of primary source exhibits for students and scholars of queer history and culture. The database uses "queer" in its broadest and most inclusive sense, to embrace topics that are gay, lesbian, bisexual, and transgender and to include work on sexual and gender formations that are queer but not necessarily LGBT. Each of the document collections in the database will include a critical introductory essay that helps explain the significance of the primary sources in historical terms and in relationship to previous scholarship. This database seeks to broaden the field of queer history; we therefore prioritize projects that focus on the experiences and perspectives of under-represented historical groups, including people of color, trans people, and people with disabilities. We ask as well that our guest editors consider questions about the strengths, limitations, and characteristics of their archive and explore the ways in which archives are constructed, constrained, and contested.

Queer Pasts will feature six exhibits a year; each will include a peer-reviewed introduction and twenty to forty related primary sources. Arellano and I will produce some of the exhibits, but most will be curated by guest editors.

In negotiating our contract with the publisher, I confronted many of the same difficult choices discussed by Susan Stryker and Paisley Currah in their introduction to the first issue of *Transgender Studies Quarterly*. Like *TSQ* and *Women and Social Movements*, *Queer Pasts* will not be an open-access publication, at least not at first. It will be available by subscription and the pricing structure will be oriented primarily to college, university, and public libraries. In this sense, it is difficult to characterize *Queer Pasts* as a public history project. With respect to the politics of this, on the one hand subscription-based "products," including most scholarly journals, are common in the academic marketplace. In addition, I am grateful for the technical expertise and institutional resources that ProQuest will bring to *Queer Pasts* and we are exploring options for developing open-access components. I also am pleased that we negotiated relatively generous compensation for our guest editors, especially because of what this might mean for unemployed or under-employed queer historians, and I appreciate that we will have a small budget to compensate LGBT archives, artists, photographers, and publishers for their contributions. I wish that corporate donors, individual philanthropists, government agencies, and private foundations would fund more open-access LGBT public history projects, but until they do, the models developed by *TSQ* and *Queer Pasts* are good alternatives. On the other hand, I support open-access scholarship, believe in the democratic mission of websites such as OutHistory, and want *Queer Pasts* to reach the largest possible audience. In the end, I decided to move forward with *Queer Pasts* and hope we can make it more accessible in the future.

All of this has been playing out during a period when the philanthropic arm of one of the world's largest corporations announced what was probably the best-funded LGBT public history project to date. In 2017, Google.org announced that it was awarding a $1 million grant to New York City's LGBT Community Center, which in partnership with the National Park Foundation would develop a project to commemorate the 1969 Stonewall Riots. Google.org followed up with an additional $500,000 in 2019. One component of the project was a major oral history initiative (completed in partnership with the Tenement Museum); one goal was to "extend the reach of Stonewall National Monument beyond its physical location"; one result was "Stonewall Forever," an online platform described as "a living monument to 50 years of pride."[27] All of this interested me as a historian of Stonewall, a queer oral historian, and a board member of a Bay Area LGBT historical organization that has long hoped to gain greater financial support from major corporations based in our region. It interested me because of a talk that historian Kevin Murphy gave at the 2019 Queer History Conference, which raised provocative questions about the politics of Stonewall-related collaborations with the National Park Service, an agency of the federal government with a problematic history of gender and sexual policing. It interested me because of similar concerns that have been expressed, most commonly in relation to LGBT pride events, about corporate sponsorships, capitalist priorities, and collaborations with the state. And it interested me because of my long-standing belief that some of the best work in queer history emerges when academic and public historians collaborate.[28]

There is much to admire and respect in "Stonewall Forever" and the other results of Google.org's major support for commemorations of Stonewall: there are valuable oral histories, informative historical exhibits, a compelling documentary film, and a living history project that will incorporate public contributions. I say this even though I would quibble with some of the "facts" presented on the website and some of the information contained in related materials produced by project funders and partners. With respect to the pre-Stonewall era, for example, the Annual Reminder demonstrations in Philadelphia did not begin in 1964 (they began in 1965). The activists who participated in the 1966 sip-in at Julius did not threaten to sue if they were denied service (they wanted to be denied service so they could challenge State Liquor Authority regulations). Homosexuality was not fully legalized in the United Kingdom in 1967 (decriminalization only applied to private sex in England and Wales; the age of consent for same-sex sex was set five years higher than it was for cross-sex sex; and there were additional limitations). And Richard Leitsch was not the leader of the Mattachine Society, which was based in California (he was the leader of the independent Mattachine Society of New York).

With respect to the riots themselves, the Stonewall Inn was not "one of the few places at the time where LGBTQ people could gather openly" (gay bar guides in 1969 listed hundreds of sites in New York and thousands around the country, and LGBTQ people could gather openly in millions of private homes). The police did not break down the doors of the Stonewall Inn (the raid began as an undercover operation; the police entered the bar without damaging the doors; and it was rioters who later attempted to break down the doors after the police were trapped inside). And the riot did not break out in the park across the street (it began on the sidewalks and street in front of the Stonewall). I also disagree with the choice to include visual images of protests from the 1950s, 1960s, and 1970s in a section of the "Stonewall Forever" film that otherwise focuses on the riots of 1969. The film acknowledges this briefly, but the overall effect is misleading, especially since at least one of the images is commonly misidentified as a photograph from the Stonewall Riots.

As for the post-Stonewall era, Argentine immigrant Diego Viñales did not die as a result of a subsequent March 1970 police raid on the Snake Pit (this was mistakenly reported when Viñales was impaled on a fence after he jumped out of a police station window, but Viñales survived). The Gay Liberation Front did not organize the first Christopher Street Liberation Day March (it was organized by the Christopher Street Liberation Day Committee, with support from more than fifteen LGBT organizations). And Stonewall was not the birthplace of the "modern day LGBTQ rights movement" (much of the movement wanted "liberation," not "rights," and the Stonewall uprising was preceded by two decades of LGBTQ activism).

More generally, I wish that "Stonewall Forever" had engaged more fully with recent scholarship in LGBTQ history, some of which challenges the interpretations offered on the website. I wish that there had been consultations with more experienced and knowledgeable historians (academic and nonacademic). The website references anonymous "researchers and archivists"; I recognize the name of just one historian, Jeanne Vaccaro, in the film credits and she describes her principal role as "casting" the interviews. LGBT oral historian Eric Marcus served as a project advisor, but he indicates that he was not consulted on the film or the website. I communicated with eight individuals who worked on "Stonewall Forever"; none took responsibility for the errors referenced above. It is great that Google.org places trust in community-based partners that represent disenfranchised and marginalized groups in society, which is what one of the organization's leaders explained to me, but this does not have to be done in ways that disregard and disrespect expertise. As obvious as this may sound: historical projects might benefit from the active involvement of historians.

Notwithstanding these criticisms, I regard much of "Stonewall Forever" as praiseworthy and think it is good that Google.org and the National Park Foundation partnered with an LGBT community organization to support a major project on Stonewall's history.[29] Or at least that is what I thought until I read through the "frequently asked questions" section of "Stonewall Forever" and opened up the window that promised to address the issue of "what content is not permitted" on the "living monument." This is the part of the project that allows members of the public to contribute new material. As it turns out, five types of content will not be permitted: copyrighted images, nudity, sexual content, hate speech, and violence. The reasons for these restrictions are easily imagined, but how will "Stonewall Forever" deal with submissions that critically address the hate speech and police violence that Stonewall patrons and passersby experienced in 1969, not to mention the retaliatory violence that some LGBTQ people committed at Stonewall? What will "Stonewall Forever" do with submissions that address later episodes in the long and brutal history of anti-LGBTQ hatred and violence? And why is "Stonewall Forever" banning sexual content and nudity in a living monument to gender and sexual liberation? We do not know if "Stonewall Forever" considered narrower language referencing pornography, obscenity, or sex acts (presumably the main targets of the prohibition), but what are the politics of banning "sexual content" on a living monument to Stonewall?

We need to know more before we try to answer these questions, but it is quite possible that queer scholarly activists will need to challenge and critique LGBT public history in the coming years. As we continue to advocate for desperately needed queer historical projects in the future, for example, we may need to intervene if funders and sponsors try to exercise undue influence, if queer diversity and difference are not respected, and if historical initiatives exclude historians. Whether or not such interventions become necessary, I hope that academic and public historians will continue to come together in projects that queer the past as we imagine different futures.

Acknowledgments

For their help in securing permission to reprint these essays and photographs, I thank Peter Aigner, John Anderies, Chris Bartlett, Justin Bengry, Michael Bronski, El Chenier, Michan Connor, Seth Denbo, Joseph E. B. Elliott, Beth English, Laura Ewen, Marla Erlien, Anna Faison, Alex Gagne, Stephen Hemrick, Gerard Koskovich, Malcolm Lazin, Karen Lou, Cynthia MacLeod, Helen Mahan, Shirley McKinney, David Perry, Daniel Ross, Donna Sachet, Mark Segal, Anita Shunamon, Bob Skiba, Charles Volz, and Michael Yamashita. More generally, I want to acknowledge Jonathan Ned Katz, Allison Miller, Claire Potter, and Rick Shenkman, each of whom offered helpful conversations and generous comments as I worked on this book. I also am very grateful for the research assistance of San Francisco State University graduate students Victor Aguilar, Andrew Johnson, Eric Noble, Carlos Tapia, Dylan Weir, and Jennifer Zoland.

The University of California Press, my editor Niels Hooper, editorial assistant Naja Pulliam Collins, and copy editor Gary J. Hamel provided valuable guidance and support, as did the endowment funds associated with the Jamie and Phyllis Pasker Chair in US history at San Francisco State University. I appreciate the helpful comments of two anonymous reviewers and the wise advice of Lisa Arellano and Gerard Koskovich, both of whom found time during an exceptionally strange year to read parts of the manuscript and offer astute suggestions.

Most of all, I want to thank Jorge Olivares. By the time this book enters the queer public sphere, we will have been together for twenty-five years. There is so much that I could say about the ways in which Jorge has enriched my life; most relevant here is how grateful I am for his consistent, compassionate, and constructive support of my work.

Notes

INTRODUCTION

1. For introductions to public history, see the National Council on Public History's website (https://ncph.org/), journal (https://tph.ucpress.edu/), newsletter (https://ncph.org/phn-back-issues/), and blog (https://ncph.org/history-at-work/).

2. See George Chauncey, *Why Marriage? The History Shaping Today's Debate over Gay Equality* (New York: Basic, 2004); George Chauncey, "'What Gay Studies Taught the Court': The Historians' Amicus Brief in *Lawrence v. Texas*," *GLQ* 10, no. 3 (2004): 509–538; Daniel Hurewitz, "Sexuality Scholarship as a Foundation for Change: *Lawrence v. Texas* and the Impact of the Historians' Brief," *Health and Human Rights* 7, no. 2 (2004): 205–216; Estelle B. Freedman, "When Historical Interpretation Meets Legal Advocacy: Abortion, Sodomy, and Same-Sex Marriage," in *Feminism, Sexuality, Politics* (Chapel Hill: University of North Carolina Press, 2006), 175–195; Nancy F. Cott, "Which History in *Obergefell v. Hodges*?" *Perspectives on History* 53, no. 5A (Summer 2015); Rachel Hope Cleves, "History from the Witness Stand: An Interview with George Chauncey," *Notches*, 23 June 2016, http://notchesblog.com/2016/06/23/history-from-the-witness-stand-an-interview-with-george-chauncey/.

3. For introductions to queer public history, see Lisa Duggan, "History's Gay Ghetto: The Contradictions of Growth in Lesbian and Gay History," in *Presenting the Past: Essays on History and the Public*, eds. Susan Porter Benson, Stephen Brier, and Roy Rosenzweig (Philadelphia: Temple University Press, 1986), 281–290; Susan Ferentinos, *Interpreting LGBT History at Museums and Historic Sites* (Lanham, MD: Rowman & Littlefield, 2015); Megan E.

Springate, ed., *LGBTQ America: A Theme Study of Lesbian, Gay, Bisexual, Transgender, and Queer History* (Washington, DC: National Park Foundation and National Park Service, 2016); Lara Kelland, "Public History and Queer Memory," *The Routledge History of Queer America*, ed. Don Romesburg (New York: Routledge, 2019), 371–381; "Queering Public History: The State of the Field," special issue of *The Public Historian* 41, no. 2 (May 2019); Nicole Belolan, ed., *LGBTQ Public History: Reports from the Field* (Indianapolis: National Council on Public History, October 2019); Katherine Crawford-Lackey and Megan E. Springate, eds., *Preservation and Place: Historic Preservation by and of LGBTQ Communities in the United States* (New York: Berghahn, 2019). My thinking about queer public history has been influenced by serving on the supervisory committee for Tamara de Szegheo Lang, "Contagious History: Affect and Identification in Queer Public History Exhibitions" (PhD diss., York University, 2018).

4. See Joan Nestle, "The Will to Remember: The Lesbian Herstory Archives of New York," *Feminist Review*, no. 34 (Spring 1990): 86–94; Brenda J. Marton, "History Projects, Libraries, and Archives," in *Encyclopedia of Lesbian, Gay, Bisexual and Transgender History in America*, ed. Marc Stein (New York: Scribner's, 2003), 2:43–48; Aimee Brown, "How Queer 'Pack Rats' and Activist Archivists Saved Our History: An Overview of Lesbian, Gay, Bisexual, Transgender, and Queer (LGBTQ) Archives, 1970–2008," in *Serving LGBTIQ Library and Archives Users*, ed. Ellen Greenblatt (Jefferson, NC: McFarland, 2011), 121–135; Nan Alamilla Boyd and Horacio N. Roque Ramírez, eds., *Bodies of Evidence: The Practice of Queer Oral History* (New York: Oxford University Press, 2012); Daniel Marshall, Kevin P. Murphy, and Zeb Tortorici, eds., "Queering Archives: Historical Unravelings," special issue of *Radical History Review*, no. 120 (Fall 2014); Gerard Koskovich, "Displaying the Queer Past: Purposes, Publics, and Possibilities at the GLBT History Museum," *QED: A Journal in GLBTQ Worldmaking* 1, no. 2 (2014): 61–78; Nan Alamilla Boyd, "History as Social Change: Queer Archives and Oral History Projects," in *Understanding and Teaching U.S. Lesbian, Gay, Bisexual, and Transgender History*, ed. Leila J. Rupp and Susan K. Freeman (Madison: University of Wisconsin Press, 2014), 311–319; Don Romesburg, "Presenting the Queer Past: A Case for the GLBT History Museum," *Radical History Review*, no. 120 (Fall 2014): 131–144; Daniel Marshall, Kevin P. Murphy, and Zeb Tortorici, eds., "Queering Archives: Intimate Tracings," special issue of *Radical History Review*, no. 122 (May 2015); Joan Nestle, "Who Were We to Do Such a Thing? Grassroots Necessities, Grassroots Dreaming," *Radical History Review*, no. 122 (May 2015): 233–242; Amy L. Stone and Jaime Cantrell, eds., *Out of the Closet, into the Archives: Researching Sexual Histories* (Albany: State University of New York Press, 2015); Tamara de Szegheo Lang, "The Explosion in Grandma's Attic, the Cabinet of Curiosities, and Chance Encounters at the GLBT History Museum," *Journal of the Canadian Historical Association* 26, no. 2 (2015): 83–110; Gerard Koskovich, Don Romesburg, and Amy Sueyoshi, "Curators in Conversation: Conceiving the Queer Past at the GLBT Historical Society Museum," *Museum International* 72, nos. 3–4 (2020): 66–79.

5. See James F. Brooks, "Commemorating Queer History," *The Public Historian* 41, no. 2 (May 2019), 5. The article referenced is Lauren Jae Gutterman, "OutHistory.org: An Experiment in LGBTQ Community History-Making," *The Public Historian* 32 no. 4 (Fall 2010): 96–109.

6. Megan E. Springate, "Introduction to the LGBTQ Heritage Initiative Theme Study," in Springate, *LGBTQ America*. The Stonewall Inn, site of the 1969 Stonewall Riots, was listed in 1999.

7. Duggan, "History's Gay Ghetto"; Terence O'Donnell, "Pitfalls along the Path of Public History," in Benson et al., *Presenting the Past*, 239, 244. For passing references to LGBT history, see 92 and 303. For signs of improvement, see Roy Rosenzweig and David Thelen, *The Presence of the Past: Popular Uses of History in American Life* (New York: Columbia University Press, 2000), 4, 119, 183, 200, 267–268. For similar marginalization in digital history, see Daniel J. Cohen and Roy Rosenzweig, *Digital History: A Guide to Gathering, Preserving, and Presenting the Past on the Web* (Philadelphia: University of Pennsylvania Press, 2005); Roy Rosenzweig, *Clio Wired: The Future of the Past in the Digital Age* (New York: Columbia University Press, 2011).

8. See Emma Pettit, "Why Are Students Ditching the History Major?" *The Chronicle of Higher Education*, 26 Nov. 2018; Colleen Flaherty, "The Vanishing History Major," *Inside Higher Ed*, 27 Nov. 2018; Benjamin M. Schmidt, "The History BA since the Great Recession: The 2018 AHA Majors Report," *Perspectives on History* 56, no. 9 (Dec. 2018): 19–23; Julia Brookins and Emily Swafford, "History Enrollments Hold Steady as Department Efforts Intensify," *Perspectives on History* 58, no. 1 (Jan. 2020): 20–23; Julia Brookins, "History Enrollment Edges Slightly Lower," *Perspectives on History* 59, no. 1 (Jan. 2021): 21–24.

9. Gerard Koskovich, "The History of Queer History: One Hundred Years of the Search for Shared Heritage," in *Preservation and Place*, 30–84.

10. Duggan, "History's Gay Ghetto"; Martin Bauml Duberman, "Reclaiming the Gay Past," *Reviews in American History* 16, no. 4 (Dec. 1988): 515–525; John D'Emilio, "Not A Simple Matter: Gay History and Gay Historians," *Journal of American History* 76, no. 2 (Sep. 1989): 435–442. See also Peter Novick, *That Noble Dream: The "Objectivity Question" and the American Historical Profession* (New York: Cambridge University Press, 1988).

11. Jeffrey Escoffier, "Inside the Ivory Closet: The Challenges Facing Lesbian and Gay Studies," *Out/Look*, no. 20 (Fall 1990): 40–48; Lisa Duggan, "The Discipline Problem: Queer Theory Meets Lesbian and Gay History," *GLQ* 2, no. 3 (1995): 179–191.

12. Scott de Groot, "'A Curse on Those Who Need Heroes'? Genealogical Appropriation and the Historical Horizons of Gay Liberation, 1969–1975," *Left History* 19, no. 1 (Spring 2015): 25–55. I limit myself to US history in the discussion that follows, but many LGBT historians, in and beyond the United States, studied non-US topics.

13. Maurice Kenny, "Tinselled Bucks: An Historical Study in Indian Homosexuality," *Gay Sunshine*, nos. 26–27 (Winter 1975): 15–17; Jim Kepner, "200 Years of Oppression," *Philadelphia Gay News (PGN)*, 15 Mar. 1978, 13; 15 May 1978, 18; 15 July 1978, 11; Cherríe Moraga and Gloria Anzaldúa,

eds., *This Bridge Called My Back: Writings by Radical Women of Color* (Watertown, MA: Persephone, 1981); Barbara Smith, ed., *Home Girls: A Black Feminist Anthology* (New York: Home Girls, 1983); Joseph Beam, *In the Life: A Black Gay Anthology* (Boston: Alyson, 1986); Juanita Ramos, *Compañeras: Latina Lesbians* (New York: Latina Lesbian History Project, 1987); Will Roscoe, ed., *Living the Spirit: A Gay American Indian Anthology* (New York: St. Martin's, 1988).

14. Allan Bérubé, *Coming Out under Fire: The History of Gay Men and Women in World War II* (New York: Free Press, 1990); Michael Bronski, *Culture Clash: The Making of Gay Sensibility* (Boston: South End, 1984); Elizabeth Lapovsky Kennedy and Madeline Davis, *Boots of Leather, Slippers of Gold: The History of a Lesbian Community* (New York: Routledge, 1993); Joan Nestle, *A Restricted Country* (Ithaca, NY: Firebrand, 1987); Joan Nestle, *The Persistent Desire: A Femme-Butch Reader* (Boston: Alyson, 1992); Eric Garber, "A Spectacle in Color: The Lesbian and Gay Subculture of Jazz Age Harlem," in *Hidden from History: Reclaiming the Gay and Lesbian Past*, ed. Martin Bauml Duberman, Martha Vicinus, and George Chauncey Jr. (New York: New American Library, 1989), 318–331; Judith Schwarz, *Radical Feminists of Heterodoxy* (Norwich, VT: New Victoria, 1982); Jonathan Ned Katz, *Gay American History* (New York: Crowell, 1976); Jonathan Ned Katz, *Gay/Lesbian Almanac* (New York: Harper, 1983). On Katz, see Jim Downs, *Stand by Me: The Forgotten History of Gay Liberation* (New York: Basic, 2016), 89–112.

15. For dissertation titles and dates, see the *Dissertations and Theses* database (Proquest). For their early work on LGBT history, see Carroll Smith-Rosenberg, "The Female World of Love and Ritual: Relations between Women in Nineteenth-Century America," *Signs* 1, no. 2 (Autumn 1975): 1–29; Carroll Smith-Rosenberg, *Disorderly Conduct: Visions of Gender in Victorian America* (New York: Oxford University Press, 1985); Lillian Faderman, "The Morbidification of Love between Women by 19th-Century Sexologists," *Journal of Homosexuality* 4, no. 1 (1978): 73–90; Lillian Faderman, *Surpassing the Love of Men: Romantic Friendship and Love between Women from the Renaissance to the Present* (New York: Morrow, 1981); Blanch Wiesen Cook, "Female Support Networks and Political Activism: Lillian Wald, Crystal Eastman, Emma Goldman," *Chrysalis* 3 (Autumn 1977): 43–61; Blanche Wiesen Cook, "'Women Alone Stir My Imagination': Lesbianism and the Cultural Tradition," *Signs* 4, no. 4 (Summer 1979): 718–739; Nancy Sahli, "Smashing: Women's Relationships before the Fall," *Chrysalis* 8 (Summer 1979): 17–27; Estelle B. Freedman, "Separatism as Strategy: Female Institution Building and American Feminism, 1870–1930," *Feminist Studies* 5, no. 3 (Autumn 1979): 512–529; Estelle B. Freedman, "'Uncontrolled Desires': The Response to the Sexual Psychopath, 1920–1960," *Journal of American History* 74, no. 1 (June 1987): 83–106; Leila J. Rupp, "'Imagine My Surprise': Women's Relationships in Historical Perspective," *Frontiers* 5, no. 3 (Autumn 1980): 61–70; Paula Gunn Allen, *The Sacred Hoop: Recovering the Feminine in American Indian Traditions* (Boston: Beacon, 1986); Kennedy and Davis, *Boots of Leather*; Esther Newton, "The Mythic Mannish Lesbian: Radclyffe Hall and the New Woman," *Signs* 9, no. 4 (1984): 557–575. Faderman was trained in English

literature and Kennedy and Newton in anthropology, but they consistently were oriented to and included in conversations among historians.

16. Vern Bullough and Martha Voght, "Homosexuality and Its Confusion with the 'Secret Sin' in Pre-Freudian America," *Journal of the History of Medicine and Allied Sciences* 28, no. 2 (Apr. 1973): 143–155; Vern Bullough, "An Early American Sex Manual; or, Aristotle Who?" *Early American Literature* 7, no. 3 (Winter 1973): 236–246; Vern Bullough, "Transsexualism in History," *Archives of Sexual Behavior* 4 (1975): 561–571; Vern Bullough, "Heresy, Witchcraft, and Sexuality," *Journal of Homosexuality* 1, no. 2 (1976): 183–199; Vern Bullough, "Homosexuality and the Medical Model," *Journal of Homosexuality* 1, no. 1 (1976): 99–110; Vern Bullough, *Sexual Variance in Society and History* (New York: Wiley, 1976); Vern Bullough, *Sin, Sickness, and Sanity: A History of Sexual Attitudes* (New York: Garland, 1977); Vern Bullough and Bonnie Bullough, "Lesbianism in the 1920s and 1930s: A Newfound Study," *Signs* 2, no. 4 (Summer 1977): 895–904; Vern Bullough, *Homosexuality: A History* (New York: New American Library, 1979); Vern Bullough, "The Rockefellers and Sex Research," *Journal of Sex Research* 21, no. 2 (1985): 113–125; Vern Bullough, "Lesbianism, Homosexuality, and the American Civil Liberties Union," *Journal of Homosexuality* 13, no. 1 (Fall 1986): 23–33; John Burnham, "Early References to Homosexual Communities in American Medical Writings," *Medical Aspects of Human Sexuality* 7, no. 8 (Aug. 1973): 34–49; Robert F. Oaks, "'Things Fearful to Name': Sodomy and Buggery in Seventeenth-Century New England," *Journal of Social History* 12, no. 2 (Winter 1978): 268–281; Robert F. Oaks, "Defining Sodomy in Seventeenth-Century Massachusetts," *Journal of Homosexuality* 6, nos. 1–2 (Fall 1980/Winter 1981): 79–83; Martin Bauml Duberman, "'Writhing Bedfellows': Two Young Men from Antebellum South Carolina's Ruling Elite Share 'Extravagant Delight,'" *Journal of Homosexuality* 6, nos. 1–2 (Fall 1980/Winter 1981): 85–101; Fred Eggan, Richard O. Clemmer, and Martin Duberman, "Hopi Indians Redux," *Radical History Review*, no. 24 (1980): 177–187; Martin Bauml Duberman, *About Time: Exploring the Gay Past* (New York: Gay Presses of New York, 1986); Duberman, Vicinus, and Chauncey, eds., *Hidden from History*; Ronald Bayer, *Homosexuality and American Psychiatry* (New York: Basic, 1981); Henry Abelove, "Freud, Male Homosexuality, and the Americans," *Dissent* 33, no. 1 (Winter 1985–86): 59–69; Walter L. Williams, *The Spirit and the Flesh: Sexual Diversity in American Indian Culture* (Boston: Beacon, 1986).

17. Salvatore John Licata, "Gay Power: A History of the American Gay Movement, 1908–1974" (University of Southern California, 1978); Robert Marotta, "The Politics of Homosexuality: Homophile and Early Gay Liberation Organizations in New York City" (Harvard University, 1979); John D'Emilio, "Out of the Shadows: The Homosexual Emancipation Movement in the United States" (Columbia University, 1982); George Chauncey, "Gay New York: Urban Culture and the Making of the Gay Male World, 1890–1940" (Yale University, 1989); Susan A. Cahn, "Coming On Strong: Gender and Sexuality in Women's Sport" (University of Minnesota, 1990); Sharon Ullman, "Broken Silences: Sex and Culture in Turn of the Century America" (University

of California, Berkeley, 1990); Lisa Duggan, "The Trials of Alice Mitchell: Sex, Science, and Sensationalism in Turn of the Century America" (University of Pennsylvania, 1992). In the early 2000s, I produced a bibliography of LGBT history dissertations for the Committee on Gay and Lesbian History (now the Committee on LGBT History); for the latest version, see http://clgbthistory.org/projects/dissertations.

18. Estelle B. Freedman, "Women's Networks and Women's Loyalties: Reflections on a Tenure Case," *Frontiers* 8, no. 3 (1986): 50–54; Esther Newton, *Margaret Mead Made Me Gay: Personal Essays, Public Ideas* (Durham, NC: Duke University Press, 2000), especially 219–224, 238–242; Esther Newton, *My Butch Career: A Memoir* (Durham, NC: Duke University Press, 2018); Martin Duberman and Robert Padgug, "From the Abolitionists to Gay History: An Interview with Martin Bauml Duberman," *Radical History Review*, no. 42 (1988): 65–86; Martin Duberman, *Cures: A Gay Man's Odyssey* (New York: Penguin, 1991); Martin Duberman, *Midlife Queer: Autobiography of a Decade* (New York: Scribner, 1996); Martin Duberman, *Waiting to Land: A (Mostly) Political Memoir, 1985–2008* (New York: New Press, 2009); Martin Duberman, *The Rest of It: Hustlers, Cocaine, Depression, and Then Some, 1976–1988* (Durham, NC: Duke University Press, 2018); D'Emilio, "Not a Simple Matter"; John D'Emilio, *Making Trouble: Essays on Gay History, Politics, and the University* (New York: Routledge, 1992); John D'Emilio, *The World Turned: Essays on Gay History, Politics, and Culture* (Durham, NC: Duke University Press, 2002); John D'Emilio, *In A New Century: Essays on Queer History, Politics, and Community Life* (Madison: University of Wisconsin, 2014); Duggan, "History's Gay Ghetto"; Duggan, "The Discipline Problem."

19. One of the earliest, after Allen, was Kevin J. Mumford; see "From Vice to Vogue: Black/White Sexuality and the 1920s" (Stanford University, 1993).

20. "1974 Annual Meeting," *AHA Newsletter*, Dec. 1974, 1; "AHA Ballot," *AHA Newsletter*, Mar. 1975, 15; "Results of Mail Ballot," *AHA Newsletter*, May 1975, 1.

21. Michael Lodwick and Thomas Fiehrer, "Undoing History; or, Clio Clobbered," *AHA Newsletter*, May 1975, 4–5.

22. Allison Miller, "Scholars on the Edge: The LGBTQ Historians Task Force Report and the AHA," *Perspectives on History* 54, no. 2 (Feb. 2016); "LGBTQ Task Force Final Report," 2015, https://www.historians.org/about-aha-and-membership/governance/reports-of-committees-and-divisions/lgbtq-task-force-final-report-(2015). The AHA task force was chaired by Leisa Meyer and included Susan Stryker, Jennifer Brier, and me, along with a series of AHA vice presidents.

23. See, for example, Donn Teal, *The Gay Militants* (New York: Stein and Day, 1971); Jim Kepner, "When Did Gay Militancy Begin," *The Advocate*, 23 Dec. 1971, 2, 10; Kay Tobin and Randy Wicker, *The Gay Crusaders* (New York: Paperback Library, 1972); Randy Wicker, "The Stonewall Myth: Lies about Gay Liberation," *GAY*, 9 Apr. 1973, 4–5.

24. John D'Emilio, "Radical Beginnings," *The Body Politic*, Nov. 1978, 19–24; "Public Actions, Private Fears," *The Body Politic*, Dec. 1978, 24–29,

"Reaction, Red Baiting, and 'Respectability': Dreams Deferred 1953," *The Body Politic*, Feb. 1979, 22–27. See also D'Emilio, *Making Trouble*; D'Emilio, *The World Turned*; D'Emilio, *In A New Century*; John D'Emilio, Urvashi Vaid, and William Turner, eds., *Creating Change: Sexuality, Public Policy, and Civil Rights* (New York: St. Martin's, 2000); Allan Bérubé, *My Desire for History: Essays in Gay, Community, and Labor History* (Chapel Hill: University of North Carolina Press, 2011).

25. See Leon Bock and Thomas Kavunedus, *Struggle for Power: The Longest School Strike in New York State History* (Xlibris, 2011); Marc Stein, "Tug of War," *Peekskill Evening Star*, 16 Oct. 1977.

26. I also began writing about abortion politics; see Marc Stein, "Ten Years After: Legalized Abortion Meets 'Right to Lifers,'" *Wesleyan Argus*, 1 Feb. 1983, 3.

27. See Marjorie Hunter, "Students Lobby in Capital against Cuts in U.S. Loans," *New York Times (NYT)*, 2 Mar. 1982, D22, which stated, "The largest contingent came from Wesleyan University in Middletown, Conn. About 650 students, more than a fourth of the students at the university, came to Washington." See also Marc Stein, "Students Face Budget Cuts without United Response," *Wesleyan Argus*, 1 Mar. 1983, 3; Marc Stein, "Congress Opposes Fed Educ. Cuts," *Wesleyan Argus*, 5 Apr. 1983, 1, 6.

28. Marc Stein and Susanna Zwerling, "Case Study Analysis: Tuition and Financial Aid at Wesleyan," 25 Jan. 1984. See also Deanne Meltzer, "COPUS Wesleyan Fights for Aid in D.C. and on Campus," *Wesleyan Argus*, 15 Nov. 1983, 4; Tom Frank, "Report Raps Aid Policy," *Wesleyan Argus*, 27 Jan. 1984, 1, 3; COPUS Wesleyan, letter to the editor, *Wesleyan Argus*, 27 Jan. 1984, 2; Ted Funsten, "Wesleyan Plans Study of Student Criticisms," *Middletown Press*, 27 Jan. 1984, 1, 11; Thomas Frank, "Report Attacks Costs for Wesleyan," *Hartford Courant*, 27 Jan. 1984, B2; Danny Kelley, "WSA Meets," *Wesleyan Argus*, 31 Jan. 1984, 1, 8.

29. Anonymous, "'Gay' Oppression and Fear," *Wesleyan Argus*, 19 Apr. 1983, 3.

30. Mary Byrne, Evelyn Gonzalez, Mark Hayman, Christine Moctezuma, and Marc Stein, "Report of the Wesleyan Student Assembly's Gay and Lesbian Issues Task Force," 7 Feb. 1985.

31. Another formative experience occurred when I was involved in a dispute about Nation of Islam leader Louis Farrakhan. At a moment when US presidential candidate Jesse Jackson was receiving criticism for his ties to Farrakhan, who had made anti-Semitic statements, the main African American student group on campus requested funds from the student government to fund a speech by Farrakhan. As one of the Student Assembly's coordinators, I spoke out in favor of providing the funds, not because I supported Farrakhan but because we had recently funded presentations by controversial white speakers, including G. Gordon Liddy and General William Westmoreland. In the end, we funded the speech, a campus-wide referendum overturned funding for all student groups, the Assembly defiantly passed a nearly identical budget, and Farrakhan delivered his lecture. See Jeffrey Schmalz, "Invitation to Farrakhan

Causes Rift at Wesleyan," *NYT*, 9 Oct. 1984, B2; "Offer to Farrakhan Survives Challenge," *NYT*, 26 Oct. 1984, B2.

32. Dennis Hevesi, "Randall Forsberg, 64, Nuclear Freeze Advocate, Dies," *NYT*, 26 Oct. 2007.

33. See Marc Stein, "Gay Community News," in *Gay Histories and Cultures: An Encyclopedia*, ed. George E. Hagerty (New York: Garland, 2000), 369–370.

34. Larry Goldsmith, "An Excellent Introduction to the Social History of Sexuality," *Gay Community News (GCN)*, 10 July 1988, 9, 12; Shelley Mains and Margaret Cerullo, "From the Bedroom to the Marketplace," *GCN*, 10 July 1988, 8–9.

35. Marc Stein, "British Gay Left: An Interview with Jeffrey Weeks," *GCN*, 30 Oct. 1988, 8–9; Marc Stein, "The 'Uses' of the Holocaust and the Evolution of Larry Kramer," review of *Reports from the Holocaust*, *GCN*, 28 May 1989, 8, 11. For the complete transcript of my interview with Weeks, see *Notches: (Re)marks on the History of Sexuality*, 10 Feb. 2015, http://notchesblog.com /2015/02/10/sexual-politics-in-the-era-of-reagan-and-thatcher-marc-stein-in -conversation-with-jeffrey-weeks/.

36. Marc Stein, "History in Camouflage," review of Allan Bérubé, *Coming Out under Fire*, *GCN*, 22 July 1990, 7, 9, 12; Marc Stein, "A Century of Queerness," review of David Halperin, *One Hundred Years of Homosexuality*, *GCN*, 17 Aug. 1990, 7, 9; Marc Stein, "Dyke Queen Meets Fag Hag," review of Eve Kosofsky Sedgwick, *Epistemology of the Closet*, *GCN*, 7 July 1991, 7, 12; Marc Stein, review of Henry Abelove, *The Evangelist of Desire*, *GCN*, 13 Oct. 1991, 7, 9.

37. "Project Seeks to Avert Dearth of College Teachers," *NYT*, 26 Dec. 1985, A14; Edward Fiske, "Colleges Scrambling to Avert a Possible Faculty Shortage," *NYT*, 16 Mar. 1986, 1, 38; Steven Prokesch, "Mounting Competition for College Teachers," *NYT*, 12 Apr. 1987, EDUC28-31; Joseph Berger, "Slow Pace toward Doctorates Prompts Fears of Unfilled Jobs," *NYT*, 3 May 1989, A1, B7; Edward Fiske, "Shortages Predicted for 90's in Professors of Humanities," *NYT*, 13 Sep. 1989, A1, B10; Elizabeth Fowler, "Shortage of Ph.D.'s on Campus Seen," *NYT*, 3 Oct. 1989, D19.

38. "Hello/Goodbye," *GCN*, 23 July 1989, 4.

39. See Pierre Bourdieu, *Homo Academicus*, trans. Peter Collier (Palo Alto, CA: Stanford University Press, 1988).

PART ONE. QUEER MEMORIES OF THE 1980S

1. For alternative perspectives, see Claire Bond Potter and Renee C. Romano, eds., *Doing Recent History* (Athens: University of Georgia Press, 2012).

2. "About the OAH," https://www.oah.org/about/; "Process: A Blog for American History," http://www.processhistory.org/about/.

3. Claire Potter, "M-I-C-K-E-Y M-O-U-S-E," *Chronicle of Higher Education*, May 9, 2015, http://www.chronicle.com/blognetwork/tenuredradical/.

4. "About OutHistory," OutHistory, http://outhistory.org/about-outhistory.

PART TWO. DISCIPLINE, PUNISH, AND PROTEST

1. Lisa Duggan, "The Discipline Problem: Queer Theory Meets Lesbian and Gay History," *GLQ* 2, no. 3 (1995): 179–191.

2. I met David Johnson when I interviewed him for Marc Stein, "The New Debate on HIV Testing," *Gay Community News*, 24 July 1988, 9–10, 15.

3. See also Marc Stein, "I Dream of Sheldon," *Graduate Perspective*, Dec. 1991, 9; Stephen Sanford, "The Second Degree: Out and About," *Daily Pennsylvanian (DP)*, 10 Nov. 1993, 3.

4. Heidi Gleit, "Grad Students to Discuss the Unionization of TAs," *DP*, 17 Sep. 1992, 1, 2; Heidi Gleit, "Grad Students Form a Third Gov't Branch," *DP*, 18 Sep. 1992, 1, 4; Heidi Gleit, "Identity Crisis," *DP*, 22 Sep. 1992, 3; Marc Stein, letter to the editor, *DP*, 30 Sep. 1992, 6; Heidi Gleit, "New Graduate Student Coalition Picks Name," *DP*, 7 Oct. 1992; Heidi Gleit, "Grad Group Is Unknown to Many," *DP*, 28 Oct. 1992, 1, 5; Marc Stein, "Getting from Here to There: Notes on Organizing Graduate Students," *Graduate Perspective*, Dec. 1992, 12; Abby Beshkin, "Graduate Stipends Cut for '93–'94," *DP*, 30 Mar. 1993, 2.

5. See Lorrie Kim, "Valentine's Day Ad Stirs Campus Ruckus," *PGN*, 15 Mar. 1991, 3; Frank Broderick, "Polo Bay Called Anti-Gay over Alleged Ad Bias," *Au Courant*, 25 Mar. 1991, 3, 11; Matthew Selman, "Complaint Filed against 'DP' for Valentine's Day Ad," *DP*, 2 Apr. 1991, 1, 7; Marc Stein, letter to the editor, *DP*, 11 Apr. 1991, 7; Marc Stein, "University Coalition Files Discrimination Claim," *Graduate Perspective*, Sep. 1991, 1, 2; Helen Jung, letter to the editor, *DP*, 8 Oct. 1991, 6; Marc Stein, letter to the editor, *DP*, 17 Oct. 1991, 7; Marc Stein, et al., letter to the editor, *DP*, 6 Dec. 1991, 6; Margaret Kane, "'DP' Publishes Apology for Ad," *DP*, 9 Dec. 1991. See also Rob Steinman, "Panel Discusses Challenges of Being Gay and 'Out' at Work," *Daily Pennsylvanian*, 16 Feb. 2001, 3; Marc Stein, "Balancing LGBTQ Student Services and LGBTQ Studies," *Up & Out: The Newsletter of PennGALA*, Mar. 2002, 2, 3.

6. See Marc Stein, "Queer Anti-Violence Demo Draws Attack from Cop," *GCN*, 21 Oct. 1990, 3, 7.

7. "Robbing the Cradle," *Lingua Franca*, May 1995, 20-21.

8. See Amy Montemerlo, "Subcommittee Tackles Gay Curriculum Issue," *Colby Echo*, 19 Mar. 1998, 1, 2.

9. Alex Kellogg, "Report Reveals Tight Job Market for Historians of Gay Topics," *Chronicle of Higher Education*, 6 July 2001.

10. See Scott Jaschik, "Anti-Gay 'Flagging' at NEH?" *Inside Higher Ed*, 9 Jan. 2006, https://www.insidehighered.com/news/2006/01/09/anti-gay -flagging-neh; Linda Kerber, "Two Days in March: Historians and Humanities Advocacy Day," *Perspectives on History*, May 2006; "Statement on Peer Review," *Perspectives on History*, Sep. 2005, 64; Bruce Craig, "Results of Investigation into the Humanities Endowment," *Perspectives on History*, Oct. 2005; American Historical Association, "Statement on Peer Review for Historical Research," 2005, https://www.historians.org/jobs-and-professional -development/statements-standards-and-guidelines-of-the-discipline/statement

-on-peer-review-for-historical-research. See also Lou Chibbaro, "Bush Administration 'Flags' Research on Gay Topics," *Washington Blade*, 27 Jan. 2006.

CHAPTER 3. COMMITTEE ON LESBIAN AND GAY HISTORY SURVEY ON LGBTQ HISTORY CAREERS

1. Survey conducted August 2000 to January 2001. Analysis based on 44 of 51 responses received. Of the seven respondents whose answers are not discussed here, two did not indicate that their dissertations dealt with lgbtq history; four completed PhDs in comparative literature, sociology, art and art history, or French studies; and one completed a PhD in Europe and lives in Europe. The survey has not captured all people who have completed or are in the process of completing dissertations that deal in part or in full with lgbtq history. One person who completed such a dissertation in the 1970s has died; three people who completed such dissertations in the early 1990s did not respond. This survey also has not captured people who left their PhD programs in the course of doing dissertations on lgbtq history. At least four people did so in the 1990s. For a bibliography of lgbtq history dissertations, see the *CLGH Newsletter* 14:2 (fall 2000), 8–11 (also available on the CLGH website at www.oneinstitute.org). The survey does not cover the experiences of people who have produced scholarship in lgbtq history as independent or post-tenure scholars.

2. "Equivalent" refers to relatively secure and full-time academic appointments in the U.K.

3. According to *Perspectives*, 59–63 percent of new history PhDs from U.S. universities in 1996, 1997, and 1998 were male. See *Perspectives*, Jan. 2000, 3.

4. History includes history, history of science, and history of consciousness.

5. According to *Perspectives*, 39–41 percent of all PhDs in history from U.S. universities in 1997 and 1998 worked on U.S. dissertation topics. See *Perspectives*, Jan. 2000, 4.

6. According to *Perspectives*, the average number of years registered in graduate programs for people who completed PhDs at U.S. universities in 1998 was 8.6. See *Perspectives*, Jan. 2000, 4.

CHAPTER 4. CROSSING BORDERS

1. See Ralf Jurgens, "HIV Testing and Confidentiality: Final Report," Canadian HIV/AIDS Legal Network and Canadian AIDS Society, 1998, http://www.aidslaw.ca/Maincontent/issues/testing/08mandate2.html; AIDS Coalition to Unleash Power, "Mandatory HIV Testing of Applicants for Immigration," 2000; "Canada to Start Testing Immigrants for HIV," 4 December 2000, http://www.cnn.com/2000/Health/AIDS/12/04/canada.aids.reut/; David Garmaise, "Questions and Answers: Canada's Immigration Policies as They Affect People Living with HIV/AIDS," The Canadian HIV/AIDS Legal Network, March 2003. According to these sources, before the policy change announced in 2000 immigrants were tested for tuberculosis and syphilis; under the new policy immigrants would also be tested for HIV and hepatitis B. In adopting this policy, Canada joined 50 countries, including the United States, in requiring

HIV tests for immigrants. The United States adopted a policy of mandatory HIV testing for immigrants in 1987.

2. For recent discussions of *Boutilier*, see William T. Reynolds, "The Immigration and Nationality Act and the Rights of Homosexual Aliens," *Journal of Homosexuality* 5, 1–2 (Fall 1979–Winter 1980): 79–87; Marc Bogatin, "The Immigration and Nationality Act and the Exclusion of Homosexual Aliens: *Boutilier v. INS* Revisited," *Cardozo Law Review* 2, 2 (Winter 1981): 359–396; Rachel A. Hexter, "Immigration - Naturalization," *Suffolk Transnational Law Journal* 6, 2 (Spring 1982): 383–394; Robert Poznanski, "The Propriety of Denying Entry to Homosexual Aliens: Examining the Public Health Service's Authority over Medical Exclusions," *University of Michigan Journal of Law Reform* 17 (Winter 1984): 331–359; Samuel M. Silvers, "The Exclusion and Expulsion of Homosexual Aliens," *Columbia Human Rights Law Review* 15, 2 (Spring 1984): 295–332; Peter N. Fowler and Leonard Graff, "Gay Aliens and Immigration: Resolving the Conflict Between *Hill* and *Longstaff*," *University of Dayton Law Review* (1985): 621–644; Philip Girard, "From Subversion to Liberation: Homosexuals and the Immigration Act, 1952–1977," *Canadian Journal of Law and Society* 2 (1987): 1–27; Richard Green, "'Give Me Your Tired, Your Poor, Your Huddled Masses' (of Heterosexuals): An Analysis of American and Canadian Immigration Policy," *Anglo-American Law Review* 16 (1987): 139–159; William N. Eskridge, Jr., "Gadamer/Statutory Interpretation," *Columbia Law Review* 90 (Apr. 1990): 609–681; Shannon Minter, "Sodomy and Public Morality Offenses Under US Immigration Law: Penalizing Lesbian and Gay Identity," *Cornell International Law Journal* 26 (1993): 771–817; William N. Eskridge, Jr., *Dynamic Statutory Interpretation* (Cambridge, MA: Harvard Univ. Press, 1994), 48–80; Robert J. Foss, "The Demise of the Homosexual Exclusion: New Possibilities for Gay and Lesbian Immigration," *Harvard Civil Rights-Civil Liberties Law Review* 29, 2 (Spring 1994; dated Spring 1993 on the internet): 439–475; William B. Turner, "Lesbian/Gay Rights and Immigration Policy: Lobbying to End the Medical Model," *Journal of Policy History* 7, 2 (1995): 208–225; Eithne Luibhéid, "'Obvious Homosexuals and Homosexuals Who Cover Up: Lesbian and Gay Exclusion in US Immigration," *Radical America* 26, 2 (Apr.–Jun. 1992, published Oct. 1996): 33–40; William N. Eskridge, "Challenging the Apartheid of the Closet: Establishing Conditions for Lesbian and Gay Intimacy, Nomos, and Citizenship, 1961–1981," *Hofstra Law Review* 25 (Spring 1997): 817–960; William N. Eskridge, Jr., and Nan D. Hunter, *Sexuality, Gender, and the Law* (Westbury: Foundation, 1997), 175–189; Eithne Luibhéid, "'Looking Like A Lesbian': The Organization of Sexual Monitoring at the United States-Mexican Border," *Journal of the History of Sexuality* 8, 3 (Jan. 1998): 477–506; William N. Eskridge, Jr., *Gaylaw: Challenging the Apartheid of the Closet* (Cambridge, MA: Harvard Univ. Press, 1999), 35–36, 69–70, 132–134, 383–384; Barney Frank, "American Immigration Law: A Case Study in the Effective Use of the Political Process," in *Creating Change: Sexuality, Public Policy, and Civil Rights*, ed. John D'Emilio, William B. Turner, Urvashi Vaid (New York: St. Martin's Press, 2000), 208–235; Joyce Murdoch and Deb Price, *Courting Justice: Gay Men and Lesbians v. the Supreme Court* (New York: Basic,

2001), 103–134; Eithne Luibhéid, *Entry Denied: Controlling Sexuality at the Border* (Minneapolis: University of Minnesota Press, 2002), 77–101; Margot Canaday, "'Who Is a Homosexual?': The Consolidation of Sexual Identities in Mid-Twentieth-Century American Immigration Law," *Law and Social Inquiry* 28, 2 (Spring 2003): 351–386; Marc Stein, "Forgetting and Remembering a Deported Alien," *History News Network*, 3 November 2003, http://hnn.us /articles/ 1769.html.

3. Earlier history dissertations primarily or partially focusing on US lesbian/ gay topics include Salvatore John Licata, "Gay Power: A History of the American Gay Movement, 1908–1974," University of Southern California, History, 1978; Ramón A. Gutiérrez, "Marriage, Sex and the Family: Social Change in Colonial New Mexico, 1690–1846," University of Wisconsin, Madison, History, 1980; John D'Emilio, "Out of the Shadows: The Homosexual Emancipation Movement in the United States," Columbia University, History, 1982; George Chauncey, "Gay New York: Urban Culture and the Making of the Gay Male World, 1890–1940," Yale University, History, 1989; Susan Cahn, "Coming On Strong: Gender and Sexuality in Women's Sport," University of Minnesota, History, 1990; Sharon Ullman, "Broken Silences: Sex and Culture in Turn of the Century America," University of California, Berkeley, History, 1990; Kevin F. White, "The Flapper's Boyfriend: The Revolution in Morals and the Emergence of Modern American Male Sexuality, 1910–1930," Ohio State University, History, 1990; Will Roscoe, "The Zuni Man-Woman: An Ethnohistorical Study of a Third Gender Role," University of California at Santa Cruz, History of Consciousness, 1991; Lisa Duggan, "The Trials of Alice Mitchell: Sex, Science, and Sensationalism in Turn of the Century America," University of Pennsylvania, History, 1992; Leisa Meyer, "Creating G. I. Jane: The Women's Army Corps During World War II," University of Wisconsin at Madison, History, 1993; Kevin J. Mumford, "From Vice to Vogue: Black/White Sexuality and the 1920s," Stanford University, History 1993. For a more comprehensive and up-to-date listing of related history dissertations, see: http://www.usc.edu /isd/ archives/clh/dissertations.html.

4. For other accounts of homophobia and heterosexism in the historical profession, see Peter Boag, "Foreword," John Gerassi, *The Boys of Boise: Furor, Vice, and Folly in an American City* (1966; Seattle: University of Washington Press, 2001), vii–xvii; George Chauncey, "The Queer History and Politics of Lesbian and Gay Studies," in *Queer Frontiers: Millennial Geographies, Genders, and Generations*, ed. Joseph A. Boone et al. (Madison: University of Wisconsin Press, 2000), 298–315; John D'Emilio, *Making Trouble: Essays on Gay History, Politics, and the University* (New York: Routledge, 1992); John D'Emilio, *The World Turned: Essays on Gay History, Politics, and Culture* (Durham, NC: Duke University Press, 2002); Martin Duberman, *About Time: Exploring the Gay Past* (New York: Gay Presses of New York, 1991); Martin Duberman, *Cures: A Gay Man's Odyssey* (New York: Dutton, 1991); Martin Duberman, *Left Out: The Politics of Exclusion* (New York: Basic, 1999); Martin Duberman, *Midlife Queer: Autobiography of a Decade, 1971–1981* (New York: Scribner, 1996); Lisa Duggan and Nan D. Hunter, *Sex Wars: Sexual Dissent and Political Culture* (New York: Routledge, 1995). On homophobia

and heterosexism in academia more generally, see *The Gay Academic*, ed. Louie Crew (Palm Springs, CA: ETC, 1978); Toni A. H. McNaron, *Poisoned Ivy: Lesbian and Gay Academics Confronting Homophobia* (Philadelphia: Temple University Press, 1997).

5. Here and elsewhere in this essay I report information that I received, directly or indirectly, from members of search committees and hiring departments. In most cases I asked for and received permission to share these accounts anonymously. While members of search committees and hiring departments often operate with implicit or explicit expectations of confidentiality, these expectations generally regulate those who are doing the hiring, not those who are being interviewed. I cannot guarantee the accuracy of all of this information. It is certainly possible that I received inaccurate or partial information. That said, I do not include here information that I received that seemed untrustworthy or unreliable and most of the information reported here came from multiple sources. Also, insofar as this essay describes my subjective experiences on the job market, in some respects the question of whether the information I received was accurate is less important than the fact that I received this information.

6. "Robbing the Cradle," *Lingua Franca*, May 1995, 20–22.

7. See "Committee on Lesbian and Gay History Survey on LGBTQ History Careers," *Perspectives*, May 2001, 29–31. For a longer and more detailed version of this report, see http://www.usc.edu/isd/archives/clgh/reports.html. See also Anna Clark, "Report on the Survey of Lesbian and Gay Historians by the Committee on Women Historians," 31 January 1993; Committee on Women Historians, "Report on the Lesbian and Gay Historians Survey," *Perspectives*, April 1993, 13–15; Verta Taylor and Nicole C. Raeburn, "Identity Politics as High-Risk Activism: Career Consequences for Lesbian, Gay and Bisexual Sociologists," *Social Problems* 42, 2 (May 1995): 252–273; Committee on the Status of Lesbians and Gays in the Profession of the American Political Science Association, "Report on the Status of Lesbians and Gays in the Political Science Profession," *PS: Political Science and Politics* 28, 3 (September 1995): 561–574; Commission on Lesbian, Gay, Bisexual, and Transgendered Issues in Anthropology, *Final Report*, November 1999; Committee on the Status of Lesbian, Gay, Bisexual, and Transgendered Persons in the Discipline, "Report on the Status of Lesbian, Gay, Bisexual, and Transgendered Persons in Sociology," 16 July 2002, http://www.asanet.org/govemance/GLBTrpt.html.

CHAPTER 5. POST-TENURE LAVENDER BLUES

1. As I reported in an article published in *Perspectives*, "With only two exceptions, respondents who have completed history dissertations that are more than one-third LGBTQ in contents are not currently employed in TTE [tenure-track or equivalent] positions in which US history departments acted as the primary hiring units." Significantly, slightly more than half of the thirty-two respondents with completed dissertations were in tenure-track or equivalent positions, but the vast majority were in history departments outside the United States; in women's studies, gender studies, American Studies, or other

non-history units; or in positions in which a US history department had not acted as the primary initiator of the hiring. My conclusion was that "despite a significant increase in the number of lgbtq history PhDs produced over the past decade, U.S. history departments have not made a commensurate increase in hiring such scholars to tenure-track positions." See Marc Stein, "Committee on Lesbian and Gay History Survey on LGBTQ History Careers," *Perspectives* 39, no. 5 (May 2001): 29–31; Marc Stein, "Committee on Lesbian and Gay History Survey on LGBTQ History Careers," June 2001 [http://clgbthistory.org /projects/reports/lgbtq-history-careers].

2. See Marc Stein, "Crossing Borders: Memories, Dreams, Fantasies, and Nightmares of the History Job Market," *Left History* 9, no. 2 (Spring/Summer 2004): 119–139.

3. For early products of the research project, see "Boutilier and the U.S. Supreme Court's Sexual Revolution," *Law and History Review* 23, no. 3 (Fall 2005): 491-536; "Forgetting and Remembering a Deported Alien," *History News Network*, 3 November 2003; "Crossing the Border to Memory: In Search of Clive Michael Boutilier (1933-2003)," *torquere* 6 (2004): 91-115 (published 2005); "The U.S. Supreme Court's Sexual Counter-Revolution," *OAH Magazine of History* (forthcoming, 2006).

4. The complete set of comments sent to me via regular mail were as follows: Panelist 1: "This is not my area of expertise so I can't assess the originality of the proposal. But the argument is very compelling and sounds right on target to me. I would like to see Stein write a substantive conclusion on post 1973 developments that would include a discussion of the sodomy cases (1985 [sic], 2003) and also 'Roe's' reversal of her prior stance on adoption [sic]." Panelist 2: "Ambitious, authoritative." Panelist 3: "Timely topic. Solid research design— likely to complete on time. Ideal combination of solid research and a topic that has a broad appeal." Panelist 4: "Does it matter that he lives and teaches in Canada? 2000 book on gay history in Philadelphia. This project is conceptually broader (despite short time horizon). Seems truly revisionary and significant. A very timely topic, given debates about same sex marriage. Emphasizes history of Supreme Court decisions privileging monogamous heterosexuality." Panelist 5: "The project will change the way we think about the sexual revolution of the 1960s and 1970s; about the Warren Court; and about the culture wars of the last forty years. Furthermore, it will be of tremendous interest to a general public. Stein has an outstanding reputation as a scholar of sexuality. His first book is bold and important. This one will be even more so. The project's juxtaposition of landmark court cases relating to sexuality serves to bring into the mainstream issues that are often ghettoized, especially the history of homosexuality in the U.S. It makes a great deal of sense to study the Supreme Court's decisions and the responses to them, but I wonder if the author will be able to complete the research in that it is an overwhelming amount of material to plow through. His research design, however, is sensible. This is a project worth funding in that Stein will need a great deal of time to complete it, and if he does, it will be an important book. In time Stein will complete the project. He has a strong track record and is well-regarded. He has already given papers on the subject and the clamor for the book will drive him." Handwritten notes on this evaluation

stated, "Conversation convinced me that this project's research plan is feasible and that Stein is the right person for this project."

The query about my living and teaching in Canada (which incidentally is not supposed to disqualify me) is interesting in light of the findings of the CLGH study, which suggested that a disproportionate number of LGBTQ historians trained in the United States have obtained tenure-track positions outside the United States.

5. The panelists' institutional affiliations are as follows: Leslie Brown (Washington University), Yong Chen (University of California, Irvine), Sandra Gustafson (Notre Dame), Alexis McGrossen (Southern Methodist University), and Carla Peterson (University of Maryland).

6. Note that the overall success rate was 14 percent, whereas the American History/American Studies success rate was 9 percent. Had the American History/American Studies success rate been 14 percent, six proposals would have been funded in this category.

7. This was a curious choice of words for a project that has little to say about the visual or the anal.

8. Anne Marie Borrego, "Humanities Endowment Returns to 'Flagging' Nontraditional Projects," *Chronicle of Higher Education*, 16 Jan. 2004, A1, A20–A21. According to the article, "The practice [of flagging], which is as old as the agency itself, allows NEH officials to identify specific grant applications—often, these days, projects dealing with sexuality, race, or gender—for extra review. In some cases, flagged proposals that receive high marks from peer-review panels are rejected, while those with low marks receive funds." See also Kelly Field, "Humanities Endowment Opens Inquiry into Alleged Leak to a Reporter," *Chronicle of Higher Education*, 28 May 2004; Mary Jacoby, "Madame Cheney's Cultural Revolution," *Salon.com*, 26 Aug. 2004.

It is difficult to know with certainty whether any of the NEH 2004 faculty research awards or fellowships funded projects dealing with same-sex, intersex, or transgender sexualities. None of the titles contain the words "bisexual," "gay," "homosexual," "intersex," "lesbian," "queer," "transgender," or "transsexual." Three contain the words "sexual" or "sexuality": "Roman Imperial Family Values and Earl Christian and Jewish Sexual Politics," "Sexuality, Illegitimacy, and Family in the Hispanic World," and "Sexuality, Medicine, and American Society: Dr. Mary Calderone and the Politics of Sex." Two invoke the term "love" and one uses the term "marriage." If gender and race are defined broadly, many of the projects appear to deal with these topics; a smaller group invoke specific terms such as *fatherhood* (1), *gender* (2), *matriarchal* (1), *men* (1), *race* (5), and *women* (5). The funding of these projects does not mean that projects dealing with gender and race are not subject to heightened scrutiny (to borrow a term from legal discourse).

In 2003, no project title contained the words *sex*, *sexual*, or *sexuality* and I am not able to identify any LGBTQ studies scholars among the fellowship recipients. In 2002 no project title contained the words *sex*, *sexual*, or *sexuality*, but James N. Green, author of *Beyond Carnival: Male Homosexuality in Twentieth-Century Brazil*, was awarded a fellowship for a project titled "Crossroads of Sin and the Collision of Cultures: Pleasure and Popular Entertainment in Rio de Janeiro (1860–1920)"; Lisa Merrill, author of *When Romeo Was a Woman: Charlotte Cushman and Her Circle of Female Spectators*, was awarded a fellowship for a project titled "A Volume of the Selected Letters of Charlotte Cushman, 1816–1876"; and Gregory M. Pflugfelder, author of *Cartographies of Desire: Male-Male Sexuality in Japanese Discourse, 1600–1950*, was awarded a fellowship for a project titled "Japanese Gender and Sexuality, 1100–2000."

Of the projects that received NEH fellowship awards in 2005, with the possible exception of one that refers to eunuchs and another that refers to "singlewomen," none have titles suggesting a focus on same-sex, intersex, or transgender sexualities. One title contains the word *sexual*: "Legal Narratives of Sexual Consent and Coercion in the Early Twentieth Century." I can identify two LGBTQ studies scholar among the recipients: Judith Bennett, an expert on lesbian sexuality in medieval and early modern Europe, was awarded a fellowship for "Singlewomen and the History of Late Medieval England, c. 1300–1550," and Licia Fiol-Matta, author of *A Queer Mother for the Nation: The State and Gabriela Mistral*, was awarded a fellowship for a project titled "Remembering Cuba: Memory and Loss in Lydia Cabrera's Writings." If gender and race are defined broadly, many of the projects appear to deal with these topics; a smaller group invoke specific terms such as *female* (1), *gender* (4), *girl* (1), *race* (3), *racial* (1), and *women* (4).

9. "Statement on Peer Review," *Perspectives*, Sep. 2005, 64.

10. Jones's letter included the following statement: "You should be aware that I often speak with unsuccessful applicants on the telephone and give them a better idea of where their proposals finished in comparison with the total number of applications evaluated in their respective panels. I also give them an idea of the feasibility of being successful next time and of their need to address the criticisms of the panelists. Such advice is best given on the telephone, and for that reason I will not repeat this advice here or officially confirm or correct your understanding of our conversation in writing." For comments on Fox-Genovese's appointment to the NEH Council, see Jon Wiener, *Historians in Trouble: Plagiarism, Fraud, and Politics in the Ivory Tower* (New York: New Press, 2005), 13–30.

11. A short time later, I spoke off the record with another *Chronicle* reporter investigating flagging and related troubles at the NEH.

12. The comments forwarded to me electronically were as follows. Panelist 1 (Rating E/VG): "Sexuality and the Supreme Court—an unlikely combination—but this project on court rulings between [*sic*] 1965–1973 on the issues that still consume Americans seems to link the two with ease. Stein challenges liberal interpretations of rulings on sexual freedom and sexual citizenship and points to many conservative elements in these decisions. He seems to blame the 'media' for misleading the public in the area of 'rights' broadly defined. This project, which is well written and intellectually significant, builds upon Stein's earlier work. Looking at what he sees as the disconnect between law and public opinion and social movement activism, he is in an excellent position to take the project in interesting directions." Panelist 2 (Rating E/VG): "The applicant is likely to complete the project. The proposal seems to ignore the longer history

and context and to be driven by a specific personal agenda." Panelist 3 (Rating E/VG): "Stein 'juxtoposes [sic] liberalizing rulings on abortion, birth control, interracial marriage, and obscenity with conservative decisions on homosexuality.' The fact that he says liberalizing rather than liberal is key here. He argues that the Supreme Court did not establish a broadly libertarian or egalitarian doctrine of sexual freedom and citizenship in the 1960s–70s as some have claimed in examining [sic] the decision in the 2003 Lawrence case. Stein argues that the Court actually privileged more traditional forms of sexual expression. Furthermore, he states that liberals and conservatives worked together on this, and finally the mass media misrepresented the development of the new legal regime. In other words, we have to get the history right so as to understand properly current legal and legislative decisions. This is a highly significant project due both to its thought-provoking thesis and its innovative organization and research. Stein's contention that while there are many good accounts on the sexual revolution, none has provided deep analysis of the Court's role, appears correct. Thus this examination of the state's (specifically, a particular institution of the state) role in social reform is valuable. Stein introduces a good argument about the essentially conservative foundations of some of the reforms touted as liberal. That becomes clear when one accepts the argument/evidence that they were not about sexual freedom. That is something that appears confirmed by the Boutilier case. There seems to have been an emphasis on balancing social order and individual rights in these cases. That is born [sic] out by the focus on the right to privacy. One thing that may complicate the comparison of the Boutilier case to the others, however, and something which may explain why the Court could dismiss privacy argument in this, was the contemporary interpretation of homosexuality as a pyschological [sic] disorder. If homosexuality was defined as mental as well as social deviancy (and lawyers and judges accepted that), then the Court may have categorized the case differently from the others. That is my off-the-cuff (and maybe off-the-wall) speculation. I am sure Stein answers that in his work by incorporating social context that he could not fit in this proposal. In some ways the issue of the media's role in all this is more significant than the Court's. The media translates court rulings and law for most citizens, thus if it does not do so accurately or puts its own spin on decisions then we have a major problem. And that is what Stein suggests. Stein has done a tremendous amount of research already. His proposal indicates that he intends to do much more. That suggests that he plans to use most of the fellowship year for that; yet it appears that he has finished most of the research and that majority of the year will be spent writing. My conclusion is that he will be moving between the two and that he will be able to draft most of the manuscript. He does present a logical outline of chapters that should make the argument clear to readers. Given his previous work, the NEH can expect that he will produce a highly readable, original book that will provoke a great deal of discussion among those interested in the histories of the Court, social reform, and sexuality." Panelist 4 (Rating E): "This fellow would seem to be a major figure in the field, with an excellent publication record in the last few years in particular, one recent book. Excellent publications for this stage of his career. This essay features an unusually clear statement of what this proposal is attempting. I'm not that knowledgeable on this specific literature, so I'd defer to better placed people on this, but this certainly looks distinctive and important, and what he says about the historiography sounds right to me. It certainly seems that he has something important to say about the courts and sexuality in the crucial sixties and seventies. He certainly is right that this material is of considerable contemporary interest. His approach encompassing the social history of the law and legal activists looks interesting too, as is the whole issue of public misperceptions of court decisions. I'd be more comfortable if this fellow was himself a lawyer, given the study he is undertaking, but he certainly seems well-situated enough in the field. It isn't quite clear to me how far along this is, but everything else looks in order." Panelist 5 (Rating E): "Marc Stein's study of the Warren Court's decisions concerning sexuality promises to be a revisionist and possibly controversial work of scholarship. With a well-conceived and logically-organized project outline, he seems well on his way to completing the study. 'Inventing Rights and Wrongs' should contribute to knowledge in several areas—as legal scholarship and cultural history, for example. His research plan and chapter outline provide a clear indication of where the project is headed."

13. The panelists' institutional affiliations are as follows: Elaine Abelson (New School University), Roger Biles (East Carolina University), Edith Blumhofer (Wheaton College), Michael Fitzgerald (St. Olaf College), and Holly Mayer (Duquesne University).

14. The comment about my "personal agenda" is also interesting in the context of my concerns about the potentially conservative uses of my argument about the Supreme Court's privileging of heterosexual, marital, monogamous, and reproductive sex.

15. The AHA "Statement on Standards of Professional Conduct" (2005) can be found at http://www.historians.org/pubs/Free/ProfessionalStandards.cfm. Among the relevant passages are the following:

> Among the core principles of the historical profession that can seem counterintuitive to non-historians is the conviction, very widely if not universally shared among historians since the nineteenth century, that practicing history with integrity does not mean being neutral or having no point of view. Every work of history articulates a particular, limited perspective on the past. Historians hold this view not because they believe that all interpretations are equally valid, or that nothing can ever be known about the past, or that facts do not matter. Quite the contrary. History would be pointless if such claims were true, since its most basic premise is that within certain limits we can indeed know and make sense of past worlds and former times that now exist only as remembered traces in the present. But the very nature of our discipline means that historians also understand that all knowledge is situated in time and place, that all interpretations express a point of view, and that no mortal mind can ever aspire to omniscience. Because the record of the past is so fragmentary, absolute historical knowledge is denied us. . . .
>
> What is true of history is also true of historians. Everyone who comes to the study of history brings with them a host of identities, experiences, and interests that cannot help but affect the questions they ask of the past and the answers they wish to know. When applied with integrity and self-critical fair-mindedness, the political, social, and religious beliefs of historians can appropriately inform their historical practice.

Because the questions we ask profoundly shape everything we do—the topics we investigate, the evidence we gather, the arguments we construct, the stories we tell—it is inevitable that different historians will produce different histories.

For this reason, historians often disagree and argue with each other. That historians can sometimes differ quite vehemently not just about interpretations but even about the basic facts of what happened in the past is sometimes troubling to non-historians, especially if they imagine that history consists of a universally agreed-upon accounting of stable facts and known certainties. But universal agreement is not a condition to which historians typically aspire. Instead, we understand that interpretive disagreements are vital to the creative ferment of our profession, and can in fact contribute to some of our most original and valuable insights.

Frustrating as these disagreements and uncertainties may be even for historians, they are an irreducible feature of the discipline. In contesting each other's interpretations, professional historians recognize that the resulting disagreements can deepen and enrich historical understanding by generating new questions, new arguments, and new lines of investigation. This crucial insight underpins some of the most important shared values that define the professional conduct of historians. They believe in vigorous debate, but they also believe in civility. They rely on their own perspectives as they probe the past for meaning, but they also subject those perspectives to critical scrutiny by testing them against the views of others.

Historians celebrate intellectual communities governed by mutual respect and constructive criticism. The preeminent value of such communities is reasoned discourse—the continuous colloquy among historians holding diverse points of view who learn from each other as they pursue topics of mutual interest. A commitment to such discourse—balancing fair and honest criticism with tolerance and openness to different ideas—makes possible the fruitful exchange of views, opinions, and knowledge.

This being the case, it is worth repeating that a great many dilemmas associated with the professional practice of history can be resolved by returning to the core values that the preceding paragraphs have sought to sketch. Historians should practice their craft with integrity. They should honor the historical record. They should document their sources. They should acknowledge their debts to the work of other scholars. They should respect and welcome divergent points of view even as they argue and subject those views to critical scrutiny. They should remember that our collective enterprise depends on mutual trust. And they should never betray that trust.

See also the recent column by the president of the AHA: James J. Sheehan, "How History Can Be a Moral Science," *Perspectives*, Oct. 2005, 3–4.

16. This is not true insofar as the comment about my objectivity was an NEH staff member's interpretation of the meaning of the panelists' comment about my personal agenda.

17. Was Kolson suggesting, intentionally or not, that my proposal had been reviewed with favorable prejudice in the first year and with neutral objectivity in the subsequent one? Was he thinking of proposals that might be disadvantaged by coming before panelists who had rejected earlier iterations, which did not seem to apply in my case, since in the earlier case the panel had recommended funding for my project?

18. On Thernstrom's appointment to the NEH Council, see Wiener, *Historians in Trouble*, 58–69.

CHAPTER 6. POLITICAL HISTORY AND THE HISTORY
OF SEXUALITY

1. Fredrik Logevall and Kenneth Osgood, "The End of Political History?"
New York Times, August 29, 2016, http://www.nytimes.com/2016/08/29
/opinion/why-did-we-stop-teaching-politicalhistory.html?.

2. See Mary L. Dudziak, "Political History Is Alive and Well, and Mat-
ters More Than Ever," *Balkin.com*, August 30, 2016, https://balkin.blogspot
.com/2016/08/political-history-is-alive-and-well-and.html; Roy Rogers, "The
Strange Death(?) of Political History," *The Junto: A Group Blog on Early
American History*, September 9, 2016, https://earlyamericanists.com/2016
/09/09/the-strange-death-of-political-history/; Gabriel Rosenberg and Ariel
Ron, "Chill Out: Political History Has Never Been Better," *Lawyers, Guns &
Money*, September 1, 2016, http://www.lawyersgunsmoneyblog.com/2016/09
/chill-out-political-historyhas-never-been-better; Julian Zelizer, "Political History Is Doing AOK," *Process: A Blog for American History*, August 31, 2016,
http://www.processhistory.org/zelizer-politicalhistory/.

3. See Jeremy W. Peters, "The Decline and Fall of the 'H' Word," *New York
Times*, March 21, 2014, http://www.nytimes.com/2014/03/23/fashion/gays
-lesbians-the-term-homosexual.html.

4. Kevin Baker, "Living in L.B.J.'s America," *New York Times*, August 28,
2016, http://www.nytimes.com/2016/08/28/opinion/campaign-stops/living-in
-lbjs-america.html.

PART THREE. HISTORIES OF QUEER ACTIVISM

1. For the journal articles and book chapters, see "Sex Politics in the City of
Sisterly and Brotherly Loves," *Radical History Review*, no. 59 (Spring 1994):
60–92, reprinted in *Major Problems in the History of American Sexuality*, ed.
Kathy L. Peiss (Boston: Houghton Mifflin, 2001), 431–43; "'Birthplace of the
Nation': Imagining Lesbian and Gay Communities in Philadelphia, 1969–70,"
in *Creating a Place for Ourselves*, ed. B. Beemyn (New York: Routledge, 1997),
253–88; "Rizzo's Raiders, Beaten Beats, and Coffeehouse Culture in 1950s
Philadelphia," in *Modern American Queer History: Essays in Representation,
Lived Experience, and Public Policy*, ed. Allida M. Black (Philadelphia: Temple
University Press, 2001), 155–80.

2. Victoria Brownworth, "Chronicling the History of Philly's Gay Movement," *PGN*, 11 Jun. 1993, 44–45; Jeannine DeLombard, "20 Questions,"
Philadelphia City Paper, 27 Oct. 1995, 13.

3. See Kevin Riordan, "Spanning the Differences," *Camden Courier-Post*,
22 May 2000, C1, C2; Kevin Riordan, "Book Chronicles Phila. Movement,"
PGN, 28 Apr. 2000, 1, 14, 18; Kevin Riordan, "'Loves' Documents Gay Philadelphia," *PGN*, 5 May 2000, 45, 47; Doug Ireland, "'In the Life' in Philadelphia," *Philadelphia Inquirer*, 2 May 2000, E1, E5; Christopher King, "Marc
Stein: The Pride of Philadelphia," *Philadelphia Weekly*, 3 May 2000, 81; Lewis
Whittington, "Out-Side In," *Philadelphia Weekly*, 3 May 2000, 81; Kate Full-
brook, *Times Literary Supplement*, 26 May 2000, 33; Tom Nickels, "Not

So Friendly Philly?" *Lambda Book Report*, July 2000, 27–28; Elisa Kukla, "Comfort & Joy," *Xtra!*, 14 Dec. 2000, 15; Kevin J. Harty, "Before Center City," *Gay & Lesbian Review*, Jan. 2001, 47; Teresa DeCrescenzo, "A Look at Books," *Lesbian News*, Feb. 2001; Jesse Monteagudo, "Philly's Lavender Past," *TWN*, 15 Feb. 2001.

4. Glenn Holsten, director, *Gay Pioneers*, WHYY (TV), Philadelphia, 2001.

5. See J. Cooper Robb, "Clear Eye," *Philadelphia Weekly*, 6 Oct. 2004, 44; Natalie Hope McDonald, "Reading Out Loud," *Philadelphia City Paper*, 7 Oct. 2004, 42; Alison Dickman, "Book Documents City History," *PGN*, 8 Oct. 2004, 3, 7; Brandon Lausch, "60 Seconds," *Metro* (Philadelphia), 11 Oct. 2004, 17. See also Andrew Israel Ross, "Best. Dedication. Ever," *Air Pollution: History, Politics, Academia, Queerness, and More Hot Air*, 10 Nov. 2005.

6. See, for example, Thomas Ginsberg, "Census Finds Gays, Lesbians in Diverse and Distinct Areas," *Philadelphia Inquirer*, 16 Aug. 2001; Nia Ngina Meeks, "History Kept in the Closet: Philly's Black Gay Community Often Overlooked," *Philadelphia Tribune*, 16 Feb. 2003, 1, 9; Julia Bloch, "Philadelphia Freedom," *Curve*, Feb. 2005, 22–24; Tommi Avicolli Mecca, "In Honor of the Compton's Riot: Remembering Philly's Screaming Queens," *BeyondChron*, 23 June 2006; Natalie Pompilio, "Days without Gays Protests California's Gay Marriage Ban," *Philadelphia Inquirer*, 2 Dec. 2008; Gerry Christopher Johnson, "Divided We Dance: Black Gays Get Their Own Party Started," *Philadelphia Weekly*, 28 Apr. 2010, 7–13; Ryan Kasley, "Author Returns to Philly for LGBT History Talks," *PGN*, 26 Sep. 2014, 8; Ray Simon, "Revisiting a Pre-Stonewall LGBT Sit-In," *PGN*, 30 Oct. 2014; Bill Chenevert, "Four Years before Stonewall, the Gay Rights Struggle Started at Independence Hall," *Philadelphia Weekly*, 10 June 2015, 9; Mark E. Dixon, "LGBT Activist Jack Adair Sought Safety on the Main Line in 1960," *Mainline Today*, 10 Nov. 2017.

7. See Marc Stein, "'Where Perversion Is Taught': The Untold History of a Gay Rights Demonstration at Bucks County Community College in 1968," OutHistory, 13 Apr. 2021, https://outhistory.org/exhibits/show/wh/whe; Marc Stein, "Power, Politics, and Race in the 1968 Philadelphia Study of Prison Sexual Violence," *Queer Pasts* (Alexandria, VA: Alexander Street, 2021). See also Kevin Riordan, "Before Stonewall, LGBTQ History Was Made at Bucks County Community College," *Philadelphia Inquirer*, 16 June 2021.

8. I discuss some of this in "Canonizing Homophile Sexual Respectability: Archives, History, and Memory," *Radical History Review*, no. 120 (Fall 2014): 52–73.

9. See also Mike Hudson, "Where Did We Begin?" *The Advocate*, 12 Apr. 2005, 15; Sono Motoyama, "Controversy," *Philadelphia Daily News*, 25 Apr. 2005, 35.

10. See Susan Stryker, "Why the T in LGBT Is Here to Stay," *Salon*, 11 Oct. 2007, https://www.salon.com/2007/10/11/transgender_2/; Susan Stryker, *Transgender History* (Berkeley: Seal, 2008), 62–63; Monica Roberts, "The 1965 Dewey's Lunch Counter Sit-In," 18 Oct. 2007, *Transgriot*, https://transgriot .blogspot.com/2007/10/1965-deweys-lunch-counter-sit-it.html?m=0&amp=1.

11. Marc Stein, "Happy Anniversary to the Dewey's Sit-In," *Bay Area Reporter*, 23 April 2015; Marc Stein, "Dewey's Sit-In, Philadelphia, April 25,

1965," OutHistory, 20 Apr. 2015, http://outhistory.org/exhibits/show/deweys
-sit-in/intro.

12. See Tim Cwiek, "Historic Marker under Fire by Some LGBT Advocates,"
PGN, 11 Oct. 2018; Monica Roberts, "Dewey's Historical Marker Erases and
Gaywashes Black Trans History," *Transgriot*, 12 Oct. 2018, https://transgriot
.blogspot.com/2018/10/deweys-historical-marker-erases-and.html; Tim Cwiek,
"Will Historic Marker's Language Be Revised?" *PGN*, 2 May 2019. See also
Shai Ben-Yaacov and Annette John-Hall, "Before Stonewall and Pride, Philly
Staged LGBTQ Protests," *The Why*, WHYY, Philadelphia, 5 June 2019, https://
whyy.org/episodes/before-stonewall-and-pride-philly-staged-lgbtq-protests/;
Pat Loeb, "One of the Earliest Victories for LGBT Rights Happened at This
Philly Diner," KYW Radio, 14 June 2019, https://kywnewsradio.radio.com
/articles/news/one-earliest-victories-lgbt-rights-happened-philly-diner; Nico
Wisler, "A Footnote Not to Be Forgotten," *Queer the Table*, Heritage Radio
Network, 24 June 2019, https://heritageradionetwork.org/podcast/a-footnote
-not-to-be-forgotten/; Denio Lourenco, "5 LGBTQ Protests That Set the Stage
for Stonewall," *Vice*, 24 June 2019; Jo Yurcaba, "Different Fight, 'Same Goal':
How the Black Freedom Movement Inspired Early Gay Activists," NBC Out,
28 Feb. 2021.

13. See also Jen Colletta, "Local LGBT Activism Marks 50th Anniversary,"
PGN, 27 Aug. 2010, 9.

14. "About *Notches: Re(marks) on the History of Sexuality*," *Notches*,
http://notchesblog.com/about-2/.

15. Marc Stein, "Heterosexual Inversions: Satire, Parody, and Comedy
in the 1950s and 1960s," in *Heterosexual Histories: Collected Essays about
Sexuality, Norms, and U.S. History*, ed. Rebecca Davis and Michele Mitchell
(New York: New York University Press, 2021), 195–224.

PART FOUR. QUEER HISTORICAL INTERVENTIONS

1. For media coverage of the conference, see Jim Coyle, "History's Sexy but
Just Can't Get Enough Respect," *Toronto Star*, 13 April 2000.

2. Mission Statement, History News Network (HNN), https://historynews
network.org/mission-statement.html; M. Andrew Holowchak interview with
Rick Shenkman, "Farewell," HNN, 23 Dec. 2018, https://historynewsnetwork
.org/article/170668.

3. "Bent on Change" conference posters and programs, 2000 and 2002, in
my personal papers.

4. On the Sexuality Studies Program and the Sex Talk symposium, see my
interview with Matthew Galloway, "Here and Now" (Toronto), *CBC Radio*,
20 Apr. 2007.

5. Marc Stein, letter to the editor, *Academic Affairs*, Oct. 2007, 2; Harriet
Eisenkraft, "Living Apart, Together," *University Affairs*, June 2012, 12–17.

6. "Active History," http://activehistory.ca/about/. The website was established after another conference, "Active History: History for the Future," held
at York University's Glendon College in 2008.

7. Marc Stein, "I Dream of Sheldon," *Graduate Perspective*, Dec. 1991, 9; Marc Stein, "In My Wildest Dreams . . .," *Graduate Perspective*, Nov. 1992, 11; Marc Stein, "Teaching Across the University," *Graduate Perspective*, Feb. 1993, 9. See also Marc Stein, "If We Had Written the Declaration of Independence," HNN, 1 Nov. 2004, http://hnn.us/articles/8062.html.

8. See also Katy Steinmetz, "Why Federal Laws Don't Explicitly Ban Discrimination against LGBT Americans," *Time*, 21 Mar. 2019; Marco della Cava, "Most Americans Want Protections for LGBTQ People," *USA Today*, 20 Nov. 2020.

9. See Adam Romero, James Tysse, and Jessica Weisel, "Brief of Scholars Who Study the Transgender Population," *Carcaño v. McCrory*, Fourth Circuit Court of Appeals, 25 Oct. 2016.

10. See "AHA Urges California Legislature to Amend AB1887 for Scholars," Jan. 2021, https://www.historians.org/news-and-advocacy/aha-advocacy/aha-letter-urging-california-legislature-to-amend-ab1887-for-scholars-(january-2021); Marc Stein, "When a Boycott Blocks Queer Research," *Public Seminar*, 18 May 2021, https://publicseminar.org/essays/when-a-boycott-blocks-queer-research/.

PART FIVE. QUEER IMMIGRATION

1. See Margot Canaday, "'Who Is a Homosexual?' The Consolidation of Sexual Identities in Mid-Twentieth-Century American Immigration Law," *Law and Social Inquiry* 28 (2003): 351–86; Siobhan B. Somerville, "Queer *Loving*," *GLQ* 11 (2005): 335–70; Margot Canaday, *The Straight State: Sexuality and Citizenship in Twentieth-Century America* (Princeton, NJ: Princeton University Press, 2009).

2. Vicki Eaklor, Karen Krahulik, Leisa Meyer, and Marc Stein, letter to the editor, *Perspectives*, Mar. 2006, p. 54.

3. "*Boutilier* and the U.S. Supreme Court's Sexual Revolution," *Law and History Review* 23, no. 3 (Fall 2005): 491–536; "Crossing the Border to Memory: In Search of Clive Michael Boutilier (1933–2003)," *torquere* 6 (2004): 91–115 (published Nov. 2005); "All the Immigrants Are Straight, All the Homosexuals Are Citizens, but Some of Us Are Queer Aliens: Genealogies of Legal Strategy in *Boutilier v. INS*," *Journal of American Ethnic History* 29, no. 4 (Summer 2010): 45–77; "Sexual Rights and Wrongs: Teaching the U.S. Supreme Court's Greatest Gay and Lesbian Hits," in *Understanding and Teaching U.S. Lesbian, Gay, Bisexual, and Transgender History*, ed. Leila Rupp and Susan Freeman (Madison: University of Wisconsin Press, 2014), 238–53; "Race, Class, and the U.S. Supreme Court's Doctrine of Heteronormative Supremacy," in *Connexions: Histories of Race and Sex in North America*, ed. Jennifer Brier, Jim Downs, and Jennifer Morgan (Champaign: University of Illinois Press, 2016), 59–81.

4. See Marc Stein, *Boutilier v. the Immigration and Naturalization Service*, OutHistory, 17 May 2017, http://outhistory.org/exhibits/show/boutilier/intro; Julio Capó Jr., Eithne Luibhéid, Siobhan Somerville, Marc Stein, and

Amy Sueyoshi, "Queering Immigration in the Age of Trump: A Roundtable on *Boutilier v. INS*," *Notches: (Re)marks on the History of Sexuality*, 22 May 2017, http://notchesblog.com/2017/05/22/queering-immigration-in-the-age-of -trump-a-roundtable-on-boutilier-v-ins/.

5. See, for example, Amin Ghaziani, *There Goes the Gayborhood?* (Princeton, NJ: Princeton University Press, 2014); Martin Duberman, *Has the Gay Movement Failed?* (Berkeley: University of California Press, 2018).

6. Marc Stein, *Sexual Injustice: Supreme Court Decisions from* Griswold *to* Roe (Chapel Hill: University of North Carolina Press, 2010), 272–78.

CHAPTER 18. THE SUPREME COURT'S SEXUAL COUNTER-REVOLUTION

1. For a more in-depth discussion of the issues considered in this essay, see Marc Stein, "Boutilier and the U.S. Supreme Court's Sexual Revolution," *Law and History Review* 23 (Fall 2005): 491–536.

2. Griswold v. Connecticut, 381 U.S. 479 (1965); Loving v. Virginia, 388 U.S. 1 (1967); Roe v. Wade, 410 U.S. 113 (1973).

3. A Book Named "John Cleland's Memoirs of a Woman of Pleasure" v. Attorney General of the Commonwealth of Massachusetts (commonly referred to as *Fanny Hill*), 383 U.S. 413 (1966); *Stanley v. Georgia*, 394 U.S. 557 (1969); *Eisenstadt v. Baird*, 405 U.S. 438 (1972).

4. Bowers v. Hardwick, 478 U.S. 186 (1986).

5. A libertarian doctrine of sexual freedom would challenge the regulation of consensual sexual expression. An egalitarian doctrine of sexual freedom would challenge the favoring or privileging of certain forms of consensual sexual expression over others.

6. Ginzburg v. United States, 383 U.S. 463 (1966); Mishkin v. New York, 383 U.S. 502 (1966); Landau v. Fording, 388 U.S. 456 (1967); G.I. Distributors v. New York, 389 U.S. 905 (1967).

7. Boutilier v. Immigration and Naturalization Service, 387 U.S. 118 (1967).

8 Only three justices endorsed the plurality position, but it is regarded as the Court's main opinion because Douglas and Black concurred in the results while disagreeing with the reasoning.

9. McLaughlin v. Florida, 379 U.S. 184 (1964).

10. Paris Adult Theatre I v. Slaton, 413 U.S. 49 (1973).

11. Miller v. California, 413 U.S. 15 (1973).

12. ONE, Incorporated, v. Olesen, 355 U.S. 371 (1958); Manual Enterprises v. Day, 370 U.S. 478 (1962); Rosenberg v. Fleuti, 374 U.S. 449 (1963); Womack v. United States, 365 U.S. 859 (1961); Darnell v. United States, 375 U.S. 916 (1963).

CHAPTER 19. IMMIGRATION IS A QUEER ISSUE

1. Marc Stein, "Sexual Rights and Wrongs: Teaching the U.S. Supreme Court's Greatest Gay and Lesbian Hits," in *Understanding and Teaching U.S.*

Lesbian, Gay, Bisexual, and Transgender History, ed. Leila Rupp and Susan Freeman (Madison: University of Wisconsin Press, 2014), 238–53.

PART SIX. SEX, LAW, AND THE SUPREME COURT

1. The keynoters have been Rhonda Williams and David Cruz in 2015, Boyd Cothran and Ana Minian in 2016, Robin Kelley and Shirin Sinnar in 2017, Roxanne Dunbar Ortiz and Ian Haney Lopez in 2018, Tsianina Lomawaima and Bertrall Ross in 2019, Ellen Dubois and Rabia Belt in 2020, and Martha Jones and James Colgrove in 2021. My colleague Sarah Crabtree coordinated the conference in 2020, when I was on research leave.

2. Robin B. Johansen et al., "Brief Amicus Curiae of Professors, Institutions of Higher Education, and American Association of University Professors," *San Francisco v. Trump*, Ninth Circuit Court of Appeals, 12 Feb. 2018.

3. See "Historical Landmarks and Landscapes of LGBTQ Law," in *LGBTQ America: A Theme Study of Lesbian, Gay, Bisexual, Transgender, and Queer History*, ed. Megan Springate (Washington, DC: National Park Service, 2016), 1–47, reprinted in *Communities and Place: A Thematic Approach to the Histories of LGBTQ Communities in the United* States, ed. Katherine Crawford-Lackey and Megan E. Springate (New York: Berghahn, 2020), 104–49; "Law and Politics: 'Crooked and Perverse' Narratives of LGBT Progress," *Routledge History of Queer America*, ed. Don Romesburg (New York: Routledge, 2018), 315–30.

4. See "Sotomayor v. Roberts: Race, Affirmative Action, and Impatience," *University of North Carolina Press Blog*, 8 July 2014, http://uncpressblog .com/2014/07/08/marc-stein-sotomayor-v-roberts-race-affirmative-action-and -impatience/; "Did You Know California Requires Professors to Sign a Loyalty Oath?" HNN, 13 Sep. 2015, http://historynewsnetwork.org/article/160596; "The Supreme Court Nomination and the Politics of Checks and Balances," *AHA Today: A Blog of the American Historical Association*, 29 Feb. 2016, http:// blog.historians.org/2016/02/the-supreme-court-nomination-and-the-politics-of -checks-and-balances/; "Punish the Voting Rights Villains," *Public Seminar*, 26 May 2021, https://publicseminar.org/essays/punish-the-voting-rights-villains/. *AHA Today* began publication in 2006 and was renamed *Perspectives Daily* in 2018. This essay was a rare instance in which an editor, the AHA's Kritika Agarwal, invited me to write on a subject other than LGBT history; I was recommended by Allison Miller, editor of the AHA's monthly magazine *Perspectives on History* and perhaps the organization's first openly-queer AHA staffer. *Public Seminar*, coedited by queer historian Claire Potter, is published by the New School and describes itself as "dedicated to informing debate about the pressing issues of our times and creating a global intellectual commons."

PART SEVEN. EXHIBITING QUEER HISTORY

1. See, for example, American Association of University Professors, "In Defense of Knowledge and Higher Education," Nov. 2019, https://www.aaup

.org/report/defense-knowledge-and-higher-education; Judith Butler, "A Dissenting View from the Humanities on the AAUP's Statement on Knowledge," *Academe* 106, no. 2 (Spring 2020). On historical empiricism and objectivity, see Peter Novick, *That Noble Dream: The "Objectivity Question" and the American Historical Profession* (New York: Cambridge University Press, 1988).

2. Oral History Association, "Best Practices," https://www.oralhistory.org/best-practices/.

3. On sexual bias and selectivity in digital history, see Marc Stein, "Canonizing Homophile Sexual Respectability: Archives, History, and Memory," *Radical History Review*, no. 120 (Fall 2014): 52–73.

4. See Lauren Jae Gutterman, "OutHistory.org: An Experiment in LGBTQ Community History-Making," *Public Historian* 32 no. 4 (Fall 2010): 96–109.

5. "Dewey's Sit-in, Philadelphia, April 25, 1965," OutHistory, 20 Apr. 2015, http://outhistory.org/exhibits/show/deweys-sit-in/intro; "50th Anniversary Demonstrations, Philadelphia," OutHistory, 23 Jun. 2015, http://www.outhistory.org/exhibits/show/50th-ann; "*Boutilier v. the Immigration and Naturalization Service*," OutHistory, 17 May 2017, http://outhistory.org/exhibits/show/boutilier/intro. For the fiftieth anniversary of the Annual Reminders in 2015, I also participated in a panel discussion of Glenn Holsten's 2001 documentary, *Gay Pioneers*, at WHYY in Philadelphia.

6. See Grace Wordsworth, "Kiyoshi Kuromiya: Balancing Might with Life," *MakingQueerHistory*, 13 Jan. 2017; Derek Duquette, "What Is a Legacy?" *A Public Historian*, 23 Feb. 2019; Victoria Brownworth, "The Road to Stonewall: Anita Cornwell," *Philadelphia Gay News*, 16 May 2019; Victoria Brownworth, "The Road to Stonewall: Kiyoshi Kuromiya," *Philadelphia Gay News*, 30 May 2019; Mark A. Momjian, "Stonewall at 50: A Salute to a Pioneering Family Lawyer," *Legal Intelligencer*, 3 July 2019; Joan Lubin and Jeanne Vaccaro, "AIDS Infrastructures, Queer Networks: Architecting the Critical Path," *First Monday* 25, no. 10 (Oct. 2020); Kenrya Rankin, *Words of Change: Anti-Racism* (Seattle: Spruce, 2020); Victoria Brownworth, "Philadelphia Activist Kiyoshi Kuromiya Honored," *Philadelphia Gay News*, 5 May 2021; Daniel E. Slotnik, "Kay Tobin Lahusen, Gay Rights Activist and Photographer, Dies at 91," *New York Times*, 27 May 2021, B11; Bob Skiba, "The Philadelphia Gayborhood Guru," https://thegayborhoodguru.wordpress.com/.

7. Marc Stein, ed., "U.S. Homophile Internationalism," a special issue of *Journal of Homosexuality* 64, no. 7 (April 2017).

PART EIGHT. STONEWALL, POPULARITY, AND PUBLICITY

1. Don Romesburg, "Presenting the Queer Past: A Case for the GLBT History Museum," *Radical History Review*, no. 120 (Fall 2014), 136.

2. These goals also motivated my work on an online bibliographic supplement: "Documenting the Stonewall Riots: A Bibliography of Primary Sources," 2019, https://history.sfsu.edu/content/documenting-stonewall-riots-bibliography-primary-sources.

3. US media interest in my work began to escalate several years earlier. See, for example, Cody Fenwick, "LGBT Pride: How A Struggle Became a

Celebration," *Patch*, 18 June 2016; Tanya Bellamy-Walker, "Orlando Shooting Not the Deadliest Shooting in US History," *New York Amsterdam News*, 23 June 2016, 36; Jon Shadel, "Can Hookup Apps Inspire a Gay Political Renaissance?" *Vice*, 13 Mar. 2017; Teo Armus, "Was Walt Whitman 'Gay'? New Textbook Rules Spark LGBTQ History Debate," *NBC Out*, 22 Nov. 2017; Gabriel Arana, "The Truth about Gay Men and Pedophilia," *Into*, 16 Nov. 2017; Gabriel Arana, "White Gay Men Are Hindering Our Progress as a Queer Community," *Them*, 13 Nov. 2017; Jamie Kravitz, "The Origin of Pride Month Is Really Fascinating," *Elite Daily*, 1 June 2018.

4. See Katy Steinmetz, "Was Stonewall a Riot, an Uprising or a Rebellion?" *Time*, 24 June 2019; Denio Lourenco, "5 LGBTQ Protests That Set the Stage for Stonewall," *Vice*, 24 June 2019; Joseph D. Lyons, "Did Stonewall Start the Gay Rights Movement?" *Bustle*, 25 June 2019; Ryan Kost, "Long before Stonewall, Decades of Queer Activism," *San Francisco Chronicle*, 26 June 2019, E1–2; Rebecca Onion, "Making Stonewall Matter," *Slate*, 26 June 2019; James Kirchick, "The Struggle for Gay Rights Is Over," *Atlantic*, 28 June 2019; Michael Wilson, "The Night the Stonewall Inn Became a Proud Shrine," *NYT*, 28 June 2019, 1, 25; Robert Iafolla, "Stonewall at 50: Uprising Sparked Growth of LGBT Protections," *Bloomberg Law*, 28 June 2019. For non-U.S. media, see Christian Saint-Pierre, "Revenir Aux Sources de Stonewall," *Le Devoir*, 30 June 2019; Patsy l'Amour, "Ein Grosser Wurf," *Dschungel*, 1 July 2019; Katya Parente, "Il Cammino del Movimento LGBT dai moti di Stonewall ad Oggi," *Progetto Gionata*, 15 Nov. 2020. Print media interviews included Joanne Meyerowitz, "Stonewall: 50 Years Later," *American Historian*, May 2019, 1–2; Brian Bromberger, "Pride 2019: Book Offers Many Layers to the Stonewall Story," *Bay Area Reporter*, 25 June 2019; Ilona Westfall, "Lessons Learned," *Prizm*, June 2019, 3; Lexi Adsit, "Stonewall at 50: A Major Anniversary Offers Opportunity for New Historical Perspectives," *History Happens*, June 2019. Radio interviews included Shai Ben-Yaacov and Annette John-Hall, "Before Stonewall and Pride, Philly Staged LGBTQ Protests," *The Why*, WHYY, Philadelphia, 5 June 2019; Alison Stewart, "Stonewall Histories," *All of It*, WNYC, New York City, 14 June 2019; Brian Lehrer, "Prejudice and Price: Oral History from Stonewall 1969," *Brian Lehrer Show*, WNYC, New York City, 21 June 2019; Mitch Jeserich, "A History of the Stonewall Riots," *Letters and Politics*, KPFA, Berkeley, California, 24 June 2019; Mina Kim, "San Francisco and LGBTQ Pride," *Forum*, KQED, San Francisco, 27 June 2019; Heather McCoy, "Heather McCoy Show," KBOO, Portland (OR), 11 July 2019; "All Sides with Ann Fisher," WOSU, Columbus, 21 Oct. 2019. Podcast interviews included Tobin Low and Kathy Tu, "What Do We Have in Common?" *Nancy*, WNYC, New York, 24 June 2019; Claire Potter, "Kicking and Screaming: Stonewall at 50," *Exiles on 12th Street*, 28 June 2019. Television interviews included Steve Scully, "Stonewall Riots 50th Anniversary," *American History TV*, C-SPAN, 23 June 2019.

5. Hugh Ryan, "Voices on the Line," *Times Literary Supplement*, 25 June 2019.

6. *The Gay and Lesbian Review*, https://glreview.org/about/.

7. The Gotham Center for New York City History, https://www.gotham center.org/about/our-mission.

8. See also Alana Mohamed, "Ten Moments in NYC LGBTQ Activist History You Need to Know in Addition to Stonewall," *Gothamist*, 28 June 2019.

9. See also Sarah Hotchkiss, "Armed with Ink, 1960s Activists 'Struck Back' against Homophobic Media," WQED Arts, 13 June 2019.

CONCLUSION

1. "Pop-Up Museum of Queer History," http://www.hughryan.org/pop-up -museum. See also Hugh Ryan, "Notes on The Pop-Up Museum of Queer History," *QED: A Journal in GLBTQ Worldmaking* 1, no. 2 (Summer 2014): 79–90.

2. "GLBT Historical Society," https://www.glbthistory.org/.

3. Our Family Coalition, "About the FAIR Education Act," http://www .lgbtqhistory.org/about-fair-education-act/.

4. "Quist," https://www.quistapp.com/.

5. Allyson Mitchell and Cait McKinney, eds., *Inside Killjoy's Kastle: Dykey Ghosts, Feminist Monsters, and Other Lesbian Hauntings* (Vancouver: University of British Columbia Press, 2019).

6. Chris E. Vargas, "Museum of Transgender Hirstory and Art," http:// www.chrisevargas.com/motha; Chris E. Vargas, "Introducing the Museum of Transgender Hirstory and Art," in *Trap Door: Trans Cultural Production and the Politics of Visibility*, ed. Reina Gossett, Eric A. Stanley, and Johanna Burton (Cambridge, MA: MIT Press, 2017), 121–134.

7. Susan Stryker and Paisley Currah, "Introduction," *Transgender Studies Quarterly* 1, nos. 1–2 (May 2014): 1–18.

8. Daniel Marshall, Kevin P. Murphy, and Zeb Tortorici, eds., "Queering Archives: Historical Unravelings," *Radical History Review*, no. 120 (Fall 2014); Daniel Marshall, Kevin P. Murphy, and Zeb Tortorici, eds., "Queering Archives: Intimate Tracings," *Radical History Review*, no. 122 (May 2015).

9. New York City LGBT Historic Sites Project, https://www.nyclgbtsites .org/about/; Rainbow Heritage Network, https://rainbowheritagenetwork.org /about/.

10. "Speaking Out for Equality," National Constitution Center, https:// constitutioncenter.org/press-room/press-kit/exhibition-press-kits/speaking-out -for-equality-press-kit.

11. Megan E. Springate, ed., *LGBTQ America: A Theme Study of Lesbian, Gay, Bisexual, Transgender, and Queer History* (Washington, DC: National Park Foundation and National Park Service, 2016); "Recognizing LGBT Historic Sites Across the Country," *NYC LGBT Historic Sites Project*, 5 May 2019, https://www.nyclgbtsites.org/2019/05/05/recognizing-lgbt-historic-sites -across-the-country/.

12. Melinda Marie Jetté, ed., "Queering Public History: The State of the Field," a special issue of *The Public Historian* 41, no. 2 (May 2019); Stephen Vider, "Public Disclosures of Private Realities: HIV/AIDS and the Domestic Archive," *The Public Historian* 41, no. 2 (May 2019): 163–189.

13. Joseph Plaster, "Black Queer Performance in Baltimore's 'Cathedral of Books,'" *The Abusable Past*, Oct. 2019; "The Peabody Ballroom Experience,"

2019, https://peabodyballroom.library.jhu.edu/; "Queer Miami: A History of LGBTQ Communities," HistoryMiami Museum, 2019, https://www.history miami.org/exhibition/queer-miami/; "Queer California: Untold Stories," Oakland Museum of California, 2019, https://museumca.org/exhibit/queer -california-untold-stories.

14. *Lesbian Testimony*, https://alotarchives.org/blog; *Making Gay History*, https://makinggayhistory.com/; *Michigan LGBTQ Remember*, https://michigan lgbtqremember.com/; *Notches*, http://notchesblog.com/; *Philadelphia Gay-borhood Guru*, https://thegayborhoodguru.wordpress.com/; *Queer America*, https://www.learningforjustice.org/podcasts/queer-america; *Sexing History*, https://www.sexinghistory.com/.

15. *LGBTQ Digital History Collaboratory*, http://lgbtqdigitalcollaboratory .org/.

16. *Lavender Legacies Guide*, https://www2.archivists.org/groups/diverse -sexuality-and-gender-section/lavender-legacies-guide.

17. *The Lavender Scare*, dir. Josh Howard (2017); *The Death and Life of Marsha P. Johnson*, dir. David France (2017); *Killing Patient Zero*, dir. Laurie Lynd (2019); *Cured*, dir. Patrick Sammon and Bennett Singer (2020); *Pride*, dir. Tom Kalin, Andrew Ahn, Cheryl Dunye, Anthony Caronna and Alex Smith, Yance Ford, and Ro Haber (2021); *My Name Is Pauli Murray*, dir. Julie Cohen and Betsy West (2021).

18. See Nadja Sayej, "The Best US Exhibitions Celebrating Stonewall at 50," *Guardian*, 3 June 2019, https://www.theguardian.com/artanddesign/2019/jun /03/stonewall-50th-anniversary-best-exhibitions-museums-galleries.

19. "AHA Releases Statement on LGBTQ+ History Curriculum," May 2021, https://www.historians.org/news-and-advocacy/aha-advocacy/aha-statement -on-lgbtq-history-curriculum-(may-2021).

20. Alyssa Lukpat, "Missouri Relocates Gay History Exhibit from State Capitol," *NYT*, 4 Sep. 2021.

21. See Amin Ghaziani, *There Goes the Gayborhood?* (Princeton, NJ: Princeton University Press, 2014); Martin Duberman, *Has the Gay Movement Failed?* (Oakland: University of California Press, 2018).

22. Elspeth H. Brown, "Archival Activism, Symbolic Annihilation, and the LGBTQ2+ Community Archive," *Archivaria* 89 (Spring 2020): 6–33.

23. Myrl Beam, *Gay Inc.: The Nonprofitization of Queer Politics* (Minneapolis: University of Minnesota Press, 2018).

24. Marc Stein, "Canonizing Homophile Sexual Respectability: Archives, History, and Memory," *Radical History Review*, no. 120 (Fall 2014): 52–73.

25. Matthew S. Bajko, "San Francisco Mayor Seeks $10M for LGBTQ Museum Site," *Bay Area Reporter*, 1 June 2021.

26. "Prohibition on State-Funded and State-Sponsored Travel to States with Discriminatory Laws," https://oag.ca.gov/ab1887. See also Marc Stein, "When a Boycott Blocks Queer Research," *Public Seminar*, 18 May 2021, https:// publicseminar.org/essays/when-a-boycott-blocks-queer-research/.

27. William Floyd, "Remembering Stonewall, 1969," 18 June 2017, *Google .org*, https://blog.google/outreach-initiatives/google-org/remembering-stonewall -1969/; William Floyd, "Stonewall Forever: Honoring LGBTQ+ History through

a Living Monument," 4 June 2019, *Google.org*, https://www.blog.google /outreach-initiatives/google-org/stonewall-forever/; "Stonewall Forever," https:// stonewallforever.org/.

28. The paragraphs that follow are based in part on conversations, correspondence, and interviews with Helen Buse (New York City LGBT Community Center Communications Coordinator), David Favaloro (Tenement Museum Senior Director of Curatorial Affairs), Maab Ibrahim (Google.org Portfolio Manager), Eric Marcus (Stonewall Forever oral history consultant), Caitlin McCarthy (New York City LGBT Community Center Archives Manager), Shirley McKinney (National Park Service Superintendent), Joey Plaster (oral history consultant), and Jeanne Vaccaro (Stonewall Forever story producer). I am grateful for their willingness to discuss "Stonewall Forever" with me. I reached out to other key contributors who declined to respond.

29. I say this even though I would quibble with the National Park Service's Stonewall National Monument lesson plans, which also were funded by Google.org (https://www.nps.gov/teachers/teacher-resources.htm#q=Stonewall +National+Monument). The high school lesson plan, for example, includes multiple media accounts of the Stonewall Riots but none from the LGBT press. It also mischaracterizes reforms in the regulation of gay bars in the late 1960s. The middle school lesson plan mischaracterizes the 1966 sip-in, misnames its organizational sponsor, and mistakenly describes Stonewall as beginning "the modern struggle for the civil rights" of LGBT Americans. With respect to the elementary school lesson plan, it is not true that "in the 1960s in America almost everything about living as a Lesbian, Gay, Bisexual and Transgender (LGBT) person was illegal" or that "New York City had particularly harsh rules." It is misleading to state that the "police knocked on the door" of the Stonewall, the police "retreated into their cars and drove away" after conflict erupted, and the main lesson was that LGBT people "can organize to change unfair laws." It is not true that all major New York newspapers had headlines the next day about the "Stonewall Riots"; none did. Craig Rodwell was active in the Mattachine Society of New York, not the California-based Mattachine Society, and he did not found the first LGBT bookstore in the United States. More generally, the NPS materials minimize the extent of LGBT resistance and reform before the riots. For additional examples of problematic historical claims and interpretations, see National Park Service, *Foundation Document: Stonewall National Monument*, May 2019.

Index

Founded in 1893,
UNIVERSITY OF CALIFORNIA PRESS
publishes bold, progressive books and journals
on topics in the arts, humanities, social sciences,
and natural sciences—with a focus on social
justice issues—that inspire thought and action
among readers worldwide.

The UC PRESS FOUNDATION
raises funds to uphold the press's vital role
as an independent, nonprofit publisher, and
receives philanthropic support from a wide
range of individuals and institutions—and from
committed readers like you. To learn more, visit
ucpress.edu/supportus.

Ingram Content Group UK Ltd.
Milton Keynes UK
UKHW041901120523
421667UK00004B/87